EXAM CRAM™

Property and Casualty Insurance License

BISYS Educational Services

BISYS

QUE®

CERTIFICATION

800 East 96th Street, Indianapolis, Indiana 46240

Trademarks

Warning and Disclaimer

Bulk Sales

Que Publishing offers excellent discounts on this book when ordered in quantity for bulk purchases or special sales. For more information, please contact

> **U.S. Corporate and Government Sales**
> 1-800-382-3419
> corpsales@pearsontechgroup.com

For sales outside the U.S., please contact

> **International Sales**
> international@pearsoned.com

Publisher
Paul Boger

Executive Editor
Jeff Riley

Acquisitions Editor
Carol Ackerman

Development Editor
Ginny Bess

Managing Editor
Charlotte Clapp

Project Editor
Seth Kerney

Copy Editor
Rhonda Tinch-Mize

Indexer
Heather McNeill

Proofreader
Kathy Bidwell

Technical Editor
Teresa Chapman

Publishing Coordinator
Pamalee Nelson

Multimedia Developer
Dan Scherf

Interior Designer
Gary Adair

Cover Designer
Anne Jones

Contents at a Glance

Table of Contents

Chapter 6
Introduction to Liability Insurance **77**

Chapter 7
Dwelling Insurance **93**

Chapter 10
Miscellaneous Personal Insurance

Chapter 14
Ocean and Inland Marine Insurance 277

About the Authors

Eric Alan Anderson is Director of Insurance Education for BISYS Education Services, based in Indianapolis, Indiana. He has almost 25 years of experience creating training and test preparation materials for the financial services industry. In addition to authoring 17 insurance training texts and editing 8 others, he has written newsletters and magazine articles, and he has developed materials for audio cassette/workbook, videotape, computer disk, and the Web. He has also taught basic English skills courses at the college level and has made presentations to national conferences of insurance associations.

Jennifer Martin, CPCU, is Senior Editor of Property-Casualty Products for BISYS Education Services, based in Indianapolis, Indiana. She is the author of 17 insurance training texts and maintains 50 titles on BISYS Education Services' course list. Jennifer has also developed interactive web-based courses and written state insurance law digests, computer documentation, newsletters, online help, and corporate disaster recovery plans.

Richard A. Morin, CIC, is a contract author based in Los Angeles, California. He has 35 years of experience writing and training on a broad range of subjects for the financial services industry. For several years, he was an editor for a major insurance training publisher, and he has also worked as an insurance underwriter, a rating supervisor, and a licensed insurance and mutual fund sales representative.

About BISYS

The BISYS Group, Inc. (NYSE: BSG), headquartered in New York City, provides solutions that enable insurance companies, investment firms, and banks to expand their businesses and run their operations more profitably. BISYS currently supports more than 22,000 domestic and international financial institutions and corporate clients through several business units. **BISYS Education Services** is the nation's premier provider of licensing preparation, continuing education, and professional development courses for life, health, long-term care, annuity, and property-casualty insurance products as well as investments. This unit complements its education services with a comprehensive compliance management solution that supports insurance and investment firms and professionals with a sophisticated suite of services that automate the entire licensing process. **BISYS Insurance Services** is the nation's largest independent distributor of life insurance and provider of support services required to sell traditional and variable life and annuity products as well as long-term care and disability insurance. This unit is also the nation's second largest independent wholesale distributor of commercial property/casualty insurance. **BISYS Investment Services** group provides administration and distribution services for approximately 380 clients, representing more than 2,200 mutual funds, hedge funds, private equity funds, and other alternative investment products with approximately $750 billion in assets under administration. It also provides retirement services to more than 18,000 companies in partnership with 40 of the nation's leading banks and investment management companies, and offers analytical research and competitive information through its Financial Research Corporation (FRC) subsidiary. **BISYS Information Services** group supports approximately 1,450 banks, insurance companies, and corporations with industry-leading information processing and imaging solutions, turnkey asset retention solutions, and specialized corporate banking solutions. Additional information is available at www.bisys.com.

About the Reviewer

Teresa Chapman has been in the insurance business since 1996. Upon graduation from Ball State University in Muncie, IN, she started her career with State Farm Insurance Company as a Life and Health Underwriter. A series of moves within State Farm led to a variety of jobs, such as supervisor of Life and Health Policy Changes and Life and Health compliance officer, culminating in her decision to become a State Farm insurance agent in Carmel, IN. Teresa lives in Noblesville, IN with her husband Trent, a State Farm auto claim representative, and their son, Christian.

We Want to Hear from You!

As the reader of this book, *you* are our most important critic and commentator. We value your opinion and want to know what we're doing right, what we could do better, what areas you'd like to see us publish in, and any other words of wisdom you're willing to pass our way.

As an executive editor for Que Publishing, I welcome your comments. You can email or write me directly to let me know what you did or didn't like about this book—as well as what we can do to make our books better.

Please note that I cannot help you with technical problems related to the topic of this book. We do have a User Services group, however, where I will forward specific technical questions related to the book.

When you write, please be sure to include this book's title and author as well as your name, email address, and phone number. I will carefully review your comments and share them with the author and editors who worked on the book.

Email: feedback@quepublishing.com

Mail: Jeff Riley
              Executive Editor
              Que Publishing
              800 East 96th Street
              Indianapolis, IN 46240 USA

For more information about this book or another Que Certification title, visit our website at www.examcram2.com. Type the ISBN (excluding hyphens) or the title of a book in the Search field to find the page you're looking for.

Introduction

Welcome to *Property and Casualty Insurance License Exam Cram!* Whether this is your first or your fifteenth *Exam Cram* series book, you'll find information here that will help ensure your success as you pursue knowledge, experience, and certification. This introduction explains state insurance licensing programs in general and talks about how the *Exam Cram* series can help you prepare for your state insurance licensing exam. Chapters 1–19 are designed to remind you of everything you need to know in order to take—and pass—your state insurance licensing exam. The two practice exams at the end of the book should give you a reasonably accurate assessment of your knowledge—and, yes, we've provided the answers and their explanations to the tests. Read the book and understand the material, and you'll stand a very good chance of passing the test.

Exam Cram books help you understand and appreciate the subjects and materials you need to pass state insurance licensing exams. *Exam Cram* books are aimed strictly at test preparation and review. They do not teach you everything you need to know to pass the exam. Instead, this book presents and dissects the questions and problems you're likely to encounter on a test. We've worked to bring together as much information as possible about state insurance licensing exams into one study guide that includes everything you need to prepare the exams.

Nevertheless, to completely prepare yourself for any state insurance licensing test, we recommend that you follow the recommendations in the Self-Assessment included in this book, immediately following this introduction. The review questions, practice exams, and optional study materials described in the Self-Assessment can help you evaluate your knowledge base against the requirements for a state insurance licensing exam under both ideal and real circumstances.

Based on what you learn from the Self-Assessment, you might decide to begin your studies with some more comprehensive self-study or classroom training, some practice with state insurance exam simulators, or an audio review program. On the other hand, you might decide to pick up and read one of the many study guides available from third-party vendors on certain topics. We also recommend that you supplement your study program with a visit to your state insurance department's website to get all the details about how to obtain your insurance license as well as how to schedule and take your insurance licensing exam.

Getting an Insurance License

Licensing is the way governments ensure that only qualified individuals are allowed to practice certain important professions, such as being an insurance producer. Because insurance is regulated primarily at the state level, the rules for getting an insurance license vary somewhat from state to state.

Every state requires individuals to pass a qualification exam to get an insurance license. In addition, most states require individuals to meet a "pre-licensing education requirement" before they can take the qualification exam. In some states, the pre-licensing education requirement can be met through an approved self-study course—that is, you buy a book that has been approved in advance by the state insurance department and take an exam (not to be confused with the licensing qualification exam) that you send in to be graded. In other states, the pre-licensing education requirement can only be met by attending an approved classroom course.

This *Exam Cram* text is not approved to meet the pre-licensing education requirement in any specific state. It is designed only as a supplementary aid to help you pass the state insurance licensing exam.

Besides fulfilling any pre-licensing education requirement and passing the licensing exam, insurance license candidates must also submit a license application to their state insurance department and have it approved. In some states, the license application must be submitted before taking the license qualification exam; in some states, it must be submitted after passing the exam. Call your state insurance department's licensing division or visit its website to find out what you need to do in your state.

Taking a Licensing Exam

As with other aspects of insurance licensing, specific instructions on how to register for your qualification exam are available from the insurance department. Ask for a licensing information bulletin or a licensing candidate handbook, which will describe where and when exams are given, the fees you must pay, and the testing procedures.

One thing all state insurance qualification exams have in common is that they are "closed book" exams. You will not be allowed to take any study materials or notes into the testing room. Even phones and calculators may not be allowed. In some states, the only items exam candidates are permitted to take into the testing room are their wallet and keys.

In most states, insurance qualification exams are given on computers. However, you will not need any computer or typing skills to take the exam. You will be instructed how to answer questions and given a short practice test to get comfortable with the equipment before the actual qualification exam begins.

When you complete a computer-administered exam, the software tells you immediately whether you've passed or failed. Your states will have rules for retesting in the event you don't pass. Those rules are described in your licensing information bulletin/candidate handbook.

How to Prepare for an Exam

Whether or not your state has a pre-licensing education requirement, you'll want to study in preparation for the license qualification exam. And even if your state has a pre-licensing education requirement, you'll probably want to do some additional studying to make sure that you are fully prepared for the exam. Your options for additional study include the following:

➤ **Self-study courses:** Publishers such as BISYS Education Services offer courses designed to allow you to study on your own for the licensing qualification exam. BISYS license training packages are available in either web-based or print-based formats and contain a number of components:

> ➤ A *Property-Casualty Concepts* text that covers all the non–state-specific topics on the licensing exam

> ➤ Practice exams that help you evaluate your comprehension of the material in the *Concepts* text

> ➤ Explanations to answers on the practice exams so that you'll know why each of your responses was right or wrong

> ➤ A state insurance law digest that covers all the state-specific topics on the licensing exam

> ➤ An optional audio CD review program that reviews the key information contained in the *Concepts* text

➤ An optional exam simulator that gives you additional question-and-answer practice over the material covered in the *Concepts* text and the state insurance law digest

➤ **Classroom training:** Many colleges and commercial training companies offer classroom training for insurance license exams. Although classroom training generally costs considerably more than self-study, some individuals find that they learn best in a classroom situation. And of course, in many states, the pre-licensing education requirement must be met with classroom study in any case.

➤ **Other sources:** There's no shortage of materials available on insurance topics. Appendix B, "Need to Know More" will give you an idea of where we think you should look for further discussion.

In addition, Que Publishing's *Exam Cram* insurance licensing preparation materials are useful in your quest for insurance knowledge. *Exam Cram* books provide you with a review of the essential information you need to know to pass the tests. They focus the detailed information in the *Concepts* texts available from BISYS Education Services. Together, the BISYS Education Services license training packages and the Exam Cram review materials create a powerful exam preparation program.

This set of required and recommended materials represents an unparalleled collection of sources and resources for insurance licensing qualification and related topics. Our hope is you'll find that this book belongs in that company.

What This Book Will Not Do

This book by itself will *not* teach you everything you need to know to pass your insurance licensing exam. It does not cover the state-specific topics that appear on the exam, usually dealing with laws that apply only in your particular state. That information, although it represents a small proportion of the entire exam, is critical to passing the exam. State-specific topics are covered in the state insurance law digests available from BISYS Education Services. This book reviews the rest of what you need to know before you take the test, with the fundamental purpose dedicated to reviewing the non–state-specific information on the insurance licensing exam.

What This Book Is Designed to Do

This book uses a variety of teaching and memorization techniques to analyze the exam-related topics and to provide you with ways to input, index, and retrieve what you'll need to know in order to pass the test.

This book is designed to be read as a pointer to the areas of knowledge you will be tested on. In other words, you might want to read the book one time, just to get an insight into how comprehensive your knowledge of insurance is. The book is also designed to be read shortly before you go for the actual test and to give you a distillation of the topics covered by the exam in as few pages as possible. We think that you can use this book to get a sense of the underlying context of any topic in the chapters—or to skim read for Exam Alerts, bulleted points, summaries, and topic headings.

We've drawn on material from each state's exam outlines and from other preparation guides, in particular, BISYS Education Services' *Property-Casualty Concepts* text. Our aim is to walk you through the knowledge you will need—looking over your shoulder, so to speak—and point out those things that are important for the exam (Exam Alerts, practice questions, and so on).

We've tried to demystify insurance jargon, acronyms, terms, and concepts. Also, wherever we think you're likely to blur past an important concept, we've defined the assumptions and premises behind that concept.

About This Book

We've structured the topics in this book to build upon one another. Therefore, the topics covered in later chapters might refer to previous discussions in earlier chapters. We suggest that you read this book from front to back.

After you read the book, you can brush up on a certain area by using the Index or the Table of Contents to go straight to the topics and questions you want to reexamine. We've tried to use the headings and subheadings to provide outline information about each given topic. After you've passed the exam and obtained your insurance license, we think that you'll find this book useful as a tightly focused reference and an essential foundation of insurance information.

Chapter Formats

Each *Exam Cram* chapter follows a standard structure, along with graphical cues about especially important or useful material. The structure of a typical chapter is as follows:

➤ **Opening hotlists:** Each chapter begins with lists of the terms you'll need to understand and the concepts you'll need to master before you can be fully conversant with the chapter's subject matter.

➤ **Topical coverage:** After the opening hotlists, each chapter covers the topics related to the chapter's subject.

➤ **Alerts:** Throughout the topical coverage section, we highlight material most likely to appear on the exam by using a special Exam Alert layout that looks like this:

 This is what an Exam Alert looks like. An Exam Alert stresses concepts or terms that will most likely appear in one or more license exam questions. For that reason, we think any information found offset in Exam Alert format is worthy of unusual attentiveness on your part.

Even if material isn't flagged as an Exam Alert, *all* the content in this book is associated in some way with test-related material. What appears in the chapter content is critical knowledge.

➤ **Notes:** This book is an overall examination of entry-level insurance knowledge. As such, we'll touch on many aspects of insurance that open doors for further inquiry. Where a topic goes deeper than the scope of the book, we use notes to indicate areas of concern or further training.

 Cramming for an exam will get you through a test, but it won't make you a fully competent insurance professional. Although you can memorize just the facts you need in order to become licensed, your daily work in the field will rapidly put you in water over your head if you don't continue your insurance education.

➤ **Review questions:** At the end of each chapter is a short list of test questions related to that chapter's topic. Each question has a following explanation of both correct and incorrect answers. The practice questions highlight the areas we found to be most important on the exam.

➤ **Need to Know More:** On the CD-ROM is an appendix titled "Need To Know More." This appendix provides pointers to resources that we found to be helpful in offering further details on the book's subject matter. If you find a resource you like in this collection, use it, but don't feel compelled to use all these resources. In this appendix, we recommend resources that we have used on a regular basis, so none of the recommendations will be a waste of your time or money. These resources might go out of print or be taken down (in the case of websites), so we've tried to reference widely accepted resources.

The bulk of the book follows this chapter structure, but there are a few other elements that we would like to point out:

➤ **Practice exams:** The practice exams, which appear in Chapters 20 and 22 (with answer keys in Chapters 21 and 23), are intended to test your comprehension of the material in this book. They are also intended to be in a similar format and degree of difficulty as the questions you are likely to see on the license exam. However, because the questions on the actual exam are kept highly confidential, you should expect that the questions on the actual license exam will be ones that you have never seen before.

➤ **Quick Check answer keys:** These provide the answers to the practice exams, complete with explanations of both the correct and incorrect responses.

➤ **Glossary:** This is an extensive glossary of important terms used in this book.

➤ **The Cram Sheet:** This appears as a tear-away sheet, inside the front cover of this *Exam Cram* book. It is a valuable tool that represents a collection of the most difficult-to-remember facts, terms, and concepts we think you should memorize before taking the test.

You might want to look at the Cram Sheet in your car or in the lobby of the testing center just before you walk into the testing center. The Cram Sheet is divided under headings, so you can review the appropriate parts just before each test.

➤ **The CD:** The CD contains the BISYS Education Services Exam Simulator, Preview Edition software. The Preview Edition exhibits most of the functionality of the commercially available version, but offers a reduced number of unit review questions and a 50-question practice exam. To get the complete set of practice questions and 100-question exam functionality, visit www.bisyseducation.com or call 1-800-241-9095.

Contacting the Source

We tried to create a real-world tool that you can use to prepare for and pass your state insurance licensing exam. We're interested in any feedback you would care to share about the book, especially if you have ideas about how we can improve it for future test takers. We'll carefully consider everything you say and will respond to all reasonable suggestions and comments. You can reach us via email at customerservice@bisys-education.com.

Let us know if you found this book to be helpful in your preparation efforts. We'd also like to know how you felt about your chances of passing the exam *before* you read the book and then *after* you read the book. Of course, we'd love to hear that you passed the exam—and even if you just want to share your triumph, we'd be happy to hear from you.

Thanks for choosing us as your license exam preparation coach, and enjoy the book. We wish you luck on the exam, but we know that if you read through all the chapters and work with the product, you won't need luck— you'll pass the test on the strength of real knowledge!

Self-Assessment

....

We've included a Self-Assessment in this *Exam Cram* to help you evaluate your readiness to take and pass your state insurance license qualification exam. It should also help you understand what you need to master an entry-level knowledge of the industry in which you are about to embark on a career.

Getting Prepared

Whether you attend a class to get ready for your exam or use self-study materials, some preparation for your insurance license qualification exam is essential. You want to do everything you can to pass on your first try. That's where studying comes in.

You can get all the confidence you need from knowing that many others have gone before you. You can follow in their footsteps. If you're willing to tackle the process seriously and do what it takes to gain the necessary knowledge, you can take—and pass—the insurance license qualification exams. In fact, the *Exam Crams* and the companion state license training packages from BISYS Education Services are designed to make it as easy as possible for you to prepare for these exams, but prepare you must!

 You can obtain an outline of exam topics, practice questions, and other information about insurance qualification exams from your state insurance department's web page; or if your state has contracted with an exam administration company to administer its insurance licensing exams (which is usually the case), from the exam administrator's web page. Do a web search to find your state insurance department's web page. Your state can direct you to the exam administrator's web page, if there is one.

Put Yourself to the (Practice) Test

Included in this book are several review exam questions for each chapter and two practice exams at the end of the book. If you don't score well on the chapter questions, you can study more and then retake the review questions at the end of each chapter. After you read the chapters, take the first practice exam, and then score yourself and review some more by reading the explanations that accompany the answer key in the chapter following that exam. If you don't earn a score of at least 80% on the first practice exam, do some additional study. Go back through this book, and also consult your notes and/or your text from any licensing exam preparation course you took. Then try the second practice exam in this book. Again, shoot for a score of 80% or better on your first try.

There is no better way to assess your exam readiness than to take a good-quality practice exam and pass with a score of 80% or better on your first try for that exam. When you take the same practice exam over and over, you begin to memorize the answers to the specific questions on that exam. It might help you improve your knowledge, but it spoils the value of the exam as an indication of how well you might respond to an exam containing questions over the full range of topics on your state's exam outline. Also, even though you must score only 70% to pass the actual exam, shoot for 80% on a practice exam to leave room for the fact that you might be nervous during the actual exam and that the questions on the actual exam might be more difficult than those on your practice exam.

If you still did not score 80% or better on your first try, investigate the other study resources available (see Appendix B, "Need to Know More?").

If you've given your utmost to self-study materials and then taken the exam and failed anyway, consider taking a class. For some people, self-study is not the optimal learning format. The opportunity to interact with an instructor and fellow students can make all the difference. For information about classes available in your area, ask your state insurance department or call BISYS Education Services (1-800-241-9095) to see if there are schools nearby using BISYS insurance licensing textbooks.

One last note: Do not use practice exams as your only means of study for the exam. Next to not preparing at all, the best way to assure that you'll fail your license qualification exam is to skip studying and go directly to taking question-and-answer practice tests to assess your readiness to take the exam. Practice exams are a gauge of how well you've comprehended your study material—they are not an accurate reflection of the questions you will see on your license qualification exam.

Other Preparation

Besides studying for the exam, there are some other things you should do to make sure that you perform well on the exam:

➤ **Get a good night's sleep the night before the exam:** When you're tired, you're more likely to make careless—that is, needless—mistakes. Getting a good night's sleep will help assure that you feel refreshed and at your best.

➤ **Eat a nourishing breakfast the morning of the exam:** Your brain needs nutrients to function at its best—make sure that you provide them! At the very least, you don't want your attention to be distracted by hunger while you're trying to concentrate on a question.

➤ **Give yourself plenty of time to get to the exam site:** Rushing to get somewhere can put you in a less-than-optimum frame of mind even if you end up arriving on time. Leave early to allow for unforeseen problems such as traffic delays. If you arrive well before the exam is scheduled to start, you can always use the extra time to go over your notes.

No Experience Required

Insurance license exams are designed so that they can be passed by individuals with no insurance industry experience or formal insurance schooling other than any state-required prelicensing education requirement. So if you are completely new to this business, don't worry. Everything you need to know to pass your qualification exam can be obtained in the study materials referenced here.

In terms of having a successful insurance career after you pass your exam, the most important requirement is a sincere desire to help people solve their financial problems and reach their financial goals. However, certain backgrounds can be an asset as you start out in the job. If you have run your own business, you already understand the type of self-discipline and motivation that will help you succeed in your insurance sales activities. If you have some prior sales experience—such as a customer service representative, real estate agent, or some other sales position—you'll probably have a comfort level with meeting people to discuss and solve their needs. But again, if you're brand new to insurance or to sales, have no fear on that account. You will have ample opportunity and resources for learning everything you need to know.

Onward to Exam and Career Success!

After you've undertaken the right studies and reviewed the many sources of information to help you prepare for the license qualification exam, you'll be ready to take a practice exam. When your scores are positive enough to indicate that you will get through the exam, you're ready to go after the real thing. Good luck!

Principles of Insurance

Terms you'll need to understand:

✓ Risk
✓ Peril
✓ Hazard
✓ Insurance

Concepts you'll need to master:

✓ Methods of managing risk
✓ Law of large numbers
✓ Insurable interest
✓ Speculative risk
✓ Pure risk
✓ Insurable risk

Most people have a general understanding of the concept of insurance. Many of us have life insurance, automobile insurance, and homeowners insurance. We know that it is something we have to pay for—those annoying periodic payments known as "premiums." Yet it is something we rely on and depend on—we expect it to provide compensation for injuries or damages when a loss (such as a fire or automobile accident) occurs. Many people might not understand that the insurance business is based on a number of sound principles that not only enable but also are required for the entire social system to work.

This chapter reviews basic principles that provide a foundation for the insurance industry. They range from the concept of risk, to the idea that individuals and businesses can minimize losses by transferring and sharing risks, to the application of the law of large numbers. Various principles also determine why some risks of loss are insurable whereas others are not.

Risk

To understand what insurance is and how it works, you must first understand the concept of risk. *Risk* is the chance or uncertainty of loss. The possibility that your house might be burglarized, or that you might be hit by a car while crossing the street, represents uncertainty of loss. Both are risks.

Risk is not the loss itself, but the uncertainty that a loss might occur. Some losses of value, such as those resulting from wear and tear on a physical object, are certain to occur eventually. These are not risks. Other losses, such as damage or injuries resulting from a lightning bolt or an industrial accident, are not predictable and therefore are not certain. These are risks.

Managing Risk

All of us face risks on a daily basis. When we drive in a car, go swimming, or participate in a sports event, we are exposed to risk. Many risks are minor and do not represent significant financial losses. But people need to plan for the potentially serious financial losses that might occur.

There are several different methods for managing risks of loss. One method is simply to *avoid the risk*. For example, you can avoid the risk of being in an auto collision by never getting into a car. But it isn't practical to avoid all risks.

Various loss control efforts fall into the category of *risk reduction*. Burglar alarms, seat belts in vehicles, and fire sprinkler systems might help to prevent losses or reduce the frequency or severity of losses when they do occur.

Another method of risk management is to simply *retain a risk*—that is, simply to keep one's exposure to it. Risks can be retained in full or in part, and risk retention can be done intentionally or unintentionally. Individuals and businesses can retain risks intentionally (by self-insuring, selecting high deductibles or coinsurance amounts) or unintentionally (by failing to plan or insure, or not even being aware that an exposure exists).

A final method of managing risk is to *transfer* it to another party. This option includes, but is not limited to, insurance. With insurance, the risk is transferred to an insurance company. But other examples of risk transfer are common in business and personal relationships. For example, hold harmless agreements are often used to shift liability from an owner or contractor to a tenant or subcontractor. A *hold harmless agreement* is a contractual arrangement in which one party assumes the liability for any losses and relieves another party of any responsibility.

 Multiple methods can be employed simultaneously to manage the same risk. For example, purchasing an insurance policy to cover a significant exposure involves risk transfer, whereas selecting a high deductible in order to reduce premiums involves an element of risk retention.

Insurance

The purpose of insurance is not to avoid or eliminate risk, but to transfer risk. Although the risk is transferred to an insurance company, the risk is actually shared by a large number of insured people whose collective premiums form a pool of money from which individual losses are paid.

A formal definition of insurance defines it as a contract or device for transferring risk from a person, business, or organization to an insurer who agrees, in exchange for a premium, to pay for losses through an accumulation of premiums.

Law of Large Numbers

In order for a system of insurance to work, it has to rely on the *law of large numbers* to predict losses and develop premiums. It is necessary to accumulate a large number of similar risks with a predictable loss ratio to create the premium base from which losses can be paid. Generally, the larger the number of similar exposure units, the more predictable and accurate the estimate of expected losses.

For example, if fire frequency statistics are gathered using only four houses, the figures aren't likely to be very accurate. The four houses might not experience any fires—in which case, the frequency would be zero, which would be erroneous because some houses do experience fires. If one house experienced a fire, the frequency would be 25%, which is unrealistically high. To gather realistic figures on frequency of fire losses to houses, statistics must be kept on thousands of houses.

Elements of Insurability

Insurance is not an appropriate mechanism for protecting against all risks. There are certain rules that establish a practical basis regarding who can be insured and for what exposures. These rules determine a risk's *insurability*— that is, the ability of an individual to obtain an insurance policy to cover the risk.

Pure and Speculative Risks

Insurance cannot be used to handle *speculative risks*. Speculative risks are risks in which there exists both the possibility of gain and the possibility of loss. A poker game or a horse race, or even an investment in the stock market, are examples of speculative risks.

Insurance can only be used to manage *pure risks*, which involve the possibility of loss with no opportunity for gain. A person can buy insurance to protect against loss if a car is stolen (pure risk) but not to protect against loss if a particular football team fails to win the Super Bowl. Because there is an opportunity for gain (the football team could win), betting on a football team is not considered a pure risk.

Insurable Interest

A basic rule concerning *who* can be insured is that before anyone can benefit from insurance, the person must have a chance of financial loss or a personal or financial interest in the property or individual insured. This is called an *insurable interest*.

 Every person has an insurable interest in his own life and health and his own property. This is why individuals can buy life and health insurance for themselves or family members and property and casualty insurance to protect their homes, automobiles, and personal assets. However, the lack of insurable interest is why a person is not permitted to buy insurance to cover someone else's life or property.

If insurable interest does not exist, an insurance policy will not pay even if it has been issued. If someone purchased a homeowners policy and later sold the house and it burned to the ground, there would be no payment because the policyholder did not have a financial interest in the property. In such cases, the premium paid or a portion of it (minus expenses) would be returned and the contract would be declared void. If someone tried to purchase life insurance on an unrelated celebrity, the policy could not even be issued because of the lack of insurable interest.

Other Elements of Insurability

Additional rules govern what risks are considered suitable subjects for insurance. Risks that do not meet these criteria are probably better handled using an alternate method of risk management or might not be insurable at all (note that these are general rules and there are some exceptions):

➤ The risk of loss must be *definite* as to time and place.

➤ The loss must be *unexpected.*

➤ The risk must be large enough to create a *financial hardship* for the individual involved.

➤ The loss must be *calculable*.

➤ The cost of the insurance must be *affordable* to the insured.

➤ There must be a large number of similar risks so that the *law of large numbers* applies and losses are predictable.

➤ The risk of loss *must not be catastrophic* in nature.

There are some obvious reasons for these rules. If a loss is not definite as to time and place, the insurance policy period might not apply. Only unexpected (accidental) losses can be insured. There is no reason to insure a loss that does not create financial hardship. If premiums were not affordable, nobody would buy insurance. Catastrophic losses, such as war risks and natural disasters, are generally excluded on most insurance policies because there is no way to economically predict the extent of possible losses or develop adequate premiums. However, through insurance pools and various government subsidies, insurance is available to cover some losses because of natural disasters, such as flood or earthquake.

Other Insurance Terms

It is essential that you understand the following terms and how they relate to insurance.

Peril

Whereas risk is the uncertainty of loss, a *peril* is the actual *cause of loss*. Fire and collision are both examples of perils, as are theft, windstorm, hail, smoke, and explosion.

 Until recent decades, many insurance policies used the words "perils insured against" to describe the coverage being provided. Nearly all modern policies use the phrase "covered causes of loss" for this purpose.

Hazard

Hazard is another important term that is distinct from risk or peril. A *hazard* is anything that increases the chance of loss. Suppose that someone was injured when a furnace exploded as the result of a poorly tightened gas connection. The peril was explosion; the hazard was a poorly tightened gas connection.

Physical, Morale, and Moral Hazards

There are three significantly different types of hazards:

➤ A *physical hazard* is a hazard that arises from the condition, occupancy, or use of the property itself. An example of a physical hazard is a skateboard left on the porch steps.

➤ A *morale hazard* exists when an individual, through carelessness or by irresponsible actions, increases the possibility for a loss. An example of a morale hazard is a person who drives a car carelessly because he knows a loss will be insured if an accident occurs.

➤ A *moral hazard* stems from an individual's value system, predominantly a capacity for dishonesty. Starting a fire intentionally or faking a theft, in order to collect insurance, are examples of moral hazards.

Exam Prep Questions

1. Which of the following represents a pure risk?
   - ○ A. Terry places a bet on the outcome of a basketball game.
   - ○ B. Margaret's dog is temperamental. She's afraid that it will bite a neighbor someday and she will be held responsible.
   - ○ C. Sam transfers all of his retirement funds into a stock that he expects to rise in value.
   - ○ D. Cindy, along with 32 others, puts $100 into an Indy 500 race pool at work. The person holding the name of the winning driver will win the entire $3,300.

2. The law of large numbers
   - ○ A. prohibits insurance with extremely high premiums.
   - ○ B. states that there must be a narrow spread of risk for insurance to be effective.
   - ○ C. states that the more examples used to develop a statistic, the more reliable the statistic will be.
   - ○ D. requires all members of society with insurance exposures to purchase insurance.

3. LaTonya purchases a house from John. She borrows $75,000 from First City Bank that, along with her $25,000 down payment, equals the $100,000 purchase price of the home. Who has an insurable interest in this home? Choose all that apply.
   - ❑ A. LaTonya
   - ❑ B. John
   - ❑ C. LaTonya's son, who would like to inherit the home some day
   - ❑ D. First City Bank

4. Highpoint Industries has an automatic sprinkler system installed in its office building. This is an example of which risk management method?
   - ○ A. Avoidance
   - ○ B. Reduction
   - ○ C. Retention
   - ○ D. Transfer

5. Benson Pharmaceutical Company decides not to manufacture a new drug after determining that it has serious potential side effects. This is an example of which risk management method?
   - ○ A. Transfer
   - ○ B. Retention
   - ○ C. Avoidance
   - ○ D. Reduction

6. Because she has always been in good health, Donna decides to cancel her health insurance policy. This is an example of which risk management method?

   ○ A. Retention
   ○ B. Control
   ○ C. Avoidance
   ○ D. Transfer

7. The tread on Alan's automobile tires is very thin. This is an example of what type of hazard?

   ○ A. Physical
   ○ B. Moral
   ○ C. Morale
   ○ D. Obvious

8. Which of the following is a *hazard* as opposed to a peril?

   ○ A. Fire
   ○ B. Lightning
   ○ C. Wet pavement
   ○ D. Flood

Exam Prep Answers

1. B is correct. A pure risk is one that involves only the possibility of loss. Choices A, C, and D are examples of speculative risks in which there exists both the possibility of gain and the possibility of loss.

2. C is correct. The law of large numbers says that the more examples used to develop a statistic, the more reliable the statistic will be.

3. A and D are correct. Insurable interest exists when there is an actual economic interest in the safety or preservation of the subject of the insurance from loss or destruction or financial damage or impairment. LaTonya has an insurable interest in the home because she owns it. First City Bank has an insurable interest as long as it carries a mortgage on the home.

4. B is correct. A sprinkler system can reduce the severity of fires, but it does not prevent them altogether.

5. C is correct. By not producing the drug, Benson avoids the risk of being sued by consumers who are injured by the drug.

6. A is correct. By not carrying health insurance, Donna is retaining the risk of financial loss from unexpected medical expenses.

7. A is correct. Worn tread is a physical condition that reduces Alan's ability to control or stop his vehicle.

8. C is correct. Wet pavement is not by itself a cause of loss (or peril), but it increases the chances of automobile collisions, which are a cause of loss.

The Insurance Contract

Terms you'll need to understand:

✓ Indemnity
✓ Aleatory contract
✓ Contract of adhesion
✓ Unilateral contract
✓ Declarations
✓ Insuring agreement
✓ Conditions
✓ Exclusions

Concepts you'll need to master:

✓ Competent parties
✓ Legal purpose
✓ Offer and acceptance
✓ Consideration
✓ Utmost good faith

A *contract* is a legal agreement between two or more competent parties that promises a certain performance in exchange for a certain consideration. When an insurance company agrees to pay for an insured's losses in exchange for a certain premium, the two parties have entered into a contract. Although a contract of insurance can be oral, it is usually written in the form of an insurance policy.

Elements of a Valid Contract

Insurance contracts, like all other contracts, must exhibit certain characteristics to be legally enforceable. These characteristics are

➤ Competent parties

➤ Legal purpose

➤ Offer and acceptance (agreement)

➤ Consideration

A contract is not valid unless it is made between parties who are considered *competent* under the law. In most cases, a person who is a minor, insane, or under the influence of alcohol or drugs is considered incompetent.

The second requirement for a valid contract is that it be formed for a *legal purpose*. A contract that is against public policy or in violation of the law is not enforceable.

The third element of a valid contract, *offer and acceptance*, means that the contract must involve at least two parties: one who makes an offer and one who accepts it. This is also called an *agreement*. An offer is a promise that requires an act or another promise in exchange. Acceptance occurs when the other party agrees to the offer or does what was proposed in the offer.

The last requirement for a valid contract is that it involve *consideration*. Consideration is a thing of value exchanged for the performance promised in the contract. With insurance, the consideration that the insured gives is the premium payment. The consideration that the insurer gives is the promise to pay for certain losses suffered by the insured.

Characteristics of an Insurance Contract

Insurance contracts have some unique characteristics that are not always found in other types of contracts. These are discussed in the following sections.

Principle of Indemnity

One of the most important characteristics of an insurance contract is that it is a contract of *indemnity*. The principle of indemnity states that when a loss occurs, an individual should be restored to the approximate financial condition he or she was in before the loss.

The principle of indemnity is closely related to both the requirement of an insurable interest and the exclusion of speculative risks. An insured can only be indemnified to the extent of his or her insurable interest. Insurance is not gambling—the insured doesn't "win" or "lose." The insured might only be returned to the approximate financial condition he or she occupied before the loss occurred.

Suppose that Ben and Jerry, who are cousins, each own 50% of a $200,000 duplex, and Ben purchases a $200,000 insurance policy in his name only. If the property is totally destroyed by fire, Ben would only be entitled to collect $100,000 (the extent of his insurable interest).

 Indemnity is a general concept in the insurance business. It does not always apply exactly to loss situations. In cases in which an insured selects deductibles or coinsurance amounts, insurance payments might be less than the actual loss amount. In cases in which an insured has a valued policy or stated amount policy, the insurance settlement could actually be more than the actual loss.

Personal

An insurance contract does not insure property; it insures the person who owns the property. This means that it is a *personal* contract.

Aleatory

Under most types of contracts, the two parties exchange something of equal value—money for services, for example. But under an *aleatory* contract, one party's performance depends on an uncertain event, which means that the exchange of value might appear to be unequal. For example, under an insurance contract, the insured pays premiums, and in return for those premiums, the insurance company only makes a *promise* to pay benefits if a loss occurs. If no loss occurs, no benefits are paid—the insured will have paid money to the insurance company and never gotten any money back. On the other hand, if a large loss occurs, the insurance company may pay benefits to the insured that far exceed the amount of money he or she paid in premium. Because of this potential financial inequality based on an uncertain event, insurance contracts are aleatory contracts.

Adhesion

Insurance policies are contracts of *adhesion*, which means that one party has greater power over the other party in drafting the contract. In an insurance contract, the insurer has greater power over drafting the contract because the provisions of the contract are prepared by the insurer. The insured, who does not take part in the preparation of the contract, simply adheres to the policy terms.

 A problem that sometimes arises in insurance contracts is *ambiguity*, which occurs when the insurer doesn't make the terms and agreements of the policy perfectly clear. Because an insurance policy is an adhesion contract, the courts usually resolve any ambiguity in policy wording in favor of the insured.

Unilateral

An insurance policy is also a *unilateral* contract. "Unilateral" means "one-sided." An insurance policy is one-sided because only the insurance company is legally bound to perform its part of the agreement. If an insured pays a premium and a loss occurs, the insurer is legally bound to pay for the loss under the terms of the policy. However, insureds are not legally obligated to pay premiums. If insureds stop paying premiums, the insurance company can cancel coverage, but it can't take the insurance policy holder to court for breaking the contract.

Contract of Utmost Good Faith

Another characteristic of an insurance contract is that it is a *contract of utmost good faith*. The insurance company relies on the truthfulness and integrity of the applicant when issuing a policy. In return, the insured relies on the company's promise and capability to provide coverage and pay claims.

Conditional

An insurance policy includes a number of conditions that both the insured and the insurer must comply with. For example, if a covered loss occurs, the insured must notify the insurer about the loss, and the insurer must use the valuation methods specified in the policy to settle the loss. For this reason, an insurance policy is a *conditional* contract.

Parts of the Insurance Contract

Because an insurance policy is a legal contract, it must be very specific about the agreements between the insured and the insurer. To do this, most policies contain the following five parts:

➤ Declarations

➤ Insuring agreements

➤ Conditions

➤ Exclusions

➤ Definitions

The *declarations*, which are almost always on the first page of the policy, contain information such as the name of the insured, the address, the amount of coverage provided, a description of the property (if property is involved), and the cost of the policy.

The *insuring agreements*, the "heart" of the policy, state in general what is to be covered or, in other words, the losses for which the insured will be indemnified. This section also describes the type of property covered and the perils against which it is insured.

The *conditions* state the "ground rules" for the policy. They describe the responsibilities and the obligations of both the insurance company and the insured.

The *exclusions* describe the losses for which the insured is not covered. If an excluded loss occurs, the insured will not be indemnified.

Finally, the *definitions* section clarifies the meanings of certain terms used in the policy. For example, auto insurance policies may cover a "newly acquired auto" besides the auto listed in the declarations. The definitions section includes a definition of "newly acquired auto" so that it is understood that the term refers only to passenger vehicles and not other types of vehicle the insured might purchase.

Exam Prep Questions

1. Which of the following is not a requirement for forming a valid contract?

    ○ A. Consideration

    ○ B. Offer and acceptance

    ○ C. Competent parties

    ○ D. Signatures of the parties involved

2. What is meant by a contract of adhesion?

    ○ A. Both parties are required to provide services for the other.

    ○ B. One party draws up the contract provisions, and the other party adheres to the terms.

    ○ C. The contract can be revoked by any party at any time for any reason.

    ○ D. A contract that is formed without any consideration by either party.

3. Which of the following describes the principle of indemnity?

    ○ A. After a loss, an insured should be restored to approximately the same condition that existed before the loss.

    ○ B. Every insured will receive full compensation for all losses in all cases.

    ○ C. When property is damaged or destroyed, the insurance company must pay the full replacement cost.

    ○ D. In the case of bodily injuries, liability coverage must be available without regard to any policy exclusions.

4. Which part of an insurance policy describes what property and/or perils will be covered by the contract?

    ○ A. Definitions

    ○ B. Exclusions

    ○ C. Insuring agreement

    ○ D. Conditions

5. What is the consideration that an insurer gives to the insured under an insurance contract?

    ○ A. Stated benefits and the dates on which they are to be paid

    ○ B. The premium

    ○ C. A promise to pay for certain losses if they occur

    ○ D. A promise to be conscientious about the customer's situation

6. Under an insurance contract, the uncertainty of events can lead to unequal financial results for the two parties. This means that insurance is what kind of contract?

    ○ A. Unilateral

    ○ B. Aleatory

    ○ C. Conditional

    ○ D. Utmost good faith

7. The "ground rules" are described in which part of an insurance policy?
   - ○ A. Definitions
   - ○ B. Exclusions
   - ○ C. Insuring agreement
   - ○ D. Conditions

Exam Prep Answers

1. D is correct. The four requirements for forming a valid contract are competent parties, a legal purpose, offer and acceptance, and consideration. Oral contracts are valid. Contracts do not have to be written or include signatures (although it is a good idea to do so).

2. B is correct. Insurance policies are contracts of adhesion because the insurance company drafts the policy provisions and the insured adheres to the policy terms.

3. A is correct. The principle of indemnity states that when a loss occurs, an individual should be restored to the approximate financial condition he or she was in before the loss.

4. C is correct. The insuring agreements state what types of losses the insured will be indemnified for. This section also describes the type of property covered and the perils against which it is insured.

5. C is correct. Consideration is the thing of value exchanged under a contract. The insured's consideration is the premium; in return, the insurer promises to pay for certain losses if they occur.

6. B is correct. If no loss occurs, the insured will receive no benefits although he or she paid premiums, but if a large loss occurs, the insured might receive benefits that far exceed the premium payments.

7. D is correct. The conditions describe the responsibilities and obligations of the insurer and the insured.

Insurance Company Organization and Regulation

Terms you'll need to understand:

- ✓ Stock insurer
- ✓ Mutual insurer
- ✓ Assessment company
- ✓ Reciprocal insurer
- ✓ Lloyd's Association
- ✓ Fraternal benefit society
- ✓ Risk retention group
- ✓ Purchasing group
- ✓ Insurance agent
- ✓ Countersignature
- ✓ Express authority
- ✓ Implied authority
- ✓ Apparent authority
- ✓ Insurance solicitor
- ✓ Insurance broker
- ✓ Admitted or authorized insurer
- ✓ Nonadmitted or unauthorized insurer
- ✓ Domestic insurer
- ✓ Foreign insurer
- ✓ Alien insurer
- ✓ Twisting
- ✓ Rebating
- ✓ Producer
- ✓ Consultant
- ✓ Loss costs

Concepts you'll need to master:

- ✓ Lines of insurance
- ✓ Agency relationship
- ✓ Rate filings
- ✓ Self-insurance
- ✓ Government insurers
- ✓ Residual insurance markets
- ✓ Personal lines
- ✓ Commercial lines
- ✓ Field underwriting
- ✓ Exclusive or captive agency
- ✓ Direct writer system
- ✓ Direct response system
- ✓ Independent agency system
- ✓ Excess or surplus lines
- ✓ Loss and expense ratios
- ✓ State insurance regulation
- ✓ National Association of Insurance Commissioners

There are several types of insurance organizations and arrangements that provide insurance coverages. Not all of them are corporations (or companies) that are in business to make a profit, but most of them are. The various categories of insurers represent the different ways they raise the money necessary to begin business and enroll their prospects for insurance. Although you need to understand the nature and structure of for-profit insurance companies, you should also know that there are other markets and providers of insurance, including non-incorporated private organizations and the federal and state governments.

Types of Insurance Organizations

In this chapter, the major types of insuring organizations are reviewed first. Then we cover various aspects of insurance company operations and the nature of insurance regulation.

Stock and Mutual Companies

Let's begin with a review of the two most common types of insurance companies. The first type is called a *stock* company. When a stock company forms, it sells stock to stockholders to raise the money necessary to operate the business. Stockholders are not necessarily insured by the company, and insureds do not necessarily own stock in the company. The company is in the business of selling insurance. Profits attributed to the operation of the company are returned as dividends to the stockholders, not the insureds.

NOTE Nothing prohibits stockholders from buying insurance from their own company or insureds from buying shares of stock issued by their insurer. However, ownership of the company is completely independent from any contractual relationships the company has with policyholders as a provider of insurance.

The second type, a *mutual* insurance company, functions differently than a stock company. In a mutual company, there are no stockholders and the policyholders collectively are the owners of the company. As owners, they can vote to elect the management of the company. Profits are returned to the insureds in the form of dividends or reductions in future premiums.

Most mutual companies are *advance premium* companies that charge non-assessable premiums—that is, policyowners are never required to pay anything in addition to their premiums even if losses for the group exceed the amounts paid in during the policy period. A small number of mutual companies are assessment companies, which charge members a pro rata share of losses at the end of each policy period. The cost of coverage from an assessment company will vary each policy period and can be small or large depending on the experience of the group. Assessment mutuals are far less popular than non-assessment mutuals because most people prefer to know that they will not be assessed additional amounts regardless of the group's loss experience. Assessment mutuals provide primarily fire and windstorm insurance for small towns and farmers.

 Both stock and mutual companies are incorporated. Their marketing practices and internal operations are nearly identical. Their structures differ only in the areas of corporate ownership and management control.

Reciprocal Insurers

Although not as common as stock or mutual insurers, coverage is also provided by *reciprocal* insurers or exchanges. A member of a reciprocal agrees to *share* the insurance responsibilities with all other members of the unincorporated group. In a sense, all members insure each other and share the losses with each other. A reciprocal is managed by an *attorney-in-fact* who is empowered to handle all of the business of the reciprocal.

Lloyd's Associations

Another type of insuring organization is called a *Lloyd's Association*. The term originated with the famous insuring group Lloyd's of London, but today a number of other similar groups exist based on the same model. These are not really insurance companies. They are voluntary associations of individuals, or groups of individuals, who agree to share in insurance contracts. Each individual, or "*syndicate*," is individually responsible for the amounts of insurance they write.

Fraternal Benefit Societies

Limited types of insurance are also provided by *fraternal benefit societies*. A fraternal benefit society is an incorporated society or order, without capital stock, that is operated on the lodge system and conducted solely for the benefit of its members and their beneficiaries, and not for profit.

A type of insurance used by fraternal benefit societies is an "*open contract.*" Under this type of contract, the society's charter, constitution, and bylaws become part of the insurance contract, and any amendments to them automatically become amendments to the insurance contract. The society is contractually obligated to pay; no amendment can omit or diminish society benefits.

 Fraternals offer insurance that is available only to their members. Most write only life and health insurance.

Risk Retention Groups and Purchasing Groups

In 1981, Congress passed the Liability Risk Retention Act to give product manufacturers more options when insuring against product liability. The Act enables product manufacturers to establish group self-insurance programs or group captive insurance companies, called *risk retention groups (RRGs)*, to protect them against product liability exposures. Federal law also enables businesses in the same trade or industry with similar liability exposures to purchase liability insurance on a group basis through *purchasing groups (PGs)*. Risk retention groups and purchasing groups are regulated in the states where they are domiciled, but once formed they can transact business in all other states.

 Risk retention groups, as providers of insurance, must be licensed and authorized as liability insurers in at least one state where they operate. Purchasing groups, as buyers of insurance, are not required to be licensed or authorized.

Self-Insurance

Some businesses and individuals choose to *self-insure*. With this option, part or all the risk of loss is borne without the benefit of insurance coverage to fall back on if a loss occurs. Some large companies are self-insured because they have the resources to withstand losses and their claims experience demonstrates that it is cheaper to be self-insured than to pay for insurance coverage.

Private Versus Government Insurers

Providers of insurance can be privately owned or operated by the state or federal government. The insurers reviewed so far (stock, mutuals, reciprocals, and so on) are all examples of private insurers.

Historically, the government has often stepped in to provide insurance for catastrophic type losses that is not ordinarily available from private insurers. Sometimes it does this directly under government insurance programs; other times it makes coverage available by providing reinsurance or subsidies to private carriers. This type of insurance is sometimes called *residual market insurance*. Over the years, the federal government has provided such things as war risk insurance, nuclear energy liability insurance, flood insurance, and federal crop insurance. State governments have organized insurance pools to provide medical malpractice insurance and auto or property insurance for individuals who are such poor risks that they can't obtain coverage in the open market.

At the state level, governments have been involved in providing unemployment insurance, and in some cases, workers compensation and disability benefits, through various state funds.

Lines of Insurance

In addition to differentiating insurers according to the nature of their structural organization, another way of classifying insurance companies is by the type of insurance policies they write. Insurance coverages are often broken down in to *lines of insurance*, which are groupings of similar kinds of insurance for statistical and reporting purposes. Information about premiums and losses is frequently analyzed by line of insurance at the company level. They are also used to monitor agency operations by examining individual agencies to determine which lines of insurance are profitable and which are not.

Four Major Lines of Insurance

There are four broad categories, or lines, of insurance:

➤ Property

➤ Casualty

➤ Life

➤ Health and Disability

An insurance company that writes only one line of insurance is referred to as a *mono-line* company. An insurance company that writes more than one line of insurance is called a *multi-line* company. Many large companies write all lines of insurance.

Personal and Commercial Lines

Each of the four major categories of insurance can be further subdivided into both personal and commercial lines. *Personal lines* are property-casualty coverages that protect an individual or family. *Commercial lines* are coverages designed for businesses.

Insurance Company Organization

Whether an insurance company is mono-line or multi-line, whether it specializes in personal lines or commercial lines, it is made up of people who perform various functions. Many of them work in the background and do not have direct exposure to the general public. Yet they perform vital functions for the companies they work for.

Agents and Their Duties

Perhaps the first person most people think of when they think of insurance is the *insurance agent*. The agent, who represents the insurance company, is the most direct link between the company and its insureds. As such, the agent has many responsibilities.

An agent's primary duty is to *sell insurance*. This is the product of the insurance business. Companies need sales to have revenue to finance operations and pay claims. Agents need sales to earn the commissions that are their livelihood.

In most states, a resident agent's *countersignature* is required to validate the contract. Countersigning means the agent signs each new policy prepared by the company before delivering it to the insured.

An agent is often responsible for *field underwriting* risks. This means using pre-established criteria to seek out the type of business that is likely to be acceptable to the company. Although the company underwriter makes the final decision to accept a risk, the agent also has a responsibility to seek out quality business.

Before selling a policy, agents must obtain information on the prospect's particular exposures and review existing policies. The agent must analyze the prospect's coverage needs and make recommendations as to the amount and type of coverage appropriate for each exposure.

Agents often prepare a *quotation* that will show a prospect what the premium for the proposed coverage will be. And when the prospect buys, the agent must complete, or help the client complete, a detailed *application*. The application must be carefully, completely, and accurately filled out and submitted on a timely basis.

The agent must make sure that the client understands the type of coverage being purchased and what the insured's responsibilities are under the policy, as well as the services that will be provided by the agent and the insurance company. The agent can also be expected to deliver the policy.

Once a policy is in force, the agent has a continuing responsibility toward the insured. At least once a year, the agent should review the client's coverage and evaluate the adequacy of the coverage provided. The agent must also stay current with new coverages that might be appropriate for the client.

At any time during the policy year, the agent must be available to assist the insured with *service needs*, such as a name change or a change in the method of premium payment, and maintain accurate records of all such changes requested by the insured. The agent can also assist the insured in filing and following up on claims. Some companies give the agent authority to settle certain types of claims.

Not only does the insurance agent have a moral obligation to fulfill these duties, but there are legal obligations as well. Agents who are negligent in meeting their responsibilities can be liable for their inadvertent errors.

Errors and Omissions insurance (E&O coverage) is available for insurance agents to cover their liability for mistakes, but not for intentional actions or fraud.

Continuing Education Needs for Agents

The insurance business is constantly changing, so it's critical that insurance professionals maintain lifelong educational programs to keep their professional knowledge and skills up-to-date. Many states have *continuing education* laws that require agents to take a certain number of hours of insurance-related course work before their licenses can be renewed.

In states that do not have continuing education laws, insurance professionals must assess their own needs for continuing education and engage in ongoing improvement of their knowledge and skills. One way to do this is by earning *professional designations* from organizations such as The American Institute for Chartered Property Casualty Underwriters and the Insurance Institute of America.

These organizations have developed a variety of programs to meet the educational needs of insurance professionals. Some of the designations offered by these institutes include Chartered Property-Casualty Underwriter (CPCU), Accredited Adviser in Insurance (AAI), and Associate in Personal Insurance (API). Although not required, these designations add significantly to an agent's status and credibility.

Authority of Agents

An *agency relationship* exists when one party (an *agent*) is authorized to act on behalf of another (a *principal*). In the insurance business, the principal is the insurance company and the agent is a person authorized to act on the company's behalf. Principals grant certain powers, or authority, to their agents, and when agents act under these powers, their acts are considered to be the acts of the principal. These acts include making contracts and accepting money.

The "knowledge" of an agent is held to be the knowledge of the principal. For example, suppose that the applicant tells the agent something very important with regard to the applicant's insurability. According to the law of agency, even if the agent does not list this information on the application, the applicant is revealing the information to the insurance company through the "knowledge" of the agent.

There are three separate levels of an insurance agent's authority:

➤ Express authority

➤ Implied authority

➤ Apparent authority

Express authority is the authority specifically given to an agent, either orally or in writing, by the principal. Written authority is usually provided through an agency agreement that allows the agent to countersign, issue, and deliver policies and provide other customary services on all contracts accepted by the insurer from the agent.

Implied authority is authority given by the insurance company to the agent that is not formally expressed or communicated. This implied authority allows the agent to perform all the usual and necessary tasks to sell and service insurance contracts and to fully exercise the agent's express authority. For example, if an agent has express authority to sell a certain coverage, he or she would have the implied authority to describe the coverage to prospective customers and make decisions regarding the appropriateness of the coverage for particular customers.

Apparent authority is a doctrine which holds that an agent can have whatever authority a reasonable person would assume he or she has. In the public's eye, an agent acting under apparent authority binds the company as fully as under expressed or implied authority. For example, an agent who has an insurer's logo on his or her business and business stationery and on the sign over his or her door has the apparent authority to represent that insurer to the public. Should the insurer revoke the agent's authority to represent it, but not take care to see that the company's logo is removed from the business card, stationery, and sign over the door, the insurer could still be bound by the agent's actions on its behalf.

 The express authority of an insurance agent is the most legally determinable type of authority. The written agency agreement spells out which lines of insurance an agent is authorized to write, whether the agent has the authority to bind coverages, whether the agent can collect premiums, and whether the agent can settle small claims directly. These issues and other specific instructions given to the agent orally are clearly specified. Implied and apparent authority are not so clear-cut, and violations in these areas are usually determined by the courts.

Insurance Marketing Systems

Generally, there are four basic distribution systems used to market insurance:

➤ Exclusive agency system

➤ Direct writer system

➤ Direct response system

➤ Independent agency system

In an *exclusive* or *captive agency system*, the insurance company contracts with agencies, which are independent businesses, to represent and sell insurance on a commission basis only for that insurance company.

In the *direct writer system*, the insurance company's agents are employees of the insurance company. They can receive a salary or be paid by commission, or a combination of both.

In the *direct response system*, there are no agents. These companies sell through direct mail, over the phone, or through the Internet.

In the *independent agency system*, agencies that work independently contract with several different companies to represent and sell insurance for those companies. An agent who represents more than one company is called an *independent* or *nonexclusive agent*. Several companies can authorize the agent to sell insurance for them, but the agent remains an independent businessperson. The agent collects commissions on the policies sold, but collects no salary from the companies he or she represents.

In the exclusive agency, direct writer, and direct response systems, the insurance company owns and controls its accounts, policy records, and renewals. If the agency or employment relationship terminates, that person loses all rights and interest in company business and related commissions.

In the independent agency system, the agent owns and controls accounts, policy records, and renewals. If an independent agent's contract with a particular insurer terminates, that agent retains rights to active accounts and can place them with another insurer and continue to receive commissions.

Other Insurance Professionals

In addition to insurance agents, there are other classifications of insurance salespeople, such as solicitors, brokers, and excess or surplus lines agents. Although not every state recognizes these classifications, we'll explain briefly how these positions differ from that of a typical insurance agent.

A *solicitor*, like an agent, sells insurance and can even be authorized to collect premiums. However, a solicitor cannot issue or countersign policies—this responsibility can only be handled by an agent. So a solicitor, who often works with or for an agent, has more limited authority than the agent.

Both agents and solicitors represent insurance companies. A *broker*, on the other hand, represents the insureds. A client who is seeking insurance could contact a broker, who in turn might contact several insurance companies to find the insurance that is best for the client.

Although a broker can sometimes appear to act as an agent of the insurer in certain activities such as policy delivery, legally a broker does not represent any insurer and does not have the authority to bind an insurer to an insurance contract.

Excess or *surplus lines* are highly specialized insurance coverages, such as auto racing liability insurance or tuition refund insurance, that are often not available from any company admitted to do business in a state. An *excess* or *surplus lines agent* is an agent licensed by the state to handle the placement of such coverages with *nonadmitted companies* (ones not authorized to conduct business in the state under ordinary circumstances).

Producer is a general term used to describe someone who sells insurance, including agents, brokers, and solicitors.

Another type of insurance professional you might encounter is an insurance *consultant*. A consultant is someone who, for a fee, offers advice on the benefits, advantages, and disadvantages of various insurance policies.

 Consultants don't actually sell *insurance*; they sell *advice*.

Other Insurance Functions

Of course, agents would have nothing to sell if it weren't for the other functions taking place in the insurance company—at both its central, or "home" office and its regional or branch offices.

Underwriting Department

Underwriting is the process of selecting certain types of risks and rejecting others so that as a whole, the policies issued by the insurance company will produce the company's desired results. The underwriting department is usually made up of many individual underwriters who make the decisions about whether to accept or reject the applications sent in by agents based on the company's standards and their own judgment. They can also be called on to review loss experience, provide judgment rates, and specify the particular policy forms that are required to provide the coverages that applicants have requested.

Underwriters use the following three financial ratios to help them accomplish their task:

➤ Loss ratio

➤ Expense ratio

➤ Combined ratio

The *loss ratio* is used to compare the company's operations from year to year. It shows the percentage of losses the company incurred for every dollar of earned premium. It is calculated by dividing the amount of incurred losses by the amount of earned premium.

Earned premium is the premium that the company actually earned by providing insurance protection for the designated period of time.

Incurred losses include amounts paid on claims for covered losses and various expenses related to handling claims.

The *expense ratio* indicates the cost of doing business. It is calculated by dividing total underwriting expenses by total written premiums.

Underwriting expenses are the costs required to acquire and maintain a book of business. They include expenses for advertising, commissions, salaries, and other administrative costs, as well as regulatory costs such as taxes and licensing fees.

Written premium is the gross amount of premium income on the company's books. It includes both earned and unearned premiums. Premiums for new business, renewals, and policy endorsements make up written premium.

The *combined ratio* is simply the sum of the loss ratio and the expense ratio. Traditionally, 100% is considered to be the break-even point. A combined ratio of less than 100% indicates that the company had an underwriting profit; a ratio greater than 100% indicates a loss.

Policy Issue and Administration

After the underwriter has approved a new application or a change to a current policy, a whole series of events takes place. A *policy analyst* or *screener* checks the application to make sure that all information is correct and complete. It then goes to a *rater* who computes the premium to be charged. The policy forms can be printed by computer or assembled using preprinted forms with specific declarations and endorsements unique to that risk.

Claims Department

The claims department sees that the company's insureds are adequately indemnified for their losses. *Claim adjusters* or *representatives* are used to inspect a loss, determine whether there is coverage for the loss, estimate indemnification, and in some cases, pay for the loss immediately. Large companies have their own claim adjusters, whereas smaller companies might use the services of independent adjusters.

Actuarial and Statistical Department

The actuarial and statistical department is the "numbers" department. Using the tremendous amount of data generated by computer, together with statistics available from other companies, *actuaries* determine the rates to be charged for various types of insurance.

Accounting Department

As with any profit-oriented business, the determination of financial condition is a very important function in an insurance company. However, insurance companies must place special emphasis in this area because their finances are closely regulated by the states—for example, premiums must be credited to specific accounts, agents must be paid commissions, and proper reserves must be maintained. All these functions are handled by the accounting department.

Investment Department

The investment department oversees the funds the company needs to invest to make sure that adequate funds will be on hand to pay claims. The investment department attempts to maintain a healthy rate of return while maintaining the safety of the investment. Because money must be on hand to pay future obligations, highly speculative stocks are not appropriate, and at least some of the investments must be readily convertible to cash, as needed.

Legal Department

Because insurance policies are legal contracts, it is not surprising that insurance companies maintain a legal staff. This department interprets the various state insurance laws and helps the company keep its policies and practices in compliance. A key role is the department's involvement with court cases arising from claims. The legal department is instrumental in helping determine fair indemnification for insureds and is also involved in the company's other legal actions.

Audit Department

For certain insurance coverages, a premium is determined after or during the policy term, instead of at the beginning of the policy term. These "after-the-fact" premiums can be based on a number of factors such as payroll, number of employees, or amount of receipts. The audit department checks the accounting records of these insureds at the required intervals to obtain the necessary information used to determine these types of premium.

Loss Control Department

Whereas an insured is glad when insurance pays for a loss, he or she would rather have no loss at all. This is why prevention and control of losses are very important aspects of the insurance business. The loss control department, or "engineering department" as it might be called in some companies, inspects factories, certifies boilers, and makes recommendations to insureds as to how risks can be avoided or reduced.

Loss control is a vital function of the insurance business. Nobody wins when significant losses occur. The insurance companies would rather not have to pay large claims, and insureds who can be reimbursed for part of their loss often have to assume deductible amounts and suffer the inconvenience of disruptions resulting from the loss. Traditionally, loss control experts recommend the use of burglar alarms, sprinkler alarms, changes in operations, and other things that are designed to avoid or reduce losses.

Agency Department

This department works very closely with, and directs the operations of, the agents who represent the company. Its responsibilities include recruiting, appointing, and training, especially if an agent will be an exclusive agent. The department must monitor the sales and marketing efforts of these agents and make sure that the number and quality of agents are closely tuned to the market the company serves.

Marketing Department

Closely related to the agency department, the marketing department helps determine the company's overall marketing strategy. It develops advertising and sales aides or works closely with a separate advertising department to accomplish these goals.

Reinsurance Department

Insurance companies often purchase insurance to cover their own exposure to loss. This is called *reinsurance*. Reinsurance helps protect insurance companies from catastrophic losses and from wild fluctuations in underwriting results. This coverage can be obtained on a policy-by-policy basis or on the basis of a whole block of policies. The reinsurance can cover the initial insurer for losses above a certain amount or can call for losses to be shared on a pro rata basis.

Miscellaneous Support Departments

Like all other businesses, insurance companies have departments whose contributions help all other departments operate smoothly. They include personnel, training, management information systems (MIS), general administration, and building and maintenance departments.

Regulation of Insurance

Although some federal regulations affect insurance directly, such as the Fair Credit Reporting Act and a few programs that make coverage for catastrophic losses available, such as FEMA's (Federal Emergency Management

Agency) National Flood Insurance Program, insurance is regulated primarily at the state level.

State Insurance Regulation

Insurance is closely regulated for the good of the insurance industry and the general public. Each state has its own laws and regulations to regulate the insurance business conducted within its boundaries.

Each state has an *insurance department* headed by an official charged with the responsibility for controlling insurance matters within that state. These officials are called directors, superintendents, or commissioners of insurance, depending on the state where they hold office, but they all perform similar duties. The term "commissioner" applies in most states.

Collectively, the commissioners of all states form a body known as the *National Association of Insurance Commissioners (NAIC)*, which meets at regular intervals to exchange information and provide coordination of the regulatory measures of each state. Through its recommendations, much of the nation's insurance laws take shape. Although nonbinding on individual states, the NAIC's recommendations are generally followed.

Regulation of Companies

State regulation of insurance companies affects numerous aspects of their formation and operations, ranging from capital and surplus requirements to investment and marketing practices. State laws require the reporting of financial data and payment of premium taxes, and specifically prohibit a number of unfair or deceptive practices.

Admitted and Nonadmitted Companies

One of the duties of an insurance department is to determine which insurance companies will be allowed to do business in the state. A company that meets the insurance department's standards and is authorized to do business in a state is called an *admitted* or *authorized insurer*. An insurance company that is not authorized to do business in a state is a *nonadmitted* or *unauthorized insurer*. A nonadmitted insurer can only do business in the state under special circumstances.

Domestic, Foreign, and Alien Companies

Although a company can conduct business in several states, it is formed and incorporated in only one state. Within its home state, an insurance company is known as a *domestic* company. Within states other than the state in which it is incorporated, an insurance company is a *foreign* company. A company that is incorporated in a country other than the United States, but doing business in the states, is known as an *alien* company.

In many areas, state laws specifically differentiate between domestic companies and foreign and alien companies. Many of these differences focus on financial and reporting requirements as well as provisions for resolving legal disputes. These requirements are designed to protect the public. Although foreign and alien companies are permitted to do business within a state, special regulatory provisions that do not apply to domestic companies are necessary because the insurers are based outside of the state's jurisdiction.

Financial Regulation

In addition to examining and authorizing companies to conduct business within the state, the state insurance department keeps close watch over the financial health of all companies doing business within its boundaries.

Various regulations are designed to preserve insurance company solvency, to detect financial problems, and to protect insureds in the event that insolvency occurs. State laws impose capital and surplus requirements on insurers, require the preparation of annual financial statements, and require periodic examinations of insurers. These laws establish initial financial requirements and help in the early detection of financial problems. If an insurer falls into a hazardous financial condition, the insurance department attempts to rehabilitate the company. If an insurer becomes insolvent, the insurance department will handle the liquidation.

In many states, the public is also protected by one or more *insurance guaranty associations* that provide funds for payment of unpaid claims when an insurer becomes insolvent.

Company Ratings

There are several organizations that rate the financial strength of insurance carriers, based on an analysis of a company's claims experience, investment performance, management, and other factors. These organizations include A.M. Best, Standard & Poor, and Moody's. These ratings are one of the most widely used indicators of financial health (or the lack of it) in the insurance industry.

Regulation of Agents

Many insurance regulations are directed toward governing the qualification and behavior of insurance agents. As the primary source of contact between insurance companies and members of the general public, it is important that agents be properly educated and act in an ethical and professional manner.

Licensing

The state insurance department devotes much of its time to working with insurance agents. One of its most important duties with regard to agents is licensing. It is illegal for someone to sell insurance without first obtaining a license from the state to do so.

To make sure that agents will be prepared to undertake their substantial responsibilities, each state requires its agents to pass a licensing exam to receive a license. This exam is administered by the state insurance department.

An agent may only offer insurance in the states where he or she holds the proper license. For example, an agent who is licensed to sell insurance only in his or her resident state of Indiana could not provide insurance on an Indiana customer's lake home located in Michigan. However, the Indiana agent could obtain a nonresident agent license from Michigan, and in that case he or she could sell coverage on property located in that other state.

Codes Regulating Agents

In addition to licensing, the state is responsible for the way agents conduct business within the state. State insurance codes are very specific about the standards agents must meet.

A *fiduciary* is a person who stands in a special relationship of trust to another person. Agents have fiduciary duties toward their clients, especially regarding the handling of premiums.

Agents cannot *misrepresent* or falsely advertise the terms or benefits of a policy or the financial condition of the company. Agents must make complete, accurate statements about the product being sold.

Twisting is a form of misrepresentation in which the agent convinces the client to cancel already existing insurance and buy another policy from the agent, to the detriment of the insured. Twisting is illegal.

Rebating is giving or offering some benefit other than those specified in the policy—such as cash, gifts, or securities—to induce a customer to buy insurance. For example, an agent might kick back part of a commission to the customer, thus lowering the price of the insurance in return for the business. Rebating is illegal in all but two states.

Agents can be in violation of the law if they *unfairly discriminate* against insured people. This means that an insured cannot be given a lower or higher rate than another insured in identical circumstances. It also means that the agent cannot accept a bribe from a client to provide insurance or lower the premium.

Form and Rate Filings

Another important function performed by state insurance departments is approval, or ratification, of the policy forms, endorsements, and rates used by companies doing business in their states. *Rates* are the basic charges an insurance company sets for various types of insurance.

In some states, called *prior approval* states, the insurance company must obtain official approval before using new forms and rates.

In *file and use* states, a company can begin using forms and rates as soon as they have been filed. The state eventually reviews the filing and officially accepts or rejects it. With *use and file* states, insurers must file rates and forms within a certain period of time after they are first used.

In *open competition* states, the state allows the companies to compete openly with the forms and rates they select, subject only to requirements of adequacy and nondiscrimination.

In some states, for some lines of insurance, the use of unique state forms or rates can be *mandatory* for any company doing business in the state.

Rating Organizations

Some states establish their own rates for certain types of insurance and require all companies to use these mandatory rates. For most types of insurance, however, the company must establish the rates and submit them to the state.

Rate-making involves collecting extensive and accurate financial, operational, premium, and loss records. To assist the insurance company in collecting these statistics, certain central *service bureaus* have been established. These organizations—made up of numerous individual insurance companies—gather, pool, and analyze statistics from all the member companies. The bureau then establishes *loss costs* based on these combined figures and files them with individual states. Loss costs represent the key component of an insurance rate—how much an insurance company needs to collect to cover expected losses.

Member companies can use these loss costs combined with factors covering their own expenses and profit margins to establish finished rates. Companies must file rates with the state but can do this by referencing the service bureau's loss costs and filing their own individual factors reflecting expenses and profit. Some companies do not belong to a service organization and collect their own statistics and file independently.

Companies that use bureau filings sometimes *deviate* from the published rates by charging something either higher or lower than the recommended rate. Deviations are usually permitted within a specified range, provided that the insurer is consistent in applying the same deviation to all similar risks.

One of the largest services bureaus is the *Insurance Services Office*, commonly referred to as ISO, which files both loss costs and standardized forms on behalf of its member companies. The *National Council on Compensation Insurance, Inc. (NCCI)* is a rating bureau that has jurisdiction over the workers compensation field. The *Surety Association Of America* functions as a rating bureau for surety bonds. There are numerous other rating bureaus.

Enforcement

An important area of regulatory responsibility for the state insurance departments is enforcement of the many laws and rules that apply to the conduct of the companies, agents, and types of insurance transacted within the state. The department is responsible for seeing that the insurance business within its jurisdiction operates in compliance with these codes and standards. Reported violations must be investigated, and appropriate penalties assessed. Violations can result in fines, license suspension or revocation, suspension or revocation of a company's authority to do business in the state, and, in some cases, imprisonment.

Federal Regulation

Although most insurance operations are regulated by the states, there are some areas where the federal government has exercised its regulatory authority. For example, federal law imposes penalties for *fraud and false statements* made in connection with insurance transactions. Anyone engaged in the insurance business who makes a false material statement or report or willfully and materially overvalues any land, property, or security in connection with financial reports or documents presented to an insurance regulatory official or agency for the purpose of influencing their actions can be subject to punishment. Any insurance officer, director, or agent who willfully embezzles, abstracts, purloins, or misappropriates any of the moneys, funds, premiums, credits, or other property of an insurer can be punished accordingly. Punishments can consist of substantial fines and/or periods of imprisonment for up to 10 years.

Exam Prep Questions

1. A mutual insurance company
   - ○ A. is managed by an attorney-in-fact.
   - ○ B. pays dividends to its stockholders.
   - ○ C. is owned by its insureds.
   - ○ D. is a voluntary association of individuals that shares in writing insurance contracts for a variety of risks.

2. A nonexclusive agent
   - ○ A. represents a single insurance company.
   - ○ B. works for a direct writer.
   - ○ C. is an independent businessperson.
   - ○ D. does not collect commissions.

3. Solicitors may not
   - ○ A. issue or countersign policies.
   - ○ B. sell insurance.
   - ○ C. collect premiums.
   - ○ D. sign an application.

4. At DEF Insurance Company, agents are employees of the company who are paid a salary plus commissions. This is an example of what type of insurance marketing system?
   - ○ A. Captive
   - ○ B. Independent
   - ○ C. Direct writer
   - ○ D. Direct response

5. Which insurance company department is responsible for accepting and rejecting applications based on company standards?
   - ○ A. Underwriting
   - ○ B. Loss Control
   - ○ C. Claims
   - ○ D. Agency

6. Which insurance company department is responsible for paying insureds' covered losses?
   - ○ A. Audit
   - ○ B. Claims
   - ○ C. Underwriting
   - ○ D. Reinsurance

7. Who is responsible for licensing insurance agents?
   - ○ A. Lloyd's Associations
   - ○ B. State insurance department
   - ○ C. Interstate Commerce Commission
   - ○ D. Insurance Services Office

8. Agent Blondell is offering a free television to every applicant who agrees to buy insurance through his agency. In most states, this is an illegal practice known as
   - ○ A. rebating.
   - ○ B. twisting.
   - ○ C. misrepresentation.
   - ○ D. failure of fiduciary responsibility.

9. J&M Industries does not have a group health insurance plan for its employees. Instead, it pays employees' medical expenses out of a fund specifically created for this purpose. This is an example of
   - ○ A. fraternal insurance.
   - ○ B. self-insurance.
   - ○ C. reinsurance.
   - ○ D. government insurance.

10. Which of the following statements concerning regulation of the insurance industry is correct?
    - ○ A. The insurance industry is regulated exclusively by the federal government.
    - ○ B. The insurance industry is very loosely regulated.
    - ○ C. The state insurance department is responsible for controlling insurance matters within the state.
    - ○ D. The state insurance department serves only the interests of the insurance industry.

11. Which of the following is *not* one of the duties of an agent?
    - ○ A. Making appropriate coverage recommendations to prospective customers
    - ○ B. Writing the provisions of a customer's policy
    - ○ C. Helping prospective customers complete the application
    - ○ D. Assuring that customers understand the coverage they are purchasing

12. The written agency contract between an insurer and an agent constitutes the agent's
    - ○ A. express authority.
    - ○ B. implied authority.
    - ○ C. assertive authority.
    - ○ D. apparent authority.

13. The Excel Insurance Company is incorporated in the state of Tennessee. It is also authorized to do business in Georgia. In Georgia, Excel is known as what type of company?

   ○ A. Alien

   ○ B. Foreign

   ○ C. Domestic

   ○ D. Non-admitted

14. Can states require insurance companies to use certain forms or rates in connection with certain types of insurance?

   ○ A. No, that would be a violation of the principle of open competition.

   ○ B. No, they can only require that forms and rates be subject to prior approval.

   ○ C. No, insurers can always begin using forms and rates as soon as they are properly filed with the state.

   ○ D. Yes, some states have mandatory forms or rates for certain coverages.

Exam Prep Answers

1. C is correct. In a mutual company, insureds are also owners of the company. They can vote to elect the management of the company. Profits are returned to insureds in the form of dividends or reductions in future premiums.

2. C is correct. A nonexclusive, or independent, agent represents more than one company. This type of agent collects commissions on the policies sold, but collects no salary from the companies he or she represents.

3. A is correct. A solicitor, who often works with or for an agent, has more limited authority than the agent. A solicitor sells insurance and might even be authorized to collect premiums. However, a solicitor cannot issue or countersign policies.

4. C is correct. In the direct writer system, the insurer's agents are actually employees. They can receive a salary, be paid on commission, or both.

5. A is correct. Underwriting is the process of selecting certain types of risks and rejecting others so that the insurer will have a profitable book of business.

6. B is correct. The claims department sees that the company's insureds are adequately indemnified for their losses. Claim adjusters determine the cause of loss, whether the loss is covered by the policy, the value of the loss, and the amount of loss payable by the policy.

7. B is correct. State insurance departments devote much of their time to working with insurance agents. One of their most important duties is agent licensing.

8. A is correct. Rebating is giving or offering some benefit other than those specified in the policy, such as cash, gifts, or securities, to induce a customer to buy insurance. Rebating is illegal in all but two states.

9. B is correct. With self-insurance, part or all of the risk of loss is borne without the benefit of insurance coverage to fall back on if a loss occurs.

10. C is correct. Insurance is regulated primarily by the states. It is closely regulated for the good of the insurance industry and the general public.

11. B is correct. Agents have a responsibility to interact effectively with customers in regard to the insurance transaction, but they do not determine the provisions of the policies the insurer issues.

12. A is correct. The specific provisions of the written agency contract constitute the authority expressly given to the agent by the insurer.

13. B is correct. Insurance companies are known as domestic companies in their home states, foreign companies in other states in which they are admitted to do business, and alien companies if their home office is located in a country other than the United States.

14. D is correct. In addition to open competition, prior approval, and file-and-use rules, some states mandate the forms or rates for certain coverages.

4

Insurance Transactions

Terms you'll need to understand:

✓ Insurance application
✓ Binder
✓ Adverse selection
✓ Certificate of insurance
✓ Misrepresentation
✓ Concealment
✓ Fraud
✓ Warranty
✓ Waiver
✓ Estoppel

Concepts you'll need to master:

✓ Underwriting
✓ Regular consumer report
✓ Investigative consumer report
✓ Judgment rating
✓ Manual or class rating
✓ Merit rating
✓ Experience rating
✓ Policy period
✓ Unearned premium
✓ Short rate cancellation
✓ Pro rata cancellation
✓ Flat cancellation

A number of steps must be taken before an insurance transaction can be completed. These include making an application for insurance, underwriting the risk, and including all the steps required for forming a valid contract.

Applications

Before an insurance policy can be issued, the prospective insured must apply to the insurance company. The agent and the applicant fill out an *application* form that is then forwarded to the insurance company. The application is the insured's offer, which is one of the requirements for forming a legal contract.

The application contains underwriting information to help the company decide whether it should accept or reject the prospect's offer to become an insured. The application also contains rating information that will help the insurance company decide how much the insured will be charged if the policy is issued.

Because the application represents the company's primary source of information about the risk to be insured, it is vitally important that the agent fill out the application completely and accurately. The agent must make sure to ask the prospect each and every question on the application form, faithfully recording answers and questioning information that seems vague or inaccurate to provide as clear a picture of the risk as possible. Failure to do so can be expensive for the company, the prospect, and the agent.

Agents have errors and omissions exposure on both sides of the transaction equation. Agents might be sued for negligence by insureds if they fail to recommend needed coverages and a loss occurs. Agents might also be sued by insurance companies if they breach their authority and commit the insurer to losses that they would not otherwise be obligated to cover.

Binders

After an agent has completed the application, he or she may have the authority to issue a *binder* for insurance. This is an oral or written statement made by the agent that the insured has immediate protection that is valid for a specified time. If it is an oral statement, it must be backed up in writing as soon as possible.

A binder issued by an agent is only valid if the agent has express authority to issue the binder for the specific coverages involved. Binders that exceed an agent's authority do not directly obligate the insurance company, but can expose the agent to legal action if a loss occurs.

Binders can also be issued directly by the insurance company. This is often done to let the insured know that there is coverage, but that a few days will be required before the actual policy is issued.

A binder does not guarantee that a policy will be issued; it only guarantees temporary coverage. The insurance company has access to additional information that is not readily available to an agent. This information might convince the company to refuse to issue the policy, even though the agent has already issued a binder.

In cases in which a binder has been issued and coverage for a full policy term is denied, coverage under the binder can be cancelled by a formal cancellation or rejection notice. However, if no formal cancellation is made, coverage remains in effect until the binder expires. If the policy is issued, coverage under the binder ceases as of the effective date of the policy.

Underwriting a Policy

When the application comes to the insurance company, underwriters review it for its acceptability. In addition to the application, underwriters may turn to other sources of information to help them evaluate the risk. These may include

➤ Inspection services

➤ Government bureaus

➤ Insurance industry bureaus

➤ Financial information service organizations

➤ Previous insurers

➤ The company's own claim files

Let's look at these sources of information in more detail, beginning with the Fair Credit Reporting Act.

Fair Credit Reporting Act

When an application is submitted to an insurance company, a consumer reporting agency is often hired to obtain information about the applicant. Reports that have traditionally been called "credit reports" are actually "*consumer reports.*" In addition to a consumer's credit standing, these reports explore personal character, reputation, habits, and lifestyle.

Public reaction to the misuse of personal information led to the enactment of the federal Fair Credit Reporting Act. This Act protects consumers by requiring that the consumer be notified in certain situations and by establishing provisions for the removal of outdated and incorrect information. One of the purposes of the Act is to ensure that credit reporting agencies exercise their responsibilities with fairness, impartiality, and a respect for the consumer's right to privacy.

The Act applies to the preparation and use of two types of reports: *regular consumer reports* and *investigative consumer reports*. The two contain similar types of information, but the investigative report gathers data through personal interviews with friends, neighbors, and associates of the consumer.

Under the Act, reporting agencies can furnish reports only for specific purposes, which are spelled out in the law. A report can be provided to someone who intends to use the information for insurance underwriting purposes or in connection with employment, credit transactions, or other types of personal business transactions.

There are limits under the law as to the type of information that may be reported and the period of time during which certain kinds of information may be included. For example, consumer reports may not contain any information about bankruptcies that are more than 10 years old. Other types of adverse information, such as that pertaining to lawsuits, liens, and arrests, that is more than seven years old may not be included in most reports.

Prior to or shortly after an investigative report (but not a regular report) is ordered, the consumer must be informed in writing that the report may be made and that additional information about the nature and scope of the report is available upon written request. The *initial written notice* must be sent to the consumer no later than *three days* after the report is ordered. Many insurers provide prenotification by stating on the insurance application that an investigative report can be ordered. If a consumer requests the additional information about the nature of the report, the disclosure must be made within five days.

If a consumer is denied or charged extra for coverage, the insurance company must tell the consumer what source of information was used to make the adverse decision.

 Under the law, if a consumer challenges any information, the reporting agency is required to reinvestigate and change the report if necessary. If inaccurate information was given to any individuals or organizations within the previous six months, the consumer's side of the story must be provided to those parties.

Both reporting agencies and users of reports are subject to civil and criminal *penalties* for failure to comply with the provisions of the Act. Violations can be punished by fines and/or imprisonment.

Adverse Selection

Underwriters are responsible for protecting the insurer against *adverse selection*. Adverse selection is the tendency for people with a greater-than-average exposure to loss to purchase insurance. For example, certain parts of the country are prone to earthquakes, so people in those areas are likely to want earthquake insurance to protect their property against loss. On the other hand, people who live in areas that are not prone to earthquakes would have no need for such coverage. An insurance company that wrote a large amount of insurance in earthquake-prone areas would be subject to adverse selection. This means that the company might experience large financial losses and decreased profitability.

Rating a Policy

When an insurance company agrees to issue a policy, a premium must be determined. There are three basic ways in which a premium can be computed:

➤ Judgment rating

➤ Manual rating

➤ Merit rating

Judgment Rating

The oldest form of determining rates is called *judgment rating*. The premium is determined by considering the individual risk. No books or tables are used; premiums are established through careful judgment. For large cases, the premium would be determined by an experienced underwriter and most likely reviewed by the head of the underwriting department.

Manual Rating

The second and most common method of premium determination is called *manual* or *class rating*. The company's rates for a particular state or area are obtained by consulting a manual, which is usually stored on a computer. Rates are arranged by various categories or classes. The agent or underwriter classifies the risk according to defined criteria and then looks up the appropriate rate. The printed rate, which is a rate per unit of insurance, is then multiplied by the number of units of insurance being purchased to calculate the premium.

Merit Rating

Another means for determining premiums is known as *merit rating*. Typically, merit rating starts with class or manual rates, which are then modified to reflect the unique characteristics of the risk that are not reflected in the manual rate.

Experience rating is a form of merit rating that modifies the manual premium based on the insured's *loss experience* (the dollars paid out in claims versus the premium received) over some period of time, generally the three years *prior* to the current policy year. When past loss experience is poorer than the average loss experience expected for this class of insured, the insured will pay more than the manual premium. When the insured's past loss experience is better than average, the insured will pay less than the manual premium.

Other types of merit rating include *retrospective rating*, which bases the insured's premium on losses incurred *during* the policy period, and *schedule rating*, which applies a system of debits or credits to reflect characteristics of a particular insured.

Certificates of Insurance

After a policy has been issued, an insured might need a *certificate of insurance* as proof that the policy has been written. A certificate of insurance, which contains a general summary of the policy's coverage, is frequently required in loan transactions and other legal matters.

A member of an insured group who has received a certificate of insurance is called a "*certificate holder.*"

A certificate of insurance is not a contract of insurance, but simply evidence that a contract exists.

Misrepresentation, Concealment, and Fraud

After an applicant's offer has been accepted and the policy has been rated, issued, and countersigned, the contract can only be cancelled by the insurance company under very specific circumstances. State laws, as well as the policy itself, spell out these circumstances.

Because the insurance contract is a contract of utmost good faith, it is expected that the insured and the insurance company will be fair and honest in their dealings with each other. However, the insurance company can void the contract on the basis of misrepresentation, concealment, or fraud by the insured.

Misrepresentation is a written or verbal misstatement of a material fact involved in the contract on which the insurer relies. Misrepresentation will only void the policy if it concerns a *material fact*. A material fact is a fact that would cause an insurer to decline a risk, charge a different premium, or change the provisions of the policy that was issued.

Concealment is similar to misrepresentation, except that it involves withholding, rather than misstating, a material fact.

Fraud is a deliberate misrepresentation that causes harm. An act of fraud contains four elements:

➤ Someone deliberately lies.

➤ The intent of the lie is for someone else to rely on that lie.

➤ Another person relies on that lie.

➤ The other person suffers harm as a result of relying on that lie.

Fraud differs from misrepresentation in that misrepresentation can be either intentional or unintentional. Fraud is always intentional and involves an all-out effort by one party to deceive and cheat the other.

Representations and Warranties

Most of the statements contained in the insured's application for insurance are *representations*—that is, statements that the applicant believes are true. Under the law, a representation is not considered a matter to which the parties contract, so a policy cannot be voided on the basis of a representation.

Sometimes, however, specific agreements are made between the insured and insurer that certain conditions will be met. For example, they might require that while a business is closed, a security guard will be on duty at all times. These agreements, called *warranties*, become a part of the policy and can void the policy if they are breached, regardless of whether the breach was intentional or unintentional.

Waiver and Estoppel

The legal definition of *waiver* is the intentional relinquishment of a known right. Sometimes an insurer or its representative knowingly overlooks a condition or exclusion that would normally have been grounds for denying coverage, increasing the premium, reducing the benefits provided in the policy, or some other material change in the policy. When the insurer or its representative relinquishes the insurer's right of denial or refusal, the act becomes a waiver. Although any policy provision can be waived, the requirement of an insurable interest cannot be waived, nor can facts be waived.

If an insurance company representative intentionally or unintentionally creates the impression that a certain fact exists when it does not, and an innocent party relies on that impression and is damaged as a result, the insurance company will be *estopped* (prevented) from denying this fact. For example, if an agent states or indicates by his or her actions that a particular loss is covered, the insurance company will be estopped from denying that coverage.

Cancellation and Nonrenewal

Most insurance policies are issued with a definite effective date and expiration date. The *policy period* or *term*—the time between the effective date and the expiration date—can be six months, one year, or even three years. But at times, the insured or the insurance company might want to cancel the insurance before the policy expires.

The insured can cancel the policy by writing a letter to the insurance company or by surrendering the policy to the company. The insurance company returns any *unearned premium*; that is, any premium not yet "used up" during the policy period.

These premiums can be returned on a *short rate basis*. This means that when the insured cancels prior to the expiration date, the company not only keeps the premium for insurance already provided, but also keeps an allowance for expenses, such as issuing the policy.

The *insurance company* does not have the same freedom to cancel that the insured does. Each state has rules governing the circumstances under which a policy can be cancelled by the company. Most states do not permit arbitrary cancellation, but restrict this right to situations such as nonpayment of premium. When the company *does* cancel, various state laws and policy provisions require that the insured be notified of the cancellation in writing within a specified number of days before the effective date of cancellation.

When the insurance company cancels the policy, unearned premium is returned to the insured on a *pro rata basis*. This means that the company retains only the earned premium, and is not permitted to keep an extra amount for expenses.

Occasionally, a policy is cancelled by either the insured or the insurance company on its effective date. This is called *flat cancellation*.

When a policy reaches its expiration date, it is customary to renew the policy for another term, provided both the insured and the insurer want the coverage to continue.

Of course, the insured has the option not to renew the insurance at this point. The insurance company might also decide not to renew the policy. Although *nonrenewal* provisions are usually more liberal than cancellation requirements, the insurance company may still be limited in the reasons it may nonrenew and in how and when the insured is notified of the decision not to renew.

Exam Prep Questions

1. Which of the following statements concerning binders is correct?

   ○ A. They guarantee that a policy will be issued.

   ○ B. They can be issued by insurance companies, but not agents.

   ○ C. They expire on the effective date of the policy to which they apply, or on the expiration date of the binder if the policy is not issued.

   ○ D. They show an intent to consider issuing insurance, but do not include any commitment to provide coverage.

2. Judgment rating is based on which of the following?

   ○ A. An evaluation of the characteristics of the individual risk

   ○ B. Manual rates developed from statistical data

   ○ C. Calculation and evaluation of the insured's past loss experience

   ○ D. Loss information reported by other states

3. What rating method makes modifications to manual rates to reflect the unique characteristics of each risk?

   ○ A. Judgment

   ○ B. Merit

   ○ C. Certification

   ○ D. Manual

4. To void a policy, misrepresentation or concealment must be which of the following?

   ○ A. Concern material facts.

   ○ B. Be intentional.

   ○ C. Both A and B are correct.

   ○ D. Neither A nor B are correct.

5. An agreement between the insured and the insurer that certain conditions will be met is which of the following?

   ○ A. Misrepresentation

   ○ B. Warranty

   ○ C. Estoppel

   ○ D. Certificate of insurance

6. When an insured decides to cancel an insurance policy prior to the expiration date, the unearned premium is returned on what basis?

   ○ A. Flat basis

   ○ B. Pro rata basis

   ○ C. Short rate basis

   ○ D. Negotiated basis

7. Which one of these statements about the Fair Credit Reporting Act is not correct?

   ○ A. Prenotification is required for both regular and investigative reports.

   ○ B. Postnotification is required when insurance coverage is denied because of adverse information in a credit report.

   ○ C. An agent who obtains information from a reporting agency under false pretenses can be sent to jail and fined.

   ○ D. Consumers have the right to challenge information in investigative reports and to have incorrect information removed.

8. The insured's policy is nearing the expiration date. The insurance company doesn't want to continue the insured's coverage, so it sends the insured a notice that the policy will not continue beyond the expiration date of the policy. This is considered which of the following?

   ○ A. Flat cancellation

   ○ B. Nonrenewal

   ○ C. Pro rata cancellation

   ○ D. Unearned renewal

Exam Prep Answers

1. C is correct. An agent or an insurance company can issue a binder. A binder does not guarantee that a policy will be issued; it only guarantees temporary coverage. If the company decides to not issue the policy, coverage under the binder may be cancelled by a formal cancellation notice; however, if no formal cancellation is made, coverage remains in effect until the binder expires. If a policy is issued, coverage under the binder ceases as of the effective date of the policy.

2. A is correct. This is the oldest form of rating. The premium is determined by considering the individual risk. No books or tables are used; premiums are established through careful judgment.

3. B is correct. Experience rating, retrospective rating, and schedule rating are all types of merit rating.

4. A is correct. Misrepresentation is a written or verbal misstatement of a material fact. It can be either intentional or unintentional.

5. B is correct. A warranty becomes part of the policy. If it is breached, the insurer can void the policy.

6. C is correct. This means that the insurer can keep an allowance for expenses. When the insurance company cancels, unearned premium is returned on a pro rata basis, which means that the company retains only the earned premium.

7. A is correct. The question asks for the statement that is not correct. Prenotification is required for investigative reports, but not regular reports. The other choices are provisions contained in the Fair Credit Reporting Act.

8. B is correct. Nonrenewal occurs when the insured or the insurer decides to not continue coverage for another policy period after the current policy period expires. Flat cancellation means to cancel a policy on its effective date. Pro rata cancellation means to cancel a policy midterm so that a refund is made of unearned premium.

Introduction to Property Insurance

Terms you'll need to understand:

- ✓ Named insured
- ✓ First named insured
- ✓ Additional insured
- ✓ Policy period
- ✓ Direct loss
- ✓ Indirect loss
- ✓ Actual cash value
- ✓ Replacement cost
- ✓ Functional replacement cost
- ✓ Market value
- ✓ Deductible
- ✓ Policy period
- ✓ Policy territory

Concepts you'll need to master:

- ✓ Declarations
- ✓ Specific insurance
- ✓ Blanket insurance
- ✓ Limit of liability (or insurance)
- ✓ Valued policy
- ✓ Agreed amount contract
- ✓ Named peril policy
- ✓ Open peril policy
- ✓ Valuation of losses
- ✓ Coinsurance
- ✓ Subrogation
- ✓ Primary insurance
- ✓ Excess insurance
- ✓ Pro rata liability
- ✓ Concurrency
- ✓ Nonconcurrent policies
- ✓ Liberalization
- ✓ Vacancy
- ✓ Unoccupancy
- ✓ Reporting forms

In this chapter we'll review some of the basic features of property insurance, including some of the concepts that apply to property insurance coverages and standard policy provisions.

Not all insurance policies are alike. Our job would be easier if every company that provided homeowners insurance used the same policy. But it doesn't work that way. That isn't to say that there isn't *some* uniformity. A few types of policies have been standardized by law, and any company that writes those policies must use a standard form. Most policies are not fixed by law, although some of the individual provisions might have to comply with existing laws.

A degree of standardization has also been introduced by insurance service organizations such as the Insurance Services Office (ISO). Many insurers use ISO forms verbatim. Although companies might deviate from ISO's forms or use their own with state approval, it is customary for member companies to use the standardized forms.

 Although some insurers do develop their own policy forms independently, most use standard ISO forms or at least use them as a base. Individual companies are permitted to alter provisions and submit them for approval. The revisions they make might be minor or major. There is a great degree of standardization in the industry on basic provisions, but there are many variations. This is why it is important for agents to read the policies they are selling, and compare policies from different insurers, in order to fully understand the differences when making recommendations to insureds.

Declarations

Like all insurance contracts, property insurance contracts are made up of declarations, insuring agreements, conditions, exclusions, and definitions. The declarations provide a summary of how the contract applies and include important information that is not found in other parts of the policy (such as the identity of the named insured, the policy period, the limits of insurance, and the premium charged).

Who Is Insured

The first job of the declarations section is to state who is insured, whether it is an individual or a business. Remember, insurance contracts are personal. Even though we sometimes talk about insuring homes or other types of property, such as cars, it is the party named in the declarations who is insured, not the property.

The word "insured" can have a number of different meanings in an insurance policy. The *named insured* is the person, business, or other entity named in the declarations to whom the policy is issued. When there is more than one named insured listed on a policy, the policy can assign a higher level of duties or rights to the *first named insured*, the person listed first on the declarations page.

In some circumstances, another individual or business might be listed on the declarations or by endorsement as an *additional insured*—for example, a mortgage company that has an outstanding loan (and therefore an insurable interest) on the property.

In addition to named insureds and additional insureds who might be listed on a policy, the policy can cover other persons, businesses, or entities as insureds who are not specifically listed on the declarations or on any endorsement. For example, a homeowners policy covers all family members who reside in the same household for their personal property and liability exposures, and commercial policies can extend coverage to cover employees and others. The provisions for such coverage are usually found in the definition of "insured" in the definitions section of the policy or "who is an insured" in the individual coverage sections.

What Property Is Covered and Where

The declarations also describe the property to be insured. The description can be very specific or very broad. Insurance written with one or more limits that apply to particular items to be insured, such as a single piece of fine art or a building at a given location, is called *specific insurance*. Insurance written with a limit that applies to all kinds of property at one or more locations is called *blanket insurance*.

The term "*specific insurance*" does not mean that every item must be specifically described. Although individual items can be described on personal property floaters or some endorsements, generally insurance with various limits that apply to different classes of property is still considered to be "specific insurance." For example, a homeowners policy is generally considered to be a form of specific insurance rather than blanket coverage because separate limits apply to the dwelling, other structures, and personal property. The fact that individual items of personal property (furniture, appliances, clothing, and so on) do not have to be listed does not make a homeowners policy a blanket policy.

The term "blanket insurance" means a policy that has a single limit that applies to all property (including buildings, personal property, property of others, and so on) at a given location or multiple locations. For example, a retail store chain with four locations might want a blanket policy with a single limit to cover all of its locations so that it could transfer inventory between its stores and not have to worry about whether the individual limit of insurance at each location was adequate.

An almost endless variety of property can be insured—buildings (real property), tangible and intangible business and personal property, property owned by the insured, and nonowned property. In addition to the brief description contained in the declarations, the Insuring Agreements describe in detail the property that is covered by the policy. You'll learn more about the types of property that can be insured as you progress through the course.

When Property Is Insured

Insurance policies specify the date and time, including where and in what time zone, coverage begins and ends. This is known as the *policy period*.

In some states, the exact time of day policies start and stop is set by law to maintain uniformity between companies and to prevent gaps in coverage when an insured changes insurance companies. In most jurisdictions, policies begin and end at 12:01 a.m. (one minute after midnight) on the effective and expiration dates.

Exact dates and time are important for determining when insurance starts and ends, and it is important for agents and insureds to understand this. Suppose that Fred's homeowners insurance is expiring on July 24 and he is in the process of changing insurance companies and agents. Believing he has coverage for July 24, he asks his new agent to make his replacement policy effective July 25, and at 2:30 p.m. on July 24, Fred's home burns to the ground. Guess what Fred? You have no coverage. Fred only had coverage for one minute after July 23. Fred's new agent should have reviewed his previous policy or at least inquired about the expiration date and started the replacement policy one day earlier.

How Much Property Is Insured For

The declarations also show the *policy limit* or *limits*, also known as the *limit of coverage*, *limit of liability*, or *limit of insurance*. These limits represent the maximum amount the insurance company will pay for a loss. Within this framework, the principle of indemnity and applicable policy conditions are used to determine the exact reimbursement in the event of a loss.

For certain hard-to-value items, the insurance company might issue a *valued* or *agreed amount contract*. Valued contracts are written for a specified amount, and they list the value of the insured property as agreed to by both the insured and the insurer at policy inception. If the item is damaged, this is the amount that will be used to value the loss. This avoids the difficulty of trying to determine the value of such property after it has already been damaged or destroyed. Examples of property frequently covered on a valued basis are art work and jewelry.

Endorsements That Apply

A final item usually included in the declarations is a list of any endorsements attached to the policy. These are usually listed by form number. This gives underwriters and agents a snapshot view of what is, or should be, attached to the basic policy form. Agents should be on the lookout for any restrictive endorsements that were not requested or expected as well as any endorsements that were requested and are not actually part of the contract.

Insuring Agreements

Insuring agreements explain what property is actually covered and what perils or causes of loss the property is insured against. Limited coverage contracts might state the perils insured against (for example, a fire only contract might say that it covers loss by fire), but most modern contracts simply refer to loss by the "covered causes of loss," which are identified in the declarations and actually described elsewhere in the contract.

Property Covered

Several different coverages can be provided in a single policy. The insuring agreement describes the key *policy coverages* in detail. The insuring agreement can also specify that certain *additional coverages* apply. These coverages, which can be called "*extended coverages*," "*coverage extensions*," or "*other coverages*" in various contracts, can be included within major coverage limits or have reduced or separate limits of liability or can require the insured to meet certain special policy requirements before applying.

 Because several different coverages can be provided by a single policy, a contract might have multiple insuring agreements to separate the classes of property covered or the types of losses covered. Each insuring agreement might be followed by its own set of additional coverages.

Perils Insured Against

Policies that list the specific perils or causes of loss insured against under the contract, such as lightning, fire, and windstorm, are called *named peril* or *specified peril* policies. Named peril contracts insure property only against the perils specifically listed in the policy.

An *open peril* policy insures against all risks of physical loss, except those specifically excluded in the policy. This type of contract is sometimes called *all risk* or *special coverage*.

Direct and Indirect Loss

In addition to specifying the property covered and the perils insured against, the insuring agreement will state whether it covers direct loss, indirect loss, or both.

Most people are familiar with the concept of *direct loss*. It means direct physical loss or damage to, or complete destruction of, property. When fire damages part of your home or a burglar steals your jewelry, you have suffered a direct loss.

Many people might not be so familiar with the concept of *indirect loss*. An indirect loss is an actual financial loss that is the result of a direct loss. For this reason, indirect losses are also known as *consequential losses*. Such losses can affect individuals and families as well as business entities. If a home is damaged by fire, lightning, or explosion, the repair expenses are not the only loss. The insured's family might have to live in a hotel for months while repairs are being made. In addition to the hotel bill, the insured can incur higher costs for food, laundry services, and other things that were normally functions of living at home. If a business has a major property loss to buildings or equipment, it might have to shut down for a period of time, and might also incur extra expenses plus a loss of business income. All of these are examples of indirect losses.

 Although indirect losses do not reflect any direct damages, they do result from such damages and the exposure to these losses can be insured against. Some personal and commercial policies automatically include some coverage for indirect losses. Optional coverage for additional types of indirect losses can also be purchased, especially in the commercial lines area.

Exclusions and Limitations

Every property insurance contract contains exclusions. In a *named peril* policy, any peril that is not specifically listed as covered is automatically excluded. However, named peril policies also list additional exclusions because some kinds of property and some loss situations are not intended to be covered even when the loss is caused by a named peril.

In an *open peril* policy, the exclusions are especially important because any peril not specifically listed as excluded is insured against.

Exclusions in a policy vary with the type of property or situation the contract is designed to cover. However, there are five broad categories of exclusions that are commonly found in property policies:

➤ **Nonaccidental losses:** These losses are excluded because they are certainties, not risks. Wear and tear, deterioration, rust, corrosion, and mechanical or electrical breakdown are all examples of nonaccidental losses.

➤ **Losses controllable by the insured:** Losses that can be controlled or prevented with extra care or effort on the insured's part are often excluded. This encourages the insured to be responsible in the use of the property. Marring, scratching, and breaking or chipping of fragile objects are all examples of losses that are controllable by the insured.

➤ **Extra-hazardous perils:** Certain perils are extra-hazardous. The insurance company could provide coverage, but the unique nature of the peril requires a substantial increase in the premium the insured would pay. Extra-hazardous perils are usually excluded from the policy because most insureds would not want or need the coverage. Those insureds who do require the coverage can often obtain it through an endorsement to the policy, for which an extra premium is charged. An example of an extra-hazardous peril is an earthquake.

➤ **Catastrophic losses:** Some losses are so broad in their scope that they could bankrupt any company that insured against them. Losses arising from war or nuclear disasters are generally uninsurable because of their catastrophic nature.

➤ **Property covered in other policies:** Property customarily covered in other insurance policies is excluded. For example, a policy covering your personal property would normally exclude your car because there is a separate automobile policy to provide coverage for your vehicle.

Some policies also include *limitations* that are less sweeping than exclusions. A limitation might eliminate or reduce coverage, but only under certain circumstances or when specified conditions apply. For example, after a building has been vacant for 60 days, some types of commercial property losses will not be covered at all, whereas the amount paid for other types of losses will be reduced by 15%.

Concurrent Causation

Property insurance policy provisions and policy language underwent changes in recent years to clarify intended exclusions and avoid confusion related to *concurrent causation*. Concurrent causation refers to a situation in which two or more perils act concurrently—at the same time or in sequence—to cause a loss. This created significant problems for insurers when one peril was covered by a policy and the other was not.

The issue initially arose when some insurers were challenged to pay earthquake claims under collapse coverage. At the time, Dwelling, Homeowners, and Commercial Property policies included collapse of a building or structure as a peril insured against, whereas earthquake coverage was generally excluded. When an earthquake struck, claims were filed under the collapse coverage by insureds who did not have earthquake coverage. The insurers maintained that they never intended to provide earthquake coverage under the peril of collapse. Some courts concluded otherwise and held for the insured on the grounds that the loss was due to collapse of the building regardless of whether earthquake was a concurrent or contributing cause.

To clarify the intent of the policy, insurers removed collapse as a peril insured against and made it an additional coverage. The wording was changed to specify that collapse coverage only applies when it is caused by certain perils named in the policy, such as fire, weight of contents or people, and the use of defective construction materials.

Conditions

The conditions section of a property insurance policy lists the duties and rights of both the insured and the insurer. We've already discussed the cancellation and misrepresentation provisions. Let's consider some additional conditions often included in property insurance contracts.

Duties Following Loss

Most contracts include conditions that specify what the insured and insurer must do when a loss occurs. Together, these provisions can be referred to as *loss provisions*.

The *Duties Following Loss* condition lists the insured's responsibilities after a loss, including

➤ Giving prompt notice of claim to the insurance company or agent

➤ Protecting the property from further damage

➤ Completing a detailed *proof of loss* (an official inventory of the damage)

➤ Making the property available for inspection by the company

➤ Submitting to examination under oath if required

➤ Assisting the insurer as required during the claim investigation procedure

Valuation

The insurance company also has duties when a loss occurs. Determining adequate indemnification is an important concern. Such provisions are sometimes contained in the *Valuation* or *How Losses Will Be Paid* condition.

In general, the insured can collect the *lesser* of

➤ Insurable interest

➤ Policy limits

➤ Actual cash value

➤ Cost to repair

➤ Replacement cost

 We've already discussed the first two items on this list. An insured can never collect more than the policy limits or the insurable interest he or she has in the property. Which additional provisions, if any, apply to a loss settlement depends on the actual terms of the contract.

Actual Cash Value

Many losses are reimbursed on an *actual cash value* basis. Actual cash value, or ACV, is usually calculated by determining the item's replacement cost (what it would cost to buy a replacement) and subtracting an amount for depreciation.

Why isn't the insured reimbursed for the full replacement cost? Depreciation is subtracted because the insured has already had use of the property. If the full amount were reimbursed so that the insured could replace it with a new item, the insured would be better off after the loss than before. This violates the principle of indemnity.

Repair Cost

Although ACV is a common method for reimbursing a loss, the insured might be reimbursed on the basis of the item's *repair cost* when this amount is less than ACV. For example, if a particular item of property is 50% damaged but can be repaired for 40% of its ACV, the insurance company will pay for the actual repairs instead of settling for 50% of the ACV.

Replacement Cost and Functional Replacement Cost

In some policies, the insurance company agrees to automatically pay the replacement cost for covered losses, with no allowance for depreciation, provided the insured meets certain conditions. This is known as *replacement cost*.

Some policies pay losses on a *functional replacement cost basis*, where damaged property is repaired or replaced with less expensive, but functionally equivalent, materials. This method is used most frequently for losses to antique, ornate, or custom construction.

Market Value

Occasionally, property is insured for *market value*, or what it could be sold for at the time of the loss. Market value is different from ACV or replacement cost. Suppose that Ed spends $400,000 to build a fancy house in an open area, but then the land around it is zoned for heavy industry and a bad-smelling oil refinery is built nearby. Because Ed might have trouble finding a buyer, his house might only have a market value of $250,000 in that location, even though it would still cost about $400,000 to rebuild it if it were destroyed.

Coinsurance

Insurance companies want to encourage their policyholders to insure their property for its full value. Because partial losses are much more common than total losses, some insureds might purchase minimal insurance to take care of any possible small losses and take a chance that they would never have a total loss. If a lot of insureds were to follow this practice, the insurance company would not be able to collect enough premium to pay for the actual losses of its policyholders.

The *coinsurance* condition encourages policyholders to insure property to value. It lists the minimum amount of insurance the insured should carry on the property, which is expressed as a percentage of the property's value. For instance, a policy with an 80% coinsurance condition means that the insured must insure the property for at least 80% of its value.

As long as the insured carries the amount of insurance required by the coinsurance condition at the time of a loss, the insurer will indemnify losses up to the limits of the policy. If the insured does not carry enough insurance when a loss occurs, the company will pay only a percentage of what full contract reimbursement would otherwise have been. The percentage paid is based on the proportion that the actual amount of insurance bears to the required amount of insurance. The amount of a loss not paid by the insurer is sometimes called the *coinsurance penalty*.

> The coinsurance penalty only applies in partial loss situations. In the event of a total loss, the policy would pay the full policy limit, although it might be inadequate to cover the loss. If a building valued at $200,000 is insured under a policy with an 80% coinsurance requirement, the insured should carry at least $160,000 of coverage to avoid a coinsurance penalty. If the insured only buys $100,000 of coverage and a loss of $50,000 occurs, the insured will only collect $31,250 because of the coinsurance penalty. However, if a total loss occurs, the insurance company will pay the full policy limit of $100,000. This will not fully cover the insured's total loss because the property was seriously underinsured, not because of any coinsurance penalty.

Because it is sometimes difficult to predict property values accurately enough to avoid the possibility of a coinsurance penalty, some policies contain an *Agreed Value* or *Stated Amount* provision. This provision specifies a certain value that will meet the coinsurance requirement. As long as the policy limit equals or exceeds this amount, the insured will not be assessed a coinsurance penalty.

When Losses Are Paid

Although it might not be specifically stated in the policy, the insurer is obligated to pay covered claims promptly. Some policies provide that a claim must be paid within a certain number of days after the insurer has received proof of loss and the parties have reached agreement on the amount of the loss. Others state only that the loss must be settled within a "reasonable" time.

Pair or Set Clauses

A *Pair or Set* condition is a loss settlement condition that appears in many property contracts. It states that if part of a pair or set is lost or damaged, the loss will be valued as a fair proportion of the total value of the set before and after the loss, giving consideration to the importance of the damaged article to the set. The insurer is not obligated to pay for the loss of the whole set when only one part has been damaged, but the insurer might have to pay more than the apparent proportion of the actual loss.

Suppose that an ornamental set of candleholders is worth $1,000 to collectors as a matched set. If one of them is damaged, destroyed, or stolen, the remaining item might only be worth $250. On the surface, it might appear that the loss is $500 because one out of two items was lost. But to the insured, the loss is $750—the difference in value before and after the loss.

The pair and set clause gives the insurance company the right to try to repair or replace the item (which it might be able to do) or to settle on the basis of difference in value (in which case, it might have to pay $750).

Deductible

Many property insurance policies have a *deductible*. This means that the insured pays the first part of every loss up to the amount of the deductible. This reduces the cost of insurance by reducing the number of small claims. The amount of the deductible is specified in the declarations.

A deductible does not reduce the amount of insurance. It reduces the premium, and the higher the deductible the insured is willing to accept, the greater the premium reduction will be. For small losses, a deductible will reduce the amount of recovery and the insured will have to absorb the deductible amount. However, if a total loss occurs, the insurer will pay the full policy limit.

Salvage and Abandonment

Many property insurance policies contain a *Salvage* condition which provides that the insurance company can take possession of damaged property after payment of loss. In effect, the insurance company "buys" the damaged property by paying the insured enough to replace it. The insurance company can then sell the damaged property for whatever it will bring. In this way, salvaged goods can reduce the cost of the claim to the insurance company. If the insurance company wants to take the property as salvage but the insured wants to keep it for some reason, the insured would have to refuse the settlement or possibly renegotiate for a lesser amount to account for the salvage value.

Salvage is a right but not an obligation for the insurance company. In total loss situations, if there is some value in the materials of the destroyed property (such as scrap metal), the insurer can exercise its right to salvage. In partial loss situations, the insurer can also exercise its right to salvage by paying the amount for a total loss, taking possession of the property, and recovering the salvage value (which might consist of material values and undamaged parts that can be sold to others). Exercising the right to salvage in partial loss situations makes sense when it would be more expensive to repair the property. If damaged property has little or no salvage value, the insurance company will not exercise this option.

Although the insurance company can retain the right of salvage, it does not allow the insured to relinquish property to the company at the option of the insured. The *Abandonment* condition states that the insured may not abandon property to the company and ask to be reimbursed for its full value. It is up to the insurance company to repair or replace property or take possession and exercise its salvage right. The insured has no right to insist that the insurer take the property.

Subrogation

Most policies give the insurance company *subrogation rights*, which is the right to recover from a third party who is responsible for a loss.

Suppose that an insured suffers a loss for which he or she is not at fault, and the party who caused the damage either has no insurance or refuses to pay for the damages. The insured's insurance company can step in and pay for the damages, and then bring suit or file a claim against the other party or the other party's insurance company on the insured's behalf. This transfer to the insurance company of the insured's right of recovery against others is called *subrogation*. The subrogation condition in most policies today is usually called *Transfer of Right of Recovery Against Others to Us*.

Appraisal and Arbitration

There are times when the insured and the insurer cannot agree on the amount of indemnification. The *Appraisal* condition provides that either party can demand an appraisal of a loss. In this event, each party chooses an appraiser. The two appraisers then select an umpire—generally, another professional appraiser whose objectivity both parties trust. If the appraisers fail to agree on an amount, they submit their differences to the umpire. The decision agreed to by any two of the three is the final amount of indemnification. Each party pays its own appraiser and shares the costs of the umpire.

The *Arbitration* condition is worded similarly, but it is not limited to disputes over the value of the loss. It can also be used to resolve other areas of disagreement between the insured and the insurance company, or between the company and a third party in the case of liability insurance, or between two insurers.

Other Insurance

The *Other Insurance* condition sets out how other insurance the insured might have on the same property affects reimbursement under the policy in question when a loss occurs. This condition can also be called *Other Sources of Recovery* or *Insurance Under Two or More Coverages*. The purpose of this provision is to assure that the insured receives a fair settlement but isn't overpaid for the loss.

Primary and Excess

Some policies provide that when other insurance exists, they will pay only the excess beyond what the other insurance pays for a loss. So if company Y's policy would pay $10,000 of a $15,000 loss, company X would pay no more that $5,000 of the loss. In this example, company Y's policy is considered *primary insurance* and company X's policy is *excess insurance*.

Pro Rata Liability

Probably the most common method for handling other insurance is to agree to pay only a proportion of any loss that is also covered by other insurance. This is known as the *pro rata method*, and the proportion paid by each insurer is based on their respective limits. For instance, if an insured had 30% of the total coverage on her house with company X and 70% of the coverage with company Y and a loss occurred, company X would pay 30% of the loss and company Y would pay 70%.

The amount paid by each company is determined by adding the limits of all policies that cover the loss, and then dividing the limit of each policy by the total amount of insurance available. The figures that result are multiplied by the amount of the loss to determine each policy's payment amount.

Sometimes an insured might have two or more policies on the same property that are identical in terms of the coverage provided, and sometimes the policies are not identical. Policies that provide exactly the same coverages and insure against exactly the same perils are known as *concurrent* policies. Policies that do not provide the same coverages or do not insure against the same perils are *nonconcurrent* policies.

 "Concurrent coverage" is not the same as "concurrent causation." Both have something to do with a simultaneous occurrence, but "concurrent coverage" means that two policies cover the same perils, whereas "concurrent causation" means that a loss resulted from more than one cause.

 Nonconcurrency can result in coverage gaps or disputed payments and should be avoided. Most significantly, it can affect claim settlements. Some policies have provisions that say they will settle on a pro rata basis if other insurance is concurrent, but coverage will only apply on an excess basis if other insurance is nonconcurrent.

Liberalization

The *Liberalization* condition provides that if the insurer broadens coverage under a policy form or endorsement without requiring an additional premium, all existing similar policies or endorsements in effect will be construed to contain the same broadened coverage.

 This provision makes it unnecessary for the insurer to issue endorsements for existing policies in order to put the broader coverage into effect. This saves money by eliminating the additional printing and paper needed and the mailing costs that would otherwise be required. Insureds will receive new policies that include the updated language when they renew their coverage.

Assignment

The *Assignment* condition specifies that a policy cannot be transferred to anyone else without the written consent of the insurer except in the event of the death of the named insured. In the case of death, the rights and duties under the policy can be transferred to the insured's legal representative. This condition is commonly titled *Transfer of Rights or Duties Under This Policy*.

No Benefit to Bailee

A *bailee* is a person or organization that has temporary possession of someone else's personal property. Examples of bailees include dry cleaners and storage facilities. The *No Benefit to Bailee* condition states that the bailee is not covered under the insured's policy while the bailee has possession of the insured's property. This provision assures that the bailee cannot collect for the loss under the insured's policy because the insured will either be reimbursed directly under the policy or under a policy the bailee might have purchased to cover such losses.

Mortgage Condition

We mentioned earlier that lenders or mortgagees might have an insurable interest in property. The mortgagee is generally named in the declarations. The *Mortgage* condition, or *Loss Payable* condition, specifies the rights and duties of the *mortgagee*, or *loss payee*, under the policy. For instance, if an insured fails to file a proof of loss, the mortgagee must do so after being notified by the insurer to protect its rights under the policy. In addition, the mortgagee might be expected to pay the premium if the insured fails to do so.

The policy might provide that if some condition caused by the insured would result in the insurer denying coverage for a loss it would otherwise have covered, the mortgagee might still have protection under the policy. The policy might also provide that the insurance company has the option of paying off the mortgage and requiring the mortgagee to assign all rights to the company, thus eliminating the mortgagee's interest.

Policy Period and Policy Territory

The *Policy Period* and *Policy Territory* provisions state that a loss will not be covered unless it occurs within the policy territory while the policy is in effect. The territory can vary, but a typical policy includes the United States, Puerto Rico, and Canada. The effective date and time of coverage is listed in the declarations.

Vacancy and Unoccupancy

Because of the increased chance of loss, property insurance policies can exclude or limit coverage for losses when property is vacant or unoccupied. *Vacant* means the absence of both people and property from the premises; *unoccupied* is the absence of people.

Reporting Forms

Property contracts can be issued on a *nonreporting* or *reporting* basis. You are familiar with nonreporting policies; these are contracts for which a flat premium is charged every time the policy is renewed. Your auto and homeowners policies are examples of nonreporting forms.

Policies are often issued on a *reporting* basis when it is difficult to determine in advance what amount of coverage should be purchased. Instead of paying a flat premium, the insured pays a *deposit premium*, or *estimated premium*, and then periodically submits reports to the insurer showing the status of those factors on which the premium is based. After the insurance company has calculated the premium, it is charged against the deposit. When the deposit is used up, the insured begins to pay the premium calculated by the insurance company at the end of each reporting period.

The insurance company might conduct a *premium audit* of the insured's records before calculating a final premium and making a final adjustment.

Exam Prep Questions

1. Walt and Joanna are co-owners of a bagel shop. Both Walt and Joanna are listed in the declarations of the policy that insures the business, with Joanna's name appearing first. The declarations also list First State Bank, which has an outstanding loan on the business. Who is considered a named insured on the policy?

   ○ A. Walt only

   ○ B. Joanna only

   ○ C. Both Walt and Joanna

   ○ D. First State Bank

2. Renata's home is demolished in a fire that started when a neighbor misdirected the fireworks he set off to celebrate the Fourth of July. Renata's insurance company pays her for the damage, and then files suit against the neighbor to recover the amount it paid for the loss. This is an example of the application of what policy condition?

   ○ A. Liberalization

   ○ B. Subrogation

   ○ C. Abandonment

   ○ D. Salvage

3. Byron sells his car to his friend Annette, but does not notify his insurance company. Assuming that Byron's policy will transfer to her automatically, Annette doesn't buy insurance for the car. When the car is stolen, Annette files a claim with Byron's former insurer. The insurer denies the claim. This is an example of the application of what policy condition?

   ○ A. Assignment

   ○ B. No benefit to bailee

   ○ C. Coinsurance

   ○ D. Other insurance

4. A heavy snowfall causes the roof over Amaya's living room to collapse. The insurance company asks her to move her belongings out of the living room to protect them from further damage and put a tarp over the roof until it can be repaired. It also asks her to complete a proof of loss form listing the items that were damaged. This is an example of the application of what policy condition?

   ○ A. Appraisal

   ○ B. Arbitration

   ○ C. Duties after loss

   ○ D. Subrogation

5. Three policies, totaling $300,000 in coverage, apply to an $80,000 loss. Policy A's limit of insurance is $100,000, policy B's limit is $50,000, and policy C's limit is $150,000. Use the pro rata method to determine how much policy C would pay for this loss.

- O A. $26,640
- O B. $40,000
- O C. $13.280
- O D. $60,000

6. Which of the following would not normally be excluded under a property insurance contract?

- O A. Catastrophic losses
- O B. Nonaccidental losses
- O C. Losses to personal property
- O D. Extra-hazardous perils

7. An indirect loss is which of the following?

- O A. The cause of a direct loss
- O B. A type of loss that results from a direct loss
- O C. An insignificant property loss
- O D. Not a type of property loss

8. Consuela's Homeowners policy has an 80% Coinsurance condition. Her home's value is $125,000. What is the minimum amount of coverage she must carry to avoid a coinsurance penalty for partial losses?

- O A. $125,000
- O B. $100,000
- O C. $80,000
- O D. $75,000

9. According to the terms of the Mortgage condition, which of the following does not apply to the rights and duties of the mortgagee?

- O A. The mortgagee might have to pay the premium if the insured doesn't.
- O B. The mortgagee can file a proof of loss when the insured fails to do so to protect its rights under the policy.
- O C. The mortgagee might have coverage under the policy even if something the insured does causes a claim to be denied.
- O D. The mortgagee has no insurable interest in the covered property.

10. Jake has two insurance policies on his house. They are issued by different companies, but they are otherwise identical. The term for this is

- O A. Concurrent causation
- O B. Fraud
- O C. Concurrent coverage
- O D. Double indemnity

11. Deirdre has a complete 12-piece tea service valued at $20,000. In an explosion covered by her insurance policy, most of the tea service comes through intact, but one of the tea cups is broken beyond repair. The cup by itself would be valued at $400, but the value of Deirdre's tea service without the broken cup is $17,000. How much will Deirdre's insurance company pay for the broken cup?

   ○ A. $400
   ○ B. $3,000
   ○ C. $17,000
   ○ D. $20,000

12. Under the Appraisal condition, the insured and the insurance company each chooses an appraiser. If the appraisers do not agree, the dispute is submitted to a third individual agreed upon jointly by the insured and the insurance company. That third party is called the

   ○ A. Attorney-in-fact
   ○ B. Judge
   ○ C. Super-appraiser
   ○ D. Umpire

Exam Prep Answers

1. C is correct. The named insured is the person, business, or other entity named in the declarations to whom the policy is issued. First State Bank has an insurable interest as the mortgagee, but is not a named insured.

2. B is correct. The subrogation condition transfers the insured's right to collect from a responsible third party to the insurance company.

3. A is correct. The Assignment condition specifies that a policy cannot be transferred to anyone else without the written consent of the insurer, except in the event of the death of the named insured.

4. C is correct. Most insurance policies include conditions that specify what the insured and insurer must do when a loss occurs. The insured's responsibilities after a loss include giving notice of claim to the agent or company, protecting property from further damage, and completing a proof of loss form.

5. B is correct. Because total coverage is $300,000 and policy C provides 50% of this amount ($150,000) it is obligated to pay 50% of the loss.

6. C is correct. Property insurance policies typically exclude nonaccidental losses, losses controllable by the insured, extra-hazardous perils, catastrophic losses, and property covered in other policies.

7. B is correct. An indirect loss is one that comes as a result, or consequence, of the original loss.

8. B is correct. A Coinsurance condition requires an insured to carry a certain amount of insurance, which is expressed as a percentage of the insured property's value, in order to avoid a coinsurance penalty for partial losses. In this case, Consuela must carry insurance at least equal to 80% of the home's value, or $100,000, in order to satisfy the requirement.

9. D is correct. Lenders or mortgagees do have an insurable interest in property. The Mortgage condition specifies the rights and duties of the mortgagee under the policy. For instance, if an insured fails to file a proof of loss, the mortgagee must do so after being notified by the insurer to protect its rights under the policy. In addition, the mortgagee might be expected to pay the premium if the insured fails to do so. The policy might provide that if some condition caused by the insured would result in the insurer denying coverage for a loss it would otherwise have covered, the mortgagee might still have protection under the policy.

10. C is correct. Concurrent coverage refers to two policies that offer the same coverage against the same perils. Concurrent causation is when two perils contribute to the same loss. Having concurrent coverage is not fraudulent. Double indemnity is a provision of life insurance policies that pays an extra benefit if death results from an accident rather than an illness.

11. B is correct. Under the Pair and Set Clause, Deirdre will be compensated for the loss in the value of the set.

12. D is correct. The umpire is selected jointly by the insured and the insurance company and settles the dispute if the appraisers selected by the insured and the insurance company do not agree on the value of the loss.

Introduction to Liability Insurance

. . . .

Terms you'll need to understand:

✓ Negligence
✓ Tort
✓ Proximate cause
✓ Intervening cause
✓ Compensatory damages
✓ Punitive damages

✓ Bodily injury
✓ Property damage
✓ Personal injury
✓ Occurrence
✓ Accident

Concepts you'll need to master:

✓ Contributory negligence
✓ Comparative negligence
✓ Assumption of risk
✓ Statute of limitations
✓ Absolute liability
✓ Vicarious liability
✓ Third party losses

✓ Defense costs
✓ Supplementary payments
✓ Policy limits
✓ Split limits
✓ Single limit
✓ Aggregate limit

In contrast to property insurance, which we covered in the last chapter and under which an insured's own property is covered, insureds might also need liability insurance, which is covered in this chapter. Liability insurance is designed to protect insureds who might be responsible for losses suffered by third parties. Picture an irate citizen creeping out from under a pile of wreckage, standing shakily erect, waving a fist, and shouting, "I'm gonna sue you for everything you've got!" Who knows; perhaps the irate citizen would win the suit and leave you or your business in absolute financial ruin. It happens! To help protect people against such happenings, insurance companies provide liability insurance.

An individual can incur legal liability as a result of actions or inactions toward other people or their property, and the financial consequences can be severe. Such losses are called *liability losses*. A liability loss occurs when a person is determined to have been responsible, or liable, for loss to another person or another person's property and is required to make financial restitution.

 Liability insurance is designed to protect an insured's overall assets. Although a homeowners policy might pay to rebuild or repair a house after fire damage, and a house is an asset, the amount of the loss cannot exceed the value of the property. When a third party is injured and it is the insured's fault, there might not be any limit on the amount of loss. The loss could wipe out savings and investments, cause the sale of owned property, and even involve the attachment of future earnings.

Negligence

A person becomes liable to another by committing a *tort*. A tort is a civil wrong that violates the rights of another. Unlike the commission of a crime, in which the government prosecutes the wrongdoer, torts are a part of civil law and are concerned with the private relationships between people.

A tort can be either *intentional* or *unintentional*. Liability insurance generally provides no protection for the insured against liability arising out of *intentional* torts. It does, however, provide coverage for *unintentional* torts.

Another term for an unintentional tort is *negligence*. If the insured is to be held liable for a certain event or action, the individual must have been negligent. Negligence is the lack of reasonable care that is required to protect others from the unreasonable chance of harm.

Establishing Negligence

Generally, a court of law must determine negligence. To establish negligence, four factors must be involved:

➤ Legal duty owed

➤ Breach of legal duty owed

➤ Proximate cause

➤ Damages

Legal Duty Owed and Breach of That Duty

First, there must be a *legal duty owed* and a *breach of that duty*. The legal duty owed to different people varies, but as a general rule, each person owes a duty to another to protect the other's rights and property. Each person is expected to behave like a reasonable or prudent person, following those ordinary considerations that guide human affairs. This is sometimes known as the *reasonable* or *prudent person rule*.

What is "reasonable" or "prudent" might vary depending on the specific situation and are subject to interpretation by the courts, but generally they refer to acting to protect someone else's property or well being in a conscientious manner.

The duty owed by one person to another is sometimes expressed as a *degree of care* or *standard of care*. For instance, a property owner owes the greatest degree of care to an *invitee*, a person invited onto the premises involving potential benefit to the property owner. A little less responsibility is owed to a *licensee*, a person on the premises with the owner's consent, but for the sole benefit of the visitor. The least degree of care is owed to a *trespasser*, one who is on the premises without permission.

 The courts are not consistent in their determinations of negligence. A burglar might sue a property owner for a condition on the property that caused an injury, or a robber might sue a store owner for the use of excessive force in preventing the robbery. Although these kinds of cases are rarely successful, they do occur and this is one more reason why we need liability insurance.

Proximate Cause

To establish the fact that one person's actions toward another were negligent, and that this negligence caused damage to another person or that person's property, the negligent act and the damage must be tied together. The negligent act is then the *proximate cause* of loss.

The proximate cause of a loss is an action that, in a natural and continuous sequence, produced the loss. This sequence is unbroken by any other factors or events, and the loss would not have occurred without the proximate cause.

When an independent action breaks the chain of causation and sets in motion a new chain of events, this *intervening cause* becomes the proximate cause.

Here is an example. Farmer Jones has a grain silo that is blown over in a windstorm. Five weeks later, he allows his neighbor's cattle to feed on the water-soaked grain that was left lying on the ground. Seventeen cows contract an intestinal ailment as a result and die.

In this case, the windstorm was the proximate cause of the loss to the silo, but not the cattle. Farmer Jones's intervening negligent act (allowing the cattle to eat water-soaked grain) was the proximate cause of the loss to the cattle.

At times, additional events might occur between the proximate cause of the loss and the loss itself, but these events occur as a "chain reaction," with no other causal element interrupting the sequence.

Consider this example. Linde Gas and Electric Company had a small fire in a control unit. This fire caused a short in the electrical wiring, which made a machine stop operating. Because this machine regulated another machine, the second machine ran out of control and flipped a flywheel off its shaft, which badly damaged adjacent machinery. In this case, the fire is the proximate cause of the damage to the machinery because it started the chain reaction and there were no intervening causes.

Damages

The final factor used to establish negligence is that another party suffered *damages*. If no one was adversely affected by an individual's actions, there is no finding of negligence.

Defenses Against Negligence

There are different types of negligence, and there are various defenses against negligence under our legal system.

Contributory Negligence

Traditionally, to establish liability, an individual had to show that the other party was negligent and that he or she did not contribute to the loss through any negligence on his or her own part. So, if a person contributed to his or her own damages in any way, another party could not be held liable for them.

Some states retain this system, ruling out all liability when there has been contributory negligence by the injured party.

Comparative Negligence

In other jurisdictions, this doctrine has been softened to some degree by *comparative negligence* laws, which enable a finding of liability to be made even when both parties have contributed to the loss, with an award based on the extent of each party's negligence. For example, if party A is injured in an accident and sues party B and it is found that party A was only 60% responsible for the loss and party B was 40% responsible, party A would only be awarded 60% of the total damages claimed.

For example, if John had a $10,000 loss and was found to be 40% responsible under the comparative negligence principle, John would receive only $6,000 and would have to absorb the other $4,000 of the loss himself.

Other Defenses Against Negligence

In some states, a doctrine known as *assumption of risk* might apply. Assumption of risk applies when a person knowingly exposes himself or herself to danger or injury. When a person assumes this risk, he or she might be prevented from recovering from a negligent party. This doctrine is frequently associated with injuries incurred by spectators at sporting events.

We've already mentioned *intervening cause*. Intervening cause can also serve as a defense against liability—in some cases, it can completely eliminate liability or at least reduce the degree of liability.

For example, if Alan knew that the brake lights on his car were broken and he failed to get them fixed even though he had ample opportunity to do so, that could be cited as an intervening cause of an accident in which Deirdre, following a safe distance behind Alan, didn't stop her car in time to avoid hitting him. Fault on Deirdre's part could be reduced or vacated by a finding that Alan's negligence in fixing his brake lights was an intervening cause of the accident.

Another defense can be found in the *statutes of limitations* enacted in various states. Such laws provide that certain types of lawsuits must be filed within a specified time of the occurrence to be valid under the law.

Absolute Liability

Earlier, we said that negligence had to be present to hold someone legally liable for an action. However, there are some exceptions. *Absolute liability* is imposed by law on those participating in certain activities that are considered especially hazardous. Individuals involved in such operations can be held liable for the damages of another, even though the individual was not negligent. Absolute liability is most frequently applied to activities involving

➤ Dangerous materials

➤ Hazardous operations

➤ Dangerous animals

Another term that is sometimes used for absolute liability is *strict liability*. Strict liability is usually used in reference to products liability.

Suppose that Larry keeps seven boa constrictors in a trailer for use in his nightclub act. Despite precautions, one of the reptiles escapes and seriously injures a child. Larry might not have been personally negligent, but he could still be held responsible by virtue of absolute liability for owning the animals.

Vicarious Liability

There are times when a person might be held responsible for the negligent acts of another person. This is called *vicarious liability*, or *imputed liability*.

A very common form of vicarious liability involves the relationship between an employer and an employee. Often, the negligence of an employee can be imputed (charged) to an employer because the employer has control over the employee. For example, a pizza delivery driver might negligently cause an accident that injures two pedestrians. The employer becomes responsible for the negligence because the employee was driving a company vehicle and the accident occurred on company time.

Another common form of vicarious liability exists in parent-child relationships. There are many cases in which parents have been held liable for acts of their minor children because of a failure to supervise them or recognize a pattern of risky behavior and take corrective action.

Liability Insurance

At the beginning of this chapter, we mentioned that liability insurance is designed to protect an insured's assets from claims made by third parties who have suffered damages. Let's explore some of these concepts more fully and then review some of the features of liability insurance policies.

Third Party Losses

Liability losses are known in the insurance business as *third party losses*. The insured is the first party. The insurance company legally representing or defending the insured is the second party. The third party is the person who has suffered the injury or damage.

Types of Damages

The financial consequences of a liability loss can be devastating. If an individual is liable for the loss of another, the courts might require the individual to pay *damages* (monetary compensation) to the injured party. A number of different types of damages can be awarded.

Compensatory damages reimburse the injured party only for losses that were actually sustained. There are two types of compensatory damages: *specific* and *general*.

Specific damages include all direct and specific expenses involved in a particular loss, such as medical expenses, lost wages, funeral expenses, and the cost to repair or replace damaged property. General damages compensate for such additional things as pain and suffering and disfigurement.

If the court determines that the individual acted wantonly or willfully in causing the injured party's damages, it can also award *punitive*, or *exemplary*, *damages*. Punitive damages are intended to punish the defendant and make an example out of him or her to discourage others from behaving the same way.

All three types of damages can be awarded in a single suit. Some negligent acts are simply because of carelessness. Where only property damage has occurred, it is likely only specific damages will be awarded. Where bodily injury has occurred, specific and general damages might be awarded. However, in cases involving gross negligence (a complete disregard for the safety of others), a court can award specific, general, and punitive damages.

Insuring Agreement

Insuring agreements describe the coverage being provided, but also describe a number of related provisions, such as defense costs, interest payments on judgments, and other supplementary payments.

Coverages

Most liability policies agree to pay *on behalf of the insured* all sums for which the insured becomes legally liable to pay as damages because of bodily injury and property damage.

Terms are always defined in the policy, but in general, *bodily injury (BI)* means injury, sickness, disease, and death arising out of injury, sickness, or disease. *Property damage (PD)* means damage to or destruction of property, including loss of use of the property. Some liability policies also cover the insured's liability for *personal injury (PI)*, such as slander, libel, false arrest, and invasion of privacy. (In the insurance business, "bodily injury" and "personal injury" have different meanings and are not used interchangeably.)

 Although insurance companies pay "on behalf of the insured," the injured party must file a claim against the insured or sue the insured, not the insurance company. In fact, third parties usually have no right to sue the insurance company directly.

Defense Costs

In addition to paying for bodily injury or property damage, liability policies promise to defend the insured in any suit seeking BI or PD damages, even if the charges are totally groundless or false. Defense costs are paid in addition to payments for amounts awarded against the insured. The insurer pays for the defense, but its duty to defend ends once the amount it pays for damages equals the policy limit. For example, if an insured's policy has a $100,000 liability limit and the insurer has spend $50,000 defending the claim and has also paid $100,000 in partial settlements, the insurer's obligation to defend ends completely, as does its obligation to pay any additional amounts of the claim that remain in dispute. Once the policy limit is exhausted, any additional defense costs and amounts awarded against the insured are fully the insured's responsibility.

 Potential defense costs paid by the insurer are unlimited until the insurer's obligation to defend ends. These costs are paid outside of the policy limits for liability, and are paid in addition to any liability amounts ultimately awarded. If an insured has a $250,000 policy limit and the insurer has spent $75,000 while defending the claim, the full $250,000 limit of insurance remains available to pay any judgments.

Settlements are not always determined by a court. Although the insurance company will provide a legal defense, in some cases it might not want to. In theory, an insurer could pay more defending a claim than the limit of insurance. In reality, that is not likely. When it appears that defense costs will be excessive or that the liability of the insured is clear and the defense cannot win the case, the insurer will usually try to cut its losses by negotiating a settlement out of court in order to avoid the additional expenses of defending the claim.

Prejudgment Interest

A court will sometimes award a third party interest on an award for damages to compensate for the interest the third party might have earned if he or she had received compensation at the time of injury or damage, rather than at the time of judgment. Most liability policies cover this *prejudgment interest*. Some policies cover it in the insuring agreement along with the actual damages, up to the policy limits. Other policies might include it as a supplementary or additional payment that is not subject to the limit of liability.

Supplementary Payments

Liability policies usually provide a number of *supplementary payments* that are all paid in addition to the policy's regular limit of liability. These coverages vary from one type of liability policy to another. We already mentioned defense costs, but in general the complete list of additional payments typically includes

➤ Defense costs

➤ Expenses incurred in the investigation of a claim

➤ Premiums for certain types of bonds, such as bail bonds, appeal bonds, and release of attachment bonds

➤ First aid to others at the time of an accident

➤ Reasonable expenses incurred by the insured at the company's request in the investigation or defense of a claim

➤ Loss of earnings (such as when the insured is required to miss work for court appearances)

➤ Prejudgment interest (when it is not included in the insuring agreement as a part of damages)

➤ Postjudgment interest (interest accruing on the judgment after an award has been made, but before payment is made by the company)

Policy Limits

Even though the purpose of liability insurance is to protect the insured from financial loss by shifting the burden of payment from the insured to the company, there is a limit beyond which the company will not go. The maximum amount the company will pay on behalf of the insured is stated in the *policy limits*, which are shown in the declarations.

The policy might stipulate separate limits for BI and PD (split limits), or there might be one limit that applies to both BI and PD (single or combined single limit).

In general, these limits apply *per occurrence*. The word "occurrence" means either a loss that occurs at a specific time and place, such as when an automobile collision occurs, or a loss that occurs over a period of time because of continued or repeated exposure to the same harmful conditions, as when fumes escaping from an activity on the insured premises eventually damage the paint on a neighboring house.

Some liability coverage limits apply *per accident*—an older and more restrictive term that limits covered losses to only those that occur at a specific time and place—and does not include coverage for losses that result from continued or repeated exposure to harmful conditions over time. Historically, liability policies covered "accidents," and insurers defined that term in their contracts. In recent decades, insurers have shifted to the broader concept of providing "occurrence" coverage.

 Generally, individual states determine minimum amounts of liability coverage an auto owner is required to carry on his or her automobile insurance policy. The state minimums are generally low and not necessarily adequate for all insureds.

 Some policies still use the term "accident" because it's a more familiar term. But it is defined so that it includes repeated exposure over time and means the same as "occurrence" in other policies. Only a careful inspection of the policy definitions will determine how it should be interpreted.

Some liability policies have a *per person* limit that states how much will be paid for injury to any one person in an occurrence or accident. Others also have an *aggregate limit*. This is a limit that applies to all losses occurring within any one policy period. Each individual loss is subtracted from the aggregate limit until it is exhausted; after which, there would be no more coverage during the policy year.

With the exception of the aggregate limit, most policy limits are *restored* immediately after payment of a loss. The per occurrence limit applies separately to each loss. So, if a policy has a $50,000 occurrence limit and a $500,000 aggregate limit, up to $50,000 would be available for each claim until the aggregate limit were exhausted. Aggregate limits are restored annually with each policy renewal or anniversary.

Exclusions

All liability policies contain certain exclusions. We'll examine these in detail when we look at specific policies, but we'll mention some common exclusions here. In general, there is no coverage for

➤ Damage to property owned by the insured

➤ Damage to property in the insured's care, custody, or control

➤ Bodily injury to an insured

➤ Losses covered under workers compensation laws

➤ Losses covered under Nuclear Energy Liability policies

➤ Injuries or damages caused intentionally by the insured

Conditions

A number of conditions are commonly found in liability policies—many of which we've already discussed, such as Cancellation, Assignment and Misrepresentation, Concealment, and Fraud. But let's review two conditions that have some special provisions applicable to liability insurance.

Duties After Loss

The *Duties After Loss* condition has some unique requirements in liability policies. The insured must notify the insurance company in writing of all losses. In addition, the insured is required to forward all applicable demands, notices, or summonses and give any necessary assistance to the case, such as testifying as required. The insured cannot voluntarily assume any liability or make any restitution to another party without the knowledge and consent of the insurer.

Other Insurance

Like property policies, liability policies contain Other Insurance clauses. In addition to the methods we've already discussed for handling other insurance—such as *pro rata liability* under which multiple insurers will share a loss proportionally based on their respective limits of insurance—liability policies can provide for *contribution by equal shares*.

Under contribution by equal shares, all insurers pay equal amounts regardless of their limits of coverage, up to the limit of the policy having the smallest limit. Then that company, having paid its policy limit, stops paying and the other companies share in the remainder of the loss. This continues until each company has paid its policy limit or the loss is paid in full.

Here's an example. The insured's $24,000 liability loss is covered by two policies—one issued by company XYZ with a $5,000 limit and one issued by company PDQ with a $25,000 limit. Company XYZ would pay $5,000; company PDQ would pay $19,000 ($5,000 + $14,000). If the loss had been $4,000, company XYZ would pay $2,000 and company PDQ would pay $2,000.

Exam Prep Questions

1. Failure to use the care that is required to protect others from the unreasonable chance of harm is called what?
   - ○ A. Proximate cause
   - ○ B. Negligence
   - ○ C. A criminal act
   - ○ D. An intervening cause

2. All of the following must be present to establish negligence except which one?
   - ○ A. Proximate cause
   - ○ B. Legal duty owed and breach of duty
   - ○ C. Damages
   - ○ D. Willful action

3. An action that, in a natural and continuous sequence, produces a loss is the
   - ○ A. hazard.
   - ○ B. proximate cause.
   - ○ C. appraisal point.
   - ○ D. exposure.

4. Liability that is imposed as a matter of law without regard to negligence is called what?
   - ○ A. Vicarious liability
   - ○ B. Absolute liability
   - ○ C. Breach liability
   - ○ D. Proximate liability

5. Liability that an insured incurs because of the actions of others, such as employees, is called what?
   - ○ A. Vicarious liability
   - ○ B. Absolute liability
   - ○ C. Breach liability
   - ○ D. Proximate liability

6. Theresa, a spectator at a baseball game, is injured when an errant ball hits her in the head. She sues the stadium owners for negligence. Which one of the following defenses against negligence would the owners probably use?
   - ○ A. Assumption of risk
   - ○ B. Comparative negligence
   - ○ C. Contributory negligence
   - ○ D. Statute of limitations

7. Which one of the following illustrates the concept of contributory negligence?

   ○ A. Martin buys a tanning bed for his home. Although he follows the manufacturer's directions to the letter, he is severely burned after spending five minutes in the bed.

   ○ B. Jane goes to a hair salon to have her hair colored. The hairdresser mixes the color improperly and dyes Jane's hair purple.

   ○ C. Rosa is injured when her car is struck from behind while she is stopped at a red light.

   ○ D. Ben turns a corner too fast and strikes Reba's car, which was illegally parked in a fire lane.

8. Lee sues Pat for injuries sustained in an auto accident. During the trial, it is determined that Lee's negligence contributed to the loss. Under comparative negligence laws, what can Lee recover?

   ○ A. Lee cannot recover any damages from Pat.

   ○ B. Lee's damages will be reduced to the extent of her own liability for the loss.

   ○ C. Lee can recover the full amount of the loss from Pat.

   ○ D. Lee might only recover 50% of the damages she claims regardless of her degree of negligence.

9. As a result of a successful lawsuit, Agnes receives $10,000 to cover her specific losses, an additional $40,000 for pain and suffering, and because the defendant was considered to have acted with willful disregard for others' safety, Agnes was awarded an additional $75,000. This additional $75,000 award can best be described as what type of damages?

   ○ A. General damages

   ○ B. Compensatory damages

   ○ C. Liability damages

   ○ D. Punitive damages

10. George accidentally hits Elaine's car with his car. The accident causes $3,000 of damage to Elaine's car, plus Elaine is injured and her medical bills come to $1,000. George's car also sustains $500 damage in the accident, but George isn't hurt. What will George's auto liability coverage pay for?

    ○ A. The damage to Elaine's car only

    ○ B. The damage to Elaine's car and Elaine's medical bills only

    ○ C. The damage to George's and Elaine's cars only

    ○ D. The damage to George's and Elaine's cars, and Elaine's medical bills

Exam Prep Answers

1. B is correct. Negligence is the lack of reasonable care that is required to protect others from the unreasonable chance of harm.

2. D is correct. Negligence is the lack of reasonable care that is required to protect others from the unreasonable chance of harm. The factors used to establish negligence are legal duty owed, breach of legal duty owed, proximate cause, and damages.

3. B is correct. Proximate cause is one of the elements required to establish a charge of negligence. It is an action that, in a natural and continuous sequence, produces a loss.

4. B is correct. Absolute liability is imposed by law on those participating in certain activities that are considered to be especially hazardous. Individuals involved in such operations can be held liable for the damages of another even though the individual was not negligent.

5. A is correct. Vicarious liability is liability that a person or business incurs because of the actions of others, such as family members or employees.

6. A is correct. Assumption of risk applies when a person knowingly exposes himself or herself to danger or injury. When a person assumes this risk, he or she might be prevented from recovering from a negligent party. This doctrine is frequently associated with injuries incurred by spectators at sporting events.

7. D is correct. In this case, both parties contributed to the accident—Ben by driving too fast and Reba by illegally parking her car. In the other examples, the injured party's own negligence did not contribute to the loss.

8. B is correct. Under a comparative negligence law, a finding of liability can be made even when both parties have contributed to the loss, with an award based on the extent of each party's negligence.

9. D is correct. All of the described damages are for liability. General damages are a type of compensatory damages in which the injured party is compensated for his or her loss. Punitive damages are awarded over and above compensatory damages as a way of punishing the wrongdoer.

10. B is correct. Liability coverage does not pay for property or bodily injury to an insured—one's own property and medical insurance is needed for that.

Dwelling Insurance

Terms you'll need to understand:

✓ Dwelling
✓ Other structures
✓ Personal property
✓ Fair rental value
✓ Removal coverage
✓ Debris removal
✓ Additional living expenses
✓ Personal liability
✓ Medical payments

Concepts you'll need to master:

✓ Basic coverage
✓ Broad coverage
✓ Special coverage
✓ Extended coverage
✓ Other coverages
✓ Replacement cost coverage
✓ Broad theft coverage
✓ Limited theft coverage
✓ Additional coverages
✓ Automatic increase in insurance
✓ Dwelling under construction

A Dwelling policy provides protection for individuals and families against loss to their dwelling and personal property. If you're already familiar with homeowners insurance, which also covers dwellings and personal property, you might wonder what the difference is between the two types of policies. We review both forms in detail, but two key differences are

➤ A Dwelling policy provides more limited property coverage than a homeowners policy.

➤ An unendorsed Dwelling policy provides property coverage only, whereas a homeowners policy provides a package of property and liability coverages.

There are three separate Dwelling policy forms: the *Basic form*, the *Broad form*, and the *Special form*, each providing a higher level of coverage than the previous one.

Different editions of Dwelling policy forms are in effect in this country. In this chapter, we focus primarily on the provisions of the Dwelling 89 policy issued by the Insurance Services Office (ISO). At the end of the chapter, we briefly review the differences between the 1989 policy forms and the 2002 Dwelling forms that are in use in some states. The changes are reasonably modest. All exam prep questions and practice exam questions are based on the 1989 forms.

Eligibility and Insureds

To be covered under a Dwelling policy, the dwelling must have no more than four separate apartments and no more than a total of five roomers or boarders. (Occupants of individual family living units might rent out a room to one or more boarders.) An eligible dwelling can be a townhouse or a rowhouse (one of a continuous series of houses sharing common sidewalls). The dwelling does not have to be occupied by the owner, and it might be under construction.

A Dwelling policy can also be used to insure a mobile home meeting certain qualifications, including that it be permanently located. However, mobile homes might only be covered under the Basic policy form.

Dwelling policies can be used to insure homes that do not qualify for homeowners insurance. For example, the owner of a single family home that is rented to tenants could not insure the home under a homeowners policy, but could insure it under a Dwelling policy. Dwelling policies are also frequently used to insure vacation homes.

Eligible dwelling property does not have to be exclusively residential. Certain *incidental* business and professional occupancies are allowed. These operations must be conducted by the insured, must provide service rather than sales, and must involve no more than two people working on the premises at any one time. Examples of permitted occupancies include beauty parlors, photography studios, and professional offices.

A Dwelling policy covers the named insured and his or her spouse, as long as the spouse lives in the same household as the insured, for loss or damage to the dwelling. If personal property coverage is purchased, the policy also covers the property of all family members living in the residence.

Basic Form (DP-1)

We begin our discussion with the Dwelling policy *Basic form*, which is also known as DP-1 or DP 00 01.

Major Policy Coverages

The Basic form includes provisions to provide the following major coverages:

➤ Coverage A—Dwelling

➤ Coverage B—Other Structures

➤ Coverage C—Personal Property

➤ Coverage D—Fair Rental Value

Although all four coverages are preprinted in the policy form, the insured does not have to purchase each one. For example, an insured who owns an unfurnished house that she rents to others might choose to purchase only Coverage A—Dwelling and Coverage D—Fair Rental Value.

On Dwelling policies, each major coverage is optional and the insured must select a limit of insurance for each coverage purchased. In contrast, Homeowner policies automatically include all the major coverages listed on the policy form.

Coverage A—Dwelling covers the dwelling, structures attached to the dwelling, materials and supplies for use in the construction or repair of the dwelling or other structures at the location, and building or outdoor equipment used to service the premises.

Coverage B—Other Structures insures buildings on the premises that are sep-arated from the dwelling by a clear space or connected only by a fence, utility line, or similar connection. The building may not be used for commercial, manufacturing, or farming purposes—commercial or farming policies are designed for those risks.

Coverage C—Personal Property covers the personal property of the insured and the insured's family members that is at the described location and is usual to the dwelling occupancy. (For example, the policy wouldn't cover an auto CD player—that would have to be covered by an auto policy.) Personal prop-erty belonging to the insured's guests or servants can be covered at the insured's request. However, the following items of personal property are not covered by a dwelling policy:

➤ Money, securities, manuscripts, bullion, currency, accounts, deeds, and evidences of debt

➤ Bank notes, coins, gold other than goldware, letters of credit, medals, personal records, platinum, silver other than silverware, tickets, and stamps

➤ Books of account, drawings and other paper records, electronic data processing tapes, wires, records, discs, or other software media (does not apply to blank recording or storage media or prerecorded media)

➤ Credit cards and fund transfer cards

➤ Animals, birds, or fish

➤ Aircraft

➤ Motor vehicles other than motorized equipment used to maintain the premises

➤ Boats other than rowboats and canoes

Personal property coverage is automatically provided for property moved from the described location to another newly acquired principal residence of the insured within the same state. The amount of insurance that applies at each location will be in proportion to the value of the property at each loca-tion at any given time. For example, if 40% of the property has been moved from location A to location B at the time a loss occurs at one of the locations, only 60% of the Coverage C limit would be available at location A and only 40% of the limit would be available at location B. This provision is called *automatic removal coverage.*

Automatic removal coverage is provided to allow an insured a reasonable time to move from one residence to another without having to estimate the values at each location and report them to the insurance company a number of times. For many people, moving to a new residence is a process that can take a number of days or weeks. However, the period of time allowed for coverage at two locations is not unlimited. Coverage begins on the date property is first moved. This split-coverage provision applies for a maximum period of 30 days and does not apply beyond the policy expiration date. If property is first moved 18 days before policy expiration, the provision would apply only for the remaining 18 days of the policy term.

Coverage D—Fair Rental Value is available to provide reimbursement if a covered property loss to the dwelling or other structure makes the building uninhabitable and the insured cannot collect the rent he or she would have been able to receive if the loss had not occurred. An insured may purchase any amount of coverage that fairly reflects the potential loss of rental income. An insured who lives in one unit of a triplex while renting the other two units to others would have a greater need for this coverage than an insured who lives in a single family home and only rents a private garage to a neighbor. If a civil authority prohibits use of the insured property because a covered peril damaged a neighboring location, this coverage still applies but payments are limited to a maximum of two weeks.

Perils Insured Against

The only perils that are automatically covered under the Basic form are

➤ Fire

➤ Lightning

➤ Internal explosion

An internal explosion is an explosion that occurs in a covered building or in a building containing covered personal property. Typical losses covered would include the explosion of a furnace, stove, or hot water heater. Steam explosions are excluded if the equipment is owned, leased, or operated by the insured. Generally, endorsements are available to cover boiler/machinery that explodes.

Extended Coverage Perils

Although only fire, lightning, and internal explosions are covered automatically, the insured has some additional options with the Basic form. The insured can opt to be covered against a list of additional perils that are sometimes called the *extended coverage* perils, or EC. These additional perils include

➤ Windstorm or hail

➤ Explosion

➤ Riot or civil commotion

➤ Aircraft

➤ Vehicles

➤ Smoke

➤ Volcanic eruption

 These perils are already printed in the DP-1 policy form. However, no coverage applies unless the insured pays the additional premium and the declarations indicate that the insured has selected extended coverage.

When extended coverage has been purchased, the explosion peril replaces the more limited internal explosion peril that would otherwise apply as part of Basic coverage. The broader explosion peril encompasses both internal explosions and other types of explosions, such as an explosion at a neighboring location that causes damage on the insured's premises.

Exterior damage to the dwelling or other structures resulting from windstorm or hail is covered, but damage to fragile items outside of buildings, such as awnings, signs, and antennas is not covered against wind or hail damage.

 Damage to the interior parts of a building or personal property within a building caused by windstorm or hail is only covered if wind or hail first makes an opening that enables these elements to enter the building. If an insured leaves a window open and wind or hail damages property inside, there will be no coverage.

The vehicles peril does not apply to damage caused by a vehicle owned or operated by the insured or a resident of the household. It also does not include vehicle damage to fences, driveways, and walks. It will cover damage to the dwelling, other structures, or other property when caused by someone who is not an insured or resident.

Smoke damage from a hostile fire in the dwelling is covered, but smoke damage from fireplaces or from agricultural smudging or industrial operations is not covered.

The insured can also obtain coverage for *vandalism and malicious mischief (V&MM)* by paying an additional premium and indicating that this coverage applies in the declarations. This coverage may only be purchased in conjunction with the extended coverage perils. If EC is not purchased, V&MM coverage is not available. Vandalism and malicious mischief coverage does not cover the following:

➤ Damage to glass parts of a building other than glass building blocks

➤ Losses by theft (does not apply to building damage caused by burglars)

➤ Damages to a building that has been vacant for more than 30 consecutive days

Other Coverages

In addition to the major coverages that are available, the Basic Dwelling form provides the following *Other Coverages*:

➤ *Other Structures* provides that up to 10% of the Coverage A limit may be used to cover losses to other structures. (You might also hear the term "*appurtenant structures*" used to describe other structures.)

➤ *Debris Removal* pays for the expense of removing debris resulting from a loss that is covered by the policy.

➤ *Property Removed* covers loss to property that occurs while the property is being removed to protect it from a covered peril. This is often referred to as *removal coverage*. (Coverage for removal to protect against loss is not the same as automatic removal coverage discussed earlier, which extends personal property coverage to property moved to another primary residence.) In the Basic form, property removed is covered for up to five days. (In the Broad and Special forms, it is provided for up to 30 days.)

➤ *Reasonable Repairs* pays for the reasonable costs to make necessary repairs to protect property from further damage following a covered loss.

➤ *Improvements, Alterations, and Additions* provides coverage for insureds who are tenants for improvements or alterations to the dwelling made at the tenant's expense. Up to 10% of the Coverage C limit is available for this coverage.

➤ *Fire Department Service Charge* pays up to $500 for fire department charges incurred when the fire department is called to save or protect covered property from a peril insured against. No deductible applies to this coverage.

➤ *Worldwide Coverage* provides 10% of the Coverage C limit for personal property while it is located anywhere in the world. An example is clothing that the insured takes on vacation.

➤ *Rental Value* provides 10% of the Coverage A limit for loss of fair rental value, payable at 1/12th of the 10% limit for each month the described location is unfit for its normal use. For example, if the Coverage A limit were $120,000, the coverage for Rental Value would be $12,000 (10%). The $12,000 would not be payable all at once, but would be payable in increments of $1,000 (1/12 of the Rental Value limit) for each month that the property was unfit for occupation.

Under Other Coverages, up to 10% of the Dwelling (Coverage A) limit is available to provide coverage for Other Structures and Rental Value. The nature of these coverages is identical to Coverages B and D as described in the policy, but do not confuse the coverage provided in this section with the available major coverages. These are indeed Other Coverages, which are extensions of coverage for the dwelling and are intended to provide limited amounts of coverage for insureds with minor exposures who might not have to purchase specific amounts of Coverages B or D.

For example, if an insured has a home valued at $100,000 and insures it under Coverage A for its full value under a Dwelling policy, and also has a detached garage valued at $8,000, there is no need to purchase a separate amount of Coverage B because up to $10,000 of coverage is available to cover the garage. However, if the insured with the same dwelling had a detached multicar garage valued at $20,000, it might be wise to purchase a specific amount of additional Coverage B to fully protect the garage (in this case, an additional $10,000 because $10,000 would still be available as an extension of Dwelling coverage).

On the Basic form, payment for loss under Other Coverages for Other Structures or Rental Value apply within the limit of insurance for Coverage A and reduce the remaining amount of insurance available for damages to the dwelling. On the Broad and Special forms, both of these coverages are provided as additional insurance and do not reduce the amount of insurance available for the dwelling.

Exclusions

The Basic form excludes the following:

➤ Losses resulting from ordinances or laws that require more elaborate or expensive reconstruction or demolition than was used in the original structure. (Replacing a dwelling's regular glass with safety glass is covered.)

➤ Losses resulting from earth movement, except for direct loss by fire or explosion resulting from earth movement.

➤ Water damage in general, including flooding, water backing up in to a building, and water leaking or seeping from below the ground.

➤ Losses due to power interruption that occurs away from the insured location.

➤ Losses because of the insured's failure to protect property from loss or to save and preserve property after a loss. (For example, if wind tore the roof off the insured's house but did not damage property inside, the insured did not remove or cover the property inside, and a day later a heavy rainstorm caused damage to the property inside, the policy would not cover the property damaged by the rainstorm.)

➤ Losses resulting from war.

➤ Losses caused by nuclear hazard.

➤ Losses caused by the insured or by someone else at the insured's direction.

Conditions

Dwelling policies contain many of the standard property insurance conditions reviewed earlier. There are also several conditions concerning how losses are paid under a Dwelling form:

➤ The *Loss Settlement* condition states that covered property losses are valued at actual cash value, but not to exceed the amount necessary to repair or replace.

➤ The *Our Option* condition gives the insurer the right to repair or replace damaged property with equivalent property within 30 days of receiving the insured's statement of loss.

➤ The *Deductible* clause, which is actually listed in the declarations, states that only the amount of loss over the deductible will be paid, up to the limit of liability.

➤ The *Pair Or Set* condition states that in the case of a loss to an item that is part of a pair or set, the insurance company is not obligated to pay the value of the entire set. The company can either repair or replace part of the set or pay the difference between the actual cash value of the property before and after the loss.

➤ The *Loss Payment* condition states that the loss will be paid within 30 days after reaching an agreement with the insured.

➤ The *Other Insurance* condition states that if a loss is also covered by other insurance, the insurance company will pay only its proportion of the loss.

➤ The *Recovered Property* condition states that if the insured or insurer recover property on which the insurer has made loss payment, the other party must be notified. The insured may have the property returned—in which case, the loss payment will be adjusted—or allow the company to have it.

Broad Form (DP-2) and Special Form (DP-3)

Now that you are familiar with the Basic Dwelling form, we'll review the other Dwelling forms. Our review focuses primarily on the differences between the Basic form and the Broad and Special forms.

Covered Perils—Broad Form

Similar to the Basic form, the *Broad form (DP-2, DP 00 02)* is a *named peril* policy listing the perils that dwellings, other structures, and personal property are insured against. The Broad form automatically covers all the standard and optional perils available on the Basic form—fire, lightning, the extended coverage perils, vandalism, and malicious mischief. It also broadens some perils covered under the Basic form and adds coverage for losses caused by these additional perils:

➤ Damage to covered property caused by burglars (does not apply to theft of property)

➤ Weight of ice, snow, or sleet

➤ Falling objects

➤ Freezing of plumbing, heating, air conditioning, or automatic fire protective sprinkler systems and household appliances

➤ Sudden and accidental tearing apart, cracking or burning of steam or hot water heating, air conditioning, or automatic fire protective sprinkler systems and water heaters

➤ Sudden and accidental damage from artificially generated electrical current (does not include damage to a tube, transistor, or similar electrical component)

➤ Accidental discharge or overflow of water or steam at the described location from within a plumbing, heating, air conditioning, or automatic fire protective sprinkler system or household appliance

The weight of ice, snow, or sleet peril does not cover damage to awnings, fences, patios, pavement, swimming pools, foundations, retaining walls, bulkheads, piers, wharves, or docks.

The falling objects peril does not include damage to awnings, fences, outdoor equipment, or outdoor radio and television antennas, including their lead-in wires, masts, and towers. Damage to a building's interior or its contents is covered only if the falling object first damages the roof or an exterior wall.

The accidental discharge or overflow peril does not include continuous or repeated leakage or seepage, loss caused by freezing, or damage to the system or appliance itself.

 Damage caused by sudden discharge or overflow of water or steam is covered. Continuous or repeated leakage or seepage over an extended period is excluded because the situation should have been detected and the loss could have been prevented or minimized.

The damage by burglars and accidental discharge perils are not covered if the building has been vacant for more than 30 consecutive days.

Freezing is not covered when the dwelling is vacant, unoccupied, or under construction unless reasonable care was taken to maintain heat in the building or to shut off the water and drain the systems and appliances.

 Damage by burglars is not covered after 30 days of vacancy because long periods of vacancy create targets for burglars. Uncollected newspapers or mail and unmowed lawns send out a signal that nobody is home. The limit on accidental discharge and the exclusion of loss caused by freezing during periods of vacancy are imposed for similar reasons—in both cases, if the water supply had been shut off and the systems drained, these losses would not have occurred. These provisions are designed to encourage insureds to take reasonable precautions to avoid losses.

The Broad form expands coverage for two of the perils that are also found on the Basic form:

➤ The vehicles peril covers damage to fences, driveways, and walks when the vehicle is driven by someone who is not a resident of the insured's household. (DP-1 excludes vehicle damage to this property in all cases.) It also covers damage to other types of property, such as the dwelling or a garage, even when the vehicle is driven by an insured or a resident of the insured's household. (DP-1 excludes all vehicle damage caused by insureds or residents.)

➤ The smoke peril includes loss caused by fireplace smoke. (DP-1 does not.)

In addition to adding and expanding covered perils, the Broad form (and the Special form) narrow the exclusion for losses caused by earth movement. All dwelling forms exclude direct damage caused by earth movement, but do cover damage caused by any fire or explosion that results. That is all the Basic form will cover, but both the Broad and Special forms will additionally cover breakage of glass or safety glazing material that is part of a building, storm door, or storm window when it results from earth movement.

Covered Perils—Special Form

The *Special form (DP-3, DP 00 03)* provides *open peril* coverage for the dwelling and other structures, insuring against all risks of direct physical loss that are not specifically excluded in the policy. Personal property is covered on a named peril basis, and the covered perils are identical to those listed on the Broad form and the related exclusions are the same for Coverage C.

Under Coverages A and B, the Special form excludes the following:

➤ All property, losses, and perils not covered because of limitations of the general exclusions (as described earlier in relation to the Basic form) and the insuring agreement.

➤ Any loss involving collapse other than as provided in the Other Coverages section.

➤ Freezing of a plumbing, heating, air conditioning, or automatic fire protective sprinkler system or a household appliance, or overflow due to freezing while the dwelling is vacant, unoccupied, or under construction, unless reasonable care was taken to maintain heat in the building or to shut off the water supply and drain the systems and appliances. For example, if the insured left the heat turned on and set to something like 70 degrees as if someone were still occupying the building even though it was vacant, that would be taking reasonable care to maintain heat in the building.

➤ Freezing, thawing, pressure, or weight of water or ice to fences, pavement, patios, swimming pools, foundations, retaining walls, bulkheads, piers, wharves, or docks.

➤ Theft in or to a dwelling or structure under construction, or theft of any property that is not part of a covered building or structure.

➤ Damage by wind, hail, ice, snow, or sleet to outdoor radio and television antennas and aerials, including their lead-in wires, masts, or towers, and damage by these same perils to lawns, trees, shrubs, or plants.

➤ Vandalism, malicious mischief, theft, and attempted theft if the dwelling had been vacant for more than 30 consecutive days at the time of loss.

➤ Constant or repeated seepage or leakage of water or steam over a period of time from a plumbing, heating, air conditioning, or fire protective sprinkler system or from a household appliance.

➤ Gradual and expected losses, such as wear and tear, deterioration, inherent vice, latent defect, mechanical breakdown, smog, rust, corrosion, mold, wet or dry rot, and smoke from agricultural smudging or industrial operations.

➤ Discharge, dispersal, seepage, migration, release, or escape of pollutants, such as smoke, vapor, soot, fumes, acids, alkalis, chemicals, and waste.

➤ Settling, shrinking, bulging, or expansion, including resulting cracking of pavements, foundations, walls, floors, roofs, or ceilings.

➤ Loss caused by birds, vermin, insects, and domestic animals.

If a loss that is not otherwise excluded involves water damage from a plumbing, heating, air conditioning, or fire protective sprinkler system or household appliance, the policy covers the loss caused by water and also the cost of tearing out and replacing any part of a building necessary to repair the system or appliance. Loss to the system or appliance itself is not covered.

Major Policy Coverages

The Broad and Special Dwelling forms offer the same major policy coverages as the Basic form plus one additional coverage. The five major coverages available under DP-2 and DP-3 include

➤ Coverage A—Dwelling

➤ Coverage B—Other Structures

➤ Coverage C—Personal Property

➤ Coverage D—Fair Rental Value

➤ Coverage E—Additional Living Expense

Coverage E pays for *additional living expenses* the insured incurs after a covered loss, including reasonable motel, dining, laundry, and transportation expenses. These expenses are covered for the time needed to repair or replace the damaged property or for the insured to become settled elsewhere in permanent quarters. If a civil authority prohibits use of the insured property because a covered peril damaged a neighboring location, payments under this coverage are limited to a maximum of two weeks.

 Although provisions for Additional Living Expense are not printed on the Basic coverage form, the coverage may be added to DP-1 by endorsement (a separate page attached to the policy, usually for an additional charge).

 Payments for Fair Rental Value and Additional Living Expenses are both reimbursements for loss of use of the property, and the term "Loss of Use" is used to describe these coverages on Homeowners policies. However, these are two distinctly different coverages that apply to different situations. Fair Rental Value covers the loss of rental income only from that part of a dwelling that is rented to others. Additional Living Expenses apply only to the actual additional expenses incurred by the insured's family while they are unable to remain in their primary residence.

Other Coverages

The Broad and Special forms include some Other Coverages that are not found on the Basic form, and they expand removal coverage.

All Dwelling policies provide *removal coverage*. Under the Broad and Special forms, property removed to protect it from loss is covered for up to 30 days. Under the Basic form, in the DP-1, it is only covered for 5 days.

DP-2 and DP-3 provide all the Other Coverages found on the Basic form plus these three additional coverages:

➤ **Trees, shrubs, and other plants**: This coverage pays up to 5% of the Coverage A limit for damage to trees, shrubs, plants, or lawns caused by a specified list of perils. However, the policy will not pay more than $500 for damage to any one tree, shrub, or plant.

➤ **Collapse**: This coverage pays for loss or damage caused by collapse of a building when caused by a specified list of perils.

➤ **Glass or safety glazing material**: This coverage pays for the breakage of glass or safety glazing material and damage to other covered property caused by the glass breakage.

Replacement Cost Coverage

Both DP-2 and DP-3 settle losses to personal property at actual cash value. Losses to the dwelling and other structures, however, are paid on a replacement cost basis, with no deduction for depreciation, as long as the insured carries insurance equal to 80% or more of the full replacement cost of the building at the time of the loss.

Suppose that an insured's home has a replacement value of $100,000. To have the home restored or replaced at replacement cost, the insured must have insurance equal to or greater than 80% of $100,000, or $80,000.

If the insured does *not* carry enough insurance to qualify for replacement cost coverage, he or she will be paid the actual cash value of the loss or a proportion of the replacement cost, whichever is larger. (Of course, the insured can never receive more than the policy limit.)

Proportional replacement cost is calculated by dividing the amount of insurance the insured carries by the amount he or she is required to carry to qualify for replacement cost coverage. The figure that results is multiplied by the amount of the loss to determine the amount of reimbursement.

Suppose that an insured's home has a replacement value of $100,000. This insured has $50,000 in coverage instead of the $80,000 needed to qualify for replacement cost coverage, and the insured has a $16,000 loss. Using the proportional method, reimbursement would be $10,000 ($50,000 divided by $80,000 equals 62.5%, which multiplied by the $16,000 loss results in a $10,000 settlement). Without such a provision, insureds might not purchase enough coverage to truly replace the value of their home in the event of a total loss. Because most fire losses are not total, the insurance company would end up paying out many more dollars for less-than-total losses to insureds who had paid fewer premium dollars into the company. To pay for those losses, premiums would have to be raised and property insurance would become more costly for everyone.

Dwelling Forms Comparison

This concludes our discussion of the Dwelling forms. Before you go on to the next section, study the following comparison tables.

Table 7.1 shows the major property coverages available under each policy form. Remember that these are separate optional coverages, and an insured may buy a single coverage, any combination of coverages, or all the available coverages.

Table 7.1 Major Policy Coverages			
Coverage	**DP-1**	**DP-2**	**DP-3**
Coverage A—Dwelling	X	X	X
Coverage B—Other Structures	X	X	X
Coverage C—Personal Property	X	X	X
Coverage D—Fair Rental Value	X	X	X
Coverage E—Additional Living Expense	By endorsement	X	X

Table 7.2 shows the Other Coverages provided by each policy form. These are extensions of the major coverages purchased and apply only if the related coverages have been purchased. For example, coverage for other structures and rental value apply only if dwelling coverage (Coverage A) has been purchased. Worldwide personal property coverage and coverage for property removed to protect it from loss apply only if personal property coverage (Coverage C) has been purchased.

Table 7.2 Other Coverages			
Other Coverage	**DP-1**	**DP-2**	**DP-3**
Other Structures	X	X	X
Debris Removal	X	X	X
Improvements, Alterations, Additions	X	X	X
Worldwide Coverage	X	X	X
Rental Value	X	X	X
Fire Department Service Charge	X	X	X
Reasonable Repairs	X	X	X
Property Removed	X	X	X
Trees, Shrubs, and Other Plants		X	X
Collapse		X	X
Glass or Safety Glazing Material		X	X

Table 7.3 shows the perils covered by the various Dwelling policy forms.

Table 7.3 Perils Insured Against				
Peril	**DP-1**	**DP-2**	**DP-3**	
			Dwelling	**Personal Property**
Fire	X	X	Open peril***	X
Lightning	X	X		X
Internal Explosion	X	N/A		N/A
Riot	X*	X		X
Explosion	X*	X		X
Vehicles	X*	X		X
Civil Commotion	X*	X		X
Smoke	X*	X		X
Hail	X*	X		X
Aircraft	X*	X		X
Windstorm	X*	X		X
Volcanic Eruption	X*	X		X
V&MM	X**	X		X
Burglars		X		X
Weight of Ice, Snow, Sleet		X		X
Discharge of Water or Steam		X		X
Falling Objects		X		X
Freezing		X		X
Sudden Tearing, Cracking, Burning		X		X
Electrical Current		X		X
Fireplace Smoke		X		X

*Extended Coverage perils available for separate premium

** Available for a separate premium

***Risks of loss not otherwise excluded are covered. (This includes all of the previously listed perils plus additional unnamed perils that are not excluded.)

Dwelling Policy Endorsements

A couple of important coverages can be added to Dwelling policies by endorsement. These include Broad or Limited theft coverage and Personal Liability and Medical Payments coverage.

Broad Theft Coverage

The *Broad Theft Coverage endorsement* adds coverage for theft of personal property to a Dwelling policy. It may only be written for an owner-occupant of an insured dwelling.

The endorsement covers theft, attempted theft, and vandalism and malicious mischief as a result of theft or attempted theft. V&MM is not covered if the dwelling has been vacant for more than 30 consecutive days immediately before the loss.

Property can be covered while it is on or off the premises. Separate limits of liability apply for on- and off-premises coverage, and off-premises coverage is available only if on-premises coverage is written.

Under this endorsement, the following types of property are not covered:

➤ Animals, birds, and fish

➤ Credit cards and fund transfer cards

➤ Property while it is in the mail

➤ Aircraft and parts other than model or hobby aircraft

➤ Property held as a sample or for sale or delivery after sale

➤ Property separately described and specifically insured by other insurance

➤ Property of tenants, roomers, and boarders that are not related to an insured

➤ Business property of an insured or residence employee

➤ Property that is in the custody of a laundry, tailor, or cleaner (except for loss by burglary or robbery)

➤ Motor vehicles and their equipment (does not apply to vehicles used to service the location or to assist the handicapped)

Special maximum limits of liability apply to the following classes of property on a per occurrence basis:

➤ $200 for money or related property, coins, and precious metals

➤ $1,000 for securities, manuscripts, and other valuable paper property

➤ $1,000 for watercraft, including trailers and equipment

➤ $1,000 for trailers not used with watercraft

➤ $1,000 for jewelry, watches, furs, and precious and semiprecious stones

➤ $2,000 for firearms

➤ $2,500 for silverware, goldware, or pewterware

When theft coverage is written, a condition of the insurance is that the insured is required to notify the police when a theft loss occurs.

Limited Theft Coverage

The *Limited Theft Coverage endorsement* also adds coverage for theft of personal property to a Dwelling policy. But this form is only used to provide coverage for a nonowner occupant of a dwelling, such as a tenant, and only on-premises coverage is available. It covers the same perils—theft, attempted theft, and vandalism and malicious mischief as a result of theft or attempted theft.

The Limited Theft Coverage form includes only three special limits of liability. Each limit is the most the insurer will pay for each loss for all property in that category. The special limits of liability are

➤ $1,000 for watercraft, including trailers and equipment

➤ $1,000 for trailers not used with watercraft

➤ $2,000 for firearms

The fewer number of categories of property subject to sublimits does not mean that limited theft coverage is less restrictive than broad theft coverage because the limited form entirely excludes coverage for the other classes of property listed on the broad form. Under the Limited form, in addition to the classes of property excluded on the Broad form, there is no coverage at all for money, gold, precious metals, securities, silverware, jewelry, watches, or furs.

Personal Liability and Medical Payments to Others

An insured can also purchase coverage for *Personal Liability and Medical Payments to Others* as an endorsement to a Dwelling policy or as a separate policy. These coverages are similar to those provided in the Liability section of a homeowners policy.

Coverages

This endorsement provides two coverages:

➤ *Coverage L—Personal Liability* provides coverage for damages that the insured becomes legally obligated to pay because of bodily injury or property damage caused by an occurrence to which the coverage applies. The insurer will also defend the insured against such claims at its own expense, even if the suit is groundless or fraudulent. The basic limit for liability coverage is $100,000. This is a minimum limit, and a higher limit can be purchased.

➤ Under *Coverage M—Medical Payments to Others*, the insurer will pay all necessary medical expenses incurred within three years of an accident that causes bodily injury. This coverage applies to either of the following injuries:

   ➤ Sustained while the injured party is on the insured location with the insured's permission

   ➤ Sustained while the injured party is off the insured location if the injury arises out of a condition on the insured location, is caused by the activities of an insured, or is caused by an animal in the insured's care

The basic limit for medical payments is $1,000 per person. This is a minimum limit and a higher limit can be purchased. An insured does not have to be legally liable for coverage to apply. This coverage does not apply to any injury sustained by the insured or the insured's family members.

Additional Coverages

Coverage for Personal Liability and Medical Payments to Others also includes three additional coverages, which are provided as additional amounts of insurance outside of the limits of liability. The additional coverages are

➤ Claim expenses

➤ First aid to others

➤ Damage to the property of others

Covered claim expenses include

➤ Defense costs

➤ Court costs charged against an insured in any suit the insurer defends

➤ Premiums on bonds that do not exceed the Coverage L limit and that are required in a suit defended by the insurer

➤ Reasonable expenses incurred by the insured at the insurer's request while assisting in the claim investigation or defense, including up to $50 per day for lost earnings

➤ Postjudgment interest (that is, interest that accrues on the amount of a settlement between the time it is awarded and the time it is actually paid)

Expenses for first aid to others are covered when they are incurred by the insured for bodily injury to others that is covered by the policy.

If the insured causes damage to the property of others, the policy provides replacement cost coverage of up to $500 per occurrence.

Exclusions

Bodily injury or property damage arising out of the following are excluded under both Coverage L and Coverage M:

➤ War

➤ Losses that are expected or intended by the insured

➤ Business pursuits or the rendering of or failure to render professional services

➤ Transmission of a communicable disease by an insured

➤ Sexual molestation, corporal punishment, or physical or mental abuse

➤ Use, sale, or possession of controlled substances other than the legitimate use of prescription drugs

➤ Rental of a premises that would not be eligible for coverage under the policy

➤ A premises owned by or rented to the insured or rented by the insured to others that is not considered an insured location

➤ Ownership, maintenance, use, loading, or unloading of most types of watercraft, aircraft, or vehicles

Specific exclusions that apply only to Coverage L (Personal Liability) include liability for the following:

➤ Damage to property owned by an insured

➤ Damage to property rented to, occupied or used by, or in the care of an insured (unless the loss is caused by fire, smoke or explosion)

➤ Losses that would be covered under a Workers Compensation or similar law

➤ Loss assessments charged against the insured as a member of an association, corporation, or community of property owners

➤ Damages assumed under most contracts or agreements

➤ Injury to the insured or any relative or minor who resides in the same household

Specific exclusions that apply only to Coverage M (Medical Payments) include bodily injuries

➤ To a residence employee that occurs off the insured location and does not arise out of or in the course of work the employee performs for the insured

➤ Because of any nuclear hazard

➤ To any person other than a residence employee who regularly resides on any part of the insured location

Other Endorsements

Other endorsements that may be used with a Dwelling policy include

➤ **Automatic increase in insurance**: This provides an annual increase in the Coverage A amount of 4%, 6%, or 8%.

➤ **Dwelling under construction**: When the intended occupant of a dwelling under construction is the named insured, this endorsement may be attached to a Dwelling policy to provide coverage. The limit of liability that applies at any given time is a percentage of the policy limit based on the value of the partially completed home.

Dwelling 2002 Forms

Some states have adopted newer versions of the Dwelling forms that have a 2002 edition date. The major differences between the 1989 and 2002 forms are summarized in this section.

Coverage B

Two changes were made to the property not covered section of Coverage B—Other Structures:

➤ Structures that contain commercial, manufacturing, or farming property owned by the insured or a tenant of the dwelling are covered as long as the structure is not used to store gaseous or liquid fuel. (This limitation does not apply to fuel in a permanently installed fuel tank of a vehicle or craft parked or stored in the structure.)

➤ Grave markers, including mausoleums, are not covered.

Coverage C

The following were added to the Property Not Covered section of Coverage C—Personal Property:

➤ Hovercraft and parts (hovercraft refers to self-propelled motorized ground effect vehicles, such as air cushion vehicles and flarecraft)

➤ Water or steam (under the earlier forms, it could be argued that water became the insured's personal property after it passed through the insured's water meter; this exclusion makes the intent of the policy clear)

➤ Grave markers, including mausoleums

➤ Electronic fund transfer cards or access devices used to deposit, with-draw, or transfer funds

➤ Scrip, stored value cards, and smart cards

➤ Data stored in computers and related equipment

Other Coverages

Under the Rental Value other coverage, the percentage of the Coverage A limit that may be used for loss of fair rental value was increased from 10% to 20%.

"Collapse" is now specifically defined in the Collapse other coverage. It must involve an abrupt falling down or caving in of the building or part of the building, with the result that the building or part of the building cannot be occupied. Collapse that results from hidden decay or hidden insect or vermin damage is not covered if the insured knew about the damage before the building collapsed.

Under the Glass or Safety Glazing Material other coverage, breakage of glass or safety glazing material that is part of a covered building, storm door, or storm window caused directly by earth movement is covered. The exclusion for loss when the dwelling has been vacant for more than 30 days does not apply to glass breakage from earth movement. Also covered is direct physical loss to covered property caused solely by the pieces, fragments, or splinters of broken glass or safety glazing material that is part of a building, storm door, or storm window. Any other loss that results because the glass or safety glazing material has been broken is not covered.

The Ordinance or Law other coverage, which was previously provided through state Special Provisions endorsements, has been incorporated in the 2002 forms.

Perils Insured Against

In the 1989 forms, vandalism and malicious mischief, accidental discharge or overflow of water or steam, and damage done by burglars were not covered if the building had been vacant for more than 30 days. In the 2002 forms, the allowed vacancy period is 60 days.

The smoke peril now covers damage caused by *puffback*—the release of soot, smoke, vapor, or fumes from a furnace, boiler, or similar equipment.

The accidental discharge or overflow of water or steam peril was modified to state that the insurer will pay to tear out and replace any part of a building or other structure on the premises when necessary to repair the system or appliance from which the water or steam escaped. However, tear out and replacement for another structure is covered only if the water or steam causes actual damage to a building on the premises. Roof drains, gutters, downspouts, and similar fixtures or equipment are not considered plumbing systems or household appliances.

Several changes were made to the freezing peril. For coverage to apply, the insured is now required to use reasonable care to maintain heat in the building or shut off the water supply and drain all systems and appliances. (For automatic fire protective sprinkler systems, the insured must continue the water supply.) In the earlier forms, this requirement only applied to buildings that were vacant, unoccupied, or under construction. In addition, the exclusion for losses to buildings that are vacant, unoccupied, or under construction no longer applies.

The sudden and accidental damage from artificially generated electrical current peril was expanded to apply to electronic components or circuitry that are part of appliances, fixtures, computers, home entertainment units, or other types of electronic apparatus.

General Exclusions

The Ordinance or Law exclusion was modified to exclude ordinances or laws whose requirements result in a loss in value to the property and ordinances or laws that require the insured to test for, monitor, clean up, or otherwise respond to pollutants. The exclusion applies regardless of whether the property has been physically damaged.

Under the Earth Movement exclusion, mudslides, sinkholes, and subsidence are now excluded. The perils listed under this exclusion apply when caused by or resulting from humans, animals, or any act of nature.

Losses resulting from destruction, confiscation, or seizure of property by the government or a public authority is now excluded.

The Water Damage exclusion was modified to exclude waterborne material. It also excludes water or waterborne material that is discharged from a sump pump or related equipment. The perils listed under this exclusion apply when caused by or resulting from humans, animals, or any act of nature.

Under the Special Dwelling form (DP-3), the exclusion for freezing, thawing, pressure, or weight of water or ice now applies to footings and other structures or devices that support all or part of a building or other structure. It also applies to retaining walls and bulkheads that do not support all or part of a building or other structure.

Conditions

The Other Insurance condition now addresses losses covered under a service agreement, such as a home warranty or service plan. When a loss is also covered by a service agreement, the service agreement pays first and the Dwelling policy pays on an excess basis.

The Duties After Loss condition now specifically states that the insured must cooperate with the insurer in a claim investigation. It was also modified to state that the insurer has no duty to provide coverage under the policy if the insured's failure to comply with these duties is prejudicial to the insurer.

The Intentional Loss condition was modified to state that when an intentional loss occurs, neither the insured nor any person or organization named as an additional insured is entitled to coverage, even those who were not involved in the intentional loss.

Under the Concealment or Fraud condition, the statement that the entire policy is void if the insured engages in concealment or fraud was removed. It now states that the insurer will not provide coverage to persons insured under the policy who engage in concealment or fraud.

The Our Option condition was modified to state that the insurer may repair or replace damaged property with material or property of like kind and quality.

The time allowed to bring legal action against the insurer was increased to two years. (Previously, it was one year after the date of loss.)

A new Loss Payable clause provides that if a loss payee is listed in the Declarations for insured personal property, the loss payee is considered an insured with respect to that property and will be notified in writing if the insurer cancels or doesn't renew the policy.

Under the Loss Settlement condition in Broad and Special forms, the insured no longer has to rebuild at the same premises to qualify for replacement cost coverage; however, payment is limited to the amount it would cost to rebuild at the original premises. Replacement cost is based on the cost to use material of like kind and quality. The insurer will pay no more than actual cash value until repair or replacement is complete; after that, the loss can be settled on a replacement cost basis. However, if the cost to repair or replace the damage is less than 5% of the limit of coverage on the building and less than $2,500, the insurer will pay on a replacement cost basis regardless of whether repair or replacement is complete.

Exam Prep Questions

1. Which of the following could not be covered under a Dwelling policy?
   - ○ A. A mobile home that is not permanently located
   - ○ B. A single family home that is under construction
   - ○ C. A three-unit townhouse
   - ○ D. A home that is rented to another person

2. Which of the following coverage provisions would not be found in an unendorsed Dwelling policy form?
   - ○ A. Dwelling
   - ○ B. Other structures
   - ○ C. Liability
   - ○ D. Personal property

3. Which of these items of personal property would be covered under a Dwelling policy when Coverage C is written?
   - ○ A. A motorcycle
   - ○ B. A pet poodle
   - ○ C. A pool table
   - ○ D. A sailboat

4. A Basic Dwelling policy form automatically provides coverage for losses caused by each of the following perils except which one?
   - ○ A. Fire
   - ○ B. Lightning
   - ○ C. Internal explosion
   - ○ D. Vandalism and malicious mischief

5. The Special Dwelling policy form provides which of the following?
   - ○ A. Basic coverage for the dwelling and broad coverage for personal property
   - ○ B. Broad coverage for the dwelling and basic coverage for personal property
   - ○ C. Open peril coverage for the dwelling and broad coverage for personal property
   - ○ D. Open peril coverage for both the dwelling and personal property

6. Which of the following Other Coverages is not included in the Basic Dwelling coverage form?
   - ○ A. Fire department service charge
   - ○ B. Collapse
   - ○ C. Debris removal
   - ○ D. Reasonable repairs

7. Under which of the Dwelling policy forms may the insured be reimbursed for the replacement cost when the dwelling is destroyed?

  ○ A. All Dwelling forms
  ○ B. The Basic form only
  ○ C. The Broad and Special forms
  ○ D. The Special form only

8. An insured has a DP-3 covering a home that has a replacement value of $100,000. The insured carries $60,000 of insurance. Following a loss, the determined is made that it would cost $12,000 to replace the damaged portion of the home. How much could the insured collect, assuming the ACV of the loss is $6,000?

  ○ A. $12,000
  ○ B. $9,000
  ○ C. $6,000
  ○ D. Nothing

9. Which of the following would not be covered under Coverage A or Coverage B of a Dwelling policy?

  ○ A. A storage shed 100 feet in back of the insured's dwelling where she keeps various yard tools
  ○ B. A detached garage that has been altered to house a manufacturing operation
  ○ C. A stack of lumber placed at the edge of the insured's property that will be used to construct a storage shed
  ○ D. A water heater located in the insured's attached garage

10. Which of the following losses would not be excluded under a Basic Dwelling policy form?

  ○ A. While the insured is on vacation, a power failure that occurs away from the insured's home causes the electricity to go off in the insured's neighborhood for 10 hours. As a result, large amounts of food stored in a freezer are ruined.
  ○ B. When Languid Lake overflows, the first floor of the insured's home is flooded, causing extensive damage.
  ○ C. Following a fire, the insured suffers an additional loss because a city ordinance requires that he replace his frame dwelling with more expensive fire-resistant materials.
  ○ D. An earthquake causes a fire that destroys the insured's home.

11. The Johnsons' home is covered by a Special Dwelling policy. When a fire damages the home, the family is forced to stay at a motel for a month while repairs are made. What coverage might reimburse them for these expenses?

   ○ A. Dwelling coverage

   ○ B. Additional living expenses

   ○ C. Personal property coverage

   ○ D. Fair rental value coverage

12. Myrtle has a Dwelling policy with Broad Theft coverage applicable both on and off her premises. Which of the following theft losses would be covered?

   ○ A. A $400 handgun taken from a bureau in her home

   ○ B. Theft of personal property owned by a boarder who rents a room in Myrtle's home

   ○ C. Two credit cards taken from her desk in her home

   ○ D. A tape player removed from the dashboard of her car that was parked in her garage

Exam Prep Answers

1. A is correct. To be eligible, a mobile home must be permanently located.

2. C is correct. A Dwelling policy automatically includes coverage provisions for the dwelling, other structures, personal property, and fair rental value. Liability and medical payments coverage may only be added by endorsement.

3. C is correct. Animals, motor vehicles, and most types of boats are excluded under Coverage C.

4. D is correct. The only perils that are automatically covered under the Basic form are fire, lightning, and internal explosion.

5. C is correct. The Special form provides Broad form named peril coverage for personal property and open peril coverage for the dwelling and other structures.

6. B is correct. Coverage for collapse is provided by the Broad and Special forms, but not by the Basic form.

7. C is correct. The Broad and Special forms will pay for losses to the dwelling and other structures on a replacement cost basis if the buildings are insured for at least 80% of their replacement value. Under the Basic form, losses are paid on an actual cash value basis.

8. B is correct. To qualify for replacement cost coverage, the insured must carry insurance equal to 80% of the replacement cost of the building. Because the insured does not carry enough insurance, the loss will be paid at proportional replacement cost or ACV, whichever is larger. In this case, proportional replacement cost ($9,000) is larger than ACV ($6,000).

9. B is correct. A detached garage that is used for commercial, manufacturing, or farming purposes is not covered under a Dwelling policy.

10. D is correct. Loss by fire that results from an earthquake is covered by all Dwelling forms.

11. B is correct. Both the Broad and Special forms make coverage available for Additional Living Expense. This coverage pays for additional living expenses the insured incurs after a covered loss, including reasonable motel, dining, laundry, and transportation expenses. These expenses are covered for the time needed to repair or replace the damaged property or become settled elsewhere in permanent quarters.

12. A is correct. Credit cards, motor vehicles and their equipment, and property owned by boarders or roomers are all excluded under the Broad Theft Coverage endorsement. However, up to $2,000 of coverage is available to cover theft of firearms.

Homeowners Insurance

Terms you'll need to understand:

- ✓ Dwelling
- ✓ Other structures
- ✓ Personal property
- ✓ Loss of use
- ✓ Loss assessment
- ✓ Personal liability

- ✓ Medical payments
- ✓ Bodily injury
- ✓ Property damage
- ✓ Debris removal
- ✓ Reasonable repairs
- ✓ Personal injury

Concepts you'll need to master:

- ✓ Incidental occupancies
- ✓ Broad coverage
- ✓ Special coverage
- ✓ Tenants coverage
- ✓ Comprehensive coverage
- ✓ Unit owners coverage

- ✓ Modified coverage form
- ✓ Scheduled personal property
- ✓ Personal property replacement cost
- ✓ Dwelling under construction
- ✓ Business pursuits

Just as companies that issue both property insurance policies and casualty insurance policies are called multi-line companies, policies that contain both property and casualty coverages in a single contract are called *multi-line policies*, or *package policies*. A *homeowners policy* is a multi-line policy because it provides property and liability insurance in a single contract.

By obtaining both property and liability coverage in one policy, the insured is more likely to avoid gaps in coverage and the overlapping of coverages that often happen when several mono-line policies are purchased instead of a package policy. It also is advantageous to the insurance company because it means fewer contracts and records, simplified billing systems, and a reduction of duplicate services. These savings mean that the price will be less than the cost of separate policies offering equivalent coverage.

In this chapter, we focus on the Homeowners 2000 policy issued by ISO.

Eligibility and Insureds

Not every person or house is eligible for coverage under a homeowners policy. The rules are stricter than those that apply to Dwelling policies. The following *eligibility rules* apply:

➤ The named insured must be an owner/occupant of the dwelling or condominium or a renter who maintains a residential occupancy.

➤ The home cannot contain more than four family living units and no more than two roomers or boarders per family.

➤ Unless the insured is a renter, he or she cannot purchase coverage for personal property only.

➤ The dwelling must be used exclusively as a residence, except for certain *incidental occupancies* such as offices, professional, or private schools or studios.

➤ Farms cannot be covered under a homeowners policy; mobile homes are eligible if the Mobile Home endorsement is attached.

➤ Dwellings under construction and secondary or seasonal residences are eligible.

➤ Homes that are being purchased on an installment contract or are occupied under a trustee or life estate arrangement are eligible.

Insureds under a homeowners policy include the named insured and residents of the same household, provided that they are relatives or are under 21 and in the care of the insured or a resident relative.

Extent and Scope of Homeowners Coverage

A homeowners policy is divided into two sections: *Section I* provides *Property insurance* and *Section II* provides *Liability and Medical Payments insurance.*

Just as there are several Dwelling forms to provide increasing levels of coverage, there are different homeowners forms to vary the extent of coverage: *HO-2, HO-3, HO-4, HO-5, HO-6,* and *HO-8.*

 Each of these forms provides identical liability coverage. It is only the property coverage that varies with the homeowners form selected.

HO-2 (HO 00 02), the *Broad form,* provides broad coverage for the dwelling and personal property. The covered perils are similar to those provided by the DP-1 with the extended coverage perils and vandalism and malicious mischief (V&MM) coverage. Breakage of glass and theft are also covered. In addition, it broadens certain perils and adds other perils that are not found on Dwelling forms.

HO-3 (HO 00 03), the *Special form,* provides open peril coverage for loss to the dwelling and other structures. It provides broad coverage for personal property, which is identical to HO-2's coverage of personal property.

HO-4 (HO 00 04), the *Contents Broad form,* insures *tenants*—people who do not own the building in which they reside. It provides broad coverage for personal property only that is similar to HO-2's and HO-3's broad coverage of personal property and no coverage for the dwelling. This policy also provides liability and medical payments coverage and is also known as the *Tenants form.*

HO-5 (HO 00 05), the *Comprehensive form,* provides open peril coverage for both the dwelling and other structures and personal property.

HO-6 (HO 00 06), the *Unit-Owners form,* provides broad coverage on the personal property of condominium owners, similar to that provided under HO-2, HO-3, and HO-4. It provides a very limited amount of dwelling coverage.

HO-8 (HO 00 08), the *Modified Coverage form,* is designed for older homes with replacement values that might far exceed their market values. It provides basic coverage on the dwelling and personal property that is similar to the DP-1 with the extended coverage perils and V&MM coverage, but also includes certain restrictions on valuation of losses. In many jurisdictions, HO-8 is no longer available.

Section I—Property

The following four separate property coverages are provided by a homeowners policy under Section I:

➤ Coverage A—Dwelling

➤ Coverage B—Other Structures

➤ Coverage C—Personal Property

➤ Coverage D—Loss of Use

Coverage A—Dwelling and Coverage B— Other Structures

Coverage A—Dwelling covers the dwelling and structures attached to the dwelling, as well as materials and supplies for repair and construction of such structures if they are located on or next to the residence premises (the dwelling listed in the declarations).

Coverage B—Other Structures covers buildings on the described premises that are separated from the dwelling by clear space or are connected only by a fence or utility line.

Neither the dwelling nor other structures can be used for business purposes, except for permitted incidental occupancies. Any other structure rented to someone other than tenants of the dwelling is excluded unless the other structure is rented as a private garage.

Permitted incidental occupancies under homeowners policies are the same as those mentioned earlier in Chapter 7, "Dwelling Insurance" (beauty parlors, photo studios, professional offices, and so on).

Neither Coverage A nor Coverage B is included in HO-4 because renters and tenants can only insure their own personal property. However, HO-6, the Unit-Owners form, does include a limited amount of Coverage A for

➤ Alterations, appliances, fixtures, and improvements that are part of the building containing the residence premises

➤ Items of real property pertaining solely to the residence premises

➤ Property that is the insured's responsibility under a condo association agreement

➤ Structures other than the residence premises owned solely by the insured at the location of the residence premises

The standard Coverage A limit for the HO-6 is $1,000 per occurrence.

Coverage C—Personal Property

Coverage C—Personal Property provides coverage for personal property owned or used by an insured while it is *anywhere in the world*. At the insured's request, coverage will also apply to property owned by others while in the part of the residence premises occupied by the insured or to the property of a guest or residence employee while in any residence occupied by the insured.

Homeowner's coverage for personal property is broader than that provided by Dwelling forms, which allow only 10% of the Coverage C limit for worldwide coverage. Under homeowners policies, the full Coverage C limit applies to personal property while it is at other locations anywhere in the world.

Keep in mind that worldwide personal property coverage applies only to temporary situations. If property is normally kept at a residence other than the residence premises shown in the declarations, it is only covered for up to 10% of the Coverage C limit or $1,000, whichever is greater. However, this restriction does not apply to property being moved from the described residence premises to a new principal residence. In this situation, full coverage applies for up to 30 days from the start of the move. Another exception applies when personal property is moved from the residence premises because the residence is being repaired or is unfit to live in. In this case, the personal property has full coverage while it is at the temporary residence.

Certain classes of property are specifically excluded from coverage. Homeowners policies *do not cover* the following:

➤ Animals, birds or fish.

➤ Motorized vehicles or aircraft, including equipment and accessories.

➤ Property of boarders.

➤ Property in an apartment held for rental by the insured.

➤ Paper or electronic records containing business data, except for prerecorded programs available on the retail market.

➤ Property rented to others off the residence premises.

➤ Credit cards.

➤ Hovercraft and parts. (Hovercraft are self-propelled motorized ground effect vehicles such as air cushion vehicles and flarecraft.)

➤ Water or steam. (Under earlier versions of homeowners policies, it could be argued that water became the insured's personal property after it passed through the insured's water meter. This exclusion makes the intent of the policy clear.)

Special Limits of Liability

Certain classes of personal property are subject to special limits of liability, which are sublimits lower than the overall policy limit that applies to all personal property. These coverage restrictions are designed to encourage insureds with personal property of especially high value or of a hard-to-value nature to insure this property on a specific basis. The limitations that apply are shown in Tables 8.1 and 8.2.

Table 8.1 Personal Property with Special Limits of Liability	
Coverage Limit	**Property**
$200	Money or related property, coins, and precious metals (does not apply to tableware)
$1,500	Securities, manuscripts, and other valuable paper property (includes the cost to research, replace, or restore the information from the lost or damaged property)
$1,500	Watercraft, including trailers and equipment
$1,500	Trailers not used with watercraft
$2,500	Property on the residence premises used for business purposes
$500	Property away from the residence premises used for business purposes
$1,500	Electronic apparatus while it is in, on, or away from a motor vehicle (such as a car phone or portable CD player) provided that the apparatus can be operated by both the vehicle's power and other power sources
$1,500	Electronic apparatus and accessories used primarily for business while away from the residence premises and not in or on a motor vehicle

For the classes of personal property shown in Table 8.2, the special limits apply only to theft losses.

Table 8.2 Personal Property with Special Limits for Theft Losses Only	
Coverage Limit	Property
$1,500	Jewelry, watches, furs, and precious and semiprecious stones
$2,500	Silverware, goldware, or pewterware
$2,500	Firearms

Coverage D—Loss of Use

Coverage D—Loss of Use provides two types of coverage. First, if a covered property loss makes the residence premises uninhabitable, the policy will cover additional living expenses related to maintaining the insured's normal standard of living. Generally, insurance companies limit this coverage to a certain number of months, or a certain amount of dollars.

Second, if a covered loss to the insured's property makes a part of the residence premises that is rented to others or held for rental by the insured uninhabitable, the policy will cover the loss of fair rental value, less any expenses that do not continue while the premises is uninhabitable.

Coverage D for loss of use on a homeowners policy is identical to combined Coverages D and E on the Broad and Special Dwelling forms. It is presented as a single coverage here because all homeowners policies provide both types of coverage for loss of use.

Expenses that do not continue are not reimbursed because they do not reflect a loss. Suppose that an insured rents part of a residence to a tenant for $300 monthly and incurs monthly expenses of about $50 for providing heat and electricity to that portion of the residence. While that part of the residence is uninhabited during repairs, there is no need to provide utility services, and the insured's actual loss is only $250 a month.

Additional Coverages

In addition to the four major property coverages just reviewed, homeowners forms provide a number of Additional Coverages.

In All Homeowners Forms

The following Additional Coverages are included in all homeowners forms. Except where specifically noted, coverage is included within the policy limit and is not provided as additional insurance.

➤ *Debris Removal—General*: Pays expenses to remove debris from covered property if a covered peril caused the loss. This includes the cost to remove ash or other particles from a volcanic eruption that caused direct loss to covered property. Generally, debris removal expenses (except for fallen trees) are covered within the policy limit and not as an additional amount of insurance, but in some cases an additional amount of insurance might be available.

 If the combined property damage loss and debris removal expense exceeds the policy limit, an additional 5% of the limit will be available for debris removal expenses as an additional amount of insurance. This applies to all types of debris except fallen trees.

➤ *Debris Removal—Trees*: A separate provision applies to coverage for the removal of fallen trees. This coverage is always provided as an additional amount of insurance outside of the policy limits, but it is subject to special sublimits and conditions. The most the insurer will pay under this coverage is $1,000 per occurrence and $500 per tree. Coverage is provided for removal of one or more of the insured's trees only if felled by the specific perils of windstorm, hail, or the weight of ice, snow, or sleet. Coverage is provided for removal of a neighbor's tree(s) if felled by any peril insured against under Coverage C. Additionally, in order for this coverage to apply, one of three conditions must exist: The tree must have damaged a covered structure; the tree must be blocking a driveway on the insured's premises that prevents a motor vehicle from entering or leaving; or the tree must be blocking a ramp or other fixture that prevents a handicapped person from entering or leaving the dwelling.

➤ *Reasonable Repairs*: Pays the reasonable costs incurred by the insured for repairs necessary to protect covered property from further loss after being damaged by a covered peril.

➤ *Trees, Shrubs, and Other Plants*: Covers trees, shrubs, and plants on the residence premises for loss by fire, lightning, explosion, riot, aircraft, vehicles not owned or operated by a resident, theft, and vandalism or malicious mischief. Coverage is limited to 5% of the Coverage A limit or a maximum of $500 for any one tree, shrub, or plant. (In HO-4 and HO-6, the limit is 10% of the Coverage C limit or a maximum of $500 for any one tree, shrub, or plant.)

➤ *Fire Department Service Charge*: Pays up to $500 when called to save or protect covered property from a covered peril. No deductible applies to this coverage. This coverage is not available for property located within the limits of the city furnishing the fire department service.

➤ *Property Removed*: Covers property against direct loss from any peril while being removed from a premises endangered by a covered peril, and for up to 30 days while removed.

➤ *Credit Card, Electronic Fund Transfer Card, or Access Device, Forgery, and Counterfeit Money*: Pays up to $500 for the insured's legal obligation to pay losses resulting from

➤ Theft or unauthorized use of these cards

➤ Forgery or alteration of the insured's checks

➤ The insured's acceptance in good faith of counterfeit money

Coverage does not apply to loss arising out of business use or the dishonesty of an insured. No deductible applies to this coverage.

➤ *Loss Assessment*: Pays up to $1,000 for the insured's share of a loss assessment charged against the insured during the policy period by a corporation or association of property owners as a result of direct loss to the property owned by all members collectively and caused by a covered peril. For instance, this coverage might pay a condominium owner's assessment for repair of a community clubhouse that was damaged by lightning. The deductible applies only once, regardless of the number of assessments in a single occurrence.

➤ *Glass or Safety Glazing Material*: Covers the breakage of glass that is a part of a building, including windows and storm doors.

In Selected Homeowners Forms

Other Additional Coverages are only contained in certain homeowners forms. Table 8.3 describes these Additional Coverages and the forms in which they are included. Except where specifically noted, coverage is included in the policy limit.

Table 8.3 Additional Coverages Found in Selected Homeowners Forms		
Additional Coverage	**Forms**	**Description Of Coverage**
Collapse	HO HO-2 HO-3 HO-4 HO-5 HO-6	Pays for direct physical loss to covered property involving collapse of a building caused by a covered peril or one of the additional perils listed for this Additional Coverage.

(continued)

Table 8.3	Additional Coverages Found in Selected Homeowners Forms *(continued)*	
Additional Coverage	**Forms**	**Description Of Coverage**
Landlord's Furnishings	HO-2 HO-3 HO-5	Provides $2,500 of coverage for loss to appliances, carpeting, and other household furnishings in an apartment on the residence premises that is rented or held for rental by the insured.
Building Additions and Alterations	HO-4	Covers fixtures, installations, and improvements made or acquired at the insured's expense. Coverage is limited to 10% of the Coverage C amount.
Grave Markers	HO-2 HO-3 HO-4 HO-5 HO-6	Provides up to $5,000 for damage to grave markers and mausoleums caused by a peril covered under Coverage C.
Ordinance or Law Coverage	HO-2 HO-3 HO-4 HO-5 HO-6	Pays up to 10% of the Coverage A limit for the increased cost to repair or rebuild a dwelling or other structure to conform with applicable building or land use codes. This coverage is provided as an additional amount of insurance.

Perils Insured Against

The number and breadth of the perils insured against by each of the homeowners forms is the major distinction among the forms.

Basic Named Perils

All homeowners policies cover, at a minimum, a number of basic perils. In the year 2000, what used to be known as the Basic form (HO-1) was discontinued in most jurisdictions, but the basic perils are still listed and covered by HO-8 (the Modified coverage form) where it is available. These perils are actually covered by all homeowners policies. The Broad and Special forms simply add coverage for additional perils. The *Basic named perils* that are covered by all homeowners policies include

➤ Fire

➤ Lightning

➤ Windstorm or hail

➤ Explosion

➤ Riot or civil commotion

➤ Aircraft

➤ Vehicles

➤ Smoke

➤ Vandalism and malicious mischief

➤ Theft

➤ Volcanic eruption

Under the windstorm or hail peril, interior damage is only covered if the wind or hail first makes an opening in the building. Watercraft, outboard motors, and related equipment are covered for damage by these perils only while inside fully enclosed buildings.

 These provisions reflect the fact that property left out in the open is exposed to perils that are expected to occur from time to time, and the insurance company is not willing to cover losses that are preventable.

Vehicle damage caused by a vehicle owned or operated by any resident of the residence premises is not covered, but vehicle damage caused by a nonresident is covered.

The smoke peril also covers *puffback*—the release of soot, smoke, vapor, or fumes from a furnace, boiler, or similar equipment. Smoke from fireplaces, agricultural smudging, or industrial operations is not covered.

Vandalism or malicious mischief losses to property on the residence premises is not covered if the dwelling has been vacant for 60 consecutive days or more.

The theft peril includes loss of property from a known place when it is likely that the property has been stolen. It also includes attempted theft. It does *not* include

➤ Theft by an insured

➤ Theft from a dwelling under construction (might be covered by endorsement)

➤ Theft from a portion of the premises that the insured rents out

➤ Theft of watercraft or equipment, trailers, or campers while off premises

➤ Mysterious disappearance (vanishing of property with no explanation)

The reasons for the limitations on theft coverage should be fairly obvious. Theft by an insured is an intentional crime, not an unexpected loss. Dwellings under construction are often not secure against those who might steal building materials. When an insured rents out a room, access to the premises is given to someone else. Security for watercraft or campers of premises might be difficult to maintain. Mysterious disappearance is not always a matter of theft.

Broad Named Perils

HO-2 (the Broad form) adds some additional perils and expands the definitions of several others. The additional *Broad form named perils* are

➤ Falling objects

➤ Weight of ice, snow, or sleet

➤ Accidental discharge or overflow of water or steam from within appliances or plumbing or related systems; does not include discharge or overflow of water from a sump

➤ Sudden and accidental rupture of a heating, air conditioning, fire protective sprinkler, or hot water heating system

➤ Freezing of plumbing or related systems

➤ Sudden and accidental damage from artificially generated electrical current

In addition, HO-2 expands coverage for two perils:

➤ The *vehicles* peril includes loss to a fence, driveway, or walk caused by a vehicle owned or operated by a person who lives in the insured household.

➤ The *smoke* peril includes loss caused by fireplace smoke.

The weight of ice, snow, or sleet peril does not cover damage to awnings, fences, patios, pavement, swimming pools, foundations, retaining walls, bulkheads, piers, wharves, or docks.

Damage to a building's interior or contents by a falling object is covered only if the falling object first damages the roof or an exterior wall.

Damage to a tube, transistor, or similar electrical component by artificially generated electrical current is not covered.

The freezing of plumbing or related systems peril does not cover losses that occur while the residence is unoccupied unless the insured has either made an effort to maintain heat in the house or has shut off the water supply and drained the system and appliances of water.

HO-4, the tenant's policy, insures personal property against the same perils covered under the Broad form HO-2. (Remember, there is no Coverage A or Coverage B in HO-4.)

HO-6, the condominium unit–owner's form, insures personal property against the same perils covered by HO-2 and HO-4, with one exception. In HO-6, the accidental discharge or overflow of water or steam peril includes coverage for the costs to tear out and replace any part of the building necessary to repair the system or appliance from which the water or steam escaped. (Earlier, we discussed the limited Coverage A available under HO-6.)

Special Form Coverage

HO-3, the *Special form*, provides *open peril* coverage for the dwelling and other structures, insuring against all risks of direct physical loss that are not specifically excluded in the policy. Personal property is covered on a *named peril* basis for the same perils insured under HO-2.

Under Coverages A and B, HO-3 excludes

➤ Any loss involving collapse, other than as provided in the Other Coverages section.

➤ Freezing of a plumbing, heating, air conditioning, or automatic fire protective sprinkler system or a household appliance, or overflow due to freezing while the dwelling is vacant, unoccupied, or under construction, unless reasonable care was taken to maintain heat in the building or to shut off the water supply and drain the systems and appliances.

➤ Freezing, thawing, pressure, or weight of water or ice to fences, pavement, patios, swimming pools, foundations, retaining walls, bulkheads, piers, wharves, or docks.

➤ Theft in or to a dwelling or structure under construction, including theft of materials and supplies used in construction.

➤ Vandalism and malicious mischief when the dwelling had been vacant for more than 60 consecutive days at the time of loss (does not apply to dwellings under construction).

➤ Gradual and expected losses, such as wear and tear, deterioration, inherent vice, latent defect, mechanical breakdown, smog, rust, corrosion, mold, wet or dry rot, and smoke from agricultural smudging or industrial operations.

➤ Discharge, dispersal, seepage, migration, release, or escape of pollutants, such as smoke, vapor, soot, fumes, acids, alkalis, chemicals, and waste (does not apply when caused by a peril covered under Coverage C).

➤ Settling, shrinking, bulging, or expansion, including resulting cracking of pavement, foundations, walls, floors, roofs, or ceilings.

➤ Loss caused by birds, vermin, insects, and animals owned by the insured.

If a loss that is not otherwise excluded involves water damage from plumbing, heating, air conditioning, or fire protective sprinkler system or household appliance, the policy covers the loss caused by water and the cost of tearing out and replacing any part of a building necessary to repair the system or appliance. Loss to the system or appliance itself is not covered.

Comprehensive Coverage

Comprehensive coverage insures the dwelling, other structures, and personal property against loss by the package of "special" perils. In effect, form HO-5 provides coverage for personal property on the same basis as Coverages A and B on form HO-3, with only minor variations.

On HO-5, the coverage for theft of personal property is slightly broader than it is on HO-3. Although the special sublimits of coverage for theft of jewelry, watches, furs, precious stones, silverware, goldware, pewterware, and firearms remain the same, the comprehensive form says that these limits apply to "loss by theft, misplacing, or losing." HO-5 is the only homeowners policy insuring these personal property items against loss by what is known as "mysterious disappearance."

Certain fragile personal items, such as eyeglasses, glassware, statues, bric-a-brac, and porcelain items, are too delicate to be considered for "all risk" type coverage. HO-5 limits the coverage for these items to losses caused by the specific perils of fire; lightning; the extended coverage (EC) perils; vandalism and malicious mischief (VMM); theft; collapse of a building; water risks that are not excluded; and sudden or accidental tearing, cracking, burning, or bulging of a steam or hot water heating system, air conditioning, or fire sprinkler system, or an appliance for heating water.

If any excluded loss is followed by a loss that is not excluded, the comprehensive form does cover the additional loss.

Exclusions

All homeowners forms contain exclusions that apply to the property coverages we've just reviewed. They include exclusion of losses because of

➤ Enforcement of law or ordinance regulating construction, repair, or demolition

➤ Earth movement, including earthquake and mine subsidence

➤ Water damage, including flooding and overflow from a sump pump

➤ Power interruption that takes place off the residence premises

➤ The insured's failure to save and preserve property after a loss or to protect it from loss

➤ War

➤ Nuclear hazard

➤ Losses caused intentionally by the insured or by someone else at the insured's direction

➤ Destruction, confiscation, or seizure of property by the government or a public authority

Conditions

A homeowners policy contains many of the conditions we've already reviewed regarding the insurer's and the insured's responsibilities under the policy, including *Duties After Loss, Mortgage Condition, Pair or Set, Appraisal,* and *Other Insurance.*

The *Loss Settlement* condition is similar to the one found in the Dwelling Broad and Special forms reviewed earlier in Chapter 7. Losses to the following are paid at actual cash value, but not more than the cost to repair or replace:

➤ Personal property

➤ Awnings, carpeting, appliances, outdoor antennas, and outdoor equipment

➤ Structures that are not buildings

Losses to the dwelling and other structures are paid at replacement cost as long as the insured carries an amount of insurance equal to or greater than 80% of the building's replacement cost. If the insured carries less than 80% of replacement cost, he or she will be paid the actual cash value of the loss or a proportion of the replacement cost, **whichever is larger**. (Of course, the insured can never receive more than the policy limit.)

The formula used to determine proportional replacement cost is a typical coinsurance provision. The amount of insurance actually carried is divided by 80% of the building's replacement cost, and the resulting percentage is then multiplied by the amount of loss to determine the reimbursement.

Replacement cost coverage is only available if the actual repair or replacement is complete unless the amount payable is less than a specified amount, which is typically 5% of the limit of insurance or $2,500.

Limits of Liability—Deductible

On homeowners policies, insureds are required to select a primary amount of insurance for the major property coverage being insured. On all forms except HO-4 and HO-6, this is dwelling coverage (Coverage A). On HO-4 and HO-6, this is personal property coverage (Coverage C). The policy automatically provides minimum amounts of coverage for other property exposures based on the primary limit unless the insured chooses to purchase additional amounts of insurance. Tables 8.4 and 8.5 show how these limits of liability are determined.

Table 8.4 HO-2, HO-3, HO-5, and HO-8	
Section I Coverage	**How Policy Limit Is Calculated**
A	Primary Limit
B	One or Two Family Dwelling: 10% of Coverage A limit
	Three or Four Family Dwelling: 5% of Coverage A limit
C	One or Two Family Dwelling: 50% of Coverage A limit
	Three Family Dwelling: 30% of Coverage A limit
	Four Family Dwelling: 25% of Coverage A limit
D	HO-8: 10% of Coverage A limit
	HO-2, HO-3, and HO-5: 30% of Coverage A limit

Table 8.5 HO-4 and HO-6	
Section I Coverage	**How Policy Limit Is Calculated**
A	Not applicable (except for $1,000 Coverage A limit in HO-6)
B	Not applicable
C	Primary limit
D	HO-6: 50% of Coverage C
	HO-4: 30% of Coverage C

These limits are provided as separate amounts of insurance. Suppose that a single family home is insured under an HO-3 with a Coverage A limit of $100,000. If the house and its contents were totally destroyed by a covered loss, the insured would receive $100,000 for the house and up to $50,000 for the contents (subject to any deductibles, special limits, and other policy conditions that might apply).

The limits automatically provided are minimum limits only. If an insured has additional exposures because of high values of other structures or categories of personal property, higher limits of coverage can be purchased.

Homeowners forms also include a deductible provision that applies to the coverage under Section I. Typical deductibles are $100, $250, or $500; other deductible amounts might also be available.

Section II—Liability

Individuals face many direct and indirect exposures to liability. A homeowner might be held liable for damages arising from his or her home or yard, as when a visitor slips and falls on a freshly waxed floor or a dead tree falls on and crushes a neighbor's bicycle. An individual can also be held liable for the actions of his or her children and pets, as when a 5 year old breaks all the windows in a neighbor's garage or the family dog bites the mail carrier. Finally, an individual might be held liable for damages arising out of personal activities away from the home, such as when an individual opens an umbrella in the crowded stands at a football game, accidentally poking it in the eye of another sports fan.

All homeowners policies provide identical liability coverages regardless of the variations in property coverages. Section II is the same on all forms and the provisions, conditions, definitions, and exclusions that apply are all the same.

Coverage E—Personal Liability

The following two major coverages are provided under Section II of each homeowners policy:

➤ Coverage E—Personal Liability

➤ Coverage F—Medical Payments to Others

Coverage E—Personal Liability covers damages that the insured becomes legally obligated to pay because of bodily injury or property damage caused by an occurrence to which coverage applies. As used in homeowners policies,

➤ *Bodily injury* means bodily harm, sickness, or disease, including required care, loss of services, and death.

➤ *Property damage* means physical injury to or destruction of tangible property, including loss of use.

In general, Coverage E applies to liability for bodily injury or property damage arising out of an insureds' personal, nonbusiness activities that occur anywhere. Coverage E also applies to liability for bodily injury or property damage arising from *insured locations* that include

➤ The premises described in the declarations

➤ Residences newly acquired during the policy period

➤ Locations where an insured is temporarily residing

➤ Locations an insured is renting for nonbusiness use

➤ Vacant land owned or rented by the insured

➤ The insured's land on which a residence is being built

➤ Cemetery plots or burial vaults

The policy also states that the insurance company will provide a defense for the insured at the insurer's expense, even when the charges are groundless. The insurer's duty to defend ends when the amount it pays for damages reaches the policy limit.

The basic liability limit provided for all bodily injury or property damage arising out of any one occurrence is $100,000. (This is a minimum limit, and higher amounts can be purchased.) In addition to actual damages, liability coverage includes any prejudgment interest awarded on any amount of a judgment the insurer is obligated to pay.

Coverage F—Medical Payments to Others

Coverage F—Medical Payments to Others pays all necessary medical expenses incurred within *three years* of an accident that causes bodily injury. This coverage applies to injuries

➤ Sustained while the injured party is *on an insured location* with any insured's permission.

➤ Sustained while the injured party is *off the insured location* if the injury arises out of a condition on the insured location, or on a location immediately adjoining the insured location; is caused by the activities of an insured or any residence employee in the course of his or her employment; or is caused by an animal owned by or in the care of any insured.

Medical payments coverage is not designed to cover injuries to insureds or regular residents of the insured premises, and such injuries are excluded except for injury to resident employees (who are covered). For this reason, Coverage F is sometimes called *Guest Medical* coverage.

Notice that there is *no requirement* under Coverage F that the insured be legally liable for the injuries. Coverage F covers injuries to others that occur on the insured's premises or result from the insured's activities, regardless of whether the insured is liable.

Coverage F has a basic limit of $1,000 per person per accident. Higher limits can be purchased.

Exclusions

Some important exclusions apply to both personal liability and medical payments, Coverages E and F, including

➤ Liability for injury or damage that is expected or intended by the insured

➤ Bodily injury or property damage arising out of business pursuits or the rendering of or failure to render professional services

➤ Bodily injury or property damage arising out of the rental of any part of the premises, except for the rental of part of an insured location as a residence

➤ Liability arising out of ownership, maintenance, use, loading, or unloading of aircraft, watercraft, and motor vehicles

➤ Liability arising out of war and war-like acts, such as insurrection and rebellion

➤ Liability arising out of the transmission of a communicable disease by an insured

➤ Liability arising out of sexual molestation, corporal punishment, or physical or mental abuse

➤ Liability arising out of the use, sale, manufacture, delivery, transfer, or possession of a controlled substance (does not apply to the legitimate use of prescription drugs)

There are some exceptions to the exclusion for liability arising out of the use of watercraft. Liability arising out of the following is covered by the policy:

➤ Watercraft that are not sailing vessels and are powered by inboard or inboard-outboard motors or engines that have 50 horsepower or less and are not owned by the insured or that have more than 50 horsepower and are not owned by or rented to an insured

➤ Watercraft that are not sailing vessels and are powered by one or more outboard engines or motors with 25 total horsepower or less, more than 25 total horsepower if the engines or motors are not owned by the insured, or more than 25 total horsepower and owned by the insured if the insured acquired the engines or motors during the policy period or owned the engines or motors prior to the policy period and either listed them on the declarations or asked the insurer to provide insurance on them within 45 days of their acquisition

➤ Sailing vessels that are less than 26 feet long or are more than 26 feet long but are not owned by or rented to an insured

➤ Watercraft that are in storage

The following additional exclusions apply only to the personal liability insurance. Under Coverage E, there is no coverage

➤ For any loss assessment charged against the insured as a member of an association, corporation, or community of property owners.

➤ Assumed under a contract or agreement, except contracts that relate directly to the insured location or contracts in which the liability of others is assumed prior to an occurrence.

➤ For property damage to property owned by, used by, or in the care of the insured.

➤ For bodily injury or property damage that is covered under a Nuclear Energy Liability policy.

The following additional exclusions apply only to the medical payments insurance. Under Coverage F, there is no coverage for

➤ Bodily injury to a residence employee that occurs off the insured location and does not arise out of or in the course of work the employee performs for the insured.

➤ Bodily injury because of nuclear reaction, radiation, or radioactive contamination, including any consequential injuries.

Additional Coverages

In addition to the major liability coverages, Section II of a homeowners policy also provides the following four coverages:

➤ *Claim Expenses*: This coverage reimburses the insured for defense costs, premiums for bonds required in a suit the insurer defends, postjudgment interest on damage awards, and reasonable expenses incurred by the insured at the company's request, including loss of earnings of up to $250 per day.

➤ *First Aid Expenses*: This coverage reimburses the insured for expenses the insured incurs for first aid to others at the time of an accident.

➤ *Damage To Property of Others*: This coverage pays up to $1,000 per occurrence for property damaged or destroyed by an insured, *without regard to legal liability*. This covers an insured's "moral obligation" to pay for damage to property that the insured might have borrowed or rented. Property owned by any insured is excluded, but unlike the major coverage for personal liability, other property in an insured's care, custody, or control is covered under this provision. When a loss is also payable under Section I of the homeowners policy, this Additional Coverage applies on an excess basis.

➤ *Loss Assessment*: This coverage pays up to $1,000 of the insured's share of any loss assessment charged during the policy period against the insured by a corporation or association of property owners when the assessment is made as a result of an occurrence to which Section II applies or as a result of liability for the act of a director, officer, or trustee acting in that capacity for the homeowners.

All of the Additional Coverages are provided *in addition to* the stated limits of limit of liability for the major coverages. So, if an insured had a $100,000 personal liability limit and a $100,000 judgment against her, the insurance company would still pay the full amount of the judgment *plus* the claim expenses. Any payments for first aid or damage to the property of others will not reduce the limit of insurance for damages under other coverage sections of the policy.

Conditions

Let's now look at the conditions contained in the homeowners policy.

Section II

Section II of a homeowners policy contains many of the conditions we've already reviewed, including an *Other Insurance* condition. In a homeowners policy, Coverage E is considered to be excess insurance over any other insurance, except for liability insurance specifically written to be excess over the limits of liability that apply to the homeowners policy.

Sections I and II

In addition to the conditions that apply separately to Sections I and II of a homeowners policy, there are general conditions that apply to both sections.

These conditions include *Policy Changes*, *Assignment*, *Concealment or Fraud*, *Liberalization*, *Subrogation*, *Policy Period*, and *Cancellation*.

Under the *Cancellation* condition, the insurance company can cancel for any reason with 10 days' written notice to the insured during the first 60 days of a policy term. After that, the company can only cancel for the following reasons:

➤ Material misrepresentation by the insured (30 days' notice required)

➤ Substantial change in risk insured (30 days' notice required)

➤ Nonpayment of premium (10 days' notice required)

The insurance company retains the right of nonrenewal, with 30 days' written notice to the insured required.

Although this condition appears in the standard policy forms, some state laws might require different cancellation procedures for policies issued in those states.

Homeowners Endorsements

Homeowners policies are designed for use by the "average" homeowner. Many homeowners, however, have special needs. To meet these needs, there are numerous endorsements that can be attached to a homeowners policy to modify coverage. Various endorsements are available to alter coverage provisions by adding coverages, changing valuation or settlement provisions, or removing exclusions.

Section I Endorsements

The *Scheduled Personal Property* endorsement provides a separate schedule of insurance for one or more of the following nine major categories of valuable property:

➤ Jewelry

➤ Furs and fur-trimmed garments

➤ Cameras, projectors, films, and related equipment

➤ Musical instruments

➤ Silverware

➤ Golf equipment

➤ Fine arts

➤ Postage stamps

➤ Coins

Many of these items represent property that has only a limited amount of coverage under a homeowners policy. The limits might be suitable for an average homeowner, but might not be adequate for an individual who owns significant amounts of property in these categories. The endorsement allows an insured to separately schedule one or more of these major categories of property with a separate amount of insurance for each category scheduled.

After the insured schedules items of personal property on this endorsement, the property is not subject to the coverage limitations that apply to unscheduled personal property under a homeowners policy. In addition, coverage is provided on an open peril basis with no deductible, even if the endorsement is attached to a named perils homeowners policy. Depending on the type of property scheduled, losses can be paid on an actual cash value, market value, repair or replacement cost, or value basis.

The *Personal Property Replacement Cost* endorsement provides that the policy will reimburse losses to personal property on a replacement cost basis, rather than actual cash value, in the same way that homeowners forms reimburse loss to dwellings and other structures. Some property is excluded, such as obsolete articles, antiques, fine arts, and paintings that cannot be easily replaced.

The *Permitted Incidental Occupancies* endorsement overrides the exclusions under the homeowners forms that apply to the insured's business activities conducted *on the residence premises*. For instance, this endorsement eliminates the Coverage B exclusion for using another structure for business purposes. It also eliminates the $2,500 limit for business property on the residence premises with regard to furniture, supplies, and equipment used in the business listed in the endorsement. It also eliminates the Section II exclusion of liability and medical payments coverage in connection with business pursuits for the described business.

None of the homeowners forms covers earthquake losses, but the coverage is available. To add earthquake as a covered peril, an insured must purchase an *Earthquake* endorsement.

Finally, the insured can purchase the *Home Day Care Coverage* endorsement to extend homeowners coverage to this type of business. The premium for this coverage is based on the number of children the insured cares for.

Section II Endorsements

A number of homeowners endorsements also affect Section II.

You will recall that the homeowners forms provide only limited liability coverage for watercraft. With the *Watercraft* endorsement, an insured can purchase coverage for

➤ Watercraft up to 26 feet long powered by outboard engines or motors exceeding 25 horsepower

➤ Watercraft powered by inboard or inboard-outboard engines or motors

➤ Sailboats more than 26 feet long

An unendorsed homeowners policy provides no coverage for liability arising out of business-related perils other than for permitted incidental occupancies. The *Business Pursuits* endorsement provides liability coverage for a business conducted *away from the residence premises.*

A homeowners policy provides no protection against personal injuries such as libel, slander, false arrest, invasion of privacy, or malicious prosecution. The *Personal Injury* endorsement modifies the definition of bodily injury to include personal injury.

Limited Fungi, Wet or Dry Rot, or Bacteria Coverage

This endorsement adds coverage to the property and/or liability sections of the policy for property damage and liability losses arising out of fungi, wet or dry rot, or bacteria. It is used only with the HO-3 and HO-5 policy forms. The limits for the coverages are scheduled in the endorsement.

Fungi is defined as any type or form of fungus, including mold or mildew. Under Section II, the definition does not include fungi that are on or part of a good or product intended for consumption. Bacteria and wet or dry rot are not defined.

Table 8.6 Property Coverage Provided by the Homeowners Forms						
	HO-2		**HO-3**		**HO-4**	
	Dwelling	Personal Property	Dwelling	Personal Property	Dwelling	Personal Property
Special			✓			
Broad	✓	✓		✓		✓
Basic						

*Provides only limited dwelling coverage

For purposes of simplification, we use the word "mold" in this section.

Under Section I, this coverage is added to the additional coverages section. It states that the amount shown in the schedule is the most the insurer will pay for

➤ All loss payable under Section I caused by mold

➤ Cost to remove mold from covered property

➤ Cost to tear out and replace any part of the building or other covered property as needed to gain access to the mold

Coverage only applies if the loss or costs resulted from a covered peril that occurred during the policy period. The insured must have used all reasonable means to save and preserve the property from further damage when the covered loss occurred.

The amount shown in the schedule is the most the insurer will pay for losses under this additional coverage, regardless of the number of locations insured or the number of claims made. This coverage does not increase the policy limit that applies to the damaged covered property.

Under Section II, the limit of liability condition is modified to state that the insurer's total liability under Coverage E for all damages arising directly or indirectly out of the actual, alleged, or threatened contact with mold will not be more than the sublimit for this coverage shown in the schedule. The sublimit does not increase the Coverage E limit and applies separately to each consecutive annual period.

Homeowners Forms Comparison

Tables 8.6–8.8 compare the features of the different homeowners forms.

HO-5		HO-6		HO-8	
Dwelling	Personal Property	Dwelling*	Personal Property	Dwelling	Personal Property
✓	✓				
			✓		
				✓	✓

Peril	HO-2	HO-3	
		Dwelling	Personal Property
Fire	✓	Open Peril*	✓
Lightning	✓		✓
Windstorm or Hail	✓		✓
Explosion	✓		✓
Riot or Civil Commotion	✓		✓
Aircraft	✓		✓
Vehicles	✓		✓
Smoke	✓		✓
Vandalism and Malicious Mischief	✓		✓
Theft	✓		✓
Volcanic Eruption	✓		✓
Falling Objects	✓		✓
Weight of Ice, Snow, or Sleet	✓		✓
Discharge of Water or Steam	✓		✓
Sudden, Accidental Rupture	✓		✓
Freezing of Plumbing and Related Systems	✓		✓
Artificially Generated Electrical Current	✓		✓

Table 8.7   Perils Insured Against

*Risks of loss not otherwise excluded are covered.

**Does not include losses to fences, driveways, or walks caused by vehicles owned or operated by residents of insured household.

HO-4	HO-5		HO-6	HO-8
	Dwelling	Personal Property		
✓	Open Peril*	Open Peril*	✓	✓
✓			✓	✓
✓			✓	✓
✓			✓	✓
✓			✓	✓
✓			✓	✓
✓			✓	✓**
✓			✓	✓***
✓			✓	✓
✓			✓	✓
✓			✓	✓
✓			✓	
✓			✓	
✓			✓****	
✓			✓	
✓			✓	
✓			✓	

***Does not include damage from fireplace smoke.

****Includes costs to tear out and replace area of the building to repair system or appliance.

Table 8.8 Additional Coverages						
Additional Coverage	HO-2	HO-3	HO-4	HO-5	HO-6	HO-8
Debris Removal	✓	✓	✓	✓	✓	✓
Reasonable Repairs	✓	✓	✓	✓	✓	✓
Trees, Shrubs, and Other Plants	✓	✓	✓	✓	✓	✓
Fire Department Service Charge	✓	✓	✓	✓	✓	✓
Property Removed	✓	✓	✓	✓	✓	✓
Credit Card, Fund Transfer Card, Forgery, and Counterfeit Money	✓	✓	✓	✓	✓	✓
Loss Assessment	✓	✓	✓	✓	✓	✓
Glass or Safety Glazing Material	✓	✓	✓	✓	✓	✓
Collapse	✓	✓	✓	✓	✓	
Ordinance or Law Coverage	✓	✓	✓	✓	✓	
Landlord's Furnishings	✓	✓		✓		
Building Additions and Alterations			✓			
Grave Markers	✓	✓	✓	✓	✓	

Exam Prep Questions

1. A homeowner who wants the maximum protection for her home and personal property should purchase the
   - ○ A. HO-4.
   - ○ B. HO-2.
   - ○ C. HO-3.
   - ○ D. HO-5.

2. An individual lives in an apartment. Which homeowners form should he purchase to cover his personal property?
   - ○ A. HO-4
   - ○ B. HO-6
   - ○ C. HO-8
   - ○ D. HO-3

3. Which homeowners form provides broad coverage for both the dwelling and its contents?
   - ○ A. HO-3
   - ○ B. HO-2
   - ○ C. HO-6
   - ○ D. HO-8

4. Which of the following could be covered by an unendorsed homeowners policy?
   - ❑ A. Mobile home
   - ❑ B. Home that is rented to another person
   - ❑ C. Home occupied by the insured and two boarders
   - ❑ D. Home that is owned and occupied by the insured

5. In the homeowners forms,
   - ❑ A. the property coverage varies in each form.
   - ❑ B. the property coverage is the same in each form.
   - ❑ C. the liability coverage varies in each form.
   - ❑ D. the liability coverage is the same in each form.

6. The Additional Coverage for collapse is included in which homeowners form(s)?
   - ❑ A. All forms
   - ❑ B. HO-4 only
   - ❑ C. HO-2 and HO-3
   - ❑ D. All forms except the HO-8

7. Which of the following classes of personal property are subject to special sublimits of coverage under a homeowners policy?

❑   A. Animals, birds, and fish

❑   B. Money

❑   C. Watercraft

❑   D. Trailers

8. Under a homeowners policy, which of the following classes of personal property have special limits for theft losses, but not for other types of losses?

❑   A. Money

❑   B. Firearms

❑   C. Silverware

❑   D. Jewelry

9. Which of these statements concerning Medical Payments to Others coverage are correct?

❑   A. Injury to an insured is not covered.

❑   B. The insured does not have to be legally liable for coverage to be available.

❑   C. Injuries that occur off the insured location are never covered.

❑   D. Medical payments are covered only if the expenses are reported within six months of the occurrence.

10. Which of these statements concerning personal liability coverage are correct?

❑   A. It covers damages that the insured becomes legally obligated to pay because of bodily injury or property damage.

❑   B. The insurer will not defend liability claims brought against the insured that are groundless or false.

❑   C. It applies to the insured's personal, nonbusiness activities that occur anywhere.

❑   D. It covers damages resulting from intentional acts of an insured.

11. Which of these statements about Coverage C of a homeowners policy are correct?

❑   A. It only covers the insured's personal property while it is at the residence premises.

❑   B. At the insured's request, coverage applies to a guest's property while the guest is in the insured's residence.

❑   C. Property normally kept at a residence other than the residence premises is covered for 10% of the Coverage C limit or $1,000, whichever is greater.

❑   D. There is no coverage for property being moved from the residence premises to a new principal residence.

12. A homeowners policy has been in force 30 days, and the company discovers that the insured has misrepresented certain material facts. The insurer wants to cancel the policy. Under what circumstances may it do so?

   ○ A. The company must wait until the policy has been in force for 60 days before it may cancel.

   ○ B. The company must give the insured 30 days written notice of cancellation.

   ○ C. The company must give the insured 10 days written notice of cancellation.

   ○ D. Under no circumstances; a policy cannot be cancelled because of material misrepresentation by the insured.

13. What is the limit on coverage for grave markers under the homeowners policy?

   ○ A. $1,000

   ○ B. $2,000

   ○ C. $2,500

   ○ D. $5,000

14. Which of the following cannot be covered by a homeowners Watercraft Liability endorsement?

   ○ A. A 30-foot boat powered by a 25 horsepower outboard engine

   ○ B. A 28-foot sailboat

   ○ C. A 28-foot inboard motorboat

   ○ D. A 25-foot boat powered by a 30 horsepower outboard engine

Exam Prep Answers

1. D is correct. The HO-5, the Comprehensive form, provides open peril coverage for dwellings, other structures, and personal property.

2. A is correct. The HO-4 is designed for tenants. It provides broad coverage for personal property and no coverage for the dwelling.

3. B is correct. HO-2 provides broad coverage for the dwelling and personal property. HO-3 provides open peril coverage for the dwelling; HO-6 offers only limited coverage for the dwelling and broad coverage for personal property; and HO-8 provides only basic coverage.

4. C and D are correct. Up to two boarders per family are allowed if the home is also occupied by the insured. An endorsement is required to insure a mobile home under a homeowners policy. The insured must live in the dwelling to qualify for homeowners coverage.

5. A and D are correct. The liability coverage is identical in all of the homeowners forms. It is only the property coverage that varies with the homeowners form selected.

6. D is correct. The Collapse additional coverage is included in all of the homeowners forms except the HO-8.

7. B, C, and D are correct. Loss of animals, birds, and fish are excluded entirely. All the other answer choices are subject to special sublimits of liability.

8. B, C, and D are correct. The following classes of property have special limits for theft losses, but not for other types of losses: jewelry, watches, furs, and precious and semiprecious stones; silverware, goldware, or pewterware; and firearms. The limit for the loss of money is $200 per occurrence regardless of the cause of loss.

9. A and B are correct. Injuries to the named insured or regular residents, other than resident employees, are not covered. Injuries sustained while the injured party is off the insured location are covered if certain conditions are met. There is no requirement under Coverage F that the insured be legally liable for the injuries. Medical payments coverage is available for expenses incurred within three years of the accident date.

10. A and C are correct. The insurance company will provide a defense for the insured at the insurer's expense, even when the charges are groundless. Damages resulting from intentional acts by an insured are not covered.

11. B and C are correct. Personal property is covered while it is away from the residence premises. When property is being moved to a new principal residence, full coverage applies for 30 days from the start of the move. Coverage for property belonging to an insured's guest or residence employee is available on request, but is not automatically provided.

12. C is correct. The insurance company may cancel a policy for any reason with 10 days' written notice to the insured during the first 60 days of a policy term.

13. D is correct. The homeowners policy includes coverage for up to $5,000 for damage to grave markers.

14. A is correct. The Watercraft Liability endorsement covers watercraft up to 26 feet long powered by outboard engines exceeding 25 horsepower, inboard-powered watercraft, or sailboats more than 26 feet long.

Personal Auto Insurance

Terms you'll need to understand:

- ✓ Named insured
- ✓ Family member
- ✓ Bodily injury
- ✓ Occupying
- ✓ Property damage
- ✓ Covered auto
- ✓ Temporary substitute auto
- ✓ Collision
- ✓ Other than collision
- ✓ Nonowned auto
- ✓ Policy territory
- ✓ Miscellaneous type vehicles

Concepts you'll need to master:

- ✓ Liability coverage
- ✓ Medical payments coverage
- ✓ Uninsured motorists coverage
- ✓ Underinsured motorists coverage
- ✓ Coverage for damage to your auto
- ✓ Who is an insured (under each coverage)
- ✓ Supplementary payments
- ✓ Financial responsibility
- ✓ Out of state coverage
- ✓ Other insurance
- ✓ Transportation expenses
- ✓ Joint ownership coverage
- ✓ Towing and labor costs
- ✓ Extended nonowner coverage
- ✓ Named nonowner coverage
- ✓ No-fault insurance
- ✓ Assigned risk plans

There are two major automobile exposures for which individuals seek protection. First, people want to be protected against their *liability* in case they injure someone or damage someone else's property through the use of their automobile. Second, people want protection for *damage to their own automobile* in case the auto is damaged in an accident or suffers other types of damage, such as fire or theft.

Because homeowners forms specifically exclude auto exposures, they must be covered separately, usually through a policy called the *Personal Auto policy*, or *PAP*. Because PAP contains both property and liability coverage, it is considered a package policy. In this chapter, we review the 1998 Personal Auto policy issued by ISO.

Organization and Eligibility

The Personal Auto policy consists of a *declarations page* and a *policy form*. The policy form contains four separate coverages, each with its own insuring agreement, exclusions, and conditions. They are

➤ Part A—Liability Coverage

➤ Part B—Medical Payments Coverage

➤ Part C—Uninsured Motorists Coverage

➤ Part D—Coverage for Damage to Your Auto (Physical Damage)

Many Personal Auto policies are written to include all the available coverages, but an insured does not have to purchase each one. Part A—Liability coverage can be written alone or with any of the other coverages. Medical Payments coverage, Part B, is optional, but it can only be written if the policy includes Liability coverage. Part C—Uninsured Motorists coverage can only be written in conjunction with Liability coverage and is subject to other laws that vary from state to state. It is mandatory in some states; in others, the insured can reject the coverage in writing. Either or both of the coverages under Part D (Collision and Other Than Collision) can be written alone or with Liability coverage.

A Personal Auto policy can be issued to an individual or to a husband and wife residing in the same household.

Definitions

The Definitions section of the Personal Auto policy defines certain key terms used in the policy. These terms help clarify the intent of various coverages and conditions.

The policy uses the words "you" and "your" to refer to the *named insured* shown in the declarations and his or her spouse. To be covered, the spouse must reside in the same household as the insured. However, if a separation occurs during the policy period or prior to the effective date of the policy, the spouse is still considered an insured for the lesser of

➤ 90 days

➤ The effective date of a new policy listing the spouse as a named insured

➤ The end of the policy period

A *family member* is any person related to the named insured who is a resident of the insured's household. This includes those related by blood, marriage, or adoption and includes a ward or foster child.

Bodily injury (BI) means bodily harm, sickness, or disease, including death that results from any of these.

Occupying means that a person is

➤ In a vehicle

➤ Upon a vehicle

➤ Getting in, on, out, or off a vehicle

Property damage (PD) means physical injury to, destruction of, or loss of use of tangible property.

The named insured's *covered auto* includes

➤ Any vehicle listed in the declarations. Vehicles eligible to be listed include *private passenger autos*, which are four-wheel motor vehicles, pickup trucks, and vans that are under a certain weight and are not used for business purposes. (Exceptions are made for vehicles used for farming or ranching, which are not considered business use under the PAP and may be covered.) The vehicles must be owned or leased under a long-term contract of six months or more.

➤ Any private passenger auto, pickup, or van the named insured acquires during the policy period.

➤ Any *trailer* owned by the named insured. This includes farm wagons or implements while towed by a vehicle listed in the declarations.

➤ Any auto or trailer not owned by the named insured that is being used as a temporary substitute for a vehicle shown in the declarations that is out of use because of breakdown, repair, servicing, loss, or destruction.

Notice that newly acquired autos qualify as covered autos. However, coverage is contingent on certain reporting requirements, as discussed in the following sections.

For Liability, Medical Payments, and Uninsured Motorists Coverage

If the newly acquired auto *replaces* one listed in the declarations, the new auto automatically has the broadest coverage provided for any vehicle already listed in the declarations until the end of the policy period.

If the new auto *does not replace* one that is already insured, coverage must be requested within 14 days after acquiring the auto in order for coverage to apply from the date the vehicle was acquired.

 In practice, this time limit might vary from company to company—14 days is the time limit in the ISO form, and it is the figure you might be tested on in your exam, but some companies allow 28 days.

For Physical Damage Coverage

For Physical Damage coverage, it doesn't matter if the new auto is a replacement or additional auto. If the insured already has at least one vehicle insured for Physical Damage coverage under the policy, coverage begins on the date the auto is acquired, as long as the insured requests coverage within 14 days after acquiring the auto. The new auto will then automatically have the broadest coverage provided for any vehicle already listed in the declarations.

 As with liability coverage, this time limit might vary from company to company— 14 days is the time limit in the ISO form and is the figure you might be tested on in your exam, but some companies allow 28 days.

If the insured does *not* already have Physical Damage coverage on an auto, coverage must be requested *by the end of the fourth day* after acquiring the auto. The fourth day generally ends at 12:01 a.m. on the fourth day.

For example, if an insured purchased a car at 8:00 p.m. on May 10, he or she would have until one minute after midnight on May 14 to request Physical Damage coverage for that car if that coverage was not already part of his or her policy. If a loss occurs in the time before the insured requests coverage, a $500 deductible applies.

Coverage for newly acquired vehicles begins on the date of acquisition only if the insured complies with any reporting requirements. If an insured requests coverage after any of the reporting periods specified in the policy have elapsed, coverage will begin at the time coverage is actually requested. This is true for both additional and replacement autos.

Suppose that Jose sells his small pickup truck and buys a new sports car. The pickup truck had liability with Collision and Other Than Collision coverage under a PAP. Because the sports car is a replacement for the pickup, it automatically has Liability, Medical Payments, and Uninsured Motorists coverage under the PAP until the end of the policy period. However, Jose would have to report the replacement vehicle within 14 days to have continuous coverage for Physical Damage.

Part A—Liability Coverage

Liability coverage is probably the most important PAP coverage because it covers an insured's greatest exposure—liability to others. If you smash your car into a brick wall and are not injured, the amount of loss is limited to the value of the car and the wall. But if you crash into a school bus and seriously injure 12 children, the potential liability claim could be enormous.

Coverage

Part A—Liability Coverage covers damages for bodily injury or property damage that an insured becomes legally responsible for because of an auto accident.

There are several important concepts here. First, the policy only protects those who are considered *insureds*. Second, coverage applies only to damages for which the insured is *legally responsible*. Finally, the damages must involve bodily injury or property damage and result from an *auto accident*.

The policy promises to settle or defend any claim or suit asking for such damages and promises to pay any defense costs incurred by the company. However, the duty to settle or defend ends when the limit of liability has been exhausted. Defense costs are paid in addition to the limit of insurance. There is no duty to settle or defend claims for bodily injury or property damage that are not covered under the policy.

Who Is an Insured

Now let's look at who is considered an insured under Part A of the Personal Auto policy. Although there are some exceptions that we cover later, in general the policy considers the following to be insureds:

➤ The named insured and members of his or her family while using any auto

➤ Anyone using the insured's car with the insured's permission or the reasonable belief that he or she is entitled to do so

➤ Other people or organizations to the extent that they share liability with an insured

➤ Other persons or organizations for their liability arising out of an accident involving any auto or trailer used by the insured or a family member (does not apply if the auto or trailer is owned by the person or organization in question)

Let's take a closer look at each of these groups.

First, the named insured, his or her spouse, and any family member is an insured for the ownership, maintenance, or use of *any* auto or trailer.

Suppose that the named insured's 16-year-old son borrows a neighbor's car and causes an accident. The son would be considered an insured for Liability coverage under the named insured's Personal Auto policy.

Any person using the named insured's covered auto with the insured's permission or the reasonable belief that he or she is entitled to do so is also covered for Liability insurance. For instance, a neighbor would be insured under the policy if he or she had an accident while driving the named insured's car with permission, but would not be covered under the named insured's policy while driving his or her own vehicle.

The policy also insures any person or organization who is legally responsible for the acts or omissions of *anyone insured* under Part A of the policy that result in an auto accident involving a covered auto. This is an example of *vicarious liability*.

For example, suppose that Glenda, a 17-year-old high school student insured under a PAP, is on her part-time newspaper delivery route when she injures a jogger with her car. If the jogger sued the newspaper publisher, the PAP under which Glenda is insured would cover the newspaper's liability.

In addition, the policy insures any person or organization who is legally responsible for the acts or omissions of a *named insured or family member* that result in an accident involving *any auto or trailer.* Such a person or organization is not covered, however, if they own or hire the auto or trailer.

Here's an example: Dave is on his way to a business luncheon in his own car when he hits Randall's car. Because Dave was on company business when the accident occurred, Randall sues both Dave and his employer, Rock Oil, for damages. Under these circumstances, Dave's Personal Auto policy would also cover Rock Oil's liability.

If Dave were driving a company-owned car when the accident occurred, his Personal Auto policy would not cover Rock Oil's liability. No coverage applies under Dave's policy for the organization when it owns or rents the vehicle involved in the accident. However, Dave's policy would still cover Dave if he is sued for damages as the driver of the vehicle.

Supplementary Payments

Similar to other liability policies, the liability portion of the Personal Auto policy contains Supplementary Payments that are paid in addition to the policy's limit of liability. They include

➤ Up to $250 for the cost of bail bonds

➤ Premiums on appeal bonds or bonds to release attachments

➤ Postjudgment interest (prejudgment interest is included as part of the liability limit)

➤ Up to $200 per day for loss of earnings because of attendance at hearings or trials at the company's request

➤ Other reasonable expenses incurred by the insured at the company's request

 Many liability policies include defense costs in the supplementary payments section of the contract. The PAP does not because it includes them in the insuring agreement, where it says it will pay all defense costs in addition to the applicable limit of liability for damages.

Exclusions

A number of important exclusions help define coverage under the Liability section of the Personal Auto policy. Excluded are

➤ BI or PD caused intentionally by the insured.

➤ Damage to property owned or being transported by the insured.

➤ Damage to property rented to, used by, or in the care of the insured.

➤ BI to an insured's employees. (These losses are covered under workers compensation.)

➤ Liability arising out of an insured's ownership or operation of a vehicle used as a public or livery conveyance, such as a taxi. This exclusion does not apply to a share-the-expense carpool.

➤ Liability arising while the insured auto is being used in an auto business.

➤ Use of a vehicle without permission (does not apply to family members using covered autos owned by the insured).

➤ BI or PD for which an insured is covered under a Nuclear Energy Liability policy.

➤ Motorized vehicles with fewer than four wheels or designed for use off public roads (does not apply to nonowned golf carts).

➤ Vehicles other than covered autos that are owned by the named insured or furnished for the named insured's regular use.

➤ Vehicles other than covered autos that are owned by family members or furnished for their regular use (does not apply to the named insured).

➤ Vehicles used in prearranged racing or speed contests.

The reasons for many of the exclusions should be obvious. Intentionally caused losses are not accidents. Loss or damage to an insured's own property is not a matter or legal liability. On-the-job injuries to employees should be covered by workers compensation. Vehicles that are not "covered autos" but are owned or regularly used by the insured or family members are excluded because they should have been reported and added to the policy and the insurance company is not going to provide free insurance for this exposure.

Limits of Liability

The Part A *limit of liability* is the most the company will pay for all damages resulting from any one auto accident, regardless of the number of insureds, claims filed, vehicles or premiums listed in the declarations, or vehicles involved in the accident.

Liability coverage is commonly provided on a *split limits basis*. The limits are usually expressed as a series of three numbers, such as 25/50/25. This means that the policy will pay

➤ $25,000 *per person* for bodily injury

➤ $50,000 *per accident* for bodily injury

➤ $25,000 *per accident* for property damage

Although split limits are common, single limit coverage is available. A policy written with a combined single limit of $100,000 for liability would make that amount available to pay all BI and PD claims arising out of the same accident, regardless of the split between BI and PD amounts or the number of claimants.

The policy also states that a person cannot collect duplicate payments for a loss that is covered under Part A and another coverage in the Personal Auto policy or under any Underinsured Motorists coverage provided by the policy.

Assume that the named insured's Personal Auto policy has limits of 100/300/100 for Part A. After an accident, there is a $250,000 judgment against him for injuries to one person. In this case, the policy will pay $100,000 (the policy limit for BI to one person).

Financial Responsibility

An important provision under Part A of the Personal Auto policy deals with financial responsibility laws. Almost all states have *financial responsibility laws* that require each driver to prove that he or she can pay for bodily injury or property damage liability losses arising out of auto accidents. A driver normally meets this requirement by purchasing an auto insurance policy with limits of liability that meet the minimum limits required by that state's law.

This provision states that the insurance company can *certify* the policy as proof of future financial responsibility. When it does, the policy will automatically reflect any changes in the state's financial responsibility laws.

Out of State Coverage

Vehicles are usually driven in more than one state, and the Personal Auto policy provides for such situations. The *Out of State Coverage* provision assures that the insured's Personal Auto policy will meet other states' financial responsibility requirements and other state laws concerning out-of-state drivers when the covered auto is being driven in that state.

Other Insurance

The *Other Insurance clause* for Liability coverage states that the company will pay only its share of a loss that is also covered by other insurance. The company's share is the proportion that its policy limit bears to the total of all applicable limits. However, any insurance the company provides for a vehicle that is not owned by the insured will be considered excess to other insurance.

Suppose that Alma has an accident in her car and is liable for damages of $60,000. She has a Personal Auto policy with a $50,000 single liability limit and other applicable liability insurance of $25,000. Alma's Personal Auto policy would pay $40,000 for this loss (50,000/75,000 × 60,000 = 40,000).

However, if Alma were driving a car owned by another person, the extent of liability provided by the other person's liability coverage would be calculated without reference to Alma's coverage. If the damages exceeded the amount the other person's liability coverage would pay, Alma's coverage would come into play.

Part B—Medical Payments Coverage

Medical Payments coverage is an important form of automobile insurance because it pays expenses for injuries to insureds and passengers of covered vehicles.

Coverage—Who Is an Insured

Part B—Medical Payments Coverage provides protection for the named insured, family members, and passengers in the named insured's auto for injuries received in an accident, *regardless of who was at fault.* It is not a form of liability coverage for injuries sustained by passengers in another auto involved in an accident with the insured.

Part B covers reasonable expenses for necessary medical and funeral services incurred within *three years* of the date of the accident.

Insureds for Medical Payments coverage include

➤ The named insured and any family member while occupying a motor vehicle designed for use on public roads or a trailer, or as pedestrians when struck by a vehicle designed for use on public roads or a trailer

➤ Any other person while occupying the named insured's covered auto and entitled to do so

Suppose that the named insured ran a red light while driving his covered auto and hit another vehicle. The occupants of the car he hit were badly injured. The named insured, his daughter, and two of his daughter's friends were in the insured's auto and were also injured. Medical Payments coverage would pay the medical bills for the named insured, his daughter, and her friends. It would not cover the medical bills of the other car's occupants, but if they sue for injuries, the insured's Liability coverage would apply.

Exclusions

Medical Payments coverage is subject to many of the same exclusions as Liability coverage. There is no coverage for injuries

➤ Sustained while occupying a motor vehicle with fewer than four wheels

➤ Sustained while using a covered auto as a public or livery conveyance

➤ That would be covered under workers compensation

➤ Sustained while occupying an uninsured auto owned by the insured or furnished for his or her regular use

➤ Sustained by anyone other than the named insured while occupying an uninsured auto owned by a family member or furnished for the family member's regular use

➤ Sustained while the insured is occupying a vehicle without the reasonable belief that he or she is entitled to do so (does not apply to family members using covered autos owned by the insured)

➤ Sustained while occupying a vehicle being used in the insured's business

➤ Caused by war or nuclear hazard

➤ Sustained while occupying a vehicle located for use as a residence or premises

➤ Sustained during prearranged racing or speed contests

Limits of Liability and Other Insurance

Medical Payments coverage has a single limit of liability that applies to all injuries sustained by *each person* injured in any one accident. Typical limits are $1,000, $2,000, $5,000, or $10,000. Some policies offer maximum coverages up to $100,000.

A person cannot collect duplicate payments for a loss that is covered under Part B and another coverage in the Personal Auto policy or under any Underinsured Motorists coverage provided by the policy.

The Other Insurance condition for Medical Payments coverage is identical to the one for Liability coverage.

Part C—Uninsured Motorists Coverage

Part C of the Personal Auto policy provides *Uninsured Motorists (UM) coverage*. UM coverage is another important form of automobile insurance because there are drivers who have no insurance or inadequate amounts of insurance. UM coverage will pay for certain losses the insured suffers at the hands of another driver that would have been covered by that other driver's insurance, but were not covered because that driver was uninsured.

Coverage

In most states, UM coverage indemnifies the insured for *bodily injury only* as a result of an accident with a legally liable uninsured motorist. Only compensatory damages are covered; punitive damages are specifically excluded.

Some states offer property damage coverage in addition to bodily injury coverage. This is provided by adding an endorsement to the policy. You should check the laws of your own state to determine whether UM coverage applies to bodily injury only or is also available for property damage.

Before the insured can be indemnified under Part C, four conditions must be met:

➤ The loss must be caused by an auto accident and involve bodily injury (in most states).

➤ The loss must be sustained by an insured.

➤ The insured must be legally entitled to recover for BI damages.

➤ The other vehicle must meet the definition of an uninsured vehicle.

Definition of Uninsured Motor Vehicle

The policy defines an *uninsured motor vehicle* as one that

➤ Has no Liability coverage at the time of the accident

➤ Has Liability coverage, but not enough to meet the state's financial responsibility requirement (note the difference between this and *Underinsured Motorists* coverage, described later in this unit)

➤ Is operated by an unidentified hit-and-run driver who strikes an insured or a family member, the insured's covered auto, or any auto occupied by the insured or a family member

➤ Has invalid Liability coverage at the time of the accident because the insurer is insolvent or denies coverage

This definition of "uninsured motor vehicle" does *not* apply to a vehicle or equipment that is

➤ Owned by, furnished to, or available for the regular use of the insured or any family member

➤ Owned or operated by a self-insurer, except for an insolvent self-insurer

➤ Owned by a government unit or agency

➤ Operated on rails or crawler treads

➤ Designed for use off public roads

➤ Located for use as a residence or premises

Earlier, you learned that the Out of State coverage provision automatically amends the policy limit to conform with other states' financial responsibility laws. Because of this provision, the part of the definition referencing policies with inadequate limits rarely applies to drivers insured under a Personal Auto policy. However, not all policies include an Out of State coverage provision. This part of the definition is intended to protect insureds who are involved in accidents with drivers insured by such policies.

Who Is Insured

Insureds for Uninsured Motorists coverage include

➤ The named insured and family members.

➤ Anyone occupying the named insured's covered auto.

➤ Any person entitled to recover damages because of BI caused by an uninsured motorist to the named insured, family members, or passengers in the covered auto. Examples include a parent who is entitled to recover for medical expenses incurred by a child, or a spouse who is entitled to damages for loss of a spouse's services, which is known as *loss of consortium.*

Exclusions

Uninsured Motorists coverage does not cover losses

➤ For BI sustained by an insured while occupying or when struck by an auto that is owned by the insured, but not insured for Uninsured Motorists Coverage under the policy

➤ For BI sustained by a family member while occupying or when struck by an auto owned by the named insured that has primary Uninsured Motorists Coverage under another policy

➤ That are settled without the insurer's consent

➤ That occur when the auto (either the insured's auto or a nonowned auto) is being used as a public or livery conveyance

➤ That occur while the insured is using an auto without the reasonable belief that he or she is entitled to do so (does not apply to family members using covered autos owned by the insured)

In some states, workers compensation insurers and disability insurers may have the right to subrogate against a third party who has caused an injury. In the case of an injury caused by an uninsured motorist, this right could extend to making a claim under the injured party's Uninsured Motorists coverage. However, such claims are specifically prohibited by the policy.

Limit of Liability

The Limit of Liability provision for Part C is similar to the one used for Part A. It also states that the insurance company will not

➤ Make duplicate payments for losses paid by or on behalf of the person who was responsible for the accident

➤ Pay any part of a loss that could be covered under a workers compensation or disability benefits law

Other Insurance

The Other Insurance provision for Uninsured Motorists coverage is similar to the ones used for Parts A and B. One important difference is that the amount the insured can be paid is limited to the highest single policy limit for Uninsured Motorists coverage. This prevents "stacking" of coverage— adding the limits of coverage available to provide a higher limit of coverage.

Suppose that Imelda has two Personal Auto policies, both with a $200,000 limit of liability for Uninsured Motorists coverage. She is involved in a serious accident with an uninsured driver and incurs $350,000 in medical expenses. The maximum amount she could collect under both policies for this loss is $200,000, not $400,000.

Arbitration

Part C provides specific provisions on arbitration that come in to play when the insured and the insurance company do not agree whether the insured is entitled to Uninsured Motorists coverage or the amount of damages. This provision operates the same way as the arbitration clauses we described earlier.

Part D—Coverage for Damage to Your Auto

Physical damage coverage protects the insured's vehicles against loss or damage. Many people who own late-model cars desire it because of the high cost of automobile repairs, but it is not a required coverage by the insurance companies or in most of the states. However, when new car purchases are financed, it is almost always required by the bank.

Coverage

Coverage for autos owned or used by an insured is available under the Personal Auto policy by *Part D—Coverage for Damage to Your Auto*, commonly known as *Physical Damage coverage*. Physical Damage coverage pays for direct and accidental loss to the named insured's covered auto or any nonowned auto against loss caused by

➤ Collision

➤ Other Than Collision (sometimes referred to as OTC or Comprehensive)

These coverages apply only to the vehicle itself and its attached or installed equipment and parts. They do not cover any personal property in the vehicle.

Together, these two coverages provide what amounts to open peril coverage for damage to the named insured's auto. The named insured can purchase Collision coverage only, Other Than Collision coverage only, or both coverages. The mix of coverages can also vary by car in the same policy. But only the coverages for which a premium is shown in the declarations will apply to each car scheduled in the policy.

Collision is defined as the impact of an auto covered by the policy with another object or vehicle, or the upset of a vehicle.

Other Than Collision coverage pays just about every other type of direct, accidental loss to the vehicle that is not specifically excluded by the policy. These perils are specifically listed in the policy as being Other Than Collision losses:

➤ Breakage of glass

➤ Contact with a bird or animal

➤ Explosion or earthquake

➤ Fire

➤ Hail, water, or flood

➤ Malicious mischief or vandalism

➤ Missiles or falling objects

➤ Riot or civil commotion

➤ Theft or larceny

➤ Windstorm

If glass breakage is caused by collision, the insured has the option of having it treated as a collision loss. This eliminates a double deductible when glass breakage and other collision damage occur in the same accident.

If the named insured has a covered loss in a nonowned auto, the broadest coverage that applies to any of his or her covered autos will apply to the nonowned auto. A *nonowned auto* is any private passenger auto, pickup truck, trailer, or van not owned by or available for the regular use of the named insured or a family member, such as a short-term rental car. Under Physical Damage coverage only, a *temporary substitute* auto is considered a nonowned auto instead of a covered auto.

Transportation Expenses

In addition to Collision and Other Than Collision coverage, Part D provides *Transportation Expenses coverage*. This coverage pays up to $20 per day, to a maximum of $600, for

➤ Transportation expenses incurred by the insured because of physical damage losses to the insured's covered auto

➤ Loss of use expenses for which the insured becomes legally responsible because of loss to a nonowned auto

Transportation Expenses will be paid for both Collision and Other Than Collision losses as long as the insured has purchased these coverages.

For transportation expenses arising out of the total theft of the auto, there is a 48-hour waiting period before expenses will be paid. Coverage continues until the auto is returned to use or the company pays for its loss.

For other types of losses, there is a 24-hour waiting period. Coverage is limited to the period of time reasonably required to repair or replace the auto.

Exclusions

Part D excludes losses

➤ To an auto that is being used as a public or livery conveyance.

➤ Because of and confined to wear and tear, freezing, mechanical or electrical breakdown, or road damage to tires (does not apply when the damage results from the total theft of the auto).

➤ Caused by war or nuclear perils.

➤ To all types of audio, visual, and data electronic equipment and its equipment and accessories, including radios, tape decks, CD players, phones, personal computers, VCRs, and videotapes. This exclusion does not apply to permanently installed telephones and sound equipment and accessories that are permanently installed in the auto or are removable from a permanently installed housing unit and designed to be operated by the auto's electrical system. It also does not apply to electronic equipment that is necessary for the normal operation and monitoring of the auto or is an integral part of a permanently installed housing unit for sound reproduction equipment.

➤ Because of destruction or confiscation by government or civil authorities (does not apply to the interests of any loss payee in a covered auto).

➤ To a camper body, trailer, or motor home that is not listed in the declarations. This exclusion also applies to cooking, dining, plumbing, and refrigeration facilities used with these items. However, this exclusion does not apply to trailers and their facilities and equipment that are not owned by the insured, and trailers, camper bodies, and their facilities and equipment that are acquired during the policy period if coverage is requested within 14 days after acquisition.

➤ To a nonowned auto when used by the named insured or family member without a reasonable belief that he or she is entitled to do so.

➤ To awnings, cabanas, or equipment designed to create additional living space.

➤ To custom furnishings or equipment in a pickup or van (does not apply to caps, covers, or bedliners on pickup trucks).

➤ To radar or laser detection equipment.

➤ To nonowned autos being used by any person engaged in an auto business.

➤ To nonowned autos being used in any business (does not apply to the use of a private passenger auto or trailer by the named insured or family member).

➤ To any auto being used in a prearranged racing or speed contest.

➤ To an auto rented by the named insured or a family member if the rental agency is prohibited from recovering from the insured or a family member under the provisions of state law or a rental agreement.

Other Provisions

Physical damage losses are reimbursed for actual cash value or the amount needed to repair or replace the property, whichever is less. If the insured and the insurance company do not agree on the amount that should be paid, the loss can be appraised. If the insurer pays for a loss in money, the payment will include the applicable sales tax for the damaged or stolen property.

Both Collision and Other Than Collision coverage are usually written with a deductible that applies separately to each occurrence.

In the Physical Damage part of the Personal Auto policy, the Other Insurance condition is called *Other Sources of Recovery*. It is essentially the same as the Other Insurance conditions in Part A and Part B, except that it states that the insurer will pay only its share of the loss if *any other source of recovery*, not just insurance, applies to the loss.

The *No Benefit to Bailee* condition states that a bailee cannot benefit from the insurance policy if a loss occurs to the car while it is in the bailee's possession. Examples of bailees include repair shop owners and employees of parking garages.

Parts E and F—Conditions

Parts E and F of the Personal Auto policy list conditions that apply to the policy as a whole. *Part E—Duties After an Accident or Loss* details the duties of insureds following a loss. They are similar to the duties required under other property and liability policies.

Under Uninsured Motorists coverage, the insured is required to notify the police promptly if a hit-and-run driver is involved. Under Physical Damage coverage, the insured must take reasonable steps after a loss to protect a covered auto and its equipment from further damage. Reasonable expenses required to do so will be reimbursed. In addition, the police must be notified if the car is stolen. Finally, the insurance company must be permitted to inspect or appraise the property before its repair or disposal following a loss.

Part F—General Provisions establishes conditions for the coverage and describes the duties and obligations of the insured and insurer.

The policy applies only to accidents and losses that occur during the *policy period* shown in the declarations and within the *policy territory*. The coverage territory includes the United States, its territories and possessions, and Canada. Covered autos are also insured while being transported between territorial ports.

Legal action against the insurer cannot be taken by an insured until all policy terms have been complied with. Under Part A, legal action cannot be taken against the insurer until it agrees in writing that an insured has an obligation to pay unless the amount of such an obligation has been established by judgment after a trial. No person or organization can take action against the insurer for the purpose of determining whether an insured is liable for a loss.

Policy terms cannot be *changed or waived* except by written endorsement. Any premium adjustment because of a change takes effect as of the date of change. If the policy form is revised to provide broader coverage without additional charge, all policyholders automatically and immediately benefit from the broader coverage on the date the change is implemented in their state of residence.

The insurer has *subrogation* rights under all coverages except Physical Damage coverage against a person using a covered auto with a reasonable belief of being entitled to do so.

The *termination* provision describes conditions for cancellation and nonrenewal. The *insured* can cancel the policy at any time by returning the policy or providing advance written notice of the desired cancellation date. The *insurer* must provide advance written notice of cancellation or nonrenewal. At least *10 days* notice must be given if the policy is being cancelled for nonpayment of premium or if cancellation occurs during the first 60 days of an initial policy term (a new policy that has not been renewed or continued). At least *20 days* notice must be given in all other cases.

After a policy has been in effect for 60 days, or after it has been renewed or continued, the insurer may only cancel for these reasons:

➤ Nonpayment of premium

➤ Material misrepresentation in obtaining the policy

➤ A regular operator of the vehicle has had his or her driver's license suspended or revoked

Nonrenewal by the insurance company requires at least *20 days* advance notice to the insured.

Underinsured Motorists Coverage

Earlier, we stated that a vehicle with Liability insurance in an amount equal to or greater than the state's financial responsibility limit is not considered an uninsured vehicle under Uninsured Motorists coverage. This financial responsibility limit, however, often falls far short of fully reimbursing the insured for a loss. *Underinsured Motorists coverage* fills this gap. In general terms, Underinsured Motorists coverage pays the difference between the insured's actual damages for bodily injury and the amount of Liability insurance carried by the driver who was at fault, up to the limits of the insured's Underinsured Motorists coverage.

 Underinsured Motorists coverage is subject to state law—being mandatory in some states and optional in others. It is added to a Personal Auto policy by endorsement. You should check the law in your state to determine whether this coverage is required, optional, or not available.

Suppose that the insured, who carries $100,000 of Underinsured Motorists coverage, is involved in an auto accident. The other driver, who was at fault, carries the state's required limit of $50,000 of Auto Liability insurance. The named insured's damages for bodily injury are $65,000. The insured's Underinsured Motorists coverage will pay $15,000 for this loss ($65,000 less the $50,000 limit of the at-fault driver's Liability policy).

Personal Auto Policy Endorsements

Although the Personal Auto policy provides broad coverage for an individual's auto exposures, some insureds might have additional coverage needs that can be met by adding an endorsement to the policy.

As mentioned earlier, a Personal Auto policy can be issued to an individual or a husband and wife who live in the same household. When the *Joint Ownership coverage* endorsement is attached, the policy can be issued to two or more persons who live in the same household or two or more individuals who are related in another way besides husband and wife.

The *Towing and Labor Costs* endorsement reimburses the insured for the cost of having a vehicle towed. The basic coverage limit is $25 for combined towing and labor costs each time a covered auto is disabled. Higher limits are usually available. Labor costs are covered only for work performed at the place of disablement—work performed after the vehicle is taken to a garage is not covered.

Some companies offer the *Miscellaneous Type Vehicle* endorsement, which can be added to the Personal Auto policy to provide coverage for motorcycles, mopeds, and recreational vehicles such as motor homes and golf carts. Other companies issue specialized policies to cover these vehicles rather than endorsing the standard policy.

The *Extended Nonowner coverage* endorsement expands the extensive coverage automatically provided under the Personal Auto policy for the insured and the family while driving cars other than the insured's covered autos. It eliminates most exclusions applicable to autos that are furnished or available for the regular use of the named insured or family members. For example, this endorsement would extend coverage to an individual who uses a car provided by his or her company in the course of work.

Part D of the Personal Auto policy pays up to $20 per day to a maximum of $600 for transportation expenses when a covered auto is out of service because of a covered loss. The *Optional Limits Transportation Expenses coverage* endorsement allows the insured to select the daily and maximum limits of coverage provided for transportation and loss of use expenses for scheduled and nonowned autos. The limits selected are shown in the declarations.

The *Named Nonowner coverage* endorsement can be issued to someone who does not own an automobile, but drives borrowed or rented autos. It might be used to provide coverage for an individual who drives a corporate-owned auto furnished for his or her use by an employer. Although the individual would have coverage while driving the company car under the company's auto policy, there would be no coverage for any other auto the insured might regularly or occasionally drive. This endorsement to the Personal Auto policy provides such coverage. If the insured acquires a private passenger auto, pickup, panel truck, or van during the policy period, the endorsement will automatically cover it for 14 days if no other insurance applies.

No-Fault Insurance

You've learned that an insured's Auto Liability insurance only pays for losses that the insured is legally liable for. But in many cases, this traditional fault system has created a backlog in the courts and excessive costs—all to determine who is at fault.

In an attempt to deal with these problems, some states have adopted *no-fault laws*. Under these laws, an insured driver is reimbursed by his or her own insurance company for medical expenses and loss of wages, *regardless of who was at fault in the auto accident*. Subrogation from the other company is not allowed.

Suppose that Samuel's car crosses the center line and strikes Mohammed's car head-on. If this accident occurred in a state with a pure no-fault law, Mohammed's insurance company would reimburse him for the injuries he sustained in the accident and Mohammed would be prevented from suing the other driver who normally would have been declared at fault. With pure no-fault, there is no reimbursement for pain and suffering losses.

But at this time, a pure no-fault plan does not exist in any state. What does exist is a variety of modified no-fault plans that allow one party to sue another if the injuries are severe or if medical expenses exceed a specified amount. For example, one state's no-fault law provides that one party can sue another for pain and suffering if the medical expenses exceed $2,000 or if there has been death, disfigurement, dismemberment, or a fracture.

No-fault plans are not standardized at this time. If your state has a no-fault law, you need to learn how it works.

Assigned Risk Plans

For some drivers, it has become increasingly difficult to obtain automobile insurance. In no small part, this is because most of these drivers are *not* average drivers. Because of poor driving records, most companies will not accept them because their loss experience is much greater than the average driver. However, it is certainly in society's best interest to have all drivers insured so that they are able to live up to their financial responsibilities when accidents do occur.

Assigned Risk Plans, or *Automobile Insurance Plans*, are voluntary agreements between insurance companies licensed in a particular state. These companies agree to share the poor risks among themselves. Because these risks are randomly assigned to the participating companies, they are called "assigned risks." Each company accepts its share of assigned risk drivers according to the size of the individual insurance company.

In most cases, drivers in the Assigned Risk Plan only have to be issued BI and PD Liability coverage in the minimum amount required by state law. In some states, Physical Damage and Medical Payments coverage can also be issued.

There are several other methods besides Assigned Risk Plans used to provide insurance for drivers whose records exclude them from obtaining coverage through normal channels. For instance, one state operates its own insurance company to handle such drivers. You should become familiar with the type of plan used in your state.

Exam Prep Questions

1. Ann's auto was damaged when it was struck by another car whose driver ran a stop sign. Which part of Ann's Personal Auto policy will cover the damage to her car?

   ○ A. Collision Coverage of Part D—Coverage for Damage to Your Auto
   ○ B. Other Than Collision Coverage of Part D—Coverage for Damage to Your Auto
   ○ C. Part A—Liability Coverage
   ○ D. Part C—Uninsured Motorists Coverage

2. Which of the following would be eligible for a Personal Auto policy?

   ❑ A. McGuffin's Linen Service Company
   ❑ B. Nancy Hardwicke
   ❑ C. John and Suzette Oglesby, a married couple who live together
   ❑ D. Don Wilson's 16-wheel big rig, which he owns

3. Which of the following autos owned by the named insured could be covered under a Personal Auto policy?

   ❑ A. Pickup truck used on the insured's farm
   ❑ B. Station wagon
   ❑ C. Chevrolet sedan
   ❑ D. Panel truck used to make deliveries for the insured's small manufacturing operation

4. If the named insured acquires a new car that does not replace a previously insured auto, what must the insured do to obtain liability coverage for the auto under her Personal Auto policy from the day it is acquired?

   ○ A. Nothing—coverage is automatic
   ○ B. Submit a new policy application
   ○ C. Notify the company of the new car within 14 days of the purchase
   ○ D. Notify the company immediately; no coverage applies until the company is notified

5. Which of the following could be covered under the Liability section of a named insured's Personal Auto policy?

   ○ A. Injuries a named insured receives in a car accident
   ○ B. Injuries to a person struck by the named insured's auto
   ○ C. Injuries to a member of the named insured's family who was a passenger in the named insured's car when it overturned
   ○ D. Damage to personal property being transported when the car was involved in a collision

6. Which of the following individuals have Liability coverage under Mr. Stump's Personal Auto policy?

❑ A. Edna, Mr. Stump's wife, who resides with him

❑ B. Mr. Stump's 16-year-old son, who lives at home

❑ C. A neighbor who borrows Stump's car with Stump's permission

❑ D. A group of teenagers who steal Mr. Stump's car from a parking lot and take it for a joy ride

7. Medical Payments coverage provides protection for all of the following *except* which one?

○ A. The insured

○ B. The insured's family

○ C. Passengers in the insured's vehicle

○ D. Occupants of a vehicle that is struck by the insured's vehicle

8. Which of the following could be considered an uninsured motorist?

❑ A. Motorist who has less insurance than required by the state's financial responsibility law

❑ B. Driver whose insurance company is insolvent

❑ C. Motorist who has enough insurance to meet the state's financial responsibility law, but not enough to fully reimburse the insured for his or her injuries

❑ D. Unidentified hit-and-run driver

9. Which of the following losses could be paid under Uninsured Motorists coverage? (Assume that there are no endorsements attached to the policy.)

○ A. Tabb, the insured, drives the wrong way down a one-way street and collides with another car. Tabb is seriously injured. The driver of the other car has no Liability insurance.

○ B. Barb, the insured, is hit by a drunk driver who is uninsured. She is not injured, but her car is totaled.

○ C. Leslie, the insured, is injured when she is struck by a car that runs a red light. The driver has no Liability insurance.

○ D. Bernard, the insured, is on his way to work when his vehicle is rear-ended by a car that was following too closely. Bernard suffers a back injury. The driver of the other car carries the minimum amount of insurance required in the state.

10. Which of the following losses would be paid under the Other Than Collision coverage of the Personal Auto policy?

○ A. A radiator develops a leak after the car has 100,000 miles on it.

○ B. The insured's car is stolen and never recovered.

○ C. The insured's auto skids on icy pavement and flips over.

○ D. The insured's auto is damaged when it is hit by another car that runs a red light.

11. An Assigned Risk Plan covers which of the following?

   ○ A. Insureds who are uninsurable in the standard market

   ○ B. Insureds who do not own their own autos

   ○ C. Insurance companies for losses involving government-owned automobiles

   ○ D. Insureds who cannot afford standard rates

12. Which of the following losses would be excluded under Part D of a Personal Auto policy?

   ❑ A. When the insured fails to pay his taxes, the IRS confiscates and sells his car.

   ❑ B. The insured's car is stolen on a cold winter day. The thieves run down the battery, and then abandon the car in a field. Before the car is discovered, the battery freezes and is ruined.

   ❑ C. The insured's cell phone that she sometimes carries in her car is damaged in a collision.

   ❑ D. Custom carpeting that the named insured added to his van is damaged in a flood.

13. Mary's Liability coverage limits are 50/100/50. A driver who was injured in an accident caused by Mary obtains a $75,000 judgment against her. Postjudgment interest of $5,000 accrues between the time the judgment was entered by the court and the time the insurer pays. What is the total amount Mary's insurance company will pay for this loss?

   ○ A. $50,000

   ○ B. $55,000

   ○ C. $75,000

   ○ D. $80,000

14. Vanessa's Liability coverage has split limits of 100/300/50. How much coverage does Vanessa have for property damage liability?

   ○ A. $5,000

   ○ B. $50,000

   ○ C. $100,000

   ○ D. $300,000

Exam Prep Answers

1. A is correct. This would be considered a collision loss under Part D of the Personal Auto policy because it involves the impact of an auto covered by the policy with another vehicle. Part A—Liability coverage would not cover damage to the insured's own car. Part C—Uninsured Motorists coverage applies only to bodily injury in most states.

2. B and C are correct. Choice A is not correct because the auto is owned by a business. Choice D is not correct because a PAP can only insure four-wheel vehicles.

3. A, B, and C are correct. Choice D is not correct because the auto is used for business purposes.

4. C is correct. The Personal Auto policy considers newly acquired cars to be covered autos. How coverage applies depends on several factors, such as the policy coverage, whether the car is a replacement auto, and when the insurer is notified about the new car.

5. B is correct. Part A—Liability coverage covers damages for bodily injury or property damage that an insured becomes legally responsible for because of an auto accident. Injuries to the named insured or his or her family members would be covered under Part B—Medical Payments coverage. Loss of personal property of an insured is not a matter of legal liability, and is not covered.

6. A, B, and C are correct. Under Part A, the named insured, his or her spouse, or any family member is insured for the ownership, maintenance, or use of any auto or trailer. A family member is any person related to the named insured who is a resident of the insured's household. An individual who uses a vehicle without permission is not covered under Part A, unless that person is a family member using a covered auto owned by the insured.

7. D is correct. Medical Payments coverage provides protection for the named insured, family members, and passengers in the named insured's auto for injuries received in an accident, regardless of who was at fault. It is not a form of Liability coverage for injuries sustained by passengers in another auto involved in an accident with the insured.

8. A, B, and D are correct. Choice C is an example of an underinsured motorist.

9. C is correct. Choice A is not correct because the uninsured driver was not liable for the accident. Choice B is not correct because the loss does not involve bodily injury. Choice D is not correct because the driver who caused the accident is not an uninsured motorist.

10. B is correct. Choice A is not correct because mechanical breakdown is excluded by the policy. Choice C and Choice D are not correct because they are collision losses.

11. A is correct. Assigned Risk Plans insure motorists with poor driving records who are unacceptable risks for most insurance companies.

12. A, C, and D are correct. Damage due to freezing is normally excluded under Part D. However, an exception is made when the damage results from the total theft of the auto.

13. B is correct. The policy will pay up to its liability limit of $50,000 plus the postjudgment interest of $5,000.

14. B is correct. The last figure is the Property Damage limit.

Miscellaneous Personal Insurance

Terms you'll need to understand:

✓ Flood
✓ Layup warranty
✓ Navigational limits
✓ Self-insured retention
✓ FAIR (Fair Access to Insurance Requirements) plan

Concepts you'll need to master:

✓ Emergency flood insurance program
✓ Regular flood insurance program
✓ Write your own program
✓ Inland marine floaters
✓ Personal property form
✓ Personal effects form
✓ Personal watercraft insurance
✓ Umbrella insurance
✓ Excess liability coverage

Although the personal lines policies we've reviewed so far insure a number of personal loss exposures, they also exclude or limit coverage for certain exposures. For example, Dwelling and homeowners policies both exclude losses caused by floods, and a homeowners policy provides only limited coverage for watercraft and certain types of valuable personal property. In this chapter, we review some specialized personal insurance policies that were developed to cover these exposures.

Flood Insurance

Flood insurance coverage was generally unavailable until the federal government became involved. In 1968, Congress created the *National Flood Insurance Program (NFIP)* to make flood insurance available to eligible communities through federal subsidization. The program is managed by the *Federal Insurance Administration (FIA)*, which is a branch of the *Federal Emergency Management Agency (FEMA)*.

Eligibility

In most cases, communities voluntarily apply for coverage through the NFIP. However, the government might also determine that a community is flood prone and require it to comply with federal flood program standards.

Almost any building that is walled and roofed, is principally above ground, and is fixed to a permanent site is eligible to be covered under a Flood policy. A policy can cover a building, its contents, or both.

Coverage

Two types of flood insurance programs are available: *emergency* and *regular*. The emergency program goes into effect when the community applies to the NFIP and remains in effect until the government finalizes the flood insurance rates for that community. Under the emergency program, insureds can purchase limited amounts of flood insurance for buildings and contents at subsidized rates. When the regular program goes into effect, additional coverage can be purchased. Table 10.1 shows the maximum limits of flood insurance available for single-family residential homes.

Table 10.1 Maximum Limits for Flood Insurance Coverage		
	Emergency Program	**Regular Program**
Building	$35,000	$250,000
Contents (Personal Property)	$10,000	$100,000

Both building and contents coverage have deductibles. The standard deductible for each coverage is $1,000 under the emergency program and $500 under the regular program. The deductible applies separately to each building loss and each contents loss on a per occurrence basis. Higher deductibles are available.

The NFIP's policies cover described property against all direct loss by or from flood at the described location. Indirect financial loss or loss of use is not covered. Property is also covered at another place, either above ground or outside of the special flood hazard area, for 45 days when removed by the insured to protect it from flood. Personal property must be in a building or otherwise protected from the elements while it is removed from the described location.

"Flood" is defined in the policies to include

➤ An overflow of inland or tidal waters

➤ An unusual and rapid accumulation or runoff of surface water

➤ Mudslides or mudflows on usually dry land areas

➤ Collapse of land as a result of excessive erosion due to flood

 The flood peril as defined relates only to various environmental conditions. Flood policies do not cover losses resulting from the backup of water from sewers or drains because this often results from a failure to keep drains clear or blockage by tree roots at a single location, and these are not considered to be "flood" losses. These losses might be covered by other property insurance.

Property Not Covered

Flood policies do not cover

➤ Accounts, bills, currency, deeds, evidences of debt, money, securities, bullion, and manuscripts

➤ Lawns, trees, shrubs, plants, growing crops, and livestock

➤ Aircraft, self-propelled vehicles, and motor vehicles

➤ Fences, retaining walls, outdoor swimming pools, bulkheads, wharves, piers, bridges, docks, and other open structures on or over water

➤ Underground structures and equipment, such as wells and septic tanks

➤ Newly constructed buildings that are in, on, or over water

➤ Structures that are primarily containers, such as gas or liquid storage tanks (does not apply to silos, grain storage buildings, or their contents)

Many of these exclusions are also found on other property insurance policies. Accounts, bills, currency, money, and securities are often excluded because the losses are difficult to verify. Growing crops, livestock, aircraft, and vehicles are excluded because other insurance policies are specifically designed to cover such exposures. A few of the exclusions, such as underground structures and newly constructed buildings over water, are unique to flood insurance coverage.

Other Provisions

Single family dwellings (other than mobile homes) are the only buildings that can be insured on a replacement cost basis under a Flood policy. *Replacement cost* coverage is automatically provided when the building is insured for at least 80% of its replacement value or for the maximum amount of insurance allowed by the Flood program. All other losses are paid on an actual cash value basis.

Debris removal expenses are covered if the amount of expenses plus the amount of the direct loss do not exceed the policy limit.

Write Your Own Program

NFIP policies can be sold by private insurance companies through the FIA's *Write Your Own program*. Under this system, the FIA sets rates, eligibility requirements, and coverage limitations. The participating insurer collects premiums and pays for losses out of these premiums. If the amount of losses exceeds the amount of premium collected, the FIA pays the difference. If the insurer collects more in premiums than it pays out in losses, the excess must be returned to the government.

Application Procedures

Applications for the NFIP must be completed in full and must be accompanied by payment in full of the gross policy premium for coverage to go into effect. Payment of partial deposit premiums is not permitted.

Coverage does not take effect until after a waiting period of 30 days following the date of application, with the following exceptions:

➤ There is no waiting period when the initial purchase of Flood insurance is made in connection with a loan.

➤ When a community first enters the Emergency or Regular program, during the first 30 days, policies take effect at 12:01 a.m. on the day after the application and premium payment are mailed.

➤ When an existing Flood policy is assigned to a property purchaser prior to transfer of title, coverage takes effect on the date title is transferred.

➤ After a policy is in effect, requested changes in coverage take effect at 12:01 a.m. on the fifth day after the date that the request and premium payment are mailed.

 During an applicable waiting period, binders cannot be issued to provide flood coverage.

Earthquake Insurance

Dwelling and homeowners policies do not cover the earthquake peril. Many insureds do not need this coverage; however, many companies are willing to offer earthquake insurance separately to those insureds who want it, either as an endorsement to their Dwelling or homeowners policy or as a separate policy.

Earthquake insurance generally covers damage to a structure, its contents, or both as the result of an earthquake. All earthquake shocks that occur within a 72-hour period constitute a single earthquake.

In some states, such as California, insurance companies are required to offer an earthquake endorsement, but it is not automatically included with property insurance policies.

Mobile Home Insurance

Eligibility rules for the standard homeowners policy specifically exclude mobile homes. Although mobile homes share many characteristics of dwellings, they also have many unique exposures: high susceptibility to wind and fire damage and exposure to loss by collision or upset while the unit is being transported. A Dwelling policy can be used to provide property coverage for mobile homes, but only the Basic form can be used and only mobile homes permanently placed on foundations are eligible. The HO-4 form can be used to cover the contents of a mobile home, but not the mobile home itself.

Many companies and rating organizations have developed a separate *Mobile Home package policy*. In addition, ISO has developed a *Mobile Homeowners endorsement* that can be attached to an HO-2 or HO-3 to modify coverage for mobile homeowners. Coverage is provided for

➤ The mobile home and all equipment and accessories originally built into the unit

➤ Equipment, additions, and appurtenant structures not originally included with the unit, such as shelters, cabanas, awnings, carports, and water pumps

➤ Additional living expenses

Damage to the mobile home from collision or upset while it is in transit is available as an optional coverage. Up to 10% of the coverage on the mobile home can be extended to cover other structures.

Liability coverage is similar to Section II of the homeowners policy, which covers liability.

Personal Inland Marine Insurance

A homeowners policy can cover many of the risks to which an average household is exposed. But there are certain risks for which the insured will require additional coverage outside of a homeowners policy. The homeowners forms contain exclusions and limitations for certain types of property that are particularly susceptible to loss, difficult to value, or of extremely high value. And in some cases, an individual who has no homeowners insurance might need coverage for personal property.

Broader coverage for personal property can be obtained through *personal inland marine* forms. Inland Marine insurance originally developed from Ocean Marine insurance, which provides very broad coverage for property being transported over water. Inland Marine insurance provides the same type of broad, flexible coverage for portable personal property. Because they provide coverage that moves with the property to protect it at various locations, inland marine forms are sometimes called *floaters*.

The three most commonly used personal inland marine forms are

➤ Personal Articles form

➤ Personal Property form

➤ Personal Effects form

To form a policy, the form must be attached to the personal inland marine form, a skeleton policy containing basic conditions that apply to all personal inland marine coverages.

Personal inland marine floaters provide open peril coverage, although a few exclusions apply, such as those shown in the following list:

➤ Gradual deterioration

➤ Inherent vice (a condition or defect that exists within the property)

➤ Insects

➤ Nuclear hazard

➤ Vermin

➤ War

➤ Wear and tear

Like many other Property policies, personal inland marine floaters contain a *pair or set* condition stating that the insurance company will not be liable for the entire value of a set when only a part of it is damaged. Inland marine floaters give the company two reimbursement options in this situation:

➤ Repair, replace, or restore the set

➤ Pay the insured the difference between the actual cash value of the full set and the actual cash value of the undamaged part

Personal Inland Marine Forms

A number of Personal Inland Marine policies are available. These include personal articles floaters, personal property floaters, and personal effects floaters.

Personal Articles Form

The *Personal Articles form* provides coverage for nine optional classes of personal property—the same nine categories covered under the Homeowners Scheduled Personal Property endorsement: jewelry, furs, cameras, musical instruments, silverware, golf equipment, fine arts, stamps, and coins. Generally, an appraisal is required when the Personal Articles form is issued to aid in developing an accurate description of covered property and to arrive at the proper value for which the property should be insured.

However, the Personal Articles form is not a valued policy. For purposes of loss settlement, the value is determined at the time of loss. In general, the company will reimburse the insured for the lesser of

➤ Actual cash value

➤ Cost to repair

➤ Cost to replace with a substantially identical item

➤ Amount of insurance specified in the policy

Another important feature of the Personal Articles form is that it provides automatic coverage for certain classes of newly acquired property when the property is in a category of property that is already insured. Automatic coverage is available for

➤ Jewelry

➤ Furs

➤ Cameras

➤ Musical instruments

➤ Fine arts

For all property except fine arts, coverage applies for 30 days; the property is covered for 25% of the applicable limit of insurance or $10,000, whichever is less. For fine arts, coverage applies for 90 days and coverage is provided for up to 25% of the applicable limit of insurance.

Coverage for newly acquired property ceases after the 30- or 90-day period unless the insured notifies the insurance company about the property during this time period.

Personal Property Form

The *Personal Property form* provides open peril coverage on a blanket basis for most kinds of personal property found in a typical home. It is similar to the coverage provided for personal property under Coverage C in a homeowners policy endorsed to provide open peril coverage for personal property. The Personal Property floater is most frequently issued to condominium or apartment dwellers who cannot obtain this open peril coverage for personal property under HO-4 or HO-6.

Property is divided into 13 basic categories (including an "all other personal property" category), and a separate limit of insurance is assigned to each category. Particularly valuable property can be scheduled separately.

Personal Effects Form

The *Personal Effects form* is designed for individuals and families who want to insure their personal belongings while traveling. Open peril coverage on an unscheduled basis is provided for the types of property usually carried by tourists, such as clothing, cameras, sports equipment, and souvenirs.

Specifically excluded are valuable papers, tickets, passports, currency, contact lenses, artificial limbs, and salesperson's samples. Property is excluded from coverage while on the insured's premises or while in storage. Insureds who travel frequently might carry this coverage on a permanent basis. Often, however, the coverage is taken out for a short term to cover a specific trip.

Personal Watercraft Insurance

A homeowners policy provides only limited coverage for watercraft. Property coverage is subject to a special limit of $1,000, and coverage might be totally excluded for certain perils. Liability coverage is excluded for boats with motors of more than specified horsepower or boats of more than a specified length.

Boatowners and Outboard Motor and Boat Policies

Insureds typically need more coverage for this exposure than that provided by a homeowners policy, particularly those who own larger or more powerful boats. This coverage can be provided through Inland Marine forms, Ocean Marine policies, or specialized policies.

Regardless of the type of coverage purchased, certain conditions and exclusions are almost always part of a Personal Watercraft policy. They stipulate that the craft must be used solely for private pleasure purposes and that coverage will not apply if the boat is hired out, chartered, or used to transport people or property for a fee. Coverage is usually excluded when the watercraft is being used in an *official* race or speed contest. (Unofficial events are not excluded.)

Boatowners/Watercraft Package policies, developed by individual insurance companies, combine Property, Liability, and Medical Payments insurance on an open peril basis. They are used to insure boats under a specified length—

such as 30 feet—or under a maximum dollar value, such as $25,000. Losses are usually paid on an actual cash value basis.

Outboard Motor and Boat insurance can be written to cover the physical damage exposure of boats. This insurance is commonly provided under open peril Inland Marine floaters. Outboard policies typically cover motors, motor boats, accessories, and trailers. Losses are usually paid on an actual cash value basis. Many provide a limited amount of coverage for collision damage to another vessel. When these policies are written, it is customary for the insured to have Liability coverage under a homeowners policy or separate liability policy.

Personal Yacht Policies

Personal Yacht policies are Ocean Marine forms that provide a package of property and liability coverages. Most inboard boats, sailboats with inboard auxiliary power, and large pleasure boats are insured under Personal Yacht policies. Smaller boats that are in good condition and have some value can also be covered under these policies.

When smaller vessels are insured on a Personal Yacht form, coverage is usually limited to property coverage on the hull, with or without coverage for a trailer. The liability exposure is usually covered under a homeowners or separate liability policy. Owners of larger vessels are more likely to purchase the complete package of Yacht coverages, which includes

➤ Hull insurance (pays replacement cost for partial losses and on a valued basis for total losses)

➤ Boat trailer insurance (pays on actual cash value basis)

➤ Protection and Indemnity, or P&I (a form of bodily injury and property damage Liability insurance)

➤ Medical Payments coverage

➤ Federal Longshore and Harbor Workers Compensation insurance (provides benefits for maritime workers)

This coverage is usually provided on an open peril basis.

Hull coverage on a Yacht policy contains a *collision clause*, which covers the insured's liability for collision damage to other vessels. This is an additional amount of insurance, and it is equal to the amount of coverage written on the hull. P&I coverage for collision damage to another vessel begins after the insurance provided by the collision clause is exhausted.

A *water skiing clause* commonly excludes coverage for any person skiing or otherwise being towed by the vessel until they are back on board or have landed safely somewhere.

The *layup warranty* applies when the yacht is located in a safe berth for storage and is not being used, such as during the winter months. It provides for a return of premium because of the reduced risk of loss.

Every Yacht policy has *navigational limits*, a clause that defines an area in which the yacht is permitted to operate. Losses that occur outside these limits are not covered unless the insurer has granted permission for the insured to do so.

Personal Umbrella Insurance

Some insureds need more extensive liability coverage than can be provided by personal lines policies. This need can be met through a *Personal Umbrella* policy, which has two important purposes:

➤ Provides additional liability insurance over and above the basic coverage provided by underlying liability insurance

➤ Covers some losses that are excluded by the underlying liability insurance

Coverage limits for a Personal Umbrella policy range from $1 million to $5 million.

Excess Liability Coverage

Let's examine how a Personal Umbrella provides excess liability coverage. Suppose that an insured has the following liability coverage: a $1 million limit under a Personal Umbrella, a $100,000 liability limit under a homeowners policy, and a $100,000 liability limit under a Personal Auto policy.

For a loss payable under the homeowners policy, the insured would have an additional $1 million of coverage after the $100,000 limit under the homeowners contract had been exhausted. On a $300,000 loss, the homeowners contract would pay $100,000, and the Umbrella policy would pay $200,000. For a loss payable under the Auto policy, this same Personal Umbrella policy would pay up to an additional $1 million, but only after the $100,000 limit of the underlying Auto policy was used up.

Because of the pivotal role played by the underlying policies, the insured must identify any underlying liability insurance to the insurer before an

Umbrella policy is issued. If the insured allows an underlying policy to lapse or be reduced in coverage, the insured would be responsible for paying damages up to the underlying policy's limit before the Umbrella policy would take over.

Suppose that the insured has a homeowners policy with $200,000 in liability coverage and a $1 million Umbrella policy. If the insured has a $100,000 liability loss payable under the homeowners policy, the homeowners policy would pay $100,000 and the Umbrella would pay nothing because the loss is fully covered by the underlying insurance.

If this same insured has a $300,000 liability loss that would have been payable under the homeowners policy, except the insured allowed the homeowners policy to lapse, the Umbrella would pay $100,000. If the insured allows an underlying policy to lapse, he or she must pay damages up to the underlying policy's limit before the Umbrella policy will pay.

Coverage for Excluded Losses

A Personal Umbrella might also cover losses that are excluded by the underlying policy. For this type of coverage, the insured must select a *retention limit*. Retention limits, which vary from $250 to $10,000, work like deductibles. They are sometimes referred to as *self-insured retentions* because they represent the amount of loss the insured must cover out of pocket. Self-insured retentions do not apply to losses that are covered under the underlying liability coverage.

Of course, even an Umbrella policy has exclusions, such as intentional acts, liability covered under workers compensation, and liability arising out of business pursuits. When a loss is excluded under both the underlying policy and the Umbrella, no coverage is available.

FAIR Plans

The extensive inner city rioting that took place in the United States in the mid-1960s led to the withdrawal from those areas of much of the availability of property insurance. This made it very difficult for mortgage companies and lenders to operate in those areas and, thus, difficult for individuals to meet insurance requirements and remain in those areas. This compounded the downward trend of inner city areas.

In response, the government acted in 1968 to provide riot insurance under a federal reinsurance plan. To obtain this insurance, states were required to develop plans through which inner city property could be insured at reasonable rates. Such plans are called *FAIR (Fair Access to Insurance Requirements) Plans*. Although the original legislation under which the plans were created has been repealed, FAIR plans still exist in many states.

Although it is not a type of insurance policy, the FAIR concept addresses the entire issue of availability of property insurance. Essentially, a FAIR Plan makes insurance available to risks that were previously considered uninsurable because of *environmental hazards*. These are defined as conditions surrounding the property of an insured that might increase the chance of a loss, but that are not within the control of the property owner or tenant occupying that property.

Under a FAIR Plan, no application for insurance can be rejected simply because of environmental hazards that are beyond the insured's control, although the property might be subject to inspection before it is accepted in the Plan.

Exam Prep Questions

1. What is the standard deductible under the regular program of the National Flood Insurance Program?
   - ○ A. $1,000
   - ○ B. $500
   - ○ C. $250
   - ○ D. $100

2. Who administers the NFIP?
   - ○ A. State insurance department
   - ○ B. Federal government
   - ○ C. Private insurance companies
   - ○ D. The National Association of Insurance Commissioners

3. What is the maximum amount of coverage that can be purchased for a single-family home under the emergency Flood insurance program?
   - ○ A. $35,000 for buildings and $10,000 for contents
   - ○ B. $250,000 for buildings and $100,000 for contents
   - ○ C. $100,000 for buildings; contents coverage is not available under the emergency program
   - ○ D. $100,000 for contents; building coverage is not available under the emergency program

4. Coverage for earthquake losses is which of the following?
   - ❑ A. Included in an unendorsed Dwelling or homeowners policy
   - ❑ B. Provided by the federal government
   - ❑ C. Available by adding an endorsement to the Dwelling or homeowners policy
   - ❑ D. Available by purchasing a separate policy

5. Mobile home policies include which of the following?
   - ❑ A. Include Liability coverage that is similar to Section II of the homeowners policy
   - ❑ B. Might include collision coverage
   - ❑ C. Cover the mobile home unit, but not its contents
   - ❑ D. Do not cover additional living expenses

6. Adequate coverage for large, powerful boats is provided by which of the following?
   - ○ A. A homeowners policy
   - ○ B. A homeowners policy with the Watercraft endorsement attached
   - ○ C. Specialized personal watercraft policies, such as Outboard Motor and Boat, Boatowners, or Personal Yacht policies
   - ○ D. The reinsurance component of FAIR Plans

7. A typical Outboard Motor and Boat policy provides which of the following coverages?
   - ○ A. Liability
   - ○ B. Medical Payments
   - ○ C. Physical Damage
   - ○ D. All of the above

8. Under a National Flood Insurance policy, losses to which of the following could be paid on a replacement cost basis?
   - ○ A. Personal property
   - ○ B. Single family homes
   - ○ C. Mobile homes
   - ○ D. Both A and B

9. Unless an exception applies, when does coverage under an NFIP policy begin?
   - ○ A. As soon as the gross policy premium is received
   - ○ B. Five days after the application and premium payment are mailed
   - ○ C. Thirty days after the date of application
   - ○ D. On the date the flood insurance application is mailed

10. Which of the following losses are excluded under most Yacht policies?
   - ○ A. Injury suffered by a passenger in a waterskiing accident
   - ○ B. Collision damage to another boat for which the insured is liable
   - ○ C. Both A and B
   - ○ D. Neither A nor B

Exam Prep Answers

1. B is correct. The standard deductible is $500 under the regular program and $1,000 under the emergency program. Higher deductibles are available.

2. B is correct. The federal government created the NFIP to make Flood insurance available to eligible communities through federal subsidization. It is managed by the Federal Insurance Administration.

3. A is correct. When the regular program goes into effect, additional coverage can be purchased: up to $250,000 for building coverage and up to $100,000 for contents.

4. C and D are correct. Dwelling and homeowners policies do not cover the earthquake peril. This coverage is provided by adding an endorsement to the Dwelling or homeowners policy or buying a separate policy.

5. A and B are correct. Mobile home policies include coverage for contents and additional living expenses.

6. C is correct. A homeowners policy provides only limited coverage for watercraft. Property coverage is subject to a special limit of $1,500, and coverage can be totally excluded for certain perils. Liability coverage is excluded for boats with motors of more than specified horsepower or boats of more than a specified length. Insureds typically need more coverage for this exposure than that provided by a homeowners policy, particularly those who own larger or more powerful boats. This coverage can be provided through Inland Marine forms, Ocean Marine policies, or specialized policies.

7. C is correct. This insurance is written to cover the physical damage exposure of boats. It is commonly provided under open peril Inland Marine floaters.

8. B is correct. Single-family dwellings (other than mobile homes) are the only buildings that can be insured on a replacement cost basis under a flood policy. All other losses are paid on an actual cash value basis.

9. C is correct. Unless an exception applies, coverage does not take effect until after a waiting period of 30 days following the date of application. Binders may not be issued during the waiting period to provide Flood coverage.

10. A is correct. The collision clause on a Yacht policy covers the insured's liability for collision damage to other vehicles. The waterskiing clause commonly excludes coverage for any person skiing or otherwise being towed by the vessel until they are back on board or have landed safely somewhere.

The Commercial Package Policy

Terms you'll need to understand:

✓ Coverage part
✓ Mono-line policy
✓ Multi-line policy
✓ Package policy
✓ Interline endorsements
✓ First named insured

Concepts you'll need to master:

✓ Commercial package policy
✓ Eligible commercial coverages
✓ Common policy declarations
✓ Common policy conditions

Throughout the remainder of this course, we review insurance policies designed for businesses. Because businesses share many of the same exposures to risks as individuals, you will find many similarities between personal and commercial forms. But businesses also have many unique exposures that require different policies or modifications of the coverages we've already reviewed.

Just as families often choose the convenience of package policies such as a homeowners policy or Personal Auto policy, businesses often choose to purchase several different lines of coverage in a single policy.

Commercial policies are not always written as package policies. Some commercial policies are written as *mono-line policies* that cover only one line of insurance. However, most businesses do purchase *multi-line policies* that cover two or more lines of insurance. The multi-line policies are true package policies and offer many advantages.

One of the most important commercial packages is ISO's *Commercial Package policy*. The Commercial Package policy, or *CPP*, can be used to provide almost any type of commercial insurance the business might need. Almost all commercial risks are eligible for coverage under the CPP.

Similar to all package policies, the CPP offers advantages to both the insured and the insurer. Repetitive information is eliminated, and the policy is easier to understand. Because of the economies an insurance company can realize when carrying several different lines of coverage for the same insured, the company is also able to make package discounts to the insured, which provides further incentive for a package plan.

Eligible Coverages

The CPP can include almost any commercial coverage a business might need, with the exception of Ocean Marine and Aviation insurance. (These coverages are usually written separately by specialty carriers.) A commercial package policy can include any combination of the following coverages:

➤ Commercial property coverage

➤ Commercial general liability coverage

➤ Commercial auto coverage

➤ Commercial crime coverage

➤ Commercial inland marine coverage

➤ Boiler and machinery coverage

➤ Professional liability coverage

➤ Employment practices liability coverage

➤ Farm coverage

The forms and endorsements applicable to each line of insurance that is eligible for coverage under the CPP are collectively known as a *coverage part*.

A CPP consists of

➤ Common Policy Declarations

➤ Common Policy Conditions

➤ Two or more coverage parts

 The same forms and endorsements are used to construct mono-line and package policies. Both must include the Common Policy Declarations and Common Policy Conditions. The only difference is that a mono-line policy includes a single coverage part, whereas a package policy includes two or more coverage parts.

A CPP might also contain *interline endorsements*—endorsements that can be used with more than one line of insurance. Some interline endorsements are mandatory, whereas others are optional.

The Nuclear Energy Liability Exclusion endorsement is an example of an interline endorsement. Lines of insurance that provide liability coverage generally exclude nuclear energy liability because there is a Nuclear Energy Liability specifically designed to cover that exposure. Therefore, a Nuclear Energy Liability Exclusion endorsement is generally attached to forms for several different lines of insurance: Commercial Auto, Commercial General Liability, Businessowners, Farm Coverage, and several others.

Common Policy Declarations

Although we review the individual coverage parts of the CPP in subsequent chapters, in this chapter we review the two general forms that are a part of every CPP and are also included in any mono-line policy issued using CPP forms: the Common Policy Declarations and the Common Policy Conditions.

The *Common Policy Declarations* contains information about who is insured, when he or she is insured, and for what lines he or she is insured. It includes

➤ The name and mailing address of the named insured

➤ The policy period, including the time and date coverage begins and ends

➤ A description of the covered business

➤ The coverage parts purchased and their premiums

➤ A list of forms applicable to all coverage parts

Common Policy Conditions

The *Common Policy Conditions* apply to all the coverage parts contained in the CPP.

Under the Common Policy Conditions, certain responsibilities and obligations—those having to do with premium payments, receipt of cancellation notices, and changes to the policy's terms—are assigned to the *first named insured*, the person whose name is listed first in the declarations. It is necessary to specify the first named insured because the CPP might be issued to more than one named insured, such as business partners. Without the responsibility for certain important matters resting on one specified individual, all the listed insureds might assume that one of the other insureds was taking care of something when in fact no one was.

Cancellation

The *Cancellation* condition sets forth the circumstances under which the policy may be cancelled. The first named insured must cancel the policy in writing, and any premium refund due will be sent to the first named insured. This refund might be less than a pro rata refund to make up for the expense of issuing the contract.

If the insurance company cancels, it must mail a written notice to the last known address of the first named insured. Ten days' notice is required for cancellation for nonpayment of premium; 30 days' notice is required for cancellation for any other reason permitted by the policy. The premium is refunded to the first named insured on a pro rata basis.

Remember that although this is the Cancellation condition that appears in the standard contract, some states might legislate unique cancellation rules for policies issued in those states.

Changes and Premiums

Along with the first named insured's right to cancel the policy go some other rights and responsibilities.

The *Changes* condition states that only the first named insured is authorized to make changes in the terms of the policy with the consent of the insurance company. Terms can be amended or waived only by an endorsement issued by the insurer that is made a part of the policy.

The *Premiums* condition states that the first named insured is responsible for the payment of all premiums and will receive any return premiums due.

Examination of Books and Records and Inspections and Surveys

The Common Policy Conditions also give the insurance company the right to obtain information that might be needed to accurately rate the policy and provide the appropriate coverage.

The *Examination of Your Books and Records* condition states that the company may examine and audit the insured's books and records at any time during the policy period, and for up to three years after the end of the policy period. This provision provides ample time for the insurance company to examine the records, but puts a limit on the time period during which the insured might be inconvenienced.

The *Inspections and Surveys* condition gives the company the right to make inspections or surveys of the insured business at any time. The company can choose to report on the conditions it finds and recommend changes. These inspections are related to insurability and premiums only and are not considered safety inspections. The insurer will not warrant that conditions are safe or healthful or comply with laws or regulations.

This condition does not apply to inspections performed to certify boilers, elevators, or pressure vessels under state or local laws.

Transfer of Rights and Duties

Finally, the *Transfer of Your Rights and Duties Under This Policy* condition states that an insured's rights and duties under the policy cannot be transferred without the written consent of the insurance company, except in the case of the death of a named insured. This is sometimes called the *Assignment* clause, and it is a common feature of both personal and commercial lines policies.

If the named insured dies, his or her rights are transferred to the deceased's legal representative, but only while he or she is acting within the scope of the duties of the legal representative. Until a legal representative is appointed, anyone having proper temporary custody of the property will have the insured's rights and duties as they relate to the property.

Exam Prep Questions

1. Which of these statements concerning the CPP are correct?
   - ❑ A. Almost all commercial risks are eligible for coverage under the CPP.
   - ❑ B. The insured can choose a variety of eligible commercial coverages to tailor the package to fit his or her specific business insurance needs.
   - ❑ C. A complete CPP includes Common Policy Declarations, Common Policy Conditions, and two or more coverage parts.
   - ❑ D. A CPP can include Ocean Marine and Aviation insurance.

2. Which of the following are contained in the Common Policy Declarations?
   - ❑ A. The policy period
   - ❑ B. The name and mailing address of the insured
   - ❑ C. Conditions specifying the insured's duties following a loss
   - ❑ D. The insured's premium for each coverage part purchased

3. Who may cancel a CPP?
   - ❑ A. Any named insured.
   - ❑ B. The insurance company.
   - ❑ C. The first named insured.
   - ❑ D. None of the above; once a policy is issued, it can never be cancelled.

4. Under a CPP, how many days advance notice is required if the insurance company is cancelling the contract for nonpayment of premium?
   - ○ A. 10 days
   - ○ B. 21 days
   - ○ C. 30 days
   - ○ D. 60 days

5. Under a CPP, how long after the end of the policy period can the insurance company examine the insured's books and records?
   - ○ A. 10 days
   - ○ B. 3 months
   - ○ C. 1 year
   - ○ D. 3 years

6. Under a CPP, when does the Inspections and Surveys condition give the insurance company the right to inspect the insured's premises?
   - ○ A. At any time
   - ○ B. Quarterly
   - ○ C. Every six months
   - ○ D. Once a year

7. What is required for an insured's rights and duties under a CPP to be transferred while the insured is alive?

   ○ A. The written consent of the insured

   ○ B. The written consent of the insurance company

   ○ C. The verbal consent of the insured

   ○ D. The written consent of the insured's legal representative

Exam Prep Answers

1. A, B, and C are correct. Ocean Marine and Aviation insurance are not eligible for the CPP.

2. A, B, and D are correct. The Common Policy Declarations contains information about who is insured, when he or she is insured, and for what lines he or she is insured. It includes the name and mailing address of the named insured, the policy period, and a summary of the premiums charged. Loss conditions are described in the policy form, not the declarations.

3. B and C are correct. Under the Common Policy Conditions, certain responsibilities and obligations are assigned to the first named insured. One of these is cancellation of the policy. The insurance company may also cancel the policy under certain circumstances.

4. A is correct. When a CPP is cancelled by the insurer for nonpayment of premium, it is required to give notice at least 10 days in advance. In all other cases of permitted cancellation by the insurer, it must give notice at least 30 days in advance.

5. D is correct. The insurance company can examine an insured's books and records up to three years after the end of the policy period.

6. A is correct. The insurance company has the right to inspect the insured's premises at any time.

7. B is correct. The insured's rights and duties under a CPP cannot be transferred without the written consent of the insurance company.

The Businessowners Policy

Terms you'll need to understand:

- ✓ Building coverage
- ✓ Business personal property
- ✓ Tenants improvements and betterments
- ✓ Debris removal
- ✓ Collapse
- ✓ Business income coverage
- ✓ Extended business income coverage
- ✓ Extra expense coverage

- ✓ Increased cost of construction
- ✓ Dependent properties
- ✓ Personal and advertising injury
- ✓ Utility services
- ✓ Protective safeguards
- ✓ Hired autos
- ✓ Nonowned autos
- ✓ Coverage territory

Concepts you'll need to master:

- ✓ Eligible occupancies
- ✓ Ineligible risks
- ✓ Covered causes of loss
- ✓ Additional coverages
- ✓ Coverage extensions
- ✓ Optional coverages

- ✓ Employee dishonesty
- ✓ Mechanical breakdown
- ✓ Internal or inside limits
- ✓ Who is an insured
- ✓ Civil authority actions

The *Businessowners policy (BOP)* is a commercial package policy that provides property and liability insurance to certain types of small businesses. Whereas the Commercial Package policy (CPP) allows the insured to pick and choose the coverages to be included in the CPP, the BOP prepackages a group of coverages desirable to small businesses.

Many companies have developed their own small Businessowners-type package policy, but in this chapter we focus on ISO's BOP.

Eligibility and Policy Organization

The eligibility rules for the BOP are more stringent than those for the CPP, which can be used to cover almost any commercial risk. Specific rules of eligibility that deal with the size of buildings and the specific type of business involved determine what risks are eligible to be covered under a BOP. The ideal BOP prospect is the small, well-managed, one-location business with easily predicted coverage needs.

Eligible Occupancies

Only certain types of businesses are eligible for coverage under current ISO rules. They include certain wholesale, processing and service, restaurant, convenience store, and contracting risks. Eligible businesses are listed in the Classification table of ISO's BOP rules.

 Unless otherwise noted, eligible risks cannot exceed 25,000 square feet in total floor area or exceed $3 million in annual gross sales at each location.

Table 12.1 summarizes the types of occupancies and size limitations that apply to risks which are eligible for Businessowner policies—it is not the Classification table that appears in ISO's Businessowner policy rules.

Table 12.1 Eligible BOP Occupancies

Occupancy	Comments
Apartments (Includes Residential Condominium Associations)	Any size building is permitted. Permitted occupancies include offices, contractors and eligible wholesaler, mercantile, processing, and service occupancies. Building owner's business personal property in the building is covered.
Condominium Commercial Unit-Owners	Business personal property of owners of condominium units used for eligible mercantile, wholesaler, processing, service, office, or contractor occupancies.
Mercantile Risks	Only certain mercantile risks are eligible. Both building and business personal property may be covered.
Motels	Both building and business personal property may be covered. Building cannot exceed three stories; no limitation on floor area. Bars and cocktail lounges are prohibited. Eligible restaurant occupancies are permitted. Seasonal operations that are closed more than 30 consecutive days are not eligible.
Offices (Including Office Condominium Associations)	Building cannot exceed six stories in height or contain more than 100,000 square feet. Permitted occupancies include offices, contractors, and eligible wholesaler, mercantile, processing, and service occupancies. Business personal property in offices that do not occupy more than 25,000 square feet in one building are eligible.
Processing and Service Risks	Only certain processing and service risks are eligible. No more than 25% of annual gross sales obtained from off-premises operations.
Self-Storage Facilities	May not exceed two stories in height; no limitation on floor area. Facilities that permit cold storage or storage of industrial materials, pollutants, chemicals, or waste are not eligible. Both building and business personal property may be covered.
Wholesale Risks	Both building and business personal property may be covered. Only certain wholesale risks are eligible. No more than 25% of annual gross sales derived from retail operations. No more than 25% of total floor area open to the public. Operations of manufacturers representatives or contractors are not eligible.

Ineligible Risks

Some classes of risks and certain types of property are specifically not eligible for the BOP as shown in the following:

➤ Auto repair or service stations, unless incidental to another otherwise eligible class

➤ Auto, motor home, mobile home, and motorcycle dealers, unless incidental to another otherwise eligible class

➤ Banks, building and loan associations, savings and loan associations, credit unions, stockbrokers, and similar financial institutions

➤ Bars and pubs

➤ Buildings occupied wholly or partially for manufacturing

➤ Condominium associations other than office or residential condominiums

➤ Household personal property

➤ Insureds whose business operations involve one or more locations that are used for manufacturing

➤ One- or two-family dwellings, unless they are garden apartments in which multiple units are grouped within a single area and are under common ownership, management, and control

➤ Parking lots or garages, unless incidental to an otherwise eligible class

➤ Places of amusement

Organization

The BOP includes the required property and liability coverages and policy conditions in one form, with certain required information about the insured contained in a separate declarations.

The *policy declarations* show the policy number, name of insurer, name of producer, name and address of the named insured, and the policy period. Spaces are provided for a description of the business, the form of business, locations of described premises, and name and address of any mortgage holder. Limits of insurance are shown for buildings and for business personal property. Any optional coverages the insured has selected are indicated on the declarations, along with the limit of insurance for those coverages.

Property Coverage

The property coverage of the BOP includes two major coverages:

➤ Coverage A—Buildings

➤ Coverage B—Business personal property

 As is the case with many property insurance policies offering multiple optional coverages, a specific limit of insurance must be shown in the declarations for each type of property that is actually covered. For example, an insured who is a tenant would not require the building coverage and would only need to show a limit for Coverage B.

Building Coverage

Building coverage applies to more than just the buildings and structures at the premises structure itself. Other items covered under the building coverage include

➤ Completed additions

➤ Permanently installed machinery and equipment

➤ Fixtures, including outdoor fixtures, such as lawnmowers, garden hoses, and snow removal equipment

➤ Personal property used to maintain or service buildings, structures, or the premises, including portable fire extinguishing equipment, outdoor furniture, floor coverings, and appliances used for refrigerating, ventilating, cooking, dishwashing, or laundering

➤ Personal property furnished by the insured in apartments, rooms, or common areas that are rented to others

The following items are also covered under the building coverage if no other insurance applies:

➤ Additions under construction

➤ Alterations and repairs to the buildings or structures

➤ Materials, equipment, supplies, and temporary structures that are on or within 100 feet of the premises and being used for additions, alterations, or repairs

Business Personal Property Coverage

Five different classes of *business personal property* are covered:

➤ Property owned and used by the insured in the business

➤ Property of others in the insured's care, custody, or control

➤ Tenants improvements and betterments

➤ Leased personal property that the insured has a contractual responsibility to insure

➤ Exterior building glass

 Business personal property is covered when it is located at the described premises and in or on a building, or in a vehicle or in the open within 100 feet of the premises. Historically, this type of property has often been referred to as "contents" of the building, but be aware that personal property does not actually have to be in a building to be covered.

Tenants improvements and betterments are fixtures, alterations, installations, or additions that tenants make to rented buildings in which they operate their businesses. For coverage to apply, these items must be permanently attached to the building, acquired, or made at the insured's expense and unable to be legally removed. Examples include when tenants have new carpeting or light fixtures installed.

Examples of *leased personal property* the insured has a contractual responsibility to insure include photocopiers and computer equipment leased under contracts that require the lessees to insure the leased property.

Exterior building glass is covered as business personal property for insureds who are tenants and do not have building coverage. The glass must be owned by the insured or in the insured's care, custody, or control.

Property Not Covered

The following property is not covered under the BOP:

➤ Accounts, bills, food stamps, other evidences of debt, accounts receivable, and valuable papers and records

➤ Aircraft

➤ Computers that are permanently installed or designed to be permanently installed in an aircraft, watercraft, motor truck, or other vehicle subject to motor vehicle registration

➤ Contraband and property being illegally traded or transported

➤ Land (including land on which the property is located), water, growing crops, and lawns

➤ Money and securities*

➤ Motor vehicles and other vehicles subject to motor vehicle registration

➤ Outdoor fences, trees, shrubs, and plants*

➤ Outdoor radio or television antennas, including satellite dishes, and their lead-in wiring, masts, or towers*

➤ Outdoor signs not attached to buildings*

➤ Watercraft while afloat, including motors, equipment, and accessories

*Except as covered under an optional coverage or coverage extension

Covered Causes of Loss

Property coverage in the BOP is provided on an *open peril* basis. This means that the policy covers any causes of loss that are not specifically excluded or limited. An endorsement can be added to the policy so that coverage is provided on a *named peril* basis, meaning that the policy covers only those causes of loss that are specifically named in the endorsement.

The specified causes of loss are

➤ Fire

➤ Lightning

➤ Explosion

➤ Windstorm or hail

➤ Smoke

➤ Aircraft or vehicles

➤ Riot or civil commotion

➤ Vandalism

➤ Leakage from fire extinguishing equipment

➤ Sinkhole collapse

➤ Volcanic action

➤ Falling objects

➤ Weight of snow, ice, or sleet

➤ Water damage

Limitations

The following limitations in the BOP either exclude certain types of losses or cap the amount of particular coverages.

Damage that occurs to *steam equipment* such as boilers, pipes, engines, or turbines is not covered if the damage results from a condition that originates
inside the equipment. There is coverage, however, that results from explosions of gases or fuel inside the furnace of a fired vessel or within the flues or
passages through which gases pass.

Damage that occurs to hot water boilers or other *water heating equipment* is
not covered if the damage results from a condition that originates inside the
equipment. There is coverage, however, for explosions.

There is no coverage for *property that is missing*, such as shortage disclosed
from an inventory, for which no physical evidence exists to show what hap-
pened to it. This limitation does not apply to money and securities when the
money and securities optional coverage is added to the policy.

There is no coverage for *property that has been transferred* to someone or
someplace outside the described premises and under unauthorized
instructions.

Damage to the *interior of a building* is covered against damage from rain,
snow, sand, sleet, ice, or dust only if the roof or walls are first damaged by a
covered cause of loss that enables these elements to enter or if the loss or
damage is caused by or results from thawing of snow, sleet, or ice on the
building.

Loss or damage to *fragile articles* that are broken is not covered unless the
damage is caused by building glass breakage or the specified causes of loss
named in the policy. Fragile articles include glassware, marbles, porcelains,
statuary, and chinaware.

 This restriction does not apply to glass that is part of a building, containers of property held for sale, or photographic or scientific instrument lenses.

For the following types of property, the amount paid for *theft* losses is limited to $2,500:

➤ Furs, fur garments, and garments trimmed with fur

➤ Jewelry, watches, watch movements, jewels, pearls, precious and semiprecious stones, bullion, gold, silver, platinum, and other precious alloys
or metals; does not apply to jewelry and watches worth $100 or less per
item

➤ Patterns, dies, molds, and forms

Exclusions

The following causes of loss are excluded in the BOP:

➤ Ordinance or law

➤ Earth movement (does not include a fire or explosion resulting from earth movement)

➤ Government action

➤ Nuclear hazard

➤ Failure of power or other utility services occurring away from the insured's premises (does not apply to loss or damage to computers and electronic media and records)

➤ War and military action

➤ Water, including flood, sewer backup, mudslides, or seepage of ground water (does not include fire, explosion, or sprinkler leakage resulting from water)

➤ Failure of computers to recognize a particular date or time

➤ Artificially generated electrical current (loss or damage to computers from artificially generated electrical current is covered if the loss results from an occurrence that took place within 100 feet of the described premises, such as an interruption of electric power supply, power surge, blackout, or brownout)

➤ Delay, loss of use, or loss of market

➤ Smoke, vapor, or gas from agricultural smudging or industrial operations

➤ Explosion of any steam boilers, pipes, engines, or turbines

➤ Water, liquids, powder, or molten material that leaks or flows from any equipment other than fire protective systems as the result of freezing unless the insured has done his or her best to maintain heat in the building or has drained the equipment and shut off the supply

➤ Dishonest or criminal acts of the insured or his or her employees

➤ Voluntarily parting with property if induced to do so by fraud or a trick

➤ Rain, snow, ice, or sleet damage to personal property left in the open

➤ Any type of collapse other than as provided as an additional coverage under the policy

➤ Pollution (unless the release, discharge, or dispersal is caused by a specified cause of loss)

➤ Failure of an insured to use all reasonable means to save and preserve property from further damage at and after the loss

➤ Errors or omissions in programming, processing, storing data, or in any computer operations or in processing or copying valuable papers and records

➤ Errors or deficiency in design, installation, testing, maintenance, modification, or repair of the insured's computer system, including electronic media and records

➤ Electrical or magnetic injury, disturbance, or erasure of electronic media and records, except as provided as a coverage extension under the policy

➤ Weather conditions that contribute to causing a loss

➤ Loss resulting from acts or decisions or the failure to act or decide

➤ Faulty planning, development, design, specifications, workmanship, or repair

➤ Rust, corrosion, fungus, decay, deterioration, and hidden or latent defects

➤ Smog

➤ Settling, cracking, shrinking, or expansion

➤ Damage caused by insects, birds, rodents, or other animals

➤ Wear and tear

Additional Coverages

Additional coverages provide coverage in specific situations. These coverages might have a separate limit of insurance or require that certain conditions be met for coverage to apply.

Debris Removal

The additional coverage *for debris removal* pays for expenses to remove debris of covered property caused by a covered cause of loss during the policy period. Expenses will be paid only if the insured reports them to the insurance company in writing within *180 days* of the date of loss or the end of the policy period, whichever is earlier. Costs to extract pollutants or remedy polluted land or water are not covered.

The most the insurer will pay for the total of the direct physical loss or damage and the debris removal expense is the limit of insurance applicable to the property that was damaged. Subject to this limit, the amount reimbursed for debris removal expenses is 25% of the amount paid for the direct physical loss plus the deductible that is applicable to that loss.

An additional $10,000 of insurance for each location in any one occurrence is available for debris removal under these circumstances:

> The direct physical loss and the debris removal expense together exhaust the limit of insurance.

> The maximum amount collectible for debris removal (25% of the loss + the deductible) is not enough to cover the debris removal expense.

If either of these conditions applies, the total payment for the direct physical loss and the debris removal expense may be up to—but cannot exceed—the policy limit plus $10,000.

Collapse

The additional coverage for "collapse" applies only when very specific conditions are met. The form defines *collapse* as an abrupt falling down or caving in of the building or part of the building that results in the building being unusable. This definition does not include a building that is in danger of collapsing or a building or part of a building that is still standing but has separated from another part of the structure or shows signs of instability such as bulging, cracking, leaning, or settling.

Collapse of a building or part of a building is covered only when it is caused by one of the specified causes of loss, building glass breakage, hidden decay, hidden insect or vermin damage, weight of people or personal property, weight of rain that collects on a roof, or use of defective materials or methods in construction, remodeling, or renovation if the collapse occurs during the course of the construction, remodeling, or renovation.

Collapse that results from hidden decay or hidden insect or vermin damage is not covered if the insured knew about the damage before the collapse occurred. If collapse occurred after construction, remodeling, or renovation was completed and was caused by a peril listed previously, the loss or damage would be covered even if the use of defective materials or methods contributed to the collapse.

Certain types of outdoor properties, even if they are otherwise covered under the policy, are covered for collapse only when they are damaged directly by a collapsed building. This includes awnings, gutters and downspouts, yard fixtures, outdoor swimming pools, piers, wharves and docks, beach or diving platforms or appurtenances, retaining walls, and walks, roadways, and other paved surfaces.

Under certain conditions, loss or damage that occurs when personal property falls down or caves in is covered even when there is no building collapse:

➤ The property must be inside a building.

➤ The collapse must result from one of the causes of loss listed previously.

➤ The property that collapses must not be one of the items of outdoor property listed previously.

 The collapse additional coverage is subject to the limits of insurance. It does not provide an additional amount of insurance.

Business Income

Under the *business income* additional coverage, the insurance company will pay for loss of business income that occurs when the insured's business operations have to be suspended after a loss and income cannot be generated.

For coverage to apply, there must be direct physical loss or damage to property at the described premises. This includes personal property in a vehicle or in the open within 100 feet of the premises.

The loss must be caused by, or result from, a covered cause of loss. Payment is made for loss during the period the property is being restored that occurs within 12 consecutive months after the date of the direct physical damage.

Also included in this additional coverage is *extended business income coverage*. This coverage extends the period for which business income loss will be paid under certain circumstances. The extended business income coverage begins after the insured's operations are resumed and continues until the insured is restored to the previous earning condition or for *30 consecutive days* (or the number of days listed in the declarations) after operations could have been resumed.

This additional coverage is not subject to the limits of insurance.

Extra Expense

The *extra expense* additional coverage allows reimbursement for additional costs an insured incurs to avoid or minimize suspending business operations after a covered loss.

If an insured spends more money than would otherwise be required in order to reduce a loss, the insurance company will reimburse specified expenses during the period of restoration.

The insurance company will pay for extra expenses that occur within 12 consecutive months after the date of the direct physical loss or damage. This coverage is in addition to the insured's limits of insurance.

Increased Cost of Construction

The *increased cost of construction* additional coverage applies only to buildings insured on a replacement cost basis. If a covered cause of loss damages a covered building, the company will pay the additional costs required to comply with an ordinance or law in repairing the damage or replacing damaged parts. This additional coverage has a limit of $10,000.

If the building is repaired or replaced at the same premises or rebuilt *at the insured's option* at another premises, the most the company will pay is the increased cost of construction at the same premises. If the *ordinance or law requires* relocation, the most the company will pay is the increased cost of construction at the new premises.

The provisions of the ordinance or law exclusion do not apply to this additional coverage to the extent that they conflict with this coverage.

Civil Authority

The *civil authority* additional coverage is available for losses that result from actions of civil authorities. The insured is covered for business income lost or extra expenses required when a civil authority denies the insured access to the described premises because property *not* at the described premises was damaged by a covered cause of loss. For example, this coverage would come in to play if the business next door to the insured's business fell into a sinkhole, and the police refused to let people into the insured's business for fear that the sinkhole might also swallow it up.

Coverage applies for a specified period. Coverage for business income begins 72 hours after the action by the civil authority and remains for up to 3 consecutive weeks. Coverage for extra expenses begins immediately after the action by the civil authority and ends either 3 consecutive weeks after that action or when the business income coverage ends, whichever is later.

Forgery and Alteration

The *forgery and alteration* additional coverage applies to an insured's loss that results directly from someone forging or altering checks, drafts, and similar items made or drawn by or on the insured or the insured's agent.

If the insured is sued for refusing to pay any of these items because it has been forged or altered, and if the insured has the insurance company's written promise to defend the insured, the insurance company will pay for any reasonable legal expenses the insured incurs in that defense. However, the most that will be paid for a loss, including legal expenses, is $2,500, unless a higher limit is shown in the declarations.

Business Income from Dependent Properties

This additional coverage covers loss of business income the insured sustains because of physical loss or damage at a *dependent property* from a covered cause of loss. A dependent property is a business that delivers materials or services to the insured, accepts the insured's products or services, manufactures products for delivery to the insured's customers, or attracts customers to the insured's business.

Coverage is limited to $5,000 unless a higher limit is shown in the declarations. Coverage begins 72 hours after the loss at the dependent property and continues until the date the damage should be repaired, rebuilt, or replaced with reasonable speed and similar quality. The amount paid will be reduced to the extent the insured can resume operations, in whole or in part, by using another source of materials or outlet for its products.

Other Additional Coverages

The *money orders and counterfeit paper currency* additional coverage provides coverage for loss that results when an insured accepts these items in good faith and in exchange for merchandise, money, or services as part of normal business transactions. A $1,000 limit applies to this additional coverage.

The *pollutant clean up and removal* additional coverage does what the debris removal additional coverage does not do: It provides limited coverage for costs to extract pollutants from land or water at the insured's premises as a result of a covered cause of loss. Coverage applies only under specified circumstances; there is a $10,000 limit for each separate 12-month policy period. The insured must report expenses within 180 days after the date of the loss or within 180 days of the end of the policy period, whichever is earlier.

The *preservation of property* additional coverage covers direct physical loss or damage from *any* cause of loss if the property has been removed to another location in order to preserve it from damage by a covered peril. Coverage applies while the property is being moved or while it is temporarily stored at another location, but only for 30 days after the property is first moved.

The *fire department service charges* additional coverage covers charges that might be levied because such liability was assumed by the insured under a contract or agreement before the loss or because these charges are required by local ordinance. Coverage applies when a fire department is called to save or protect covered property from a covered cause of loss. There is a $1,000 limit on the amount of insurance available.

The *water or other liquid, powder, or molten materials* additional coverage covers damage to a building that indirectly results from the escape of these items. If the damage is otherwise covered, this additional coverage pays for necessary costs to tear out and replace any part of the building to repair damage to the system from which the material escaped. The policy will also cover repair or replacement of damaged parts of fire extinguishing equipment if the damage results in discharge of any substance from an automatic fire protection system or is directly caused by freezing. The cost to repair the defect that caused the loss or damage is not covered.

The *glass expenses* additional coverage covers expenses incurred to put up temporary plates or board up openings if repair or replacement of damaged glass is delayed. It also covers expenses required to remove or replace obstructions (other than window displays) when repairing or replacing glass that is part of a building.

Finally, the *fire extinguisher systems recharge expense* additional coverage pays to recharge or replace the insured's fire extinguishers and fire extinguishing systems if they are discharged on or within 100 feet of the premises. It also covers loss or damage to covered property caused by the accidental discharge of chemicals from a fire extinguisher or fire extinguishing system.

Coverage Extensions

Coverage extensions permit an insured to extend the insurance for other specified purposes. Unless otherwise provided, coverage extensions apply to property located in or on the building covered under the policy or to property located in the open or in a vehicle within 100 feet of the premises.

Under the *newly acquired or constructed property coverage extension*, if the insured acquires a building at another location or builds a new building on the described premises, the newly acquired or constructed buildings are covered under the policy's building coverage for up to $250,000 at each location. Business personal property coverage can be extended to property, including newly acquired property, at newly acquired or constructed buildings or to newly acquired property at the described premises. Coverage for newly acquired business personal property is $100,000 at each location. Coverage applies for 30 days after the new premises or property is acquired or construction has begun on the new premises, until the policy expires, or until the insured reports values to the insurance company, whichever occurs first.

Business personal property coverage can be extended to property that is *temporarily off the premises* while in transit or at other premises not owned, leased, or operated by the insured. A $5,000 limit applies.

Coverage can be extended to apply to *outdoor property*, including outdoor fences, signs not attached to buildings, trees, shrubs and plants, and radio and television antennas, including satellite dishes. A debris removal expense is also covered. Coverage applies only for loss by fire, explosion, aircraft, lightning, and riot or civil commotion. Coverage is limited to $2,500, and not more than $500 for any one tree, shrub, or plant.

Business personal property coverage can be extended to include *personal effects* owned by the insured and the insured's officers, partners, or employees. The most the company will pay under this extension is $2,500 at each insured premises.

If the insured has business personal property coverage, the *valuable papers and records coverage extension* can be used to cover the costs to research, replace, or restore information on lost or damaged valuable papers and electronic or magnetic records for which duplicates do not exist. It does not apply to property held as samples or for delivery after sale or to property in storage away from the premises shown in the declarations. There is a maximum limit of $10,000 at each described premises, unless a higher limit is shown in the declarations. For valuable papers and records not at the described premises, the limit is $5,000.

If the insured has business personal property coverage, the *accounts receivable coverage extension* can be used to cover amounts due from customers that the insured is unable to collect because of damage from a covered loss, interest charges on loans required to offset those amounts, excess collection expenses incurred because of the loss, and other reasonable expenses required to reestablish accounts receivable records. Limits are the same as those for the valuable papers and records coverage extension: $10,000 at the described premises and $5,000 for accounts receivable not at the described premises.

Optional Coverages

A number of optional coverages are included in the BOP, but they apply only if so designated in the declarations. Optional coverages usually require an additional premium, whereas additional coverages are included at no extra charge.

Employee Dishonesty

Loss to business personal property and money and securities that results from dishonest acts of employees is covered by the *employee dishonesty* optional coverage. Coverage applies whether the employees act alone or in collusion with others, except the insured and partners of the insured. There is no coverage for loss in which the only proof is an inventory or profit and loss computation.

Coverage for an employee is cancelled immediately on discovery by the insured or any partners, members, managers, officers, or directors not in collusion with the employee of any dishonest act committed by that employee before or after he or she was hired by the insured.

The amount shown in the declarations is the most that will be paid for all loss or damage in one occurrence, no matter whether more than one person or act is involved. Only loss that occurs during the policy period is covered. The insurance company will not pay for a covered loss discovered after one year from the end of the policy period. This is known as the *discovery period*.

Under certain circumstances, the insured has coverage under the employee dishonesty optional coverage of the current policy for losses that occurred during the previous policy period that would have been covered by that policy except that the discovery period expired. The following conditions must be met for the current policy to apply:

➤ The current policy must have become effective at the time the previous policy terminated.

➤ The current policy would have covered the loss had it been in effect when the loss occurred.

Mechanical Breakdown

Under this optional coverage, the insurance company will pay for direct damage to covered property caused by a sudden and accidental breakdown of an object, as defined by the policy, which damages the object so that it needs to be repaired or replaced. The object can be one that is owned by the insured or one that is in the insured's care, custody, or control. It must be at the described premises.

The policy definition of *object* lists equipment in two main categories: certain boiler and pressure vessels and certain types of air conditioning units. The policy also defines exactly what is *not* considered an *accident*. There is no coverage for accidents that occur while an object is being tested.

The insurance company may suspend this coverage by immediately mailing written notice to the insured if it is discovered that the object is in or is exposed to a dangerous condition. If coverage is suspended, the insured will receive a pro rata refund of the premium.

Other Optional Coverages

The *outdoor signs* optional coverage provides coverage for direct physical loss or damage to all outdoor signs on the premises that are owned by or in the care, custody, or control of the insured. The limit of insurance for this optional coverage is specified in the declarations. When this optional coverage applies, all other references to outdoor signs in the policy no longer apply.

The *money and securities* optional coverage applies to loss of money and securities used in the insured's business as a result of theft, disappearance, or destruction. Coverage applies while the money and securities are

➤ At a bank or savings institution

➤ Within the living quarters of the insured, a partner, or an employee who has custody of the property

➤ At the described premises

➤ In transit between any of these places

Limits of Insurance

The most the insurer will pay for loss or damage in any one occurrence is the applicable limit of insurance in the declarations. Each coverage shown in the declarations has its own limits, and the per occurrence rule applies separately to each.

Some coverages have *internal* or *inside limits*. These limits are stipulated in the limits of insurance provision and also in various other sections of the policy, such as the covered property, additional coverages, and coverage extensions sections. An example is the $1,000 limit for the fire department service charge additional coverage.

A $1,000 per occurrence limit also applies to outdoor signs attached to buildings. The limits of insurance provision also specifies that the limits applicable to the coverage extensions, the fire department service charge additional coverage, and the pollutant cleanup and removal additional coverage are in addition to the policy's limits of insurance.

The BOP also includes a provision that addresses inflation. A percentage selected by the insured from a number of options offered by the insurance company is indicated in the declarations for the building coverage. Over the policy period, the limit of insurance gradually increases by the selected percentage until it reaches the full amount by the end of the period.

The limit for business personal property automatically increases by 25% to provide for seasonal variations, meaning that an insured is covered for a loss of up to 25% more than the stated coverage. However, the 25% increase only applies if the limit of insurance for business personal property coverage in the declarations is at least 100% of the insured's average monthly values during either the 12 months or the period of time the insured has been in business before the loss, whichever is less.

Deductible

The standard deductible for property losses is $500.

A base deductible applies to all building and business personal property coverages, including both mandatory and optional coverages. No deductible applies to the fire department service charge, extra expense, business income, civil authority, and fire extinguisher systems recharge expense additional coverages.

A separate $500 deductible applies to the money and securities, employee dishonesty, and outdoor signs optional coverages. There is also a separate $500 deductible for the glass expenses additional coverage. These deductibles are *not* in addition to the base deductible.

Liability and Medical Expenses Coverage

BOPs are structured similar to homeowner policies in the sense that they both include property and liability coverages in the same contract. The liability section of a BOP also includes coverage for medical expenses.

Liability Coverage

Business liability coverage covers the insured's legal liability that arises from *bodily injury*, *property damage*, and personal and advertising injury. Personal and advertising injury is injury, including consequential bodily injury, that arises out of any of the following offenses:

➤ False arrest, detention, or imprisonment

➤ Malicious prosecution

➤ Wrongful eviction from a place a person occupies by or on behalf of its owner, landlord, or lessor

➤ Wrongful entry into a place a person occupies by or on behalf of its owner, landlord, or lessor

➤ Invasion of the right of private occupancy of a place a person occupies by or on behalf of its owner, landlord, or lessor

➤ Oral or written publication of material that slanders or libels a person or organization, disparages a person's or organization's goods, products, or services, or violates a person's right of privacy

➤ Use of another's advertising idea in the insured's advertisement

➤ Infringement of copyright, trade dress, or slogan

 Business liability coverage is broader than the liability coverages provided by the personal lines policies reviewed in previous chapters because in addition to covering bodily injury and property damage, it also covers personal and advertising injury, which are essentially commercial exposures.

For a policy to cover any of the injuries or offenses we have described, the loss must take place in the coverage territory and occur during the policy period. The *coverage territory* for liability coverage is the following:

➤ The United States, its territories and possessions, and Canada

➤ International waters or airspace between the United States, its territories or possessions, and Canada

➤ All parts of the world if the injury or damage arises out of

> ➤ Goods or services normally made or sold by the insured in the United States, its territories and possessions, or Canada

> ➤ The activities of a person who is away from home on business in any of these places

> ➤ Personal and advertising injury offenses that take place through the Internet or similar electronic means of communication

Coverage also typically applies in all parts of the world if the insured's responsibility to pay damages is determined in a suit on the merits in the United States, its territories and possessions, or Canada or in a settlement to which the insurance company has agreed.

The insuring agreement also stipulates that losses of a continuing or ongoing nature that were—prior to the policy period—known to the insured or employees authorized to report losses are not covered.

Under liability coverage, the insurance company accepts the right and duty to defend suits that seek damages under the policy. The insurance company has the sole right to investigate and settle claims and resulting suits. However, when the limits of insurance are used up in paying judgments, settlements, or medical expenses, the insurance company's duty to defend ends.

Supplementary Payments

Supplementary payments extend the liability coverage and make certain amounts available, usually *in addition to* the limits of insurance. The BOP includes the following supplementary payments:

➤ Cost of bonds to release attachments, up to the limit of insurance.

➤ Costs the insured is required to pay because of a suit.

➤ Expenses the insurance company incurs.

➤ Interest that accrues after a judgment and before it is paid, offered, or deposited in court.

➤ Prejudgment interest the insured is required to pay, unless the insurance company makes an offer to pay the limit of insurance—then it will not pay prejudgment interest based on the period of time after that offer.

➤ Reasonable expenses the insured incurs at the insurance company's request to assist in investigating or defending a claim or suit, including $250 per day for lost earnings because of time off from work.

➤ Up to $250 for the cost of bail bonds related to violations that arise from vehicles to which bodily injury liability coverage applies.

If certain conditions are met, the insurer will pay the defense costs for an *indemnitee*—a party who is not an insured who is under contract to provide goods or services to an insured—*in addition to* the policy's limit of liability and provide a defense for the indemnitee. Among the conditions that must be met for this coverage to apply are that the insured and the indemnitee must be named in the same lawsuit and the liability assumed by the insured must be covered by the policy.

Medical Expenses Coverage

The BOP also covers specified medical expenses *without regard to who is at fault*. If other requirements are met, the policy will pay for medical expenses even if the insured would not have been legally liable for them or for the events that precipitated them. The policy will pay reasonable expenses for the following:

➤ First aid when an accident occurs

➤ Medical and surgical services

➤ Hospital services

➤ X-ray services

➤ Ambulance services

➤ Professional nursing services

➤ Dental services

➤ Funeral services

To be covered, the medical expenses must be *necessary* expenses that result from *bodily injury* that occurs on or next to premises the insured owns or rents or injury that occurs because of the insured's business operations. The accident that causes the injury must occur in the coverage territory and during the policy period, and the medical expenses must be incurred and reported to the insurance company within one year after the accident.

Medical expenses coverage is intended to pay for such expenses incurred by the *general public*. Therefore, medical expenses will generally not be paid for the following:

➤ Any insured (does not include the insured's volunteer workers)

➤ Anyone hired to work for or on behalf of any insured or any insured's tenant

➤ A person who is injured on a part of the premises the insured owns or rents and that the injured person normally occupies

➤ A person (whether he or she is an employee of the insured) whose injury calls for benefits payable under a workers compensation, disability, or similar law

➤ A person who is injured while taking part in athletics

Exclusions

For *bodily injury and property damage* liability losses, the BOP excludes liability

➤ Arising out of expected or intended injury (does not apply to bodily injury that occurs when the insured uses reasonable force to protect persons or property)

➤ Assumed under contracts or agreements (does not apply to contracts that meet the policy's definition of an insured contract or to liability the insured would have whether or not a contract or agreement existed)

➤ Related to liquor, but only for insureds whose business is manufacturing, distributing, selling, serving, or furnishing alcoholic beverages

➤ For obligations under workers compensation, disability benefits, unemployment compensation, or similar laws

➤ For BI to employees that arises out of and in the course of their employment with the insured

➤ Arising out of pollutants, including associated cleanup costs

➤ Arising out of the ownership, maintenance, and use of aircraft, autos, and watercraft

➤ Arising out of the use of mobile equipment in, or while practicing or preparing for, any prearranged race, speed or demolition contest, or any stunting activity

➤ Assumed under contract for BI or PD due to war

➤ Arising from rendering or failing to render professional services

➤ For damage to property the insured owns, rents, or occupies or property in the insured's care, custody, or control

➤ For damage to the insured's product or the insured's own work

➤ For damage to impaired property or to property that has not been physically injured arising out of a defect or deficiency in the insured's product or work or a delay or failure to perform a contract or agreement

➤ For losses, costs, or expenses incurred for the loss of use, withdrawal, recall, inspection, repair, replacement, adjustment, removal, or disposal of the insured's product, work, or impaired property

➤ For business liability or medical expenses resulting from the hazardous properties of nuclear materials

➤ For medical expenses that are included within the products-completed operations hazard, excluded under liability coverage or due to war and acts of war

The following exclusions apply specifically to *personal and advertising injury* losses. Not covered are personal and advertising injury

➤ Caused by or at the direction of the insured with the knowledge that the act would violate the rights of another and inflict personal and advertising injury

➤ That arises out of oral or written publication of material that occurs by or at the insured's direction with the insured's knowledge that it is false

➤ That arises out of oral or written publication of material that was first published before the beginning of the policy period

➤ That arises out of a criminal act committed by or at the direction of any insured

➤ For which an insured has assumed liability in a contract or agreement (does not apply to liability for damages the insured would have even if there were no contract or agreement)

➤ Arising out of breach of contract (other than an implied contract to use another's advertising idea in the insured's advertisement, which is covered)

➤ Arising out of the failure of goods, products, or services to conform with advertised quality or performance

➤ Arising out of a wrong description of the price of goods, products, or services

➤ Arising in connection with any actual, alleged, or threatened discharge, dispersal, seepage, or escape of pollutants, as well as any requests to test for, clean up, contain, or otherwise respond to pollutants

➤ Committed by insureds in the business of advertising, broadcasting, publishing, telecasting, designing websites, or providing Internet search, access, content, or service

➤ Arising out of an electronic chatroom or bulletin board the insured hosts, owns, or controls

➤ Arising out of infringement of copyright, trademark, patent, trade secret, or other intellectual property rights

➤ Arising out of the unauthorized use of another's name or product in the insured's email address, domain name, or metatags

Who Is an Insured

Who is considered an insured under the BOP depends on how the named insured is designated in the policy declarations: as an individual, partnership, joint venture, limited liability company, or as an organization other than a partnership, joint venture, or limited liability company. Table 12.2 summarizes who is insured under a BOP.

Table 12.2 Who Is an Insured		
Designation	**Who Are Insureds**	**Restrictions**
Individual	Named insured Named insured's spouse	Only in connection with sole proprietor ships.
Partnership or joint venture	Named insured Named insured's partners and their spouses Named insured's members and their spouses	Members, partners, and their spouses are insureds only in connection with conducting the business. Current or past partnerships or joint ventures are not insureds unless designated in declarations.

(continued)

Table 12.2 Who Is an Insured *(continued)*		
Designation	**Who Are Insureds**	**Restrictions**
Limited liability company	Named insured Members Managers	Members are insureds only in connection with conducting the business. Managers are insureds only in connection with their duties as managers. Current or past limited liability companies are not insureds unless designated in declarations.
Organization other than partnership, joint venture or limited liability company	Named insured Executive officers and directors Stockholders	Executive officers and directors are insureds only in connection with conducting the business. Stockholders are insureds only in connection with liability as stockholders.

Others that are considered insureds under the BOP include

➤ Named insured's *employees* (other than executive officers and managers) when acting within the scope of their employment

➤ An organization or person (other than employees) while acting as insured's *real estate manager*

➤ If the named insured dies, any person or organization that has *temporary custody of the deceased's property* (but only with regard to liability that arises out of maintenance or use of the property, and only until a legal representative has been appointed) or the insured's *legal representative* while acting within the scope of those duties

➤ Any person operating mobile equipment that is registered in the insured's name with the insured's permission

Limits of Insurance

The limits shown in the policy's declarations are the most that will be paid under the circumstances described in the policy. These limits *are* the limits, no matter how many insureds, claims, suits, people, or organizations are involved.

Table 12.3 illustrates the most the insurance company will pay under the BOP in various circumstances.

Table 12.3 Limits of Insurance	
Limit Shown in the Declarations	**Maximum Amount Payable for**
Liability and Medical Expenses	Total of all damages that arise out of bodily injury, property damage, and medical expenses in one occurrence
	Personal injury and advertising injury to one person or organization
Medical Expenses	Medical expenses for bodily injury to one person
Under Business Liability Coverage, Damage to Premises Rented or Insured	Property damage to premises the insured rents, or occupies temporarily with the owner's permission, that arises out of one fire or explosion

The policy also includes two separate *aggregate limits*: one for injury or damage under the products-completed operations hazard and another for all other injury, damage, or medical expenses except fire legal liability losses. Both of the aggregates are *two times the limit* shown in the declarations for liability and medical expenses coverage.

Conditions

There are several sets of conditions in the BOP. The conditions that apply to the entire policy are called the *common policy conditions*. There are two sets of conditions for the property coverage: the *property general conditions* and the *property loss conditions*. The liability conditions are called the *liability and medical expenses general conditions*. Most of these are standard conditions that appear in other commercial property and liability policies.

Under the property insurance loss conditions, a special limitation applies to business income losses resulting from *loss or damage to electronic media and records*. Coverage is limited to the longer of 60 consecutive days after the damage occurs or the period needed to repair, rebuild, or replace other property damaged in the same loss at the described premises.

A liability coverage condition extends coverage to meet requirements of a state's motor vehicle *financial responsibility law*. When the policy is used as proof of future financial responsibility, the insurance company agrees to interpret the policy to comply with the law to the extent of the coverage and limits of insurance the law requires. For mobile equipment, the policy will provide any coverage required by a motor vehicle law, including liability, uninsured motorists, underinsured motorists, and no-fault coverage.

Endorsements

You should be aware of the following endorsements that are commonly attached to BOPs. Endorsements for both the property and liability sections of the policy can be used to alter the coverage or to provide additional coverages.

Utility Services Endorsements

The *Utility Services—Direct Damage coverage endorsement* covers loss or damage to property caused by an interruption in water, communication, or power supply service. For coverage to apply, the property must be scheduled for coverage on the endorsement and the service interruption must be caused by a covered cause of loss.

Here's an example of a loss that would be covered under this endorsement. The insured, a photographer, has her developing equipment insured under a BOP with the Utility Services—Direct Damage endorsement. When an electrical transformer is struck by lightning, a power surge results that damages the equipment. The BOP would cover this loss.

The *Utility Services—Time Element coverage endorsement* pays for loss of business income or extra expense if damage to certain utility services property located outside the covered building by a covered cause of loss results in an interruption of service to the described premises.

Protective Safeguards Endorsement

The *Protective Safeguards endorsement* requires the insured to maintain the protective devices or services listed on the endorsement on specified property as a condition of the policy. The protective safeguards are identified by the following symbols:

➤ *P-1—Automatic Sprinkler System:* Any automatic fire protective system, including related supervisory services and connected sprinklers, pipes, pumps, and similar devices

➤ *P-2—Automatic Fire Alarm System:* An automatic fire alarm system that protects the entire building and is connected to a central station or reports to a public or private fire alarm station

➤ *P-3—Security Service:* A security service with a guard that makes hourly rounds of the premises while the business is closed

➤ *P-4—Service Contract:* A privately owned fire department that provides fire protection service to the premises

➤ *P-9:* Any other protective system described in the endorsement

The insurer will not pay for fire damage losses if the insured failed to keep the protective safeguard in working order or did not notify the insurer that the device was not working properly. When an automatic sprinkler system is shut off due to breakage, leakage, freezing, or opening of sprinkler heads, the insurer does not have to be notified if the system can be restored within 48 hours.

Hired Auto and Nonowned Auto Liability

The *Hired Auto and Nonowned Auto Liability endorsement* covers the insured's liability for one or both of the following:

➤ Bodily injury or property damage that arises out of the maintenance or use of a hired auto by the insured or the insured's employees in the course of the insured's business

➤ Bodily injury or property damage that arises out of the use of any nonowned auto in the insured's business by any person

Hired autos are autos the insured leases, hires, or borrows, but not from employees or members of their households or any partners or executive officers of the insured. *Nonowned autos* are autos not owned, leased, or borrowed by the insured but used in the business.

These coverages are purchased separately and scheduled on the endorsement. The endorsement is available only when the insured has no other commercial auto insurance.

Comparison of Commercial Package Policy and Businessowners Policy

Table 12.4 summarizes the key differences between a CPP and a BOP .

Table 12.4 Features of CPP Versus BOP		
Feature	**Commercial Package Policy**	**Businessowners Policy**
Eligibility	Almost all commercial risks	Small- to medium-sized businesses in limited occupancy classes.
		Insurer specifies limitations on size of building and specific type of business involved.
Format of Policy	Common Policy Declarations	Businessowners Common Policy Declarations
	Common Policy Conditions	Businessowners Policy Form
	Two or more coverage parts	
Coverages	All eligible coverages selected separately	Prepackaged policy containing Property and Liability coverage.

Exam Prep Questions

1. What is the largest office building risk that might be eligible for a BOP?
   - ○ A. Three stories and 50,000 square feet
   - ○ B. Three stories and 75,000 square feet
   - ○ C. Six stories and 75,000 square feet
   - ○ D. Six stories and 100,000 square feet

2. In addition to maximum floor space, the BOP eligibility rules limit eligible risks to what maximum?
   - ○ A. $5 million in annual sales
   - ○ B. $3 million in annual sales
   - ○ C. $1.5 million in annual sales
   - ○ D. $750,000 in annual sales

3. Under the additional coverages of the Businessowners property coverage, property removed to protect it from loss will be covered at another location for up to how many days?
   - ○ A. 5 days
   - ○ B. 10 days
   - ○ C. 20 days
   - ○ D. 30 days

4. What is the standard deductible for the BOP property coverage?
   - ○ A. $500
   - ○ B. $1,000
   - ○ C. $750
   - ○ D. $250

5. Which of the following statements applies to Mechanical Breakdown coverage?
   - ○ A. It is not available in a BOP.
   - ○ B. It is automatically provided in a BOP.
   - ○ C. It is an optional BOP coverage that is activated by an entry in the declarations.
   - ○ D. It is specifically designed to cover insured objects while they are being tested.

6. Which one of the following coverages is *not* included in the BOP?
   - ○ A. Bodily injury and property damage liability
   - ○ B. Personal and advertising injury liability
   - ○ C. Medical expense
   - ○ D. Professional liability

7. Which of the following would be covered under the building coverage of a BOP?
   - ❑ A. Restroom fixtures
   - ❑ B. Photocopy machines
   - ❑ C. Furnishings in the insured's private office
   - ❑ D. Carpets and floor tiles

8. Which of the following would be covered under the business personal property coverage of a BOP?
   - ❑ A. Desks, filing cabinets, and other office equipment the insured uses in her business
   - ❑ B. An enclosure around the front entry to a store that the insured tenant had built when he began leasing the building
   - ❑ C. Cans of paint that are stacked near a newly constructed outer wall prior to painting the wall
   - ❑ D. Fire extinguishers located at various places on the inside walls of the building

9. Which of the following losses would be covered under the property coverage of a BOP?
   - ❑ A. An insured moved inventory to another location to protect it from a tornado. Two days later, a sewer backup in the new location damaged that property.
   - ❑ B. An explosion at the insured's business spewed toxic chemicals onto property belonging to another company. That company's owner sues the insured for the costs to clean up the chemicals.
   - ❑ C. When a tornado damaged a nearby business, authorities closed off the area for one week to clean up the damage. The insured lost business income during that period.
   - ❑ D. Because of negligence of an employee, an explosion on the insured's premises damages a nearby building.

10. Which of the following is *not* excluded under Businessowners Liability coverage?
    - ○ A. Damages the insured causes intentionally
    - ○ B. Liquor liability for those in the business of serving liquor
    - ○ C. Liability assumed under an insured contract
    - ○ D. Damage to the insured's own work

11. What is the time limit for Extended Business Income coverage under the BOP?
    - ○ A. 30 days
    - ○ B. 45 days
    - ○ C. 60 days
    - ○ D. 90 days

12. For how long after the date of a direct physical loss will the insurance company pay for extra expenses under the extra expense additional coverage?

    ○ A. 30 days
    ○ B. 90 days
    ○ C. 180 days
    ○ D. 12 months

13. Unless a higher limit is shown in the declarations, what is the limit on coverage for business income from dependent properties?

    ○ A. $5,000
    ○ B. $10,000
    ○ C. $50,000
    ○ D. $100,000

14. What is the discovery period for coverage of losses under the employee dishonesty optional coverage?

    ○ A. One year from the date of the dishonest act
    ○ B. One year from the end of the policy period
    ○ C. Three years from the date of the dishonest act
    ○ D. Three years from the end of the policy period

15. Which of the following is covered under personal and advertising injury liability coverage in the BOP?

    ○ A. Slander and libel
    ○ B. Malicious prosecution
    ○ C. Copyright infringement
    ○ D. All of the above

Exam Prep Answers

1. D is correct. Office buildings that are no more than six stories high and contain no more than 100,000 square feet are eligible for the BOP.

2. B is correct. Certain types of wholesale, processing, and service businesses are eligible for the BOP as long as gross annual sales do not exceed $3 million.

3. D is correct. The preservation of property additional coverage covers loss from any cause of loss to property that was removed from the insured location to protect it from damage by a covered peril. Coverage applies for up to 30 days after the property is first moved.

4. A is correct. The standard deductible is $500.

5. C is correct. Optional coverages are usually preprinted in the policy, but apply only if they are designated in the declarations. Losses involving an object during testing are specifically excluded.

6. D is correct. The Businessowners Liability coverage includes the following coverages: BI liability, PD liability, personal and advertising injury liability, and medical expense.

7. A and D are correct. Property owned and used by the insured in the business, such as photocopy machines and furnishings in the insured's private office, would be covered under Business Personal Property coverage.

8. A and B are correct. Property owned and used by the insured in the business and tenants' improvements and betterments made at the tenant's expense that cannot be legally removed are covered under Business Personal Property coverage. Materials that are on or within 100 feet of the premises being used for alterations, such as the cans of paint in Choice C, are covered under Building coverage. Personal property used to maintain or service the building, such as the fire extinguishers in Choice D, are also covered under Building coverage.

9. A and C are correct. The Pollutant Cleanup and Removal additional coverage pays the costs to extract pollutants from the insured's premises, not property belonging to others. Damage to a nearby building might be the basis for a liability claim against the insured, but is not insured by the BOP property coverage.

10. C is correct. The exclusion for liability assumed under contract has some exceptions. One is liability assumed under an insured contract. All the other choices are specifically excluded.

11. A is correct. Extended Business Income coverage begins after the insured's operations are resumed and continues until the insured is restored to the previous earning condition or for 30 consecutive days (unless a different length of time is specified in the declarations).

12. D is correct. The insurance company will pay for extra expenses that occur within 12 consecutive months after the date of the direct physical loss.

13. A is correct. The default limit for coverage of business income from dependent properties is $5,000.

14. B is correct. The discovery period during which a claim for this coverage can be filed ends one year from the end of the policy period.

15. D is correct. Personal and advertising injury covers all of the items listed plus false arrest, wrongful eviction, wrongful entry, invasion of the right of private occupancy, and use of another's advertising idea in an advertisement.

Commercial Property Insurance

··

Terms you'll need to understand:

✓ Real property
✓ Business personal property
✓ Personal property of others
✓ Liberalization
✓ Agreed value
✓ Business income
✓ Period of restoration
✓ Suspension of operations
✓ Extra expense
✓ Rental value
✓ Contributing location

✓ Recipient location
✓ Manufacturing location
✓ Leader location
✓ Electronic data
✓ Nonowned, detached trailers
✓ Builders risk
✓ Coinsurance
✓ Collapse
✓ Value reporting form
✓ Spoilage endorsement

Concepts you'll need to master:

✓ Commercial property coverage part
✓ Commercial property coverage forms
✓ Causes of loss forms
✓ Additional coverages
✓ Coverage extensions
✓ Optional coverages
✓ Inflation guard coverage
✓ Replacement cost coverage

✓ Time element coverage
✓ Extended business income coverage
✓ Extended period of indemnity
✓ Maximum period of indemnity
✓ Monthly limit of indemnity
✓ Basic causes of loss
✓ Broad causes of loss
✓ Special causes of loss

One important insurance need for businesses is the need for *property insurance*: both insurance on *real property* such as office buildings, factories, and warehouses and insurance on *business personal property* such as furniture, fixtures, machinery, and inventory. The most widely used means for providing the property insurance that businesses need is the *Commercial Property coverage part* of the Commercial Package policy.

Commercial Property Coverage Part

The Commercial Property coverage part consists of a number of separate components that can be combined to provide the appropriate property coverage for a wide variety of commercial insureds. In addition to the Common Policy declarations and conditions, each Commercial Property coverage part must include

➤ Commercial Property declarations form

➤ Commercial Property conditions form

➤ One or more Commercial Property coverage forms

➤ One or more Causes of Loss forms

➤ Any mandatory endorsements

In addition to any mandatory endorsements that are required, various optional endorsements may also be attached.

Commercial Property Declarations and Coverage Forms

The *Commercial Property declarations form* provides additional information about the premises to be insured and the specific forms that will apply. It also includes the name and addresses of any mortgage holders.

The *Commercial Property coverage forms* contain descriptions of the specific coverages being provided to the business. Each Commercial Property coverage form defines what property is covered, what property is not covered, how limits and deductibles apply, and what special conditions apply.

The following list shows the Commercial Property coverage forms reviewed in this chapter:

➤ Building and Personal Property

➤ Builders Risk

➤ Condominium Association

➤ Condominium Commercial Unit-Owners

➤ Business Income with Extra Expense

➤ Business Income Without Extra Expense

➤ Extra Expense

➤ Legal Liability

Causes of Loss Forms

The *Causes of Loss forms* list the perils that the property is insured against. There are three separate Causes of Loss forms:

➤ Basic

➤ Broad

➤ Special

More than one Causes of Loss form can be attached to the coverage part, with different causes applying to various classes of property or locations. For example, Basic coverage may be written for business personal property, whereas Broad or Special coverage is written for buildings.

Commercial Property Conditions Form

The *Commercial Property conditions form* includes conditions that apply specifically to the Commercial Property coverage forms.

➤ The *Control of Property* condition states that an act of neglect by a person beyond the insured's direction or control will not affect the insurance. In addition, if the insured violates a condition of the policy with regard to a specific location, the insurance applicable to other locations will not be affected.

➤ The *Legal Action Against Us* condition gives the insured two years from the date that direct physical loss occurred to bring an action against the insurer. Such an action cannot be brought unless the insured has complied with all conditions of the policy.

➤ The *Other Insurance* condition states that when other insurance is written on the same basis, the policy prorates with the other policies—that is, it pays its proportion of the loss. If other insurance covers the same loss, but is subject to a different plan or coverage, the policy is excess over the other insurance—that is, the policy will only apply to any unpaid loss that still remains after the other policy pays up to its limit.

➤ The *Policy Period, Coverage Territory* condition states that to be covered, a loss must occur during the policy period and in the coverage territory. The coverage territory is the United States, its territories and possessions, and Canada.

➤ The *Transfer of Rights of Recovery Against Others to Us* condition gives the insurance company subrogation rights.

➤ The *Concealment or Fraud* condition states that the Commercial Property coverage part is void if the insured intentionally conceals or misrepresents a material fact concerning the coverage part, the covered property, the insured's interest in covered property, or a claim.

➤ If two or more of the policy's coverages apply to the same loss, the *Insurance Under Two or More Coverages* condition provides that the insurer will not pay more than the actual amount of loss or damage.

➤ The *No Benefit to Bailee* condition prohibits a bailee from being reimbursed by the insured's Commercial Property insurance if the insured's property is damaged or destroyed while in the bailee's custody.

➤ The *Liberalization* condition states that any revision that broadens coverage without requiring an additional premium will automatically apply to the coverage part if the revision is adopted by the insurer during the policy period or within 45 days prior to the policy's effective date.

NOTE: The purpose of the liberalization clause is to avoid the need to endorse existing policies that are already in effect when the insurer makes a change that is favorable to the insured. This is not only a matter of convenience for both parties, but it also saves money by eliminating printing and mailing costs.

Building and Personal Property Coverage Form

The most commonly purchased form, and the form that is the core of the Commercial Property coverage part, is the *Building and Personal Property coverage form*.

Property Covered

The Building and Personal Property coverage form can be used to cover buildings, the insured's business personal property, and the personal property of others located at the business premises. They are not all required; the insured can select coverage for one or more of these categories. Coverage is only provided for the specific coverages that have a limit of insurance shown in the declarations.

 Building and Personal Property coverage is subject to a deductible. The standard deductible is $500 per occurrence. Higher deductibles, which reduce the premium charged, are available.

In addition to the building itself, the *Building coverage* includes

➤ Completed additions

➤ Fixtures, including outdoor fixtures

➤ Permanently installed machinery and equipment

➤ Personal property used to maintain or service the premises, such as fire extinguishers

➤ Outdoor furniture, floor coverings, and certain appliances

➤ If not otherwise covered, additions under construction and alterations or repairs to the building, including materials, equipment, supplies, and temporary structures within 100 feet of the described premises

Business personal property is covered while it is in the building, in the open, or in a vehicle within 100 feet of the premises. It includes

➤ Furniture

➤ Fixtures

➤ Machinery

➤ Equipment

➤ Stock

➤ Other owned personal property used in the business

➤ The value of labor, parts, or services on the personal property of others

➤ If the insured is a tenant, the improvements and betterments added by the insured

➤ Leased personal property that the insured has a contractual responsibility to insure, unless it's otherwise covered

Stock is the insured's merchandise. It includes items stored or offered for sale, raw materials for manufacturing, materials in the process of being manufactured, manufactured items, and supplies used in packaging and shipping.

Improvements and betterments are fixtures, alterations, installations, or additions that are made a part of a building the insured tenant occupies but does not own and that are acquired by or made at the expense of the insured but cannot legally be removed by the insured.

Personal property of others pays for damage to property of others in the insured's care, custody, or control, regardless of whether the insured is legally liable for that loss. The person who owns the property receives payment for the loss.

Property Not Covered

The following property is excluded from coverage:

➤ Money, accounts, food stamps, notes, securities, and related property (lottery tickets held for sale are not securities and are covered)

➤ Animals, unless they are boarded or held for sale

➤ Autos for sale

➤ Bridges, roads, walks, patios, and other paved surfaces

➤ Contraband (property being illegally transported or traded)

➤ Cost of excavations and other ground preparation

➤ Foundations of buildings, structures, machinery, or boilers if their foundation is below the basement level or below ground level if there is no basement

➤ Land, water, growing crops, and lawns

➤ Personal property while it is airborne or waterborne

➤ Bulkheads, pilings, piers, wharves, and docks

➤ Property covered under another policy in which it is more specifically described

➤ Retaining walls that are not a part of the building described in the declarations

➤ Underground pipes, flues, and drains

➤ The cost to replace or restore information contained in valuable papers or records, including those that exist as electronic data, except as provided in the coverage extensions

➤ Vehicles, including watercraft and aircraft, that are licensed for use on public roads, or are principally operated away from the premises—this exclusion does not apply to

  ➤ Vehicles that are manufactured, processed, or warehoused by the insured

  ➤ Vehicles, other than autos, that the insured holds for sale

  ➤ Rowboats or canoes out of water at the described premises

➤ The following property while outside of buildings, except as provided in the coverage extensions:

  ➤ Grain, hay, straw, or other crop

  ➤ Fences

  ➤ Antennas (including satellite dishes)

  ➤ Signs that are not attached to the building

  ➤ Trees, shrubs, and plants

➤ Electronic data, except as provided as an additional coverage

Additional Coverages

In addition to the basic coverages, the Building and Personal Property coverage form provides some *additional coverages.*

Debris Removal pays expenses to remove debris of covered property caused by or resulting from a covered cause of loss. It does not cover extraction of pollutants from land or water. It pays up to 25% of the amount paid for direct loss to covered property, plus the deductible. But if the actual debris removal expense exceeds the 25% limitation, or if the sum of the direct loss and the debris removal expense exceeds the limit of insurance, the insurer will pay an additional $10,000 for debris removal expense.

Suppose that a tornado strikes the insured's business, resulting in $75,000 in damages to the building and $25,000 in debris removal expenses. The building is insured for $200,000 with a $5,000 deductible. Without the $10,000 of additional debris removal expense coverage, the insured would receive $23,750 for the debris removal expenses ($75,000×25%=$18,750; $18,750+$5,000=$23,750). But because the debris removal expenses exceed the 25% limitation, the additional debris removal expense coverage will pay up to $10,000 to cover the expense (in this case, another $1,250 in addition to the $23,750 so that the entire $25,000 debris removal expense will be paid). *Preservation of Property* pays for loss to property removed from the insured location to protect it from a peril insured against the covered property. This coverage only applies if the loss occurs within 30 days after the property was removed.

Fire Department Service Charge pays up to $1,000 for a fire department service charge. This is paid in addition to the limit of insurance; no deductible applies.

Pollutant Cleanup and Removal covers the costs to extract pollutants from land or water at the insured's premises if the pollution was caused by a covered cause of loss. This coverage is subject to a $10,000 limit per policy period that applies in addition to the policy limit. The expenses must be reported to the insurer in writing within 180 days of the loss.

The *Increased Cost of Construction* additional coverage covers the additional costs required to comply with building codes when a building is damaged by a covered cause of loss. However, it does not cover costs arising out of the enforcement of any ordinance or law that

➤ Requires demolition, repair, replacement, reconstruction, remodeling, or remediation of property because of the presence of mold

➤ Requires the insured to test for, clean up, remove, or otherwise respond to or assess the effects of mold

The coverage is available only for buildings insured on a replacement cost basis. The maximum amount payable is the lesser of 5% of the amount the building is insured for or $10,000.

The *Electronic Data* additional coverage pays to replace or restore electronic data that has been destroyed or corrupted by a covered cause of loss. Electronic data means information, facts, or computer programs stored, created, used on, or transmitted to or from computer software, CD-ROMs, hard or floppy disks, or any other repositories of computer software used with electronically controlled equipment. It does not include the insured's stock of prepackaged software.

In general, the covered causes of loss include those in the applicable Causes of Loss forms, plus collapse. Also covered are viruses or other instructions introduced to a computer system or network designed to damage or destroy any part of its system or disrupt its normal operation. There is no coverage for loss or damage caused by or resulting from manipulation of a computer system by an employee or an entity retained by the insured to inspect, design, install, maintain, repair, or replace the system.

To the extent that electronic data is not replaced or restored, the loss is valued at the cost of replacement of the media on which the data was stored with blank media that is substantially identical. The most paid under this additional coverage is $2,500 for all loss or damage sustained in any one policy year, regardless of the number of losses or the number of premises, locations, or computer systems involved. If payment for one loss does not exhaust this limit, the balance is available for subsequent loss or damage sustained in, but not after, that policy year. An occurrence that begins in one policy year and continues or results in additional loss in a subsequent policy year is treated as if all loss occurred in the year in which the occurrence began.

Coverage Extensions

Certain coverage extensions also apply, but only if the insured agrees to meet an 80% or higher coinsurance requirement or purchases a reporting form. These coverage extensions provide additional limits of insurance.

The *Newly Acquired or Constructed Property* coverage extension applies to Coverage A and Coverage B. Up to $250,000 for each new building can be extended for up to 30 days to cover new buildings being constructed at the same location, as well as buildings newly acquired at other locations intended for use as a warehouse or a use similar to that of the building described in the declarations. Business personal property insurance can be extended for up to 30 days to cover business personal property located at newly acquired locations (other than fairs, trade shows, or exhibitions) and newly acquired or constructed buildings at the location described in the declarations. This business personal property can be insured property or newly acquired property. The maximum amount payable is $100,000 at each building.

Personal Effects and Property of Others coverage provides up to $2,500 of coverage for personal effects of the named insured, partners and employees (excluding loss from theft), and personal property of others. This coverage extension is available even if the insured does not purchase personal property of others coverage, as long as the coinsurance requirement is met.

The *Valuable Papers and Records—Other Than Electronic Data* coverage extension pays up to $2,500 to replace or restore information on damaged valuable papers and records.

The *Property Off-Premises* coverage extension extends up to $10,000 in coverage for covered property that is away from the described premises. Coverage is provided while the property is

➤ Temporarily at a location the insured does not own, lease, or operate

➤ In storage at a location the insured leases

➤ At a fair, trade show, or exhibition

Property is not covered while it is in or on a vehicle or in the care of a salesperson, except while the salesperson is at a fair, trade show, or exhibition.

The *Outdoor Property* coverage extension extends a limited amount of coverage to fences, antennas, satellite dishes, signs, trees, plants, and shrubs. The maximum payable is $1,000, with a $250 limit applying to any one tree, plant, or shrub.

Another coverage extension is for *nonowned detached trailers.* Trucking companies that make deliveries to businesses sometimes leave the trailer for the insured to unload and then return later to pick up the empty trailer. Some businesses also use rented trailers as storage facilities. In both cases, although the property inside the trailer is covered by the policy, the insured is usually responsible for damage to the trailer itself while it is on the premises. This coverage extension applies to such losses.

The trailer must be in the insured's care, custody, or control at premises described in the declarations, and the insured must be contractually obligated to pay for damage to the trailer. There is no coverage for damage that occurs while the trailer is attached to a vehicle or while it is being hitched or unhitched from a vehicle. The limit is $5,000 unless a higher limit is shown in the declarations.

Conditions

In addition to the conditions listed in the Common Policy Conditions and Commercial Property Conditions forms, several important conditions are also listed in the Building and Personal Property coverage form.

The *Duties in the Event of Loss* condition states that after a loss, the insured must

➤ Notify the insurer about the loss or damage as soon as possible. The insured must provide a description of the property involved and describe how, when, and where the loss or damage occurred.

➤ Notify the police if a law might have been broken.

➤ Take reasonable steps to protect the covered property from further damage and keep a record of expenses incurred to protect the property. If possible, the insured should set the damaged property aside for examination.

➤ Provide a complete inventory at the insurer's request.

➤ Allow the insurer to inspect the property, examine books and records, and take samples of the property at its request.

➤ Testify under oath with regard to the claim if requested by the insurer.

➤ Send a signed, sworn statement of loss within 60 days of the insurance company's request.

The *Loss Payment* condition states that the insurance company will give the insured notice of how it intends to settle the loss within 30 days after it receives the insured's sworn statement of loss. As long as the insured complies with all the terms of the coverage part and reaches an agreement with the company on the amount of the loss, the insurer will pay the loss within 30 days after it receives the sworn statement of loss.

The *Valuation* condition describes how losses will be settled. Most losses are paid at actual cash value (ACV). However, if the coinsurance conditions are met and costs are $2,500 or less, the policy pays the cost of building repair or replacement without taking depreciation into account. Other factors that determine valuation include the following:

➤ *Stock* already sold is valued at its net selling price.

➤ *Glass* is valued at the cost of replacement with safety glazing material if required by law. (If replacement with safety glazing material is not required by law, glass is valued at the cost of replacement with similar materials.)

➤ *Valuable papers and records* are valued at the cost of blank materials needed to reproduce the lost records and labor to transcribe or copy the records.

➤ *Tenants improvements and betterments* are valued at ACV if the insured-tenant makes the repairs promptly or at a proportion of the original cost of the improvements if the repairs are not made promptly. If someone besides the insured, such as the building owner, pays for repairs, the insurer will pay nothing for the loss.

The *Vacancy condition* states that if a building has been vacant for more than 60 consecutive days before the loss, the insurer will not pay for loss because of vandalism, water damage, theft or attempted theft, building glass breakage, or sprinkler leakage (unless the system has been protected against freezing). In addition, any amount that would otherwise be paid for a covered loss will be reduced 15%.

Buildings under construction are not considered vacant.

The *Mortgageholders condition* promises to pay losses to any mortgageholders named in the declarations as their interest may appear. This condition protects the interest of mortgageholders by promising advance notice of cancellation. The insurer must provide 10 days' written notice if canceling for nonpayment of premium and 30 days' notice if canceling for any other reason allowed by the policy. If the insurer decides not to renew, the mortgageholder must be given at least 10 days' advance written notice.

The *Coinsurance condition* states that if the insured's amount of coverage at the time of loss does not meet the required coinsurance percentage, the company reduces the payment it would otherwise make in the same proportion as the insurance carried bears to the insurance required.

Optional Coverages

The Building and Personal Property coverage form also provides three optional coverages that must be listed in the declarations to be activated. An additional premium is charged for each optional coverage selected.

Agreed Value coverage suspends the coinsurance requirement for the covered property designated and substitutes an agreement to cover any loss in the same proportion that the limit of insurance carried bears to the stated value. The insured is required to submit a form stipulating the value of the property.

If the agreed value on an item is stated to be $50,000 and the limit is $50,000, any loss is covered in full. If the limit carried is only $25,000, only 50% of any loss would be covered. The standard Coinsurance clause pays the proportion of the loss that the limits carried bear to the value at the time of loss, rather than the agreed value.

When the insured selects *Inflation Guard coverage*, the insured and the insurance company agree on one of several percentages that will apply annually to the limits of insurance. For example, if 8% is selected, the total limits of insurance gradually increase on a pro rata basis until, at the end of the year, the available limit is 8% higher than the limits shown initially. The coverage form includes a precise formula for determining the amount of increase at any given time during the policy period.

Replacement Cost coverage overrides ACV in the Valuation condition by agreeing to pay for loss or damage to covered property on a replacement cost basis, with the exception of certain property listed in the declarations. Replacement cost coverage is subject to the same coinsurance provisions as the standard ACV valuation.

Builders Risk Coverage Form

Another form that can be added to the Commercial Property coverage part is the *Builders Risk coverage form*.

Property Covered

The Builders Risk coverage form can be used to cover commercial, residential, or farm buildings that are under construction. Coverage begins on

➤ The date construction begins if the building does not have a basement

➤ The date construction starts above the lowest basement floor if there is a basement

Coverage is written for one year, but ceases whenever any of the following occur:

➤ The property is accepted by the purchaser.

➤ Ninety days have elapsed since construction was completed.

➤ The building is occupied or put to its intended use.

➤ The insured's interest in the property ceases.

➤ The insured abandons the construction with no intention of completing it.

Coverage includes both the building under construction and its foundation. Fixtures, machinery, equipment used to service the building, and the insured's building materials and supplies can be covered if they will become a permanent part of the building and are located within 100 feet of the building.

In addition, coverage can be extended to cover building materials and supplies owned by others but in the insured's care, custody, or control, provided that they are located within 100 feet of the described building. The most that will be paid under this extension is $5,000.

The following property is not covered:

➤ Land or water

➤ Lawns, trees, shrubs, or plants when outside of buildings

➤ Radio and television antennas when outside of buildings, including lead-in wiring, masts, or towers

➤ Signs when outside of buildings and not attached to buildings (attached signs are covered)

Amount of Coverage Available

The amount of coverage available under the Builders Risk coverage form is determined in accordance with the anticipated completed value of the building under construction.

The insurance company agrees to pay the ACV of the loss; however, it will not pay a greater share of any loss than the proportion that the limit of insurance bears to the value of the building on the date of completion. This is stipulated in the *Need for Adequate Insurance* condition. Consider this example: The value of a building on its date of completion is $200,000. The limit of insurance carried is $100,000, with a $500 deductible. The amount of loss is $80,000. The company would pay $39,500. Here's how we calculated this figure:

$100,000÷$200,000=.50

$80,000×.50=$40,000

$40,000–$500=$39,500

Miscellaneous Conditions

The Builders Risk coverage form includes most of the same conditions found on the Building and Personal Property coverage form, with these variations:

➤ There is no Vacancy provision because buildings under construction are not considered vacant.

➤ There is a clause stating that all property is valued at ACV at the time of loss. Because ACV is paid for all losses, the form does not include options for replacement cost, agreed value, or inflationary adjustment.

➤ There is no Coinsurance condition. (The Need for Adequate Insurance condition serves essentially the same purpose by penalizing insureds who do not have the required amount of insurance when a loss occurs.)

Builders Risk Reporting Form

The *Builders Risk Reporting form* provides another option with regard to the amount of insurance that must be carried. When this form is attached to the Builders Risk coverage form, the insured is allowed to purchase a smaller amount of insurance that gradually increases as the value of the building under construction increases. This form requires a report of value that must be filed with the insurer each month. The insurance company will not pay more for any loss than the proportion the values last reported before the loss bears to the ACV of the covered property on the effective date of the last report.

Condominium Coverage Forms

Two condominium forms are available under the Commercial Property coverage part.

The *Condominium Association coverage form* insures a condominium association against direct physical loss or damage to

➤ Buildings

➤ Business personal property

➤ Personal property of others in the care, custody, or control of the association while it is located at the premises

It can be used to insure the condominium associations of residential or commercial condominiums. The perils insured against are contained in the Causes of Loss forms attached to the coverage.

The definition of "building" is extended to cover items such as permanently installed machinery and equipment. It also covers outdoor fixtures that are a part of the building as well as other specifically named personal property. In general, however, the definition of "building" does not include personal property owned, used, or controlled by a unit-owner. Business personal property includes only property owned by the association or owned indivisibly by all unit-owners.

The *Condominium Commercial Unit-Owners coverage form*, as its name implies, is designed for the owner of a condominium. It covers the condominium's contents and is available only for the owner of a *commercial* condominium. (Residential condo owners can obtain contents coverage with an HO-6.) It covers the unit-owner's business personal property and the personal property of others in the insured's care, custody, or control. It does not cover buildings; this coverage is typically provided under the Condominium Association coverage form issued to the Association.

In the event that both the Association and Unit-Owners forms apply to a specific loss, the Association form's coverage is primary.

Business Income Coverage Forms

Business Income coverage forms pay for loss of income the insured sustains because of a direct physical loss from a peril insured against that forces the insured to suspend operations during a period of restoration. The *period of restoration* begins on the date of the direct physical loss and ends on the date on which the property can be repaired, rebuilt, or replaced with reasonable speed. *Suspension* means a slowdown or cessation of the insured's business activities.

Coverages

The type of coverage provided under the Business Income forms is known as *time element coverage* because it provides coverage for the loss of business income over a period of time that results from direct physical loss.

The term "time element coverage" reflects the fact that the amount of a covered loss might have no relationship to the amount of actual physical damage that led to the income loss, but does depend on the time required to get the business running again. For example, in the event of fire damage, a business might have to shut down only for the time it takes to make repairs to the building. However, if a covered peril damaged or destroyed a vital piece of special equipment only manufactured in Germany, and is only manufactured to order, the business might have to shut down for many months while waiting for a replacement.

Business income includes

➤ Net income that would have been earned if the loss had not occurred

➤ The costs of continuing normal operations, including payroll

For loss of business income to be covered, the suspension of operations must result from direct physical loss to property at the described premises caused by a peril insured against in the Causes of Loss form.

There are two Business Income forms:

➤ Business Income with Extra Expense

➤ Business Income Without Extra Expense

Extra Expense is a coverage that reimburses the insured for expenses incurred to keep a business going after a loss caused by a covered peril.

The *Business Income with Extra Expense coverage form* includes an Extra Expense coverage that reimburses the insured for money spent to avoid or minimize a business shutdown. It covers only expenses the insured would not have incurred if the property had not been damaged.

The *Business Income Without Extra Expense coverage form* replaces the Extra Expense coverage with an *Expenses to Reduce Loss coverage* that covers expenses the insured incurs to reduce loss, up to the amount the loss is reduced.

With either of the Business Income forms, the insured may select

➤ Business Income coverage, including Rental Value coverage

➤ Business Income coverage, other than Rental Value coverage

➤ Rental Value coverage only

Rental Value includes the total anticipated rental income from a tenant occupancy, all amounts that are legal obligations of the tenant and would otherwise be the insured's obligations, and fair rental value of any part of the premises occupied by the insured.

Similar to the other Commercial Property forms we've reviewed, the Business Income coverage forms contain a Coinsurance clause. Coinsurance applies to Business Income coverage, but not to Extra Expense coverage.

Additional Coverages

Both Business Income forms contain certain *additional coverages*. One such coverage is *Extended Business Income*. This pays for loss of business income, even after operations have been resumed, until the business has been restored, but for no more than *30 days* from the date business is resumed.

The *Order of Civil Authority* coverage pays business income and extra expense losses incurred when a civil authority prohibits access to the described premises because property other than the described premises was damaged by a covered cause of loss. Both business income and extra expense losses are paid for up to 3 consecutive weeks. Payment for business income losses begins 72 hours after the action by the civil authority.

The *Alterations and New Buildings* coverage pays business income and extra expense losses incurred when a covered cause of loss damages a new building or an alteration or addition to an existing building. Also covered is damage to machinery, equipment, supplies, or building materials located on or within 100 feet of the described premises if these items are being used in construction, alterations, or additions or are incidental to the occupancy of new buildings. If the loss delays the start of the insured's operations, the period of restoration under this coverage begins on the date operations would have begun if the loss had not occurred.

Optional Coverages

Several *optional coverages* are also included in the Business Income coverage forms.

The *Extended Period of Indemnity* option gives the insured Extended Business Income coverage for the number of days stated in the declarations, rather than the 30 days allowed by the Extended Business Income additional coverage. For example, an insured may buy coverage for 60 days, 90 days, or some other period.

The *Maximum Period of Indemnity* optional coverage limits reimbursement for extra expenses or loss of business income to no more than the amount of loss incurred during the first 120 days following the direct loss.

The *Monthly Limit of Indemnity* optional coverage allows the insured to establish the amount of reimbursement for loss of business income during each 30-day period. The insured selects a fraction that is multiplied by the limit of insurance to determine the maximum that could be paid for each 30 days.

 The Coinsurance condition that applies to the Business Income coverage forms is waived when either the Maximum Period of Indemnity or Monthly Limit of Indemnity coverages are selected by the insured.

The insured may also select the *Agreed Value* optional coverage. This coverage requires the insured to submit a business income report/worksheet every 12 months that shows financial data for the 12 months prior to the submission, as well as estimated data for the 12 months following. As long as a new worksheet is submitted every 12 months, the Coinsurance clause will not apply. Instead, the insured is expected to carry insurance to value or the agreed value established by the worksheets. If the insured fails to file the required financial data, the Coinsurance clause is reactivated.

Business Income from Dependent Properties—Broad Form

The *Business Income from Dependent Properties—Broad Form* is a variation on the Business Income forms. It provides coverage for the following:

➤ Insureds who depend on another business as their sole supply of merchandise or raw materials can suffer a loss if their supplier is forced to cut back or eliminate shipments because of a direct physical loss. The Business Income From Dependent Properties—Broad Form protects the insured against loss because of loss at such a *contributing location*.

➤ Insureds who depend on a particular business as the primary buyer for their products are covered under this form if direct physical loss at such a *recipient location* causes the insured's earnings to suffer.

➤ Insureds might depend on a manufacturer to deliver certain products or components to the insured's customers under a sales contract. Should the *manufacturing location* be unable to fulfill the contract because of direct physical loss, insureds can suffer a loss of income that can be covered under this form.

➤ Insureds might depend on another business to attract customers to their own business. Loss to such a *leader location* can cause insureds to suffer a loss of earnings that can be covered under this form.

Extra Expense Coverage Form

Although one of the Business Income coverage forms includes Extra Expense coverage to help minimize or prevent a suspension of business, some insureds simply cannot accept such a suspension. Instead, they will do whatever is required to avoid such a shutdown. For these insureds, the need is not to protect lost income, but to cover the extra expenses needed to continue operations at any cost. Examples are public utilities, newspapers, dairies, and other businesses in which, if the business shut down, there would be a great hardship on customers or lost business that would likely never be regained.

This type of risk needs the *Extra Expense coverage form*, which provides no reimbursement for lost business income, but concentrates on reimbursing the insured for extra expenses incurred to remain in operation. The Extra Expense coverage form is a time element coverage.

Limits are applied to recovery depending on the period of restoration. For instance, limits might be stated in the declarations as 40%/80%/100%. This means that if the restoration period was

➤ *30 days or fewer*: 40% of the full amount of insurance would be paid.

➤ *31–60 days*: 80% of the full amount of insurance would be paid.

➤ *More than 60 days*: 100% of the full amount of insurance would be paid.

Legal Liability Coverage Form

Earlier, you learned that the Building and Personal Property coverage form covers damage to the property of others in the insured's care, custody, or control, regardless of whether the insured is legally liable for that loss. The Legal Liability coverage form also covers damage to property of others while in the insured's control, *but only if the insured is legally liable for the damage.*

An insured may choose this form to obtain a lower rate because it covers fewer types of losses. Payment is made on behalf of the insured. Coverage might apply to exposures arising from the insured's occupancy of another's building or from having custody of the property of others, such as customers' goods.

Causes of Loss Forms

In addition to one or more coverage forms, the Commercial Property coverage part requires a *Causes of Loss form*. Whereas the coverage forms explain what property is covered and what coverages are provided, the Causes of Loss form states what perils are insured against. It also lists specific exclusions. There are three Causes of Loss forms: Basic, Broad, and Special.

Basic

The *Causes of Loss—Basic form* is a named perils form that lists the following 11 covered perils:

➤ Fire

➤ Lightning

➤ Explosion

➤ Windstorm or hail

➤ Smoke

➤ Aircraft or vehicles

➤ Riot or civil commotion

➤ Vandalism

➤ Sprinkler leakage

➤ Sinkhole collapse

➤ Volcanic eruption

Smoke from agricultural smudging or industrial operations is not covered.

The windstorm or hail peril does not include damage caused by frost, cold weather, snow, sleet, or ice other than hail. Damage to the interior of a building or its contents is covered only when the wind or hail first creates an opening in the walls or roof.

The explosion peril includes explosion of gasses or fuel within the furnace or flues of any fired vessel.

Vehicle damage caused by vehicles the named insured owns or operates in the course of the insured's business is not covered.

The Basic form exclusions include

➤ Fungus, wet rot, dry rot, and bacteria (except as provided as an additional coverage); does not apply when resulting from fire or lightning

➤ Ordinance or law

➤ Earth movement (does not include a fire or explosion resulting from earth movement)

➤ Government action

➤ Nuclear hazard

➤ Failure of power or other utility services occurring away from the insured's premises

➤ War and military action

➤ Water, including flood, sewer backup, mudslides, or seepage of ground water

➤ Artificially generated current

➤ Rupture or bursting of water pipes (other than automatic sprinklers)

➤ Leakage or discharge of water or steam resulting from breaking of water or steam system or appliance (does not apply to automatic sprinklers), including continuous or repeated seepage or leakage or the presence or condensation of humidity, moisture, or vapor that occurs over a 14-day period or more

> ➤ Explosions of steam boilers, pipes, engines, or turbines

> ➤ Mechanical breakdown

Additional Coverage—Limited Coverage for Fungus, Wet Rot, Dry Rot, and Bacteria

The Basic form also includes the *Limited Coverage for Fungus, Wet Rot, Dry Rot, and Bacteria additional coverage.* Fungus is defined as any type or form of fungus, including mold or mildew, and any mycotoxins, spores, scents, or byproducts produced or released by fungi. For the purpose of simplification, we use the word "mold" in this section.

This additional coverage provides limited coverage for mold that results from a covered cause of loss other than fire or lightning. (Coverage for mold-related losses arising out of fire or lightning is provided elsewhere in the form.) The loss must occur during the policy period, and all reasonable means must have been used to save and preserve the property from further damage at the time of and after that occurrence. The insurer will pay for

> ➤ Direct physical loss or damage to covered property caused by mold, including the cost to remove it

> ➤ Costs to tear out and replace any part of the building or other property if needed to gain access to the mold

> ➤ Cost of testing performed after removal, repair, replacement, or restoration of the damaged property is completed, provided that there is a reason to believe that mold is present

Coverage is limited to $15,000 for all loss or damage arising out of all occurrences of covered causes of loss that take place in a 12-month period, regardless of the number of claims. The 12-month period starts with the beginning of the present annual policy period. If a particular loss results in mold, the insurer will not pay more than a total of $15,000 even if it continues to be present or active or recurs in a later policy period. This additional coverage does not increase the applicable limit of insurance on covered property.

Broad

The *Causes of Loss—Broad form* covers all the perils listed in the Basic form, as well as the following additional perils:

> ➤ Falling objects (does not cover damage to interior property unless the exterior of the building is damaged first)

> ➤ Weight of snow, ice, or sleet

➤ Water damage (accidental discharge or leakage of water or steam as a result of the cracking or breaking of a water or steam system or appliance)

Coverage also includes the cost of tearing out or replacing any part of a building to repair damage to the system from which the water or steam escaped, and costs to repair the system itself. Not covered are the costs to repair any defect that caused the loss, loss from continuous seepage over 14 days or more, or loss caused by freezing unless proper precautions were taken to prevent freezing.

Collapse Additional Coverage

The Broad form contains the Limited Mold Coverage additional coverage and another additional coverage for collapse. *Collapse* is defined as an abrupt falling down or caving in of the building or part of the building that results in the building being unusable. This definition does not include a building in danger of collapsing or a building—or part of a building—still standing that has separated from another part of the structure or showing signs of instability such as bulging, cracking, leaning, or settling.

Collapse of a building, part of a building, or a building containing covered property is covered only when it is caused by one of the specified Broad form perils or any of the following additional perils:

➤ Breakage of glass

➤ Hidden decay

➤ Hidden insect or vermin damage

➤ Weight of people or personal property

➤ Weight of rain that collects on a roof

➤ Use of defective material or methods in construction, remodeling, or renovation if the collapse occurs while the construction, remodeling, or renovation is in progress

Collapse that results from hidden decay or hidden insect or vermin damage is not covered if the insured knew about the damage before the collapse occurred. If collapse occurs after construction, remodeling, or renovation is completed and is caused by a covered peril, the loss or damage is covered even if the use of defective materials or methods contributed to the collapse.

The following types of outdoor properties, even if they are otherwise covered under the policy, are covered for collapse only when they are damaged directly by a collapsed building:

➤ Outdoor radio or television antennas, including satellite dishes, and their lead-in wiring, masts, or towers

➤ Awnings, gutters, and downspouts

➤ Yard fixtures

➤ Outdoor swimming pools

➤ Fences

➤ Piers, wharves, and docks

➤ Beach or diving platforms or appurtenances

➤ Retaining walls

➤ Walks, roadways, and other paved surfaces

Under certain conditions, loss or damage that occurs when personal property falls down or caves in is covered even when there is no building collapse:

➤ The property must be inside a building.

➤ The collapse must result from one of the specified causes of loss.

➤ The property that collapses must not be one of the items of outdoor property previously described.

Also, coverage does not apply if marring or scratching is the only damage that results from the collapse. Settling, shrinkage, expansion, cracking, bulging, leaning, sagging, or bending are not considered to be collapse.

The Collapse additional coverage does not increase the limits of insurance provided by the coverage part.

Special

The *Causes of Loss—Special form* covers any direct physical loss that is not specifically excluded or limited in the form. In other words, it provides open perils coverage. Because of this, the list of exclusions is more extensive and detailed than in the other Causes of Loss forms you've studied. In addition to some of the exclusions contained in the other forms, such as earth movement, war, and nuclear hazard, the Special form excludes

➤ Wear and tear

➤ Rust, corrosion, fungus, decay, deterioration, and hidden or latent defects

➤ Smog

➤ Pollutants (unless the release, discharge, or dispersal is caused by a specified cause of loss)

➤ Settling, cracking, shrinking, or expansion

➤ Damage caused by insects, birds, rodents, or other animals

➤ Mechanical breakdown

➤ Explosion of steam boilers, pipes, and engines

➤ Dishonest or criminal acts of the insured or the insured's employees

➤ Voluntary parting with property if induced to do so by fraud or a trick

➤ Rain, snow, ice, or sleet damage to personal property that is not in a building

➤ Loss resulting from acts or decisions or the failure to act or decide

➤ Collapse (other than that specifically included under the Collapse additional coverage)

➤ Faulty planning, development, design, specifications, workmanship, or repair

Both the Limited Mold coverage and the Collapse additional coverages are included in the Special form.

Limitations

The Special Causes of Loss form imposes limitations on coverage for certain types of losses.

The Special form covers theft, but coverage for various classes of property is limited to the following amounts:

➤ $2,500 for furs, fur garments, and garments trimmed with fur

➤ $2,500 for jewelry, watches, jewels, pearls, precious and semiprecious stones, gold, silver, and platinum (does not apply to jewelry and watches worth less than $100 per item)

➤ $2,500 for patterns, dies, molds, and forms

➤ $250 for stamps, tickets, lottery tickets held for sale, and letters of credit

The following property is covered only if the loss is caused by a specified cause of loss (the same as the Broad form perils) or breakage of building glass:

➤ Valuable papers and records, abstracts, drawings, and data processing, recording or storage media

> Animals, and then only if killed or if it is necessary to destroy them

> Breakage of fragile articles, such as statuary, marble, chinaware, and porcelain

> Building machinery, tools, and equipment that the insured owns or is entrusted with while away from the premises

Causes of Loss—Earthquake and Volcanic Eruption

None of the Causes of Loss forms cover earthquake or volcanic *eruption* (that is, damage caused by volcanic movement of the earth; volcanic *action*—damage caused by airborne shock waves, ash, or lava flow—is covered). An insured can obtain coverage for these perils by adding the *Earthquake and Volcanic Eruption endorsement* to the policy.

 This endorsement must be used in conjunction with one of the Causes of Loss forms. Although a policy can be written to cover property only for the Basic, Broad, or Special Causes of loss, under the ISO commercial lines program, earthquake coverage cannot be written alone. The Earthquake and Volcanic Eruption endorsement can only be attached to a policy that includes at least one of the other Causes of Loss forms. However, earthquake coverage might be available as a separate policy from specialty carriers.

Volcanic eruption means the eruption, explosion, or effusion (pouring forth) of a volcano. All earthquake shocks or volcanic eruptions that occur within any 168-hour period constitute a single earthquake or volcanic eruption. The expiration of the policy does not reduce the 168-hour period.

An insured can choose to limit coverage to sprinkler leakage caused by an earthquake or volcanic eruption and not cover other losses resulting from these perils. This is indicated by entering *earthquake—sprinkler leakage only* in the policy declarations. The 168-hour time period for earthquake shocks and volcanic eruptions also applies to this optional coverage.

Comparison of Causes of Loss

Table 13.1 summarizes the perils covered by the Basic, Broad, and Special Causes of Loss forms and the Earthquake and Volcanic Eruption endorsement.

Peril	Basic	Broad	Special	Earthquake and Volcanic Eruption Endorsement*
			Open Peril**	
Fire	✓	✓		
Lightning	✓	✓		
Explosion	✓	✓		
Windstorm or Hail	✓	✓		
Smoke	✓	✓		
Aircraft or Vehicles	✓	✓		
Riot or Civil Commotion	✓	✓		
Vandalism	✓	✓		
Sprinkler Leakage	✓	✓		
Sinkhole Collapse	✓	✓		
Volcanic Action	✓	✓		
Limited Mold Coverage***	✓	✓	✓	
Falling Objects		✓		
Weight of Snow, Ice, Sleet		✓		
Water Damage		✓		
Collapse***		✓	✓	
Earthquake				✓
Volcanic Eruption				✓

Table 13.1   Perils Insured Against

*Must be used in conjunction with Basic, Broad, or Special Causes of Loss form.

**Risks of loss not otherwise excluded are covered.

***Additional coverage.

Endorsements

Several endorsements can be added to the Commercial Property coverage part.

Value Reporting Endorsements

Some businesses might insure property for which values fluctuate regularly or property that is moved from one location to another from time to time. For these insureds, the *Value Reporting form* is used to provide coverage based on actual values at certain locations at specific times. The insured purchases a somewhat higher amount of insurance than he or she thinks will be needed, and then reports actual values at each location on a regular basis, paying premium on the basis of these reports at the end of the policy period based on average exposures. Coverage amounts are also adjusted accordingly, reducing the risk that the insured will be underinsured or overinsured at any one location. Property that can be covered by the Value Reporting form includes business personal property, stock, and the personal property of others.

A variation of the reporting form is the *Peak Season endorsement*, which allows the insured to carry increased coverage during certain seasons of the year when inventory or other covered property is higher than usual.

Ordinance or Law Coverage Endorsement

The ordinance or law policy exclusion prohibits payment for increased costs because of building regulations or demolition laws. The *Ordinance or Law Coverage endorsement* offsets this exclusion by providing coverage when an insured's loss is increased because of such laws.

Both demolition costs and increased construction costs are covered if they are required or regulated by law or ordinance. Loss in value of the undamaged portion of the building as a consequence of enforcement of such an ordinance or law is also covered. However, the endorsement does not cover costs resulting from the enforcement of laws regarding pollutants, such as laws concerning pollution cleanup or removal.

Spoilage Endorsement

The *Spoilage endorsement* can be added to the Building and Personal Property or Condominium Commercial Unit-Owners coverage forms to provide coverage for the insured's perishable stock—personal property that must be maintained under controlled conditions to protect it from loss or damage.

Exam Prep Questions

1. Which of the following perils are covered in the Causes of Loss—Basic form?
   - ○ A. Collapse
   - ○ B. Explosion
   - ○ C. Volcanic eruption
   - ○ D. Nuclear hazard

2. Under the Earthquake and Volcanic Eruption endorsement, all earthquake shocks or volcanic eruptions that occur within a certain number of hours constitute a single earthquake or volcanic eruption. What is that time period?
   - ○ A. 40 hours
   - ○ B. 72 hours
   - ○ C. 168 hours
   - ○ D. 24 hours

3. Which Causes of Loss form provides open peril coverage?
   - ○ A. Basic
   - ○ B. Broad
   - ○ C. Special
   - ○ D. Both Basic and Broad

4. Loss caused by sprinkler leakage is covered under which Commercial Property Causes of Loss forms?
   - ○ A. Basic
   - ○ B. Broad
   - ○ C. Special
   - ○ D. All of the above

5. Which Commercial Property Causes of Loss forms cover collapse?
   - ❑ A. Basic
   - ❑ B. Broad
   - ❑ C. Special
   - ❑ D. All of the above

6. Which of the following would be covered under the building coverage of the Building and Personal Property coverage form?
   - ❑ A. Inventory stored at the insured's warehouse
   - ❑ B. An addition to the insured's store on which construction has just begun
   - ❑ C. Fire extinguishers located in the insured's factory
   - ❑ D. Office furniture and supplies kept in the insured's building.

7. The insured's business sustains $25,000 damage in a fire. The fire department that was called to the scene billed the insured $1,000. The business is insured under the Building and Personal Property coverage form for $500,000 with a $5,000 deductible. How much will the insurance company pay for this loss?

   ○ A. $21,000

   ○ B. $20,000

   ○ C. $24,000

   ○ D. $26,000

8. Which of the following properties would *not* be excluded under the Building and Personal Property coverage form?

   ○ A. Lawn

   ○ B. Driveway

   ○ C. Private company jet

   ○ D. Animals held for sale

9. When are losses under the Building and Personal Property coverage form paid at replacement or repair cost?

   ○ A. Always

   ○ B. Never

   ○ C. If the insured meets the coinsurance requirements and costs are $2,500 or less

   ○ D. Whenever the total amount of loss does not exceed 25% of the policy limit

10. Which of the following have special loss valuation requirements under the Building and Personal Property coverage form?

   ❑ A. Buildings

   ❑ B. Furniture and fixtures

   ❑ C. Glass

   ❑ D. Valuable papers and records

11. Which of the following losses would be excluded under the Building and Personal Property coverage form if the insured building had been vacant for more than 60 days before the loss occurred?

   ❑ A. Attempted theft

   ❑ B. Sprinkler leakage when the insured had protected the system against freezing

   ❑ C. Vandalism

   ❑ D. Glass breakage

12. Which of the following is covered under the Builders Risk coverage form?
    - ○ A. Building under construction
    - ○ B. Foundation of the building under construction
    - ○ C. Fixtures, machinery, and equipment used to service the building if they will become a permanent part of the building and are located within 100 feet of the building
    - ○ D. All of the above

13. Up to what percent of the amount paid for direct loss will the insurance company pay for debris removal expense under the Business and Personal Property coverage form?
    - ○ A. 5
    - ○ B. 10
    - ○ C. 20
    - ○ D. 25

14. What is the limit on Pollutant Cleanup and Removal coverage under the Business and Personal Property coverage form?
    - ○ A. $10,000
    - ○ B. $20,000
    - ○ C. $25,000
    - ○ D. $50,000

15. What is the per-year policy limit for coverage of electronic data under the Business and Personal Property coverage form?
    - ○ A. $1,000
    - ○ B. $2,500
    - ○ C. $5,000
    - ○ D. $7,500

Exam Prep Answers

1. B is correct. Coverage for collapse is provided as an additional coverage in the Broad and Special Causes of Loss forms only. Volcanic eruption is covered under the Earthquake and Volcanic Eruption endorsement. (The other Causes of Loss forms cover volcanic action, which is not the same thing as volcanic eruption.) Loss arising out of a nuclear hazard is excluded under all Causes of Loss forms.

2. C is correct. Under this endorsement, all earthquake shocks or volcanic eruptions that occur within any 168-hour period constitute a single earthquake or volcanic eruption.

3. C is correct. The Basic and Broad Causes of Loss forms are named peril forms.

4. D is correct. All of the Causes of Loss forms cover sprinkler leakage.

5. B and C are correct. Collapse is not covered under the Basic Causes of Loss form.

6. B and C are correct. Inventory, furniture, and supplies would be covered under business personal property coverage.

7. A is correct. Fire department service charges are paid in addition to the limit of insurance, with no deductible.

8. D is correct. The first three choices are excluded, but animals are not excluded if they are boarded or held for sale.

9. C is correct. Most losses are paid at actual cash value. However, if the Coinsurance conditions are met and costs are $2,500 or less, the policy will pay the cost of building repair or replacement without taking depreciation into account.

10. C and D are correct. Stock, glass, valuable papers and records, and tenants improvements and betterments all have special valuation requirements.

11. A, C, and D are correct. Damage because of attempted theft, vandalism, or glass breakage is excluded after 60 days of vacancy. Damage in a vacant building because of sprinkler leakage is covered if the system was protected against freezing.

12. D is correct. The Builders Risk coverage form covers the building under construction and its foundation. Fixtures, machinery, equipment used to service the building, and the insured's building materials and supplies can be covered if they will become a permanent part of the building and are located within 100 feet of the building.

13. D is correct. Under the Business and Personal Property coverage form, the insurance company will pay up to 25% of the amount paid for a direct loss for debris removal expense. An additional $10,000 of coverage is available if the debris removal expense exceeds the 25% limit or the total loss exceeds the policy limits.

14. A is correct. The policy will pay up to $10,000 for pollutant cleanup and removal if the pollution was caused by a covered peril.

15. B is correct. The Business and Personal Property coverage form will only pay up to $2,500 in any one policy year for losses to electronic data.

Ocean and Inland Marine Insurance

Terms you'll need to understand:

- ✓ Hull insurance
- ✓ Cargo insurance
- ✓ Freight insurance
- ✓ Protection and indemnity insurance
- ✓ Trip or voyage coverage
- ✓ Open cargo coverage
- ✓ Perils of the sea

- ✓ Jettison
- ✓ Barratry
- ✓ General average loss
- ✓ Particular average loss
- ✓ Annual transit policy
- ✓ Trip transit policy
- ✓ Motor truck cargo policy

Concepts you'll need to master:

- ✓ Warehouse to warehouse coverage
- ✓ Implied warranties
- ✓ Nationwide definition
- ✓ Commercial property floaters
- ✓ Filed versus nonfiled forms
- ✓ Domestic shipments

- ✓ Instrumentalities of transportation and communication
- ✓ Bailee's customer policies
- ✓ Equipment floaters
- ✓ Business floaters
- ✓ Dealers policies

Marine insurance is a type of insurance that protects property wherever it is—on land or sea. There are two types of Marine insurance: *Ocean Marine* and *Inland Marine*. The origin of marine coverages stems from its relationship to transportation. Initially, Marine insurance covered property in transit by sea. The field gradually expanded to cover property while being loaded and unloaded, while sitting on docks or in warehouses, and while being transported over land between points of origin and destination. Eventually, it evolved even further to include almost any type of property that is capable of being moved and structures at fixed locations that have some relationship to elements of transportation. In addition to property coverage, some marine policies include elements of liability coverage. As it exists today, it is a very broad field of insurance offering a great deal of flexibility for covering a variety of risks.

Ocean Marine Insurance

We'll begin by studying Ocean Marine insurance, which covers cargo and ships in transit over sea. It is one of the oldest types of insurance and one of the first to provide open peril coverage for the insured's property. There are no standardized forms.

Categories of Ocean Marine Insurance

There are four categories of Ocean Marine insurance: Hull insurance, Cargo insurance, Freight insurance, and *Protection and Indemnity (P&I)*.

Hull insurance provides *Physical Damage coverage* for the ship itself while in transit on oceans, rivers, and lakes. Coverage can be obtained for a single vessel or an entire fleet. *Limited Liability insurance* can also be included through the *Running Down clause*, which protects the owner if he or she is held liable for the negligent operation of the vessel in damaging another ship.

Cargo insurance covers goods while they are in transit over water. Through the use of the *Warehouse to Warehouse clause*, coverage can also be extended to include coverage from the property's point of origination to its point of destination. Coverage can be purchased on a *trip* or *voyage basis*, or it can be purchased on an *open cargo basis*. An insured who frequently ships cargoes, such as an importer or exporter, would arrange for open cargo coverage.

 The Warehouse to Warehouse clause not only includes ocean travel, but also any incidental journey by land. For instance, the inland trip from the warehouse to the shipping dock, or from the dock to the warehouse, would be covered even if it involved a considerable number of miles.

Trip or voyage coverage protects only a specific shipment. An open cargo policy applies for a period of time, such as a policy year, and automatically protects shipments as soon as the insured's interest begins.

Freight insurance protects the insured against the loss of shipping costs. This coverage can be written separately or included with Hull insurance or Cargo insurance, depending on how the shipping costs are handled. When shipping is prepaid by the owner of the cargo, he or she would lose the shipping charges if the cargo is lost. In these cases, it is common for the owner to purchase Freight coverage along with the Cargo insurance. Alternatively, if the freight is not prepaid and the cargo is lost, it is the shipper or vessel owner who would stand to lose. A ship owner can protect against this loss by adding Freight insurance to the Hull coverage.

Finally, *Protection and Indemnity (P&I) insurance* provides Marine Liability insurance. P&I protects against liability for

➤ Job-related injuries to sailors

➤ Injuries to stevedores, longshore workers, or harbor workers

➤ Damage to cargo through negligence

➤ Damage to other property not caused by collision

➤ Damage to other property or another boat resulting from collision

Characteristics of Ocean Marine Insurance

To fully understand Ocean Marine insurance, you need a thorough understanding of the terminology and practices that are a part of the shipping industry and the marine trade—a task that goes beyond the scope of this book. We can, however, introduce you to a few of the more important characteristics of Ocean Marine insurance.

Ocean Marine insurance can be issued on a named peril or open peril basis. Waterborne properties are subject to a wide variety of perils, such as fire, explosion, pilferage, contact with other cargo, and leakage or damage by ship sweat (condensation that forms on the inside walls of the ship's hull). They are also subject to a group of perils known as *perils of the sea*. These perils, which often result from stormy weather, include

➤ Unusual wind or wave action

➤ Stranding (such as when a ship becomes immobilized on a sandbar or goes up a waterway and can't return)

➤ Lightning

➤ Collision

➤ Sinking

Another peril covered under Ocean Marine contracts is *jettison*. Jettison is a voluntary action to rid the ship of cargo to prevent further peril. Jettison is permitted if the action is taken to save the remaining property. The loss incurred by sacrificing a portion of the cargo will be reimbursed.

Another peril unique to Ocean Marine forms is called *barratry*. Barratry refers to illegal acts committed willfully by the ship's master or crew for the purpose of damaging the ship or its cargo. It includes hijacking, abandonment, or embezzlement.

In Marine insurance, the term used to indicate a partial loss is *average*. Jettison is known as a *general average loss*. This means that partial loss resulting from a sacrifice of cargo to save remaining property is shared by all other property owners, including the owners of the ship. Each owner shares in the general average loss in proportion to his or her total property interest, regardless of which owner's property was actually jettisoned.

Any other partial loss that does not arise from a general sacrifice of property is known as a *particular average loss*. There is no distribution of the loss among all property owners for particular average; instead, each owner bears whatever loss his or her own property sustained.

Because of the far ranging travels of ships and their cargoes, Ocean Marine insurers are particularly dependent on *implied warranties*. Implied warranties are not written into the policy, but they carry the same weight as those that are written. Breach of an implied warranty can void the contract. These warranties include

➤ **Seaworthiness:** The vessel must be fit for the voyage, not overloaded, and have a competent crew.

➤ **Conditions of cargo:** The cargo must be warranted to be sound and packed properly.

➤ **Legality:** The trip must involve a lawful enterprise.

➤ **No deviation in voyage:** The ship must follow an agreed route, with no changes in destination and no untoward delays.

 Reliance on implied warranties is intended to support both safety and public policies. The insurer has a right to expect that the vessel is fit, that the crew is properly trained, and that the purpose of the voyage is not to circumvent laws. If a ship is dangerously overloaded or is carrying illegal contraband, the insurer will not cover any losses that occur.

Inland Marine Insurance

Inland Marine insurance first developed as an extension of Ocean Marine insurance to provide coverage for cargo that travels over land instead of by sea. From there, however, Inland Marine insurance branched out to provide very broad coverage on a wide variety of portable property in addition to the coverage it continues to provide for cargo in transit.

Nationwide Definition

To help identify the kinds of risks that are eligible for either Ocean or Inland Marine insurance, the insurance industry developed the *Nationwide Definition*. The Definition lists six categories of eligible Marine risks:

➤ Imports

➤ Exports

➤ Domestic shipments

➤ Instrumentalities of transportation or communication

➤ Personal property floater risks

➤ Commercial property floater risks

The first two categories, imports and exports, are covered by Ocean Marine insurance. Personal property floater risks are covered by Personal Inland Marine insurance, which we studied in Chapter 10, "Miscellaneous Personal Insurance." The three remaining categories represent the following risks, which are eligible for Commercial Inland Marine insurance:

➤ Domestic shipments

➤ Instrumentalities of transportation or communication

➤ Commercial property floater risks

A wide variety of seemingly unrelated risks falls into the categories eligible for Commercial Inland Marine coverage. Usually, the characteristic that makes them eligible is an element of portability, although there are exceptions. But as a general rule, Inland Marine insurance does not cover stationary property such as real estate, furniture, fixtures, or merchandise while it is being manufactured.

Domestic shipments are covered through a variety of Inland Marine *Transportation forms* that cover property being transported.

Instrumentalities of transportation or communication include forms that cover property related to transportation or communication, such as bridges, pipelines, and television towers.

Commercial property floater risks embrace a number of subcategories of Inland Marine forms, including *Bailee's Customer forms*, *Equipment forms*, *Business floaters*, and *Dealers policies*.

Filed and Nonfiled Forms

Because Inland Marine insurance can cover such a wide variety of mobile property, there is no one standard policy. Instead, each type of property requires a unique policy form, with each company preparing its own contracts. The only exception is *filed (controlled) classes* of Inland Marine insurance that can be written under the ISO Commercial Inland Marine coverage part of the Commercial Package policy. They include these coverage forms:

➤ Mail

➤ Physicians and surgeons equipment

➤ Theatrical property

➤ Film

➤ Commercial articles

➤ Accounts receivable

➤ Valuable papers and records

➤ Signs

➤ Jewelers block

➤ Floor plan

➤ Equipment dealers

➤ Camera and musical instrument dealers

Nonstandardized forms for other Inland Marine coverages not specifically listed are known as *nonfiled classes* or *forms*.

Filed Forms

We'll begin by looking at filed forms, those that can be written under the ISO Commercial Package Policy program.

Commercial Inland Marine Coverage Part

The Commercial Inland Marine coverage part requires the following forms in addition to the Common Policy declarations and the Common Policy conditions:

➤ Commercial Inland Marine declarations form

➤ Commercial Inland Marine conditions form

➤ One or more of the 12 filed coverage forms we listed earlier

When Inland Marine coverage is issued as a mono-line policy, the Commercial Inland Marine declarations form may be combined with the Common Policy declarations to form a single declarations form.

All the filed coverage forms provide open peril coverage that is typical of Inland Marine coverages. Nonfiled forms may be written on a named peril or open peril basis.

Commercial Inland Marine Conditions

The *Commercial Inland Marine conditions* are divided into two sections: *Loss Conditions* and *General Conditions*. Many of the conditions are similar to those contained in other policies, such as Abandonment, Pairs, Sets or Parts, Appraisal, and No Benefit to Bailee.

The *Insured's Duties in the Event of Loss* are similar to what is found in other Property forms. The insured must

➤ Notify the police if a law might have been broken

➤ Give the insurer prompt notice of the loss and describe the property involved

➤ Give the insurer a description of how, when, and where the loss occurred as soon as possible

➤ Take reasonable steps to protect the property from further damage, set damaged property aside if feasible, and keep a record of expenses related to the loss

➤ Make no statement that assumes any obligation or admits any liability without the insurer's consent

➤ Permit the insurer to inspect the property and records proving loss

➤ Submit to questioning under oath if requested

➤ Send a signed, sworn statement of loss within 60 days after it is request-ed by the insurer

➤ Promptly send the insurer any legal papers or notices concerning the loss

➤ Cooperate with the investigation or settlement of the claim

The *Other Insurance* condition states that if the insured has other insurance written *on the same basis* as the Commercial Inland Marine form, the Commercial Inland Marine form pays on a *pro rata basis.* If the other cover-age is *not written on the same basis,* Commercial Inland Marine coverage is excess over any other insurance that applies to the loss, regardless of whether the insured can collect under the other insurance.

The *Reinstatement of Limit After Loss* condition provides that the limit of insurance will not be reduced by payment of any claim, except for a total loss of a scheduled item. When this occurs, the insurer will refund the unearned premium on that item.

Losses are valued on an actual cash value basis or the cost to restore or replace the property, whichever is less. The property's value is determined at the time of the loss.

Mail Coverage Form

In this section, we look at each of the filed Commercial Inland Marine cov-erage forms. Then, we look at some of the key nonfiled forms written in the industry. The first coverage form we talk about falls into the *Domestic ship-ments (Transportation forms)* category of the Nationwide Definition.

The *Mail coverage form* provides open peril coverage against loss to property in transit by registered mail, first class mail, certified mail, or express mail. Covered property includes bonds, stock certificates, certificates of deposit and other securities, stamps, money orders, checks, and other documents and papers of value except food stamps, unsold traveler's checks, and money. When sent by registered mail, covered property also includes bullion, plat-inum, and other precious metals, jewelry, watches, precious and semiprecious stones, unsold traveler's checks, food stamps, and money.

Property is covered while it is in the care, custody, and control of a govern-ment postal service and while in transit by a common carrier or messenger to and from a government post office. Property is covered until it is deliv-ered to the address shown on the package or returned to the sender in the event of nondelivery.

If the value of any mailing was not recorded properly because of error or oversight, the insurer will pay the actual value of the property in the event of loss if promptly notified after discovery of the error or oversight. However, if the value of property in any one shipping exceeds the limit of insurance, the insurer will only pay the proportion of a loss that the limit of insurance bears to the actual value.

In the event of loss, the value of covered property is its actual value, but not less than its market value, on the date of mailing. Coverage is always written on a reporting basis, with reports required within 30 days after the end of each reporting period.

Physicians and Surgeons Equipment Coverage Form

There are no filed forms that fall under the *Instrumentalities of transportation and communication* category of the Nationwide Definition. The remaining filed forms all fall within the final category of the Definition: *Commercial property floater risks.* As we've already mentioned, this category can be further divided into several subcategories. We look first at the *Equipment floater* sub-category.

The *Physicians and Surgeons Equipment coverage form* covers medical and dental instruments on and off the premises, as well as furniture and fixtures at the office and the insured's interest in improvements and betterments. Medical and dental equipment of others used by the insured is also covered at the insured's option. Radium is not covered.

The form provides open peril coverage, with the following exclusions:

➤ Government action

➤ Nuclear hazard

➤ War and military action

➤ Marring, scratching, or exposure to light

➤ Breakage of tubes, bulbs, lamps, or articles made primarily of glass (does not apply to lenses)

➤ Delay, loss of use, loss of market, or any consequential loss

➤ Dishonest or criminal acts committed by the insured, the insured's employees, or anyone else with an interest in the property or to whom the property is entrusted (does not apply to carriers for hire or acts of destruction by employees)

➤ Artificially generated current that creates a short circuit or other electric disturbance within an article covered by the policy

➤ Voluntarily parting with property if induced to do so by a fraudulent scheme, trick, or false pretense

➤ Unauthorized instructions to transfer property to another person or place

➤ Neglect of an insured to protect property at the time of loss or after a loss

➤ Weather conditions

➤ Acts or decisions, or the failure to act or decide, of any person, group, or government body

➤ Faulty, inadequate, or defective planning, zoning, workmanship, repair, construction, materials, or maintenance

➤ Wear and tear, inherent vice, hidden or latent defect, or gradual deterioration

➤ Mechanical breakdown

➤ Insects, vermin, or rodents

➤ Corrosion, rust, dampness, cold, or heat

The Physicians and Surgeons Equipment coverage form also covers collapse of a building or structure when it is caused by one of the perils specified in the form and damage caused by theft or attempted theft to the building.

The insured must maintain any *protective safeguards* (such as a security service or automatic fire alarm system) that were in effect at the beginning of the policy period. If the insured fails to keep these safeguards in working condition and in operation when the business is closed, coverage at that location is suspended until the protective safeguards are back in operation.

Theatrical Property Coverage Form

Another Equipment floater, the *Theatrical Property coverage form,* covers scenery, props, and costumes used by a theater group in a specific production identified in the declarations. Also covered is theatrical property in the insured's care, custody, or control or on which the insured has made partial payments. The form does not cover

➤ Buildings or their improvements and betterments

➤ Vehicles (unless actually used on the stage in the covered production)

➤ Jewelry with precious or semiprecious stones, metals, or alloys

➤ Accounts, bills, currency, deeds, money, securities, and admission tickets

➤ Animals

➤ Contraband

➤ Property being illegally transported or traded

The form provides open peril coverage and contains many of the exclusions we've described in relation to other Commercial Inland Marine forms. In addition, the form excludes

➤ Theft from an unlocked, unattended vehicle

➤ Unexplained disappearance

➤ Shortage found upon taking inventory

Collapse of a building or structure is also covered when it is caused by one of the perils specified in the form.

Film Coverage Form

The *Film coverage form* is also considered an Equipment floater. It provides open peril coverage for exposed motion picture film, soundtracks, video-tapes, and magnetic tapes that are used in the production scheduled in the declarations and that the insured owns or has in his or her custody or control. It does not cover cutouts, unused footage, positive prints or films, or library stock.

In addition to the exclusions found in all Commercial Inland Marine forms, the Film coverage form excludes loss resulting from

➤ Deterioration, atmospheric dampness, or changes in temperature

➤ Exposure of negative film to light

➤ Use of developing chemicals

➤ Developing, cutting, or printing of film or other laboratory work

➤ Electric or magnetic injury, disturbance, or erasure of electronic recordings or videotape (does not apply to damage caused by lightning)

Collapse coverage is included.

Covered property is valued on the basis of the cost of reproducing the lost or damaged property plus any reduction in value of undamaged parts of a production. The cost of the story, scenario, music rights, continuity, permanent sets, owned wardrobes, and props are not considered when valuing the property. The insured must use any means available to re-create the damaged property to reduce the amount of loss. Payment cannot exceed the value of the covered production as shown in the insured's books.

Property is covered until the full quota of positive prints or films is completed, the insured's interest in the property ends, or the policy expires or is cancelled, whichever occurs first.

The coverage territory includes the United States, its territories and possessions, and Canada. Property is also covered when it is located within 50 miles of these areas.

The insured is required to keep accurate business records and retain them for at least three years after the policy ends. The insured must also send the insurer a written report for each production when it is no longer covered under the policy. The report must include the actual cost, overhead expenses, and other expenses of the completed production and a list of each studio, laboratory, vault, and cutting room used and the period of time the policy covered property at these locations. The actual premium charged is based on this report, using the rates in effect at the time the coverage began. The premium is adjusted to reflect any difference between the actual premium owed and the premium paid.

Commercial Articles Coverage Form

The final coverage form in the Equipment floater subcategory is the *Commercial Articles coverage form*. It covers the interests of the owner of commercial cameras, musical instruments, and related equipment, as well as similar property of others that is in the insured's care, custody, or control.

The form provides open peril coverage, with essentially the same exclusions as other Commercial Inland Marine forms. Property is covered worldwide. It also covers collapse.

Additional acquired property is automatically covered for up to 30 days if it is a type of property already covered by the form. In the event of loss, the insurer will pay the lesser of 25% of the policy limit or $10,000. The insured is required to report any additional acquired property within 30 days and pay any additional premium required. If not reported, coverage automatically ends after 30 days.

Accounts Receivable Coverage Form

There are three *Business floaters* that fall within the Commercial property floater risk category of the Nationwide Definition: the Accounts Receivable coverage form, the Valuable Papers and Records coverage form, and the Sign coverage form.

The *Accounts Receivable coverage form* reimburses the insured for amounts that can't be collected from customers because of damage to the company's accounts receivable records. It also covers extra collection expenses and interest on any loans the insured must obtain to stay in business while collections are impaired. Accounts receivable records kept in storage away from the premises are not covered.

In addition to the usual exclusions, the Accounts Receivable coverage form does not cover loss resulting from

➤ Alteration, falsification, concealment, or destruction of accounts receivable records done to conceal wrongful acts

➤ Bookkeeping, accounting, or billing errors or omissions

➤ Electrical or magnetic injury, disturbance, or erasure of electronic recordings caused by

 ➤ Programming errors or faulty machine instructions

 ➤ Faulty installation or maintenance of data processing equipment or components

 ➤ An occurrence that takes place more than 100 feet from the insured's premises

 ➤ Interruption of electrical power supply, power surge, blackout, or brownout that occurs more than 100 feet from the insured's premises

Any loss that requires an audit of records or inventory computation to prove its existence is not covered.

In addition to the collapse coverage provided by other Commercial Inland Marine forms, the Accounts Receivable coverage form covers loss of records when removed from the premises to protect them from imminent loss. Removal coverage applies only if the insured gives written notice of the removal within 10 days.

If the insured cannot accurately establish the amount of accounts receivable outstanding at the time of loss, the average monthly amounts receivable for the preceding 12-month period will be used. That amount is then adjusted for normal fluctuations in the amount receivable or demonstrated variance from the average for the month in which the loss occurred. The following will be subtracted from the total amount of accounts receivable:

➤ The amount of accounts for which there is no loss

➤ The amount of accounts that the insured is able to reestablish and collect

➤ An amount to allow for probable bad debts that the insured is normally unable to collect

➤ Unearned interest and service charges

To the extent that any loss is paid by the insurer, any later recovery of amounts receivable must be returned to the insurer. Recoveries in excess of the amount paid by the insurer do not have to be returned.

The insured must keep all accounts receivable records in receptacles described in the declarations when the business is closed and when the records are not in use.

Valuable Papers and Records Coverage Form

Another form in the business floaters category is the *Valuable Papers and Records coverage form*, which reimburses the insured for the cost of replacing damaged items such as manuscripts, films, maps, drawings, deeds, and books that belong to the insured or are in the insured's care, custody, or control. Money and securities are not covered.

The collapse and removal coverages previously described in this section are included. The form also pays up to $5,000 for loss to covered property while it is away from the premises unless a higher limit is specified in the declarations.

Important exclusions include errors or omissions in processing or copying and electrical or magnetic injury, disturbance, or erasure of electronic recordings.

The value of each item of property that is specifically declared and described in the declarations is the applicable limit for that item. If property is recovered after the loss is settled, the insured may choose to have the property returned, with an adjustment made to the amount already paid.

The insured must keep all valuable papers and records in receptacles described in the declarations when the business is closed and when the records are not in use.

Signs Coverage Form

The final form in the Business floaters category is the *Signs coverage form*, which insures businesses against loss to neon, fluorescent, automatic, or mechanical electric signs and lights. The form covers the insured's signs and similar property of others in the insured's care, custody, or control.

Breakage during transportation or during installation, repairing, or dismantling is not covered. Also excluded is artificially generated current that creates a short circuit or other electric disturbance within a covered item.

The standard collapse coverage is included.

Jewelers Block Coverage Form

There are several filed forms in the *Dealers policy* subcategory of Commercial property floater risks. These policies represent an exception to the general rule of mobile property. Although dealers do need occasional coverage for property away from the premises, their primary coverage need is for damage to merchandise while on the business premises.

The first Dealers policy we cover is the *Jewelers Block coverage form*, which covers

➤ The insured's stock in trade, which includes jewelry, precious and semi-precious stones, precious metals and alloys, and other stock used in the business

➤ Merchandise that has been sold but has not yet been delivered to the customer, and therefore remains on the insured's property

➤ Similar property of others *who are not in the jewelry trade* in the insured's care, custody, or control

➤ Similar property of others *in the jewelry trade* in the insured's care, custody, or control, but only to the extent of the insured's legal liability for the property or the amount of money actually advanced by the insured

The form does not cover property

➤ Sold under a deferred sales payment agreement after it leaves the insured's premises

➤ At an exhibition promoted or financially assisted by a trade association or public authority

➤ Exhibited in showcases or show windows away from the premises

➤ While being worn by the insured, an employee, or a family member of either (does not apply to watches worn solely for purposes of adjustment)

➤ In transit by

   ➤ mail (unless sent by registered mail)

   ➤ express carriers, railroads, or waterborne or air carriers (does not apply to property accompanied by a passenger and transported by passenger parcel or baggage services)

   ➤ motor carriers (does not apply to shipments by a carrier operating exclusively as a merchant's parcel delivery service, by an armored car service, or by parcel transportation or baggage services of passenger bus lines)

The Jewelers Block coverage form contains two optional coverages. *Show Windows coverage* covers theft of stock from a show window when the window is cut or smashed. *Money coverage* covers theft of money from locked safes or vaults on the insured's premises. The form also covers collapse of a building or structure when it is caused by one of the perils specified in the form and damage caused by theft or attempted theft to the building.

In addition to the exclusions common to Commercial Inland Marine forms, the Jewelers Block coverage form excludes

➤ Water damage to property at the insured's premises

➤ Theft from any vehicle unless the insured, an employee, or other person whose only duty is to attend the vehicle is actually in or on the vehicle when the theft occurs (does not apply to property in the custody of the post office or other carriers)

➤ Unexplained disappearance

➤ Shortage found upon taking inventory

➤ Shortage of property claimed to have been shipped when the package is received in good condition with the seals unbroken

➤ Dishonest or criminal acts committed by the insured, his or her employees, or anyone else to whom the property is entrusted

➤ Insufficient or defective packing

➤ Breakage of fragile articles

In the event of loss, the value of the property is determined at the time of loss and is the lesser of

➤ Actual cash value

➤ Cost to restore the property to its condition immediately before the loss

➤ Cost to replace the property

➤ The lowest figure listed in the insured's inventories, stock books, stock papers, or lists existing at the time of loss

Antique or historical value is not considered in the value of the property.

The insured must maintain any *protective safeguards* (such as a security service or automatic fire alarm system) that were in effect at the beginning of the policy period. If the insured fails to keep these safeguards in working condition and in operation when the business is closed, coverage at that location is suspended until the protective safeguards are back in operation.

The insured must take a physical inventory at least once every 12 months and maintain detailed records of inventory, purchases, sales, property of others, and property off premises. These records must be retained for 3 years after the policy ends.

Floor Plan Coverage Form

Another type of Inland Marine Dealers policy is the *Floor Plan coverage form*. It covers stock that is subject to a floor plan arrangement in which a dealer borrows money from a lender with which to pay for merchandise. This "encumbered" merchandise can then be insured under a Floor Plan policy. Coverage might be written to cover the interest of the dealer, the lending institution, or both. Property is not covered after the insured's interest in it ceases or after it is sold, delivered, or otherwise disposed of.

Excluded are

➤ Water damage to property at the insured's premises

➤ Bankruptcy, foreclosure, or similar proceedings

➤ Artificially generated current that creates a short circuit or other electrical disturbance within an article covered by the policy

➤ Breakage of glass or other fragile articles

➤ Damage to property in the open caused by rain, hail, sleet, snow, or freezing

Collapse coverage is included.

The condition regarding maintaining inventory records discussed previously in this section also applies to the Floor Plan coverage form.

A number of conditions appear in the Floor Plan coverage form that are not included in the other Commercial Inland Marine forms. The *Transit Coverage in the Event of Cancellation* condition states that if the policy is cancelled, property already in transit will be covered until it reaches its destination.

When coverage is written on a *dual interest basis*, the policy provisions are binding on all parties. However, the protection given a secured lender will not be impaired by failure of another party to comply with policy provisions if the secured lender diligently tried to comply with all provisions.

Coverage is written on a *reporting basis*. The insured must file reports of values within 30 days after the end of each month. Premiums will be computed according to monthly rates. The insurer is not liable for loss in excess of the amount of insurance written even if reported values exceed the limit of insurance.

If the insured has not filed any report at the time of a loss, the insurer is only liable for 90% of the limit of insurance written. If the insured fails to make a report when required, the insurer is only liable for the amount last reported. The penalty for underreporting values is a proportional reduction in recovery for a loss. Coverage is rerated at each anniversary. The insured must furnish information required for rerating purposes within 30 days after each anniversary.

Equipment Dealers Coverage Form

The *Equipment Dealers coverage form* is used to cover dealers of mobile equipment and construction equipment. It covers the dealer's stock in trade consisting primarily of mobile agricultural equipment and construction equipment. It also covers property of others in the dealer's care, custody or control. It does not cover

➤ Automobiles, trucks, motorcycles, aircraft, and watercraft

➤ Money, securities, accounts, and bills

➤ Property in the course of manufacture

➤ Property that is leased, rented, or sold, including property sold under a deferred payment sales agreement

➤ Furniture, fixtures, office supplies, improvements and betterments, machinery, tools, patterns, dies, molds, and models

➤ Property of others described in the declarations

Important exclusions include

➤ Water damage to property at the premises

➤ Unexplained disappearance

➤ Shortages found upon taking inventory

➤ Artificially generated current that creates a short circuit or electrical disturbance within an article covered by the policy

The form includes Collapse coverage and covers damage caused by theft or attempted theft to the building.

Debris Removal coverage pays expenses to remove the debris of covered property that is damaged by a covered cause of loss, subject to a limit of 25% of the amount paid for the direct physical loss plus the amount of the deductible. However, if the amount of the debris removal expenses and the direct loss exceeds the limit of insurance, or if the total debris removal expense exceeds the 25% limitation, the insurer will pay up to an additional $5,000 for debris removal costs. The expenses must be reported to the insurer within 180 days of the date of loss or the end of the policy period, whichever is earlier.

Pollutant Cleanup and Removal coverage pays expenses to extract pollutants from land or water if the release or discharge of the pollutants resulted from a covered cause of loss that occurred during the policy period. The most the insurer will pay is $10,000 for all such expenses arising during each separate 12-month period of coverage under the policy. The expenses must be reported to the insurer within 180 days of the date of loss or the end of the policy period, whichever is earlier.

The conditions regarding protective safeguards and maintaining inventory records discussed earlier also apply to the Equipment Dealers coverage form.

The value of *unsold property* is the lesser of ACV, the cost to restore the property, or the cost to replace it. Property that is *sold but not delivered* is valued at its net selling price after all allowances and discounts. The value of property of others in the insured's care, custody, or control is the lesser of the amount for which the insured is liable or ACV. The value of the insured's labor and materials is considered both cases.

Camera and Musical Instrument Dealers Coverage Form

The final form in the Dealers category is the *Camera and Musical Instrument Dealers coverage form*. It covers the insured's stock in trade as well as customer property in the insured's care, custody, or control, such as an instrument or camera that is being repaired, cleaned, or adjusted. It does not cover

➤ Property that has been sold and delivered to customers, including property sold under a deferred payment sales agreement

➤ Money, securities, accounts, or bills

➤ Furniture, fixtures, office supplies, improvements and betterments, machinery, patterns, molds, and models

➤ Property that is in the mail (does not apply to property sent by registered or government insured mail)

Excluded are

➤ Earthquake damage to property at the insured's premises

➤ Water damage to property at the insured's premises

➤ Theft from an unattended, unlocked vehicle with no visible signs of forced entry

➤ Marring and scratching

➤ Exposure to light

➤ Breakage of tubes, bulbs, lamps, or items made largely of glass (except lenses)

➤ Unexplained disappearance

➤ Shortage found upon taking inventory

➤ Artificially generated current that creates a short circuit or other electrical disturbance within an item covered under the policy

Collapse and theft damage coverages are included. The conditions concerning protective safeguards and maintaining inventory records also apply to this form.

Losses to unsold property, sold property, and property of others are valued on the same basis as the Equipment Dealers coverage form. For negatives, positives, or prints, their value is the cost of unexposed film or developing paper, including labor and materials.

Nonfiled Forms

Now that you're familiar with some popular filed Inland Marine forms, we'll turn our attention to nonfiled forms: those that cannot be included in the ISO Commercial Package policy.

Domestic Shipments

The Domestic shipments category of the Nationwide Definition includes a number of nonfiled Inland Marine Transportation forms that provide coverage for shipments traveling by truck, train, air, or mail. We've already mentioned the filed Mail coverage form and the nonfiled Parcel Post policy.

Businesses that ship or receive merchandise need coverage against loss to their cargoes while they are in transit. Common carriers—those who hold themselves out to the public to ship goods—must accept a certain amount of liability for losses to cargo. (These obligations are set forth in the *bill of lading* that must be issued to each business for whom the carrier ships goods.) However, there are many losses for which the carrier is not responsible. Even when the carrier is liable for loss to cargo in its custody, reimbursement of the loss might be uncertain. The various Inland Marine Transportation forms were developed to cover this exposure.

The *Annual Transit policy* protects the shipper or receiver of goods against loss to goods in transit. Coverage is available on a named peril basis, protecting against such losses as fire, windstorm, collision, and theft, or on an open peril basis. The policy covers all the insured's incoming or outgoing shipments during the year.

The *Trip Transit policy* is similar to the Annual Transit policy. However, it is used to insure single shipments of goods for companies that have only occasional shipments to insure. Coverage extends from the time and point of origination to the time and point of destination.

The nonfiled *Motor Truck Cargo policy* covers cargo while it is being transported in a truck. It protects the *carrier*, instead of the shipper, for liability for loss to domestic shipments in transit. The carrier has a responsibility to deliver goods entrusted to it unharmed. There are only a few things, such as *acts of God* (floods, tornadoes) or the *shipper's own neglect* (poor packing), for which the carrier is not liable. This form is sometimes called the *Motor Truck Cargo—Truckers form*.

A variation of Motor Truck Cargo insurance provides coverage known as *owner's goods on owner's trucks* to companies that transport their own goods. It provides direct damage coverage instead of liability coverage. This form might also be called the *Motor Truck Cargo—Shipper's form* or the *Motor Truck*

Cargo—Owner's form. Some companies issue a *Motor Truck Cargo—Combination form* that provides both liability coverage for the shipment of another's goods and direct damage coverage for the shipment of the insured's own goods on its own trucks.

Instrumentalities of Transportation and Communication

The next category of the Nationwide Definition, Instrumentalities of transportation and communication, includes forms covering property such as bridges, tunnels, oil pipelines, loading docks, and radio and TV towers.

 Although this property itself is not portable, it is directly connected with elements of transportation and is subject to many of the same perils as property in transit. For example, bridges and tunnels support vehicle traffic, pipelines transport oil or gas, and radio and TV towers are used to transport data.

Commercial Property Floater Risks

A number of nonfiled forms fall under the Commercial property floater risk category of the Nationwide Definition.

Bailee's Customer Policies

Bailee's policies are a subcategory for which there are no filed forms but for which there are several important nonfiled forms.

Bailment is the delivery of property by the owner to someone else to be held for some special purpose, and then returned to the owner. An example of bailment is leaving your shoes at the repair shop to have them reheeled. The *bailee* is the one who receives the property; the one who owns the property is called the *bailor.*

Just as carriers have a responsibility for the safety of property in their custody, bailees also have a responsibility for property in their custody. If the property is damaged through the bailee's own fault, he or she will be liable to the customer for damage. But even when the property is damaged in a fire or some other disaster that is not the bailee's fault, the customer will expect to get the property back undamaged or be compensated for the loss. To retain the goodwill of the customer, the bailee will probably reimburse the customer. The *Bailee's Customer policy* reimburses the insured for damage to a customer's property that is in his or her care, regardless of whether the insured is liable for the damage, as long as the damage resulted from a covered peril.

Several different Bailee's Customer policies are available that are tailored to specific businesses, such as the *Cleaners, Dyers, and Laundries policy*. One unique peril covered by this form is *confusion of goods*, which covers the loss that can occur when the resulting damage from another loss has made it impossible to identify which garments belong to a particular customer.

Equipment Floaters

There are a number of nonfiled Equipment floaters—one of the most important of which is the *Contractors Equipment floater*.

The Contractors Equipment floater covers the heavy machinery, equipment, and tools a customer needs to conduct business. It covers the contractor on an open peril or named peril basis for loss to all types of tools, machinery, and equipment owned, rented, or borrowed by the insured. The property is protected from loss by fire, landslide, theft, and other perils while it is on the job site, on the way to and from a job site, and in temporary storage. Neither the Commercial Property nor the Commercial Auto policies provide the extensive coverage that can be obtained under the Contractors Equipment floater.

Business Floaters

We've already discussed several filed Business floaters. There are also two nonfiled forms in this subcategory of Commercial property floater risks.

A firm selling refrigeration systems, elevators, or other pieces of large equipment might have a great deal of property on location awaiting or in the process of installation. Such installation and final testing can take months— even years. The *Installation policy* is an Inland Marine coverage that insures against loss to machinery, equipment, building materials, and supplies in transit to or being used with or during the course of installation, testing, building, renovating, or repair. It can be issued to cover the interest of the owner, the seller, or the contractor.

The *Electronic Data Processing Equipment floater* provides open peril coverage for computer hardware, software, and data that is owned by the insured or in the insured's care, custody, or control. Property in transit is covered. Optional breakdown coverage insures against damage to the equipment caused by mechanical breakdown, electrical disturbances, and temperature changes. Extra expense and business interruption coverage is also included.

Dealers Policies

In addition to the filed Dealers policies we've covered, nonfiled policies can be written for a number of dealers, including art, stamp, coin, and antique dealers. These policies are generally written on an open peril basis and cover property on the premises, off the premises, and while in transit provided that certain conditions are met.

Exam Prep Questions

1. A voluntary action to rid the ship of cargo to prevent further damage is called what?

   - ○ A. Jettison
   - ○ B. Particular average
   - ○ C. Barratry
   - ○ D. General average

2. The Motor Truck Cargo policy does which of the following?

   - ○ A. Insures a truck carrier for liability arising out of the transportation of cargo
   - ○ B. Covers any loss to cargo in transit, regardless of whether the carrier is liable for damage
   - ○ C. Insures the shipper for all incoming or outgoing shipments during the policy term
   - ○ D. Provides coverage for a shipper on a single shipment of goods

3. If the insurance company requests a proof of loss on a Commercial Inland Marine claim, the insured must submit it within how many days?

   - ○ A. 10 days
   - ○ B. 30 days
   - ○ C. 60 days
   - ○ D. 90 days

4. Which of these statements about the Mail coverage form are correct? Select all that apply.

   - ❏ A. It covers bonds, securities, and checks when they are sent by first class or certified mail.
   - ❏ B. Food stamps and money are always excluded under the policy.
   - ❏ C. Property is covered on a named peril basis.
   - ❏ D. Losses are valued on the basis of the property's actual value, but not less than its market value, on the date of mailing.

5. Which of the following can be covered under the Physicians and Surgeons Equipment coverage form? Select all that apply.

   - ❏ A. Medical instruments that are on the premises
   - ❏ B. Dental instruments that are off the premises
   - ❏ C. Radium
   - ❏ D. All of the above

6. Which of the following losses could be covered under the Theatrical Property coverage form?

   ○ A. Theft of costumes from an unlocked vehicle

   ○ B. Damage to a vehicle used as a prop in the production

   ○ C. Destruction of admission tickets for the production in a fire

   ○ D. All of the above

7. Which of the following properties can be covered under the Film coverage form? Select all that apply.

   ❑ A. Positive prints

   ❑ B. Motion picture film

   ❑ C. Soundtrack

   ❑ D. Unused footage

8. Which of these losses is covered under the Signs coverage form? Select all that apply.

   ❑ A. The electric sign above the insured's business is destroyed when it is blown down in a thunderstorm.

   ❑ B. The insured's neon sign is damaged when vandals throw rocks at it.

   ❑ C. A power surge blows out several tubes in the insured's fluorescent sign.

   ❑ D. All of the above.

9. Which of these losses is covered under the Jewelers Block coverage form, assuming that the insured has purchased all available optional coverages? Select all that apply.

   ❑ A. Theft of money from a locked vault on the insured's premises

   ❑ B. Theft of money from an unlocked vault on the insured's premises

   ❑ C. Theft of covered property from an unattended auto

   ❑ D. Theft of items on display in a show window when the window is smashed

10. How often is the insured required to submit reports of values under the Floor Plan coverage form?

   ○ A. Quarterly

   ○ B. Monthly

   ○ C. Annually

   ○ D. Weekly

11. Which of these losses would be covered under the Camera and Musical Instrument Dealers coverage form?

   ○ A. When the insured plugs in an electric guitar to demonstrate it for a customer, there is a short circuit that damages the guitar's wiring.

   ○ B. A clerk drops a camera when arranging digital cameras in a show window. The lens shatters.

   ○ C. Both A and B.

   ○ D. Neither A nor B.

12. The Electronic Data Processing Equipment floater covers what? Select all that apply.

❏ A. Computer hardware, but not software or data.

❏ B. Property in transit.

❏ C. It does not cover computer equipment that is in the insured's care, custody, or control.

❏ D. It can contain breakdown coverage.

Exam Prep Answers

1. A is correct. Jettison is a voluntary action to rid the ship of cargo to prevent further peril. Jettison is permitted if the action is taken to save the remaining property. The loss incurred by sacrificing a portion of the cargo will be reimbursed.

2. A is correct. This form protects the carrier, instead of the shipper, for liability for loss to domestic shipments in transit.

3. C is correct. The Commercial Inland Marine Conditions form states that the insured must send a signed, sworn statement of loss within 60 days after the insurer requests it.

4. A and D are correct. The Mail coverage form provides open peril coverage against loss to property in transit by registered, first class, certified, or express mail. Food stamps and money can be covered when sent by registered mail.

5. A and B are correct. This form covers medical and dental instruments on and off the premises, furniture and fixtures at the office, and the insured's interest in improvements and betterments. Radium is not covered.

6. B is correct. Vehicles are covered if they are actually used on the stage in the covered production. Admission tickets are not covered property. Loss by theft from an unlocked, unattended vehicle is excluded.

7. B and C are correct. The Film coverage form covers exposed motion picture film, soundtracks, videotapes, and magnetic tapes used in the production scheduled in the declarations and that the insured owns or has in his or her custody or control. It does not cover cutouts, unused footage, positive prints or films, or library stock.

8. A and B are correct. Loss caused by artificially generated current that creates a short circuit or other electrical disturbance within a covered item is not covered.

9. A and D are correct. The Show Windows optional coverage covers theft of stock from a show window when the window is cut or smashed. Money coverage covers theft of money from locked safes or vaults on the insured's premises. Theft from any vehicle is excluded unless the insured, an employee, or other person whose only duty is to attend the vehicle is actually in or on the vehicle when the theft occurs.

10. B is correct. Coverage under the Floor Plan form is written on a reporting basis. The insured must file reports of values within 30 days after the end of each month.

11. B is correct. This form excludes loss arising out of artificially generated current that creates a short circuit or other electrical disturbance within an item covered under the policy.

12. B and D are correct. The Electronic Data Processing Equipment floater provides open peril coverage for computer hardware, software, and data that is owned by the insured or in the insured's care, custody, or control. Property in transit is covered. Optional breakdown coverage insures against damage to the equipment caused by mechanical breakdown, electrical disturbances, and temperature changes.

Commercial General Liability Insurance

Terms you'll need to understand:

✓ Business liability exposure
✓ Premises and operations exposure
✓ Products-completed operations
✓ Indirect or contingent liability
✓ Retroactive date

✓ Bodily injury
✓ Property damage
✓ Occurrence
✓ Coverage territory
✓ Personal and advertising injury

Concepts you'll need to master:

✓ Occurrence coverage
✓ Claims-made coverage
✓ Coverage trigger
✓ Extended reporting periods
✓ Basic extended reporting period
✓ Supplemental extended reporting period
✓ Supplementary payments
✓ General aggregate limit
✓ Products-completed operations aggregate limit

✓ Personal and advertising injury limit
✓ Per occurrence limit
✓ Damages to premises rented to insured limit
✓ Medical expense limit
✓ Other insurance—contribution by equal shares
✓ Other insurance—contribution by limits

This chapter reviews Commercial General Liability coverages, which might be one of the most important forms of insurance for many businesses because of the potential of liability losses that could result in large settlements against the insured. The primary purpose of commercial liability insurance is to protect business assets and enable an enterprise to survive when accidents or injuries occur.

Business Liability Exposures

Commercial General Liability (CGL) insurance covers business liability exposures. Business liability is liability that arises out of the conduct of a business. Every business has a number of potential liability exposures, which we'll describe in this chapter.

Premises and Operations Exposure

One of the most significant exposures a business has is its *premises and operations exposure*: liability arising out of the business location or the activities of the business. This includes liability for bodily injury, property damage, and personal and advertising injury. Personal and advertising injury includes such things as slander, libel, copyright infringement, invasion of privacy, false arrest, wrongful entry onto another's premises, and malicious prosecution.

One example of the premises and operations liability exposure is a claim against Sandle Appliances for injuries a customer suffers when she slips and falls on a newly waxed floor inside the store. Another example is a claim against Breckenridge Manufacturers for libelous statements made about a competitor's products.

Products-Completed Operations Exposure

A business can also be exposed to liability by defects in its *products or completed operations*. Examples of this exposure include a claim against Hooks Bakery for injury resulting from the sale of spoiled cream puffs and a claim against Magic Carpets Inc. for injury that results when a customer steps on a carpet tack left behind by Magic's workers.

Indirect or Contingent Liability Exposure

A business may not only be held liable for its own actions, but in certain cases, it may be held liable for the actions of others. A business may have *indirect* or *contingent liability* for the actions of its employees, agents, contractors, or subcontractors. An example is a claim against First National Bank when a passerby is injured at the construction site of a new bank branch being built by Rolland Construction Company. Rolland Construction might be held directly liable, and First National Bank might also be held liable because Rolland was under contract by First National at the time. This indirect liability exposure is sometimes called *owners and contractors protective*.

Exposures Covered by Commercial General Liability Insurance

There are other types of liability exposures faced by businesses, including

➤ Work-related injuries to employees

➤ Pollution

➤ Contractual agreements in which the insured assumes liability

➤ Ownership, maintenance, or use of autos, watercraft, and aircraft

 Because of the unique nature of these liability exposures, they are either excluded outright from Commercial General Liability coverage or may be covered only in certain circumstances or for limited amounts. More complete protection for these liability exposures is usually available under contracts specifically designed to cover them. For example, work-related injuries to employees should be covered by Workers Compensation insurance, separate Pollution Liability coverage forms may be attached to a policy, and automobile exposures should be covered by Commercial Automobile insurance.

A business's liability for the premises and operations exposure, products-completed operations exposure, and indirect/contingent liability exposure can all be covered by a Commercial General Liability (CGL) policy.

Commercial General Liability Coverage Part

Commercial General Liability insurance may be included in a Commercial Package Policy or may be issued as a standalone policy. The coverage provided by the liability section of the Businessowners policy is similar to that provided by the CGL.

A Commercial General Liability coverage part must include the following:

➤ Common Policy declarations

➤ Common Policy conditions

➤ CGL declarations

➤ One or more CGL coverage forms

➤ Any mandatory endorsements

There are two primary CGL coverage forms: the *occurrence form* and the *claims-made form*. Although the two forms contain basically the same coverages, exclusions and conditions, they differ in how coverage under the form is activated, or "triggered."

Occurrence Form

Traditionally, liability policies have been written on an occurrence basis. This is a concept you should be familiar with. All the policies you have studied so far only cover losses that "occur" during the policy period and within the policy territory.

 Coverage under the occurrence form is triggered by damage or injury that happens during the policy period. The policy inception date and expiration date set clear boundaries for the application of the coverage.

Suppose that Joe Street is injured when a small piece of steel from the defective motor of a Niftycare lawnmower hits him in the eye. Provided the claim is otherwise covered, Niftycare's occurrence policy that was in effect at the time the injury occurred will apply to the loss, whether Joe makes his claim against Niftycare during the policy period or years later. There is coverage for any covered occurrence that happens during the policy period, even if the claim is made after the policy expires.

Suppose that on April 7, 2002, a ladder on which Brian Barker is standing falls apart. He lands on his back and complains of some slight pain, but nothing major. Because the injury seems so slight, Brian does not file a claim for the injury. In 2004, however, he experiences recurring back pain and consults a physician, who decides that the problem is a result of the 2002 injury. Brian files a claim against the manufacturer of the defective ladder, Newstep Ladder Company. Newstep had an occurrence CGL with Company A from 1997–2003; it took out a new occurrence CGL with Company B in 2004.

Company A would pay for Brian's injury because it occurred in 2002 when its policy was in effect.

Claims-Made Form

The occurrence form is suitable for many insureds, but for others, it is not the best choice.

Consider an individual who owns and renovates rental properties. From 1961–1971, he painted his properties with a lead-based spray made by a well-known manufacturer. In 1998, he is diagnosed as having developed lead poisoning from exposure to the lead-based paint. This individual might be able to recover damages from the paint manufacturer under all of the occurrence policies in effect between 1961 and 1971. This insurance can be interpreted in several ways as to how it should be paid, and the insurance companies might not have set aside adequate reserves to take care of such long-range exposures because there is no way of adequately predicting such losses. The claims-made form was developed to address these types of considerations.

 Coverage under the claims-made form is triggered when a claim is first made against the insured during the policy period, even if the actual injury or damage occurred at another time. This means that if Joe Street from our earlier example files a claim against Niftycare and it had claims-made coverage, it would be covered under the policy in effect when the claim is filed, rather than the policy in effect when the injury occurred. Under the claims-made form, claims filed during the policy period are covered, even when the occurrence took place prior to the effective date of the policy.

Retroactive Date

Although we said that a claim made during the policy period is covered by a claims-made form, even if the injury did not occur during that period, there might be a cutoff date sometime prior to the beginning of the policy period before which a claims-made policy will not pay. This is known as the *retroactive date*, and it provides some measure of protection for the insurer against previous losses that might have occurred before the claims-made form was written.

The retroactive date is listed in the CGL declarations. The insured has three options for the retroactive date:

➤ Use the same date as the policy-effective date

➤ Use an earlier date than the policy-effective date

➤ Use no retroactive date

An agent must be careful when selling a new CGL to avoid creating a coverage gap (a period of time during which the insured is without coverage). For instance, if the expiring policy is a claims-made form and it is replaced with another claims-made form, the retroactive date of the new policy should be the same as the old one to avoid a coverage gap.

Advancing the retroactive date can create a coverage gap. To avoid this situation, the rules by which claims-made CGL coverage is governed require that the insured give *written consent* to advancing the retroactive date. And, even with the insured's consent, the retroactive date can be advanced only for one of the following reasons:

➤ A different insurance company writes the new policy.

➤ A substantive change in the insured's operations has resulted in a greater exposure to loss.

➤ The insured did not provide the insurer with information the insured knew or should have known that would have been material to the insurance company's decision to accept the risk, or the insured did not provide information requested by the insurance company.

➤ The insured the policy period is covered by a claims-made form, even requests that the retroactive date be advanced.

Extended Reporting Periods

A gap can also occur when a claims-made policy is replaced by an occurrence form. However, a special feature built in to the claims-made form, called the the policy period is covered by a claims-made form, even *extended reporting period*, can help close potential coverage gaps.

Extended reporting periods (ERPs) provide coverage for claims made after the policy's expiration date. The policy provides an extended reporting period if

➤ The claims-made form is cancelled or not renewed.

➤ The insurer renews or replaces the form with insurance that has a retroactive date later than the date shown in the declarations of the current form.

➤ The insurer renews or replaces the form with an occurrence form.

Once an extended reporting period is in effect, it cannot be cancelled.

A basic extended reporting period of either 60 days or 5 years is available automatically and free of charge under specified conditions.

Let's first consider the 60-day basic ERP. When a claims-made policy is terminated, a 60-day basic ERP automatically becomes available. The insured does not have to apply for it, and no premium is charged. It provides automatic coverage for any valid claim made during the 60 days after the policy expires, as long as the incident occurred between the expiring policy's retroactive date and its expiration date.

Now, suppose that the insured is aware of an event that took place before the claims-made policy expired, but suspects that claims might first come in after the 60-day basic ERP. The insured has up to 60 days following policy expiration to report the occurrence or offense to the insurer. In this case, the 5-year basic ERP automatically applies. Claims for damages arising from the reported occurrence can be brought any time during the 5-year period.

A *Supplemental Extended Reporting Period endorsement* is also available. It provides an unlimited extension of the reporting period, although the event causing the claim must still occur between the retroactive date and the policy expiration date. This ERP takes effect at the end of either the 60-day or 5-year ERP, whichever applies. The insured must request this endorsement and pay an additional premium.

Extended reporting periods are commonly referred to as "tail coverage" because they cover losses that might trickle in after the end of a policy period. With liability insurance, there is often a delay between the occurrence of injuries and the actual reporting of claims. Occurrence forms have built-in tail coverage because the policy in effect at the time of a covered injury always applies. This is not true with claims-made coverage. If a claims-made policy is terminated or replaced with a different form of coverage, it is important to anticipate possible future claims and consider purchasing the Supplemental ERP in addition to the Basic ERP, which is automatically provided.

Definitions

Both versions of the CGL forms contain a Definitions section that helps clarify the intent of various coverages and conditions. This section is identical in both the occurrence and claims-made forms. In the following section of this chapter, we'll explain some of those definitions.

By insurance standards, an *auto* is a land motor vehicle, trailer, or semitrailer designed for travel on public roads, including any attached machinery or equipment. It does not include mobile equipment.

Mobile equipment is any of the following types of land vehicles, including any attached machinery or equipment:

➤ Bulldozers, farm machinery, forklifts, and other vehicles designed for use principally off public roads

➤ Vehicles maintained for use solely on or next to premises the insured owns or rents

➤ Vehicles that travel on crawler treads

➤ Vehicles, self-propelled or not, maintained primarily to provide mobility to permanently mounted power cranes, shovels, loaders, diggers, or drills or road construction or resurfacing equipment such as graders, scrapers, or rollers

➤ Vehicles that are not self-propelled and are maintained primarily to provide mobility to permanently attached equipment such as air compressors, pumps, and generators or cherry pickers and similar devices used to raise or lower workers

➤ Any vehicle that does not fit any of the previous descriptions and is maintained primarily for purposes other than the transportation of persons or cargo

Certain self-propelled vehicles are *not* mobile equipment and are considered autos:

➤ Self-propelled vehicles with permanently attached equipment designed primarily for snow removal, road maintenance (other than construction or resurfacing), or street cleaning

➤ Cherry pickers and similar devices that are mounted on automobile or truck chassis and used to raise or lower workers

➤ Self-propelled vehicles with attached air compressors, pumps, or generators

The definitions of "auto" and "mobile equipment" are mutually exclusive, and they are identical on CGL coverage forms and Commercial Auto coverage forms. This is to create a clear distinction between automobile and general liability coverages.

The *insured's product* includes any goods or products, other than real property, that are manufactured, sold, handled, distributed, or disposed of by the insured, others trading under the insured's name, or a person or organization whose business or assets the insured has acquired. It also includes

➤ Containers, materials, parts, or equipment furnished in connection with the product

➤ Warranties or representations made at any time with respect to the fitness, quality, durability, or performance of any part of the product

➤ The providing of or failure to provide warnings or instructions

The *insured's work* means work or operations performed by or on behalf of the insured and materials, parts, or equipment furnished in connection with such work or operations. It also includes warranties or representations made at any time with respect to the fitness, quality, durability, or performance of the insured's work and the providing of or failure to provide warnings or instructions.

Impaired property means tangible property other than the insured's product or the insured's work that cannot be used or is less useful because

➤ It incorporates the insured's product or work that is known or thought to be defective, deficient, inadequate, or dangerous.

➤ The insured failed to fulfill the terms of a contract or agreement.

The property is impaired only if it is currently in a state in which it cannot be used, but it can be restored to use by repair, replacement, adjustment, or removal of the insured's product or work, or by the insured fulfilling the terms of the contract or agreement.

Coverage territory usually means the described territory of the United States of America, including its territories and possessions, and Canada. It also means international waters or airspace if the injury or damage does not occur in the course of travel or transportation to or from any place not included in the described territory.

When the insured is determined to be responsible for damages in a lawsuit in the described territory, or in a settlement the insurer agrees to, the coverage territory includes all parts of the world if injury or damage arises out of

➤ Goods or products made or sold in the described territory

➤ Activities of a person whose home is in the described territory, but who is—for a short time—out of the described territory on business for the insured

➤ Personal and advertising offenses that take place through the Internet

Loading or unloading means handling of property in these circumstances:

➤ After it is accepted for movement into or onto an aircraft, watercraft, or auto

➤ While it is in or on an aircraft, watercraft, or auto

➤ While it is being moved from an aircraft, watercraft, or auto to the place where it is finally delivered

The definition of "loading or unloading" does not include the movement of property by a mechanical device, other than a hand truck, that is not attached to the aircraft, watercraft, or auto.

Pollutants are any solid, liquid, gaseous or thermal irritant or contaminant, including smoke, vapor, soot, fumes, acids, alkalis, chemicals, and waste. Waste includes materials to be recycled, reconditioned, or reclaimed.

The *products-completed operations hazard* includes all bodily injury (BI) and property damage (PD) occurring away from the premises owned or rented by the insured, and arising out of the insured's product or work, other than products that are still in the insured's physical possession and work that has not yet been completed or abandoned. Until the insured actually transfers products to others or completes work, liability exposures do not fall within the products-completed operations hazard.

A *leased worker* is a person leased to the named insured by a labor leasing firm under an agreement between the insured and labor leasing firm to perform duties related to the conduct of the insured's business.

A *temporary worker* is a person who is furnished to the insured to substitute for a permanent employee on leave or to meet seasonal or short-term work-load conditions.

The definition of *employee* includes leased workers, but not temporary workers.

A *volunteer worker* is a person who is not an employee, who donates his or her time and who is not paid by the insured or anyone else for work performed. A volunteer worker acts at the direction of the insured to perform duties determined by the insured.

CGL Coverages Provided

The CGL forms provide three coverages:

➤ Coverage A—Bodily Injury and Property Damage Liability

➤ Coverage B—Personal and Advertising Injury Liability

➤ Coverage C—Medical Payments

Coverage A—Bodily Injury and Property Damage Liability

Coverage A—Bodily Injury and Property Damage Liability pays those sums the insured becomes legally obligated to pay as damages because of bodily injury (BI) or property damage (PD) to which the insurance applies. To be covered, the BI or PD must be caused by an *occurrence*, which is defined in the CGL as an accident, including continuous or repeated exposure to the same general harmful conditions.

Remember that the occurrence form covers only BI or PD that occurs during the policy period. The insuring agreement of the occurrence form also stipulates that losses of a continuing or ongoing nature that were—prior to the policy period—known to the insured or employees authorized to report losses are not covered. The claims-made form covers BI or PD that occurred on or after the retroactive date, if any, and for which a claim for damages is first made against the insured during the policy period. A claim is considered to have been made when notice of the claim is received and recorded by any insured or by the insurer, whichever comes first.

In addition to paying those sums the insured is legally obligated to pay, the company has the right and duty to defend an insured against any suit alleging liability for damages to which the policy applies.

Exclusions—Coverage A

A number of important exclusions apply to Coverage A, including liability, such as the following:

➤ Liability arising out of intentional injury

➤ Liability that the insured assumes under a contract or agreement

➤ For those in the alcoholic beverage business, any liability imposed by law concerning alcoholic beverages

➤ Liability for work-related injuries covered under workers compensation or employer's liability laws

➤ Liability for most pollution losses that result in bodily injury, property damage, or clean-up costs

➤ Liability resulting from the maintenance, operation, or use of aircraft, autos, or watercraft, except as specified in the policy

The exclusion for liability assumed under contract has some important exceptions. Liability that the insured would have incurred even without assuming it under contract and liability assumed under insured, or incidental, contracts is covered. Insured contracts include leases, sidetrack agreements, easement agreements, contracts with municipalities required by ordinance, elevator maintenance agreements, and contracts relating to the insured's business under which the insured assumes another's liability.

As part of an insured contract, the insured might also assume liability for any defense costs incurred by or for a third party. These costs are considered covered damages if they are related to a loss that is insured by the policy. Because these costs are classified as covered damages, they reduce the policy's limit of liability. Under certain circumstances, the insurer can sometimes pay these costs *in addition to* the policy's limit of liability.

Also excluded under Coverage A is liability

➤ Arising out of the transportation of mobile equipment by auto or the use of mobile equipment in any prearranged racing or related activity, or while practicing or preparing for such an activity

➤ Assumed under a contract for war or warlike acts

➤ For damage to property owned, rented, or occupied by the insured or in the insured's care, custody, or control (does not apply to property and its contents for premises rented to the insured for seven consecutive days or less)

➤ For damage to the insured's own product arising out of the product itself

➤ For damage to the insured's own work

➤ For claims based on defects, deficiencies, inadequacies, or dangerous conditions in the insured's products or work and delays or failures to properly perform contracts

➤ Related to recall of the insured's products or work because of a known or suspected defect

➤ For bodily injury arising out of personal and advertising injury

An exception to certain exclusions under Coverage A protects the insured against legal liability for negligent acts that result in fire damage to a premises rented to the insured or temporarily occupied by the insured with the owner's permission.

Coverage B—Personal and Advertising Injury Liability

Coverage B provides Personal and Advertising Injury Liability coverage. It covers liability arising out of offenses such as libel or slander. Similar to Coverage A, Personal and Advertising Injury Liability coverage may be offered on either an occurrence or claims-made basis.

Exclusions—Coverage B

Liability arising out of any of the following is excluded under Coverage B:

➤ Knowingly inflicting injury that violates the rights of another

➤ Oral or written publication of material that the insured knows is false, but publishes anyway

➤ Material that was published before the effective date of the policy

➤ Criminal acts committed by or at the direction of the insured

➤ Liability assumed under contract, except for liability the insured would have incurred even without assuming it under contract

➤ Breach of contract

➤ Failure of goods, products, or services to conform with advertised quality or performance

➤ Incorrect price descriptions of goods, products, or services

➤ Any offense committed by an insured who is involved in the business of advertising, publishing, broadcasting, telecasting, or designing or determining content of websites for others

➤ Infringement of copyright, patent, trademark, trade secret, or other intellectual property rights (does not apply to infringement in the insured's advertisement of copyright, trade dress, or slogan)

➤ Any offense committed by an insured whose business is an Internet search, access, content, or service provider

➤ An electronic chatroom or bulletin board the insured hosts or owns, or over which the insured exercises control

➤ Unauthorized use of another's name or product in the insured's email address, domain name, or metatag

Coverage B also contains a blanket exclusion for *any type of pollution loss*. You might be wondering why an exclusion for pollution losses is needed for Coverage B. In the past, some insureds were able to recover pollution liability losses under Coverage B because the policy's definition of personal injury includes "wrongful entry into another's premises." The CGL now contains a pollution exclusion for Coverage B to prevent insureds from obtaining personal and advertising injury coverage for pollution liability.

Coverage A and B Supplementary Payments

The following *Supplementary Payments* are also available for Coverage A and B. These are paid in addition to the amounts paid for Liability claims under Coverages A and B and do not reduce the limits of insurance available for these coverages. Following are supplementary payments:

➤ All expenses incurred by the insurance company

➤ Up to $250 for the cost of bail bonds

➤ Cost of bonds to release attachments

➤ Reasonable expenses incurred by the insured to assist in the investigation and defense of a claim, including up to $250 per day for loss of earnings

➤ All costs taxed against the insured in a suit

➤ Prejudgment and postjudgment interest

➤ Defense costs for an indemnitee

Earlier, you learned that a third party's defense costs assumed by the insured under an insured contract are covered damages if they are related to a loss that is insured by the policy. Because these costs are classified as covered damages, they reduce the policy's limit of liability. The Supplementary Payments section provides that if certain conditions are met, the insurer will

➤ Pay the defense costs for an indemnitee—a party who is not an insured who is under contract to provide goods or services to an insured—in addition to the policy's limit of liability

➤ Provide a defense for the indemnitee

Among the conditions that must be met for this coverage to apply are that the insured and the indemnitee must be named in the same lawsuit and the liability assumed by the insured must be covered by the policy.

Coverage C—Medical Payments

Coverage C of the CGL coverage forms is Medical Payments. It pays for medical expenses incurred for bodily injury caused by an accident on premises the insured owns or rents, on ways next to premises the insured owns or rents, or arising from the insured's operations. To be covered, the expenses must be incurred and reported to the insurer within one year of the date of the accident. Medical payments are made without regard to fault, unlike other coverages under the CGL forms.

Exclusions—Coverage C

Excluded under Coverage C of the CGL are injuries

➤ To any insured or to a tenant or employee of the insured, including a person injured on a part of the insured's premises that he or she normally occupies (does not apply to the insured's volunteer workers)

➤ Payable under workers compensation or related laws

➤ Occurring to a person while he or she is taking part in athletics

➤ Included in the products-completed operations hazard (these would be paid under Coverage A)

➤ Excluded under Coverage A

➤ Related to war

Who Is an Insured?

This section describes various persons or entities that may be insureds under the policy.

Named Insured

In the CGL, who is considered an insured under the policy depends on how the named insured is designated in the CGL declarations: as an individual, partnership or joint venture, limited liability company, trust or organization other than a partnership, or joint venture or limited liability company. The potential insureds under a CGL policy are summarized in Table 15.1.

Table 15.1 Who Is An Insured		
Designation in Declarations	**Insureds**	**Restrictions**
Individual	Named insured Named insured's spouse	Only in connection with sole proprietorships.
Partnership or joint venture	Named insured Named insured's members and their spouses Named insured's partners and their spouses	Members, partners, and their spouses are insureds only in connection with conducting the business.
Limited liability company (a company structured like a corporation, but with additional tax and liability advantages for its members)	Named insured Members Managers	Members are insureds only in connection with conducting the business. Managers are insureds only in connection with their duties as managers.
Organization other than partnership, joint venture, or limited liability company	Named insured Executive officers and directors Stockholders	Executive officers and directors are insureds only in connection with conducting the business. Stockholders are insureds only in connection with liability as stockholders.
Trust	Named insured Trustees	Trustees are insureds only in connection with their duties as trustees.

Others Who May Be Insured

Each of the following is also an insured under CGL coverage:

➤ The named insured's employees for acts within the scope of their employment or while performing duties related to the conduct of the insured's business (does not include executive officers of a corporation or managers of a limited liability company)

➤ The insured's volunteer workers while performing duties related to the insured's business

➤ A nonemployee or organization while acting as real estate manager for the named insured

➤ If the named insured dies

> ➤ Any person or organization having temporary custody of the named insured's property, but only with respect to liability arising out of the maintenance or use of that property and only until a legal representative has been appointed for the insured
>
> ➤ The insured's legal representative with respect to those duties

➤ Any person driving mobile equipment that is registered to the named insured along a public highway with the insured's permission, and any person or organization responsible for the driver's conduct with respect to liability arising out of the operation of the equipment

Newly Acquired Organizations

CGL forms automatically cover newly formed or acquired organizations as a named insured under certain circumstances:

➤ The named insured must maintain ownership or majority interest of the new organization.

➤ No other similar insurance must be available to the organization.

➤ Automatic coverage is provided for 90 days or until the end of the policy period, whichever is earlier.

➤ Coverages A and B do not cover losses that occurred before the organization was acquired or formed.

Coverage continues after the automatic period expires if the insured reports the new organization to the insurer.

Coverage is not automatically provided for newly acquired or formed partnerships, joint ventures, or limited liability companies.

Limits of Insurance

The limits of insurance shown in the declarations are the most that will be paid, regardless of the number of insureds, claims made, suits brought, or persons bringing suit. Several different coverage limits and sublimits apply to payments made under the CGL.

The *General Aggregate Limit* is the most that will be paid for the sum of Coverages A, B, and C, except for damages arising out of the products-completed operations hazard. This limit can be modified by endorsement so that it applies separately to each of the insured's locations or projects.

A separate *Products-Completed Operations Aggregate Limit* represents the most that will be paid under Coverage A because of injury and damage arising out of the products-completed operations hazard.

The *Personal and Advertising Injury Limit* represents the most that will be paid under Coverage B for the sum of all damages because of personal injury or advertising injury sustained by any one person or organization. This limit is also subject to the overall General Aggregate Limit.

The *Per Occurrence Limit* is the most that will be paid for the sum of damages under Coverages A and C because of all bodily injury, property damage, and medical payments arising out of any one occurrence. This limit is also subject to either the General Aggregate Limit or the Products-Completed Operations Aggregate Limit, whichever is applicable.

The *Damage to Premises Rented to the Insured Limit* represents the most that will be paid under Coverage A for liability for fire damage to premises rented to the insured or occupied by the named insured with the owner's permission arising out of any one fire. This sublimit is also subject to the Per Occurrence Limit and the General Aggregate Limit.

Finally, the *Medical Expense Limit* is the most that will be paid under Coverage C for all medical expenses because of bodily injury sustained by any one person. This sublimit is also subject to the Per Occurrence and General Aggregate Limits.

 All limits apply separately to each consecutive annual period. If a multiyear policy is issued, all limits are reinstated on each anniversary date.

If the insured purchases the Supplemental ERP endorsement for the claims-made form, separate aggregate limits apply to claims first received and recorded during the supplemental extended reporting period.

Conditions

Some of the CGL conditions are common to other types of coverages, such as provisions for taking legal actions and provisions for subrogation. However, the following conditions have some provisions that are unique to CGL coverage.

Duties in the Event of Occurrence, Offense, Claim, or Suit

The insured has certain duties in the event of an occurrence, offense, claim, or suit.

The insured must notify the insurer as soon as practicable of an occurrence or offense that might result in a claim, including how, when, and where it took place, the names and addresses of any injured persons and witnesses, and the nature and location of any injury or damage arising out of the occurrence. (Under the claims-made form, notice of an occurrence is *not* notice of a claim.)

If a claim is made or suit brought against any insured, the insured must immediately record the specifics of the claim or suit and the date it was received and notify the insurer as soon as practicable. The insured must also see to it that the insurer receives written notice of any claim or suit as soon as practicable.

The insured must also

➤ Immediately send the insurer copies of any demands, notices, or other legal papers received in connection with a claim or suit

➤ Authorize the insurer to obtain records

➤ Cooperate with the insurer in the investigation, settlement, or defense of a claim

➤ At the company's request, assist the insurer in the enforcement of any right against someone who might be liable to the insured

➤ Not voluntarily make a payment, assume any obligation, or incur any expense—other than expenses for first aid—without the insurer's consent, except at the insured's own cost

Nonrenewal

The *When We Do Not Renew* condition states that if the insurance company decides to not renew the CGL policy, it must mail or deliver written notice of nonrenewal to the first named insured at least 30 days before the expiration date of the policy.

Other Insurance

The *Other Insurance* condition states that when the insured's CGL is primary and other primary insurance applies to the same loss, the loss will be divided between the policies by one of two methods:

➤ Contribution by equal shares

➤ Contribution by limits

Under *contribution by equal shares*, all insurers contribute equally up to the limit of the policy with the lowest limit. At that point, the insurer with the lowest limit stops paying because it has already paid its policy's limit, and the other insurers share the remainder of the loss. This continues either until the loss is paid in full or each company has paid its limit.

Here's an example. The insured has primary coverage with two companies. Company A's policy has limits of $25,000; Company B's limits are $50,000. Both policies permit contribution by equal shares. If a $60,000 covered loss occurred, Company A would pay up to its limits ($25,000) and Company B would pay $35,000.

Contribution by equal shares applies when all policies involved specify this method of handling other insurance. If they don't, *contribution by limits* applies. Contribution by limits is a method you are already familiar with for apportioning losses. Each company pays a proportion of the loss equal to the proportion its policy limits bear to the total amount of insurance available.

 CGL coverage is excess over some types of insurance, such as Builders Risk and Commercial Property coverage on the insured's own work. In such cases, the CGL coverage does not apply until the other applicable insurance limits are exhausted.

Claim Information

The *Your Right to Claim and Occurrence Information* condition is included in the claims-made form, but not the occurrence form. It provides that the insurer give the first named insured certain information relating to the current CGL claims-made form and any previous claims-made forms the insurer has issued to the insured during the previous three years. The information includes

➤ A list or record of each occurrence not previously reported to any other insurer of which this insurer has been notified according to policy provisions

➤ A summary, by policy year, of payments made and amounts reserved under any applicable General Aggregate Limit and Products-Completed Operations Aggregate Limit

If the insurer cancels or doesn't renew the policy, it will provide this information no later than 30 days prior to termination. In other circumstances, the insurer will provide the information only if it receives a written request from the first named insured within 60 days after the end of the policy period. The information will be provided within 45 days of the request.

Other Commercial General Liability Coverage Forms and Endorsements

Several CGL forms and endorsements are commonly used:

➤ The *Pollution Liability Coverage Extension endorsement* overrides the Coverage A exclusion for BI or PD claims arising out of pollution losses. It does not, however, provide coverage for cleanup costs associated with pollution losses.

➤ The standard CGL coverage forms cover the insured's liability for operations of independent contractors. The *Owners and Contractors Protective Liability (OCP) coverage form* is specifically designed to provide this coverage. It is purchased by someone other than the named insured to protect the insured against liability arising out of work performed for the insured by an independent contractor. It is most frequently used to protect an owner for liability arising out of operations being performed by a general contractor. Coverage applies only to the specific location and contractor named in the declarations and is written on an occurrence basis.

➤ The *Liquor Liability coverage form* covers insureds who are in the liquor business. It covers liability for contributing to a person's intoxication or for providing liquor in violation of the law for businesses engaged in the liquor business. The standard forms exclude this liability, which is sometimes called *dram shop liability*. Coverage can be purchased on either a claims-made or occurrence basis.

➤ The *Pollution Liability coverage form* and the *Pollution Liability-Limited coverage form* cover certain pollution losses excluded under the standard form. Each covers pollution incidents, which are emissions of pollutants into or on land, the atmosphere, or water that cause environmental damage. The only difference is the Pollution Liability-Limited form does not cover cleanup costs, and the Pollution Liability form does. Both Pollution forms are only written on a claims-made basis.

Exam Prep Questions

1. Which of the following are true about the 60-day basic extended reporting period? Select all that apply.
   - ❑ A. It becomes effective automatically if needed when a claims-made policy expires.
   - ❑ B. The insured must request it in writing within 60 days after the policy expires.
   - ❑ C. It does not require an additional premium.
   - ❑ D. No separate endorsement is required to provide this extended reporting period.

2. What is the purpose of a retroactive date in the claims-made form?
   - ○ A. Extends the period of time in which a claim can be covered under the policy
   - ○ B. Stipulates a date as the first date on which an event can occur and be covered by the policy if a claim is filed
   - ○ C. Extends the policy period
   - ○ D. Stipulates a date after which any loss that occurs will not be covered

3. Which of the following is a personal and advertising injury?
   - ○ A. Broken leg
   - ○ B. Death
   - ○ C. Calling a client a cheat and a fraud
   - ○ D. Dog bite

4. Which of the following are usually excluded under Coverage A of the Commercial General Liability policy? Select all that apply.
   - ❑ A. Property damage to property owned by the insured
   - ❑ B. Property damage to property in the care, custody, or control of the insured
   - ❑ C. Bodily injury sustained by an insured while using the insured's product
   - ❑ D. Bodily injury to a customer who is injured in an accident on the insured's premises

5. All of the following reduce the CGL's General Aggregate Limit except which of the following?
   - ○ A. Medical Payments sublimit
   - ○ B. Personal and Advertising Injury limit
   - ○ C. Fire Damage limit
   - ○ D. Products-Completed Operations limit

6. A woman is injured when she breaks a tooth on a rock that mysterious-ly found its way into a box of cereal. This is an example of which of the following?

   ○ A. Premises and operations exposure

   ○ B. Products-completed operations exposure

   ○ C. Contingent liability exposure

   ○ D. Contractual liability exposure

7. Which of the following business liability exposures are either excluded altogether from the CGL or covered only in certain circumstances? Select all that apply.

   ❑ A. Premises and operations

   ❑ B. Indirect/contingent liability

   ❑ C. Pollution

   ❑ D. Work-related injuries to employees

8. Which one of the following is not required in a CGL coverage part?

   ○ A. CGL declarations

   ○ B. One or more CGL coverage forms

   ○ C. Causes of Loss form

   ○ D. Common Policy Conditions

9. Which of the following would be considered mobile equipment under the Commercial General Liability coverage form? Select all that apply.

   ❑ A. Truck used to transport personnel to construction sites

   ❑ B. Road construction grader

   ❑ C. Bulldozer

   ❑ D. Self-propelled vehicles designed for snow removal

10. Which of the following are excluded under Coverage A of the CGL?

    ○ A. Damage the insured causes intentionally

    ○ B. Pollution losses caused by the insured

    ○ C. Liquor liability for those in the business of serving liquor

    ○ D. All of the above

11. Which of the following would be excluded under Coverage C of the CGL? Select all that apply.

    ❑ A. A shopper is injured in the insured's retail store when a box falls on him from an overhead shelf.

    ❑ B. The insured sponsors a foot race on the land surrounding his retail store. A participant is injured during the race.

    ❑ C. An individual hired by the insured to paint her business office falls off a ladder and is injured.

    ❑ D. One of the insured's employees is injured while on the job.

12. If an insurer decides to not renew the CGL policy, how many days notice of nonrenewal must be provided to the first named insured?

   ○ A. 10 days
   ○ B. 7 days
   ○ C. 20 days
   ○ D. 30 days

Exam Prep Answers

1. A, C, and D are correct. When a claims-made policy is terminated, a 60-day basic ERP automatically becomes available. The insured does not have to apply for it, and no premium is charged. It provides automatic coverage for any valid claim made during the 60 days after the policy expires, as long as the incident occurred between the expiring policy's retroactive date and its expiration date.

2. B is correct. The retroactive date provides some protection against losses that occurred before the claims-made form was written.

3. C is correct. The other answer choices are examples of bodily injury.

4. A and B are correct. Coverage A excludes property damage to property owned by the insured and property damage to property in the care, custody, or control of the insured. Because Coverage A provides third-party liability coverage, injury to an insured is not covered.

5. D is correct. There is a separate Products-Completed Operations Aggregate limit that is not subject to the General Aggregate limit.

6. B is correct. The products-completed operations hazard includes all BI and PD occurring away from the premises owned or rented by the insured, and arising out of the insured's product or work, other than products that are still in the insured's physical possession and work that has not yet been completed or abandoned.

7. C and D are correct. Businesses face a number of liability exposures, including work-related injuries to employees; pollution; contractual agreements in which the insured assumes liability; and ownership, maintenance, or use of autos, watercraft, and aircraft. However, because of the unique nature of these liability exposures, they are either excluded outright from the CGL policy or may be covered only in certain circumstances or for limited amounts. More complete protection for these liability exposures is available under contracts specifically designed to cover them.

8. C is correct. Causes of Loss forms are not used with the CGL coverage part.

9. B and C are correct. Both of these items are specifically listed in the policy's definition of mobile equipment. An auto is a land motor vehicle, trailer, or semitrailer designed for travel on public roads, including any attached machinery or equipment.

10. D is correct. All of these losses are specifically excluded under Coverage A.

11. A, C, and D are correct. Coverage C excludes injuries to the insured's employees and injuries that occur while participating in athletics.

12. D is correct. The nonrenewal condition states that if the insurer decides to not renew the CGL policy, it must mail or deliver written notice of nonrenewal to the first named insured at least 30 days before the expiration date of the policy.

Commercial Auto Insurance

. . . .

Terms you'll need to understand:

- ✓ Bodily injury
- ✓ Property damage
- ✓ Comprehensive coverage
- ✓ Specified causes of loss coverage
- ✓ Collision
- ✓ Covered autos

- ✓ Garagekeepers coverage
- ✓ Trailer interchange coverage
- ✓ Individual named insured
- ✓ Covered pollution cost or expense
- ✓ Direct damage garagekeeper's
- ✓ Business auto liability

Concepts you'll need to master:

- ✓ Commercial auto coverage part
- ✓ Business auto coverage
- ✓ Who is an insured
- ✓ Covered auto symbols
- ✓ Business auto physical damage coverage

- ✓ Garage coverage
- ✓ Truckers coverage
- ✓ Motor carrier coverage
- ✓ Drive other car coverage
- ✓ Employees as additional insureds

Businesses, similar to individuals, need both liability and physical damage coverage for losses that arise out of autos owned by or used in the business. In this chapter, we focus on automobile coverages designed to cover the private passenger and commercial auto exposures of businesses that can be insured under a Commercial Auto Coverage part of the Commercial Package Policy.

Commercial Auto Coverage Part

Commercial Auto coverage can be written as a mono-line policy or included in a Commercial Package Policy. A Commercial Auto coverage part must contain the following:

➤ Common Policy declarations

➤ Common Policy conditions

➤ One or more of five separate coverage forms: Business Auto, Business Auto Physical Damage, Garage, Truckers, or Motor Carrier

➤ Appropriate declarations for the coverage forms selected

The *Business Auto Physical Damage form* covers the insured's owned or hired business autos for physical damage only. We discuss the remaining forms in more detail. The text focuses on the Business Auto coverage form; our discussion of the other Commercial Auto coverage forms is limited to the ways in which they *differ* from the Business Auto form.

Business Auto Coverage Form

The *Business Auto coverage form* is used to insure the private passenger and commercial auto exposures of all businesses other than garages, truckers, and motor carriers. Because of the specialized nature of these businesses and their unique coverage needs, separate forms were designed to cover these risks.

The Business Auto coverage form includes

➤ Liability coverage

➤ Physical Damage coverage (Comprehensive or Specified Causes of Loss and Collision)

Uninsured Motorists, Medical Payments, and Underinsured Motorists coverages are not included in the Business Auto form, but can be added by endorsement.

Definitions

The *Definitions* section of the Business Auto coverage form defines certain key terms used in the policy. These terms help clarify the intent of various coverages and conditions, as you will see as you progress through this chapter.

For insurance purposes, the definition of *auto* is a land motor vehicle, trailer, or semitrailer designed for travel on public roads. It generally does not include mobile equipment. An exception is made under the policy's Liability coverage when mobile equipment is being towed or carried by a covered auto. This provision fills an insurance gap because the Commercial General Liability policy excludes coverage for mobile equipment while it is being transported by an auto that is owned or operated by an insured. Other exposures arising out of mobile equipment are covered under Commercial General Liability insurance.

Bodily injury (BI) means bodily injury, sickness, or disease, including death resulting from any of these. *Property damage (PD)* means damage to or loss of use of tangible property.

Covered pollution cost or expense means costs arising out of any statutory or regulatory requirement or any order by a government authority demanding that the insured test for, monitor, clean up, remove, contain, treat, detoxify or neutralize, or respond to or assess the effects of pollutants. It does not include the costs arising out of the escape of pollutants that are in property being transported or towed by; handled into, onto, or from the covered auto, or otherwise in the course of transit by the insured; or being stored, disposed of, treated, or processed in or on the covered auto. Also excluded are pollutants released before the property is moved to the place where they are accepted by the insured for movement into the covered auto and after the pollutants are delivered by the insured. This exclusion does not apply to fuels, lubricants, fluids, exhaust gases, or other pollutants necessary for or resulting from the normal operation of a covered auto or its parts.

Diminution of value is an actual or perceived loss in resale or market value that results from a direct, accidental loss.

Pollutants means any solid, liquid, gaseous, or thermal irritant or contaminant, including smoke, vapor, soot, fumes, acids, alkalis, chemicals, and waste. Waste includes materials to be recycled, reconditioned, or reclaimed.

In Chapter 15, "Commercial General Liability Insurance," you learned the definition of *mobile equipment*. This definition is identical in the Business Auto and Commercial General Liability coverage forms. This enables the two coverages to fit together precisely and removes any doubt about which coverage applies to autos and which applies to mobile equipment.

Covered Autos

The insured selects what autos are to be considered *covered autos* for each coverage. These selections are contained in the Business Auto declarations and are based on a numerical symbol system described in the policy. The insured can select from the symbols shown in Table 16.1.

Table 16.1 Business Auto Coverage Symbols		
Symbol	Type of Auto Selected	Description
1	Any auto	Any auto the insured will use during the policy period, including autos that are owned, leased, hired, rented, or borrowed
		Used to designate Liability coverage only
2	Owned autos only	Any auto the insured owns
		Designates other coverages besides Liability coverage
3	Owned private passenger autos only	Any private passenger auto the insured owns
		Designates any coverage provided by the Business Auto coverage form
4	Owned autos other than private passenger autos only	Other types of vehicles the insured owns, such as trucks, trailers, buses, and motorcycles
		Designates any coverage provided by the Business Auto coverage form
5	Owned autos subject to no-fault law	Designates owned autos required to have no-fault benefits in a particular state
6	Owned autos subject to compulsory Uninsured Motorists law	Designates owned autos required to have Uninsured Motorists coverage in a particular state
7	Specifically described autos	Applies only to autos specifically listed in the Business Auto coverage form declarations

(continued)

Table 16.1	Business Auto Coverage Symbols *(continued)*	
Symbol	Type of Auto Selected	Description
8	Hired autos only	Designates Liability and/or Physical Damage coverage only
		Used only for autos the insured has leased, hired, rented, or borrowed
		Does not include autos rented or borrowed from employees or members of their households
9	Nonowned autos only	Used only for autos used in the insured's business that are not leased, hired, rented, or borrowed
		Includes autos owned by employees, but used in the insured's business or personal affairs
		Designates Liability coverage only

Coverage can be tailored to the needs of the insured by selection of the appropriate symbols. Various symbols can be used for different coverages.

 The broadest coverage available is reflected by symbol 1 because "any auto" includes all owned, hired, and nonowned autos. Symbol 7 is the most restrictive because it applies only to specifically described autos.

With the exception of specifically described autos, autos acquired during the policy period are automatically covered. For specifically described autos, an auto acquired during the policy period is a covered auto for a particular coverage only if the insured already insures all autos for this coverage or if it replaces a covered auto and the insured notifies the insurer within 30 days of acquisition.

If the insured has liability coverage under the policy, the following vehicles are also covered autos for liability coverage:

➤ Temporary substitute autos

➤ Trailers with a load capacity of 2,000 pounds or less

➤ Mobile equipment while it is being towed or carried by a covered auto

Liability Coverage

The liability coverage in the Business Auto coverage form is similar to that provided by the Personal Auto policy. The policy agrees to pay all sums that an insured legally must pay as damages because of BI or PD to which the insurance applies caused by an accident involving the ownership, maintenance, or use of a covered auto. Coverage for defense costs and supplementary payments is also included.

The insurer also agrees to pay all sums an insured legally must pay as a *covered pollution cost or expense* to which the policy applies. The pollution cost must be caused by an accident and result from the ownership, maintenance, or use of covered autos. The insurer will pay for covered pollution costs only if there is BI or PD caused by the same accident. Coverage for liability for pollution cleanup costs is also included under specific circumstances.

Who Is an Insured

In addition to the named insured, others have liability coverage while using a covered auto with permission. The policy also covers those who become liable for the conduct of an insured.

Those who are *not insureds* include

➤ The owner of an auto hired or borrowed from an employee or family member

➤ A person who is working in an auto-type business

➤ A person, other than an employee or lessee, who is moving property to or from a covered auto

Exclusions

Business Auto Liability coverage contains many of the same exclusions as Personal Auto Liability coverage as well as some unique exclusions, including liability for the following:

➤ Expected or intended injuries

➤ Assumed under contract or agreement (does not apply to liability the insured would have had if there were no contract or agreement or contracts that meet the policy's definition of an insured contract)

➤ For work-related injuries to employees, including those covered under workers compensation and related laws and injuries caused to an employee by another employee

➤ For damage to property owned by, transported by, or in the care, custody, or control of the insured

➤ For damage arising out of the movement of property by a mechanical device

➤ For BI or PD arising out of the operation of self-propelled vehicles with attached cherry pickers that are used to raise or lower workers or that have permanently attached equipment, such as air compressors, pumps, and generators

➤ For completed operations

➤ For pollution damage, except as specifically provided in the policy

➤ Assumed under a contract for war or war-like acts

➤ For covered autos while being used for—or while practicing or preparing for—organized or professional racing, demolition, or stunting activities

Supplementary Payments

In addition to damages for BI and PD liability, the liability section of the Business Auto coverage form covers the following as *Supplementary Payments*:

➤ Expenses the insurer incurs

➤ Cost of bail bonds up to $2,000 for violations because of a covered accident

➤ Cost of bonds to release attachments, but only within the limit of insurance

➤ Expenses the insured incurs at the insurer's request, including the insured's lost earnings up to $250 a day because of time off from work

➤ Costs the insured is required to pay because of a lawsuit

➤ Interest that accrues after a judgment and before it is paid

All Supplementary Payments are provided in addition to the limit of insurance and do not reduce the coverage available to cover damages awarded against the insured.

Out of State Coverage Extensions

The Business Auto coverage form provides for situations in which a business's autos are driven in more than one state. The *Out of State Coverage Extensions* modify the policy's Liability coverage to meet other states' financial responsibility requirements and other state laws concerning out-of-state drivers when the covered auto is being driven in that state.

Worldwide Liability Coverage

The coverage territory for the Business Auto coverage form includes the United States, its territories and possessions, and Canada.

In addition, the form provides worldwide Liability coverage for private passenger autos the insured hires, leases, rents, or borrows without a driver for a period of 30 days or fewer. The insured's liability must be determined in a settlement agreed to by the insurer or in a lawsuit filed in the United States, its territories and possessions, or Canada.

Physical Damage Coverage

The *Physical Damage* portion of the Business Auto coverage form contains three principal coverages:

➤ *Comprehensive*: Covers any loss, other than collision or overturn, that is not excluded by the policy

➤ *Specified Causes of Loss*: More limited type of Comprehensive coverage that covers only these perils:

  ➤ Earthquake

  ➤ Explosion

  ➤ Fire

  ➤ Flood

  ➤ Hail

  ➤ Lightning

  ➤ Sinking, burning, collision, or derailment of a conveyance transporting the covered auto (such as a ship)

  ➤ Theft

  ➤ Vandalism or mischief

  ➤ Windstorm

➤ *Collision*: Covers overturn of the covered auto and collision with another object

The insured can select various Physical Damage coverage options for different vehicles. For example, some vehicles might be insured for Comprehensive and Collision losses, whereas others are insured only for the Specified Causes of Loss.

Collision and Comprehensive coverages are written with a deductible such as $500 or $1,000—the amount of which the insured can choose. Under Comprehensive coverage, the deductible does not apply to loss caused by fire or lightning. Under Specified Causes of Loss coverage, a $25 deductible applies to loss by vandalism or mischief. No other losses have a deductible under this coverage.

If the insured carries Comprehensive coverage, losses from glass breakage, falling objects or missiles, and hitting a bird or animal are treated as Comprehensive losses. This usually works to the insured's advantage because Comprehensive coverage is usually written with a lower deductible than Collision coverage. However, the insured can also have glass breakage paid as a Collision loss. This removes a possible double deductible if the glass breakage results from a collusion that includes other damage.

Coverage for *towing and labor costs* incurred is also available when a covered private passenger auto is disabled.

A *coverage extension* for *transportation expenses* covers expenses incurred because of the theft of the insured's vehicle. Coverage begins 48 hours after the theft and ends when the auto is returned or the insurer pays the loss. Coverage is limited to a maximum of $20 per day, or a total of $600.

Another coverage extension covers *loss of use* expenses for rented autos that the insured is legally responsible to pay under a contract or agreement. Coverage is limited to $20 per day, to a maximum of $600.

Exclusions

The Physical Damage coverage exclusions are similar to those found in the Physical Damage section of the Personal Auto policy, including loss to or because of the following:

➤ Sound reproducing and receiving equipment, tapes, and records

➤ Wear and tear, freezing, mechanical or electrical breakdown, or road damage to tires

➤ War

➤ Nuclear events

➤ Covered autos while being used for—or while practicing or preparing for—organized or professional racing, demolition, or stunting activities

➤ Diminution in value

Conditions

The conditions in the Business Auto coverage form are similar to those you have studied in relation to other insurance contracts. In this section, we briefly cover those that are unique to the Business Auto coverage form.

The insurer has three options for *settling physical damage claims*:

➤ Pay for, repair, or replace the damaged or stolen property

➤ Return stolen property to the insured at the company's expense and pay for any damages resulting from the theft

➤ Take the damaged or stolen property at an agreed or appraised value

In the event of a total loss, depreciation and physical condition are considered when determining actual cash value. If a repair or replacement results in better than like kind or quality, the amount of the betterment is not covered.

The insured cannot take *legal action against the insurance company* unless the insured has fully complied with all terms of the policy. If the lawsuit relates to the policy's Liability coverage, the insurer must also agree in writing that the insured is obligated to pay or the amount of judgment must have been determined after a trial.

The *other insurance* condition states that the Business Auto coverage form provides *primary coverage* for covered autos owned by the insured and, for liability losses, covered trailers that are connected to covered autos owned by the insured. The coverage is *excess* for losses involving nonowned covered autos and covered trailers while they are connected to nonowned motor vehicles.

When the Business Auto coverage form and another insurance cover on the same basis, either primary or excess, the Business Auto coverage form pays only its proportionate share of the loss.

If *more than one policy or coverage form* issued by the same insurer applies to a loss, the amount that the insured can be paid is limited to the highest single policy limit.

Garage Coverage Form

Because automobile-type businesses such as car dealerships, gas stations, and parking garages are excluded by the Business Auto coverage form, these risks must be covered under a separate *Garage coverage form*. This form provides

➤ Liability coverage

➤ Garagekeepers coverage

➤ Physical Damage coverage

 On the exam, make sure that you read the question you are answering carefully to determine which coverage the question is based on. For example, don't read too quickly and mistake the "Business Auto coverage form" for the "Business Auto Physical Damage form" or the liability coverage provided under the Garage Coverage form for "Garagekeepers coverage."

Uninsured Motorists, Underinsured Motorists, and Medical Payments coverage can be added by endorsement.

Covered Autos

As in the Business Auto coverage form, the Garage Coverage form uses a numerical system to determine which autos are covered autos. It is similar to the one used for the Business Auto coverage form, except the numbers are different. Two symbols are unique to the Garage coverage form:

➤ *Symbol 30*: Coverage for customers' autos left with the insured for service, repair, storage, or safekeeping (this is Garagekeepers coverage, which we review later)

➤ *Symbol 31*: Physical Damage coverage only for dealers' autos and autos held for sale by dealers, nondealers, or trailer dealers

Liability Coverage

The Garage coverage form covers both auto and business liability arising out of

➤ The ownership, maintenance, or use of covered autos (*Garage Operations—Covered Autos*)

➤ Garage operations (*Garage Operations—Other Than Covered Autos*)

Those protected as insureds under the Garage coverage form for Garage Operations—Covered Autos are essentially the same as those insured for liability under the Business Auto coverage form, with one important exception. For auto dealer risks, garage customers are not covered if they have their own Liability coverage. If customers do not have Liability coverage of their own, the Garage form protects them, but only up to the minimum limits of financial responsibility. The insured has the option of adding coverage for customers up to the full limits of the policy.

For Garage Operations—Other Than Covered Autos, those considered insureds include the named insured, his or her employees, and the business' directors and shareholders while acting within the scope of their duties.

The Garage coverage form contains many of the same Liability exclusions as the Business Auto coverage form. It also contains some general liability-type exclusions such as damage to the property of others in the insured's care, custody, or control, property damage to the insured's own products, or work and product or work recalls.

Garagekeepers Coverage

The Liability section of the Garage coverage form excludes liability for damage to property of others in the care, custody, or control of the insured. For garages, this excludes a significant business exposure: the garage's liability for customers' autos in its care or custody. Coverage for this specific exposure is provided under the *Garagekeepers insurance* section of the Garage coverage form.

Garagekeepers insurance covers the insured's liability for damage to customers' property that the insured has for servicing, repair, parking, or storage. The insured also has the option of purchasing *Direct Damage Garagekeepers* insurance, which pays for physical damage to customers' property in the insured's custody, whether or not the insured is liable. Direct Damage Garagekeepers insurance can be provided on either a primary or excess basis; the causes of loss that can be covered include Comprehensive or Specified Causes of Loss and Collision.

Physical Damage Coverage

Garage Physical Damage coverage offers the same coverages as the Business Auto coverage form: either Comprehensive or Specified Causes of Loss and Collision. It specifically excludes *false pretense coverage*—coverage for losses when a dealer is deceived into voluntarily parting with a covered auto. (Such coverage is available by endorsement.)

Typically, auto dealers purchase Physical Damage coverage on a blanket basis, meaning that all vehicles owned by the insured are covered without specifying the exact number. A few specialized exclusions apply to this *blanket coverage*, including

➤ Expected profits

➤ Collision damage to autos being driven or transported from the point of purchase or distribution to the point of destination if this distance is 50 miles or more

Truckers Coverage Form

The Business Auto coverage form specifically excludes businesses that set themselves out for hire to haul the goods of others. So truckers must obtain coverage for their vehicles under the *Truckers coverage form*, a modified version of the Business Auto coverage form that takes into consideration the special practices and regulations that apply to the trucking industry.

The Truckers coverage form includes three coverages:

➤ Liability

➤ Trailer Interchange

➤ Physical Damage

The liability and physical damage coverages are similar to those provided under the Business Auto coverage form.

Covered Autos

Similar to the other Commercial Auto coverage forms you've studied so far, the Truckers coverage form uses a numerical system to determine which autos are covered. It is similar to the one used for the Business Auto coverage form, except that the numbers are different and the "owned auto" options do not include private passenger autos. It also contains two symbols to provide Trailer Interchange coverage:

➤ *Symbol 48*: Trailers borrowed or leased by the named insured for which liability for loss has been assumed under a written trailer interchange agreement. This only applies to the Comprehensive, Specified Causes of Loss or Collision coverages of Trailer Interchange coverage.

➤ *Symbol 49*: Trailers owned or hired by the named insured while the trailers are in someone else's possession under a written trailer interchange agreement.

Trailer Interchange Coverage

Truckers frequently need to borrow or hire a trailer from another trucking business for use in their own business. Under the Business Auto coverage form, damage to such property is excluded from coverage. Under the Truckers coverage form, *Trailer Interchange insurance* covers damage to a specific trailer under the policy of the trucker in whose possession the trailer is at the time of loss, provided that

➤ The trucker is liable under a written interchange agreement.

➤ The damage is caused by a covered peril.

Motor Carrier Coverage Form

The *Motor Carrier coverage form* is an alternative to the Truckers coverage form. Whereas a trucker is a person hired to haul the goods of others, a *motor carrier* is anyone who transports property by auto in a commercial enterprise, regardless of whether he or she was hired for that purpose.

Because this broad definition encompasses truckers, those who are eligible for coverage under the Truckers coverage form could also be covered under the Motor Carrier coverage form. However, those who are eligible for coverage under the Motor Carrier form can only be covered under the Truckers form if they transport goods for others by hire.

 For the exam, keep in mind that the Motor Carrier coverage form has broader eligibility than the Trucker's coverage form.

With the exception of those who can be covered under the form, the Motor Carrier coverage form is practically identical to the Truckers coverage form. Like the Truckers coverage form, it provides Trailer Interchange coverage. Unlike the Truckers form, owned private passenger autos can be covered autos in the Motor Carrier coverage form.

Motor Carrier Act of 1980

Truckers and other commercial carriers are subject to a number of regulations, such as the *Motor Carrier Act of 1980*, that require trucking companies to certify that they are capable of meeting financial obligations if they become liable for injury or damage arising from their trucking operations.

The most common method for satisfying these requirements is to obtain adequate Truckers coverage to cover the automobile exposure, as well as *Commercial Inland Marine Motor Truck Cargo* insurance to cover the liability for cargo being hauled. If insurance is used to establish proof of financial responsibility, the *MCS-90 endorsement* must be attached to the policy. This endorsement provides public liability coverage for bodily injury, property damage, and environmental restoration.

The limits of liability required by the Motor Carrier Act affect vehicles that have a gross vehicle weight of 10,000 pounds or more. The required limits are divided into three categories, depending on the kind of hazardous cargo hauled:

➤ $750,000 for interstate transportation of nonhazardous property

➤ $1,000,000 for interstate or intrastate transportation of oil or other hazardous wastes

➤ $5,000,000 for interstate or intrastate transportation of large quantities of certain hazardous materials, such as compressed gas, radioactive materials, explosives, or oil

Vehicles that have a gross vehicle weight of less than 10,000 pounds must comply with the financial responsibility limit of $5,000,000 if the vehicle hauls explosives, any quantity of poison gas, or large quantities of radioactive materials.

Endorsements

A number of endorsements can be added to the Commercial Auto coverage forms. A review of some of the most commonly used commercial auto endorsements follows.

Drive Other Car Coverage Endorsement

The *Drive Other Car—Broadened Coverage for Named Individuals (DOC)* endorsement extends the definition of a covered auto to include autos the named insured does not own, hire, or borrow while being used by the person named in the endorsement. Coverage does not apply to autos owned by the person named in the endorsement or a family member.

DOC coverage might be especially important if the named insured under a Business Auto coverage form is furnishing an auto to an employee who has no Personal Auto insurance. Although the employee would have coverage under the Business Auto form while using the furnished auto or any other auto owned, hired, or borrowed by the named insured, the employee would have no coverage under the Business Auto form for an auto he or she borrowed or rented unless the DOC endorsement was attached to the Business Auto form.

Individual Named Insured

The *Individual Named Insured* endorsement extends Personal Auto-type coverage to immediate family members of the named insured.

For example, consider a sole proprietor who operates a business and has Business Auto coverage, but no Personal Auto insurance. Under the Business Auto policy, the sole proprietor would have coverage for any auto. The sole proprietor's family members would have coverage while using autos owned, hired, or borrowed by the named insured and while using nonowned autos in the insured's business. However, they would have no coverage for their personal use of nonowned autos. Attaching the Individual Named Insured endorsement to the Business Auto coverage form extends coverage for the use of any auto to family members, subject to certain exclusions. It provides very similar coverage to that provided by the Personal Auto policy.

Employees as Additional Insureds

If a business has broad coverage for all autos, it would be covered in any lawsuit arising out of an accident involving owned, hired, borrowed, or nonowned autos, including autos owned by employees while used for business purposes. Although the employees are insured under the Business Auto Liability section while driving autos owned by the business, they are not insured while driving their own cars in the course of business. If a suit against a business also named an employee as the driver and owner of a vehicle, the Business Auto coverage form would only protect the business. If the employee has Personal Auto coverage, it would provide some protection, but claims resulting from a business-related accident might involve amounts well above the employee's coverage limits.

Employees can be protected under the Business Auto coverage form with the *Employees as Additional Insureds* endorsement. It states that any employee is an insured while using an auto the business does not own, hire, or borrow when the autos are used in the business or personal affairs of the named insured.

This coverage insures employees for the business use of their own autos or autos owned by the employee's family members. It does not protect family members who own a vehicle being used by an employee.

Other Endorsements

As we mentioned earlier, the insured can also add *Medical Payments, Uninsured Motorists,* and *Underinsured Motorists* coverage by endorsement. These endorsements provide coverage similar to that provided for Personal Auto coverage.

Leased vehicles can be considered owned vehicles for coverage purposes by attaching the *Additional Insured—Lessor endorsement* to the policy.

An endorsement can be used to add coverage for *specified hired autos*. When attached to a policy, the hired autos scheduled in the endorsement are treated as if they were covered automobiles owned by the named insured.

Finally, when the *Mobile Equipment* endorsement is attached, mobile equipment is considered a covered auto.

Exam Prep Questions

1. Which of the following coverages are provided by Business Auto Physical Damage coverage?

   ❑   A.   Collision
   ❑   B.   Transportation Expenses
   ❑   C.   Comprehensive
   ❑   D.   Garagekeepers Insurance

2. Which portion of the Garage coverage form covers liability for damage to property of others in the insured's care, custody, or control?

   ○   A.   Liability
   ○   B.   Garagekeepers
   ○   C.   Physical Damage
   ○   D.   Both A and B

3. Trailer Interchange coverage is included in which of the following forms?

   ❑   A.   All Commercial Auto coverage forms
   ❑   B.   The Truckers coverage form
   ❑   C.   The Motor Carrier coverage form
   ❑   D.   The Garage coverage form

4. The Garage coverage form covers liability arising out of which of the following?

   ❑   A.   Ownership, maintenance, or use of covered autos
   ❑   B.   Garage operations
   ❑   C.   A trailer interchange agreement
   ❑   D.   Advertising injury

5. Which of the following perils are included in the Business Auto coverage form's Specified Causes of Loss coverage?

   ❑   A.   Collision
   ❑   B.   Earthquake
   ❑   C.   Flood
   ❑   D.   Theft

6. Which of the following statements concerning Business Auto Liability coverage are correct?

   ❑   A.   It covers BI or PD caused by an accident.
   ❑   B.   It does not cover pollution losses.
   ❑   C.   It only covers sums for which the insured is legally liable.
   ❑   D.   The BI or PD must result from the ownership, maintenance, or use of a covered auto.

7. Who of the following would be considered an insured under Business Auto Liability coverage?

   ❑ A. The named insured

   ❑ B. Others while using a covered auto with permission

   ❑ C. The owner of a borrowed auto

   ❑ D. Others who become liable for the conduct of an insured

8. Which of the following are excluded under Business Auto Liability coverage?

   ❑ A. Liability assumed under a contract that is considered an insured contract

   ❑ B. Damage to the insured's own auto

   ❑ C. Injury to employees covered by workers compensation laws

   ❑ D. Liability for property in the insured's custody

9. Which of the following losses would be paid under the Business Auto coverage form's Comprehensive coverage?

   ○ A. Gradual corrosion of the grillwork on a covered auto because of continuous exposure to salt air

   ○ B. Overturn of a covered auto

   ○ C. Collision damage to a covered auto

   ○ D. Theft of a covered auto

10. Which of the following businesses might be covered under a Garage coverage form?

   ❑ A. Used car dealer

   ❑ B. Catering company

   ❑ C. Auto body shop

   ❑ D. Service station

11. Which of the following coverages are included in an unendorsed Garage coverage form?

   ❑ A. Garagekeepers

   ❑ B. Uninsured Motorists

   ❑ C. Liability

   ❑ D. Physical Damage

12. Which of the following can be considered covered autos only under the Garage coverage form?

   ❑ A. Customers' autos left with the insured for service

   ❑ B. Autos the insured has leased to use in the business

   ❑ C. Autos held for sale by a dealer

   ❑ D. Autos owned by the insured and used in the insured's business

13. Which of the following Commercial Auto coverage forms does not offer liability coverage?

   ○ A. Business Auto

   ○ B. Business Auto Physical Damage

   ○ C. Garage

   ○ D. Trucker's

14. Which of the following would be included in an unendorsed Business Auto coverage policy? Select all that apply.

   ❑ A. Liability coverage

   ❑ B. Physical Damage coverage

   ❑ C. Uninsured Motorists coverage

   ❑ D. Medical Payments coverage

Exam Prep Answers

1. A, B, and C are correct. The Physical Damage portion of the Business Auto coverage form contains three principal coverages: Comprehensive, Specified Causes of Loss (a more limited type of Comprehensive coverage), and Collision. Transportation expenses are covered as part of Physical Damage coverage. Garagekeepers insurance is not included in the Business Auto coverage form.

2. B is correct. The Liability section of the Garage coverage form excludes liability for damage to customers' autos in the insured's custody. Coverage for this exposure is provided under the Garagekeepers section of the Garage form.

3. B and C are correct. Trailer Interchange coverage covers damage to a specific trailer under the policy of the trucker who has possession of the trailer at the time of loss, as long as certain conditions are met. It is included in the Truckers and Motor Carrier coverage forms.

4. A and B are correct. Trailer Interchange coverage and advertising injury are not included in the Garage coverage form.

5. B, C, and D are correct. Specified Causes of Loss coverage is a limited type of Comprehensive coverage. It covers fire, lightning, explosion, theft, windstorm, hail, earthquake, flood, vandalism, or mischief, as well as sinking, burning, collision, or derailment of a conveyance transporting the covered auto.

6. A, C, and D are correct. This coverage pays all sums an insured legally must pay as a covered pollution cost or expense to which the policy applies as long as certain conditions are met.

7. A, B, and D are correct. The owner of a hired or borrowed auto is not an insured for Liability coverage while using the covered auto.

8. B, C, and D are correct. The exclusion for liability assumed under contract or agreement does not apply to contracts that meet the policy's definition of an insured contract.

9. D is correct. Losses from wear and tear are excluded. The other two losses are considered collision losses.

10. A, C, and D are correct. The Garage coverage form is designed to cover automobile-type businesses, such as car dealerships, gas stations, and parking garages. These types of businesses cannot be covered under the Business Auto coverage form.

11. A, C, and D are correct. The Garage coverage form includes Liability, Garagekeepers, and Physical Damage coverage. Medical Payments, Uninsured Motorist, and Underinsured Motorists coverage may be added by endorsement.

12. A and C are correct. There are two covered auto symbols that are unique to the Garage coverage form. Symbol 30 is used for customers' autos left with the insured for service, repair, storage, or safekeeping. Symbol 31 is used for Physical Damage coverage only for the dealers' autos and autos held for sale by dealers, nondealers, or trailer dealers.

13. B is correct. Business Auto Physical Damage covers losses to the insured's own vehicles, not losses to other's vehicles the insured might become liable for.

14. A and B are correct. Uninsured Motorists and Medical Payments coverage are available only by endorsement.

Commercial Crime Insurance

. . . .

Terms you'll need to understand:

- ✓ Burglary
- ✓ Safe burglary
- ✓ Robbery
- ✓ Theft
- ✓ Forgery
- ✓ Custodian
- ✓ Messenger
- ✓ Watchperson
- ✓ Employee benefit plan

- ✓ Money
- ✓ Securities
- ✓ Property other than money or securities
- ✓ Computer fraud
- ✓ Extortion
- ✓ Principal
- ✓ Surety
- ✓ Obligee

Concepts you'll need to master:

- ✓ Loss sustained form
- ✓ Discovery form
- ✓ Employee theft
- ✓ Forgery or alteration
- ✓ Inside the premises
- ✓ Outside the premises

- ✓ Fidelity bond
- ✓ Name schedule bond
- ✓ Position schedule bond
- ✓ Commercial blanket bond
- ✓ Blanket position bond

In this chapter, we review *Commercial Crime insurance*—insurance designed to protect businesses and government entities against property loss resulting from crimes such as burglary, robbery, theft, and employee dishonesty.

Crime coverage can be provided as a mono-line policy or as part of a Commercial Package policy. However, unlike the other Commercial lines coverages you've studied up to this point, the same forms are *not* used for package policies and mono-line policies. For Crime insurance, "coverage" forms are used for package policies and "policy" forms are the mono-line versions. The primary difference is that a separate Common Policy Conditions form is not required for a mono-line policy because these conditions are incorporated into the policy forms. For a Commercial Package policy, separate forms are required.

Types of Crime Forms

There are separate Crime forms for commercial businesses and government entities. We focus primarily on forms written for businesses.

Each Crime form is available in two versions: a *loss sustained* form and a *discovery* form. The difference between the forms is what triggers coverage. The most commonly used forms are shown in Table 17.1.

Table 17.1 Commonly Used Crime Forms		
	Mono-line Policies	**Package Policies**
Commercial	Commercial Crime Policy—Discovery Version	Commercial Crime Coverage Form—Discovery Version
	Commercial Crime Policy—Loss Sustained Version	Commercial Crime Coverage Form—Loss Sustained Version
Government	Government Crime Policy—Discovery Version	Government Crime Coverage Form—Discovery Version
	Government Crime Policy—Loss Sustained Version	Government Crime Coverage Form—Loss Sustained Version

Separate Employee Theft and Forgery policies are also available, and other coverages may be added by endorsement.

Loss Sustained Form

Crime insurance written under a *loss sustained form* covers losses that are *sustained* during the policy period and *discovered* either during the policy period or up to one year after the policy expires. This one-year discovery period terminates immediately when the insured obtains other Commercial Crime insurance.

The policy does not extend coverage beyond the policy expiration date. Losses that occur after policy expiration are not covered. But losses that occur during the policy period and are discovered within one year after policy expiration are covered.

Suppose that a pet supply store is insured under the loss sustained version of the Crime policy. The policy period is January 1, 2003 to January 1, 2004. A loss occurs on April 6, 2003, but is not discovered until September 7, 2004. The Crime policy covers this loss because the loss occurred during the policy period and was discovered within one year after the policy expiration date.

The *Loss Sustained During Prior Insurance condition*, which appears only in the loss sustained forms, states that the policy will pay for a loss that occurred during the term of a previous policy but was discovered during the term of the present policy. For coverage to apply, three conditions must be met:

➤ The discovery period under the previous policy has expired.

➤ The current policy became effective on the date the prior policy expired.

➤ The loss is covered under both the current and previous policies.

The most that will be paid for the loss is the *lesser* of the current or previous policy limit.

Suppose that the insured's Commercial Crime policy with Company A had an effective date of January 1, 2003 and expired January 1, 2004. The insured then purchased a policy from Company B, which was effective from January 1, 2004 to January 1, 2005, and then renewed for another year. The insured had a crime loss that occurred in February 2003, but was not discovered until March 2005. The policies from both companies were written on a loss sustained basis. Assume that, without regard to the date, the loss would have been covered under either policy. This loss would be covered under Company B's policy.

Discovery Form

Certain crime losses, such as extortion and embezzlement, might not be discovered until weeks, months, or years after they occur. Crime insurance written on a *discovery* basis covers losses that are *sustained at any time* and *discovered* either during the policy period or up to 60 days after the policy expires (up to one year for losses related to employee benefit plans). A loss is "discovered" when the insured

➤ First becomes aware that a loss has occurred or will occur, even if the actual amount of loss or details concerning the loss are not known

➤ Receives notice of an actual or potential claim for a covered loss

The extended time periods to discover losses terminate immediately when the insured obtains other Commercial Crime insurance.

Definitions

All of the Crime forms include a definitions section that defines certain key terms used in the policy. These terms help clarify the intent of various coverages and conditions, as you will see as you progress through this chapter.

Types of Crimes

Although *burglary* is not specifically defined in the Crime forms, it still has a specific meaning in the insurance industry. Burglary is the taking of property from inside the premises by a person unlawfully entering or leaving the premises. There must be evidence of forcible entry or exit, such as marks made by tools, explosives, chemicals, or electricity.

Safe burglary is the taking of property from within a locked safe or vault by a person unlawfully entering the safe or vault as evidenced by marks of forcible entry on the exterior of the safe or vault. It also includes the taking of the entire safe or vault from inside the premises.

Robbery is the unlawful taking of property from the care and custody of another person. The robber must have caused or threatened to cause bodily harm to the person being robbed or must have committed an obviously unlawful act that is witnessed by the person being robbed.

Theft means the unlawful taking of money, securities, or other property. This broad term includes burglary, safe burglary, and robbery. But unlike burglary, safe burglary, and robbery—which usually involve the use of force—theft also includes the taking of property by stealth (action designed to escape notice).

 NOTE | Theft (larceny) means any act of stealing. It is the broadest category of covered crimes because it includes all of the more narrowly defined categories, such as burglary, robbery, and forgery, and goes beyond them in scope.

Forgery is signing the name of another person or organization with the intent to deceive.

Other Definitions

A *custodian* is someone who has care or custody of property *inside* the premises. It includes the insured, the insured's partners or members, or any employee. It does not include a watchperson or janitor.

A *messenger* is someone who has care and custody of property while it is *outside* the premises. It can include the insured, a relative of the insured, the insured's partners or members, or any employee.

A *watchperson* is someone retained specifically by the insured whose sole duty is to have care and custody of property inside the premises.

An *employee benefit plan* is any welfare or pension plan subject to the Employee Retirement Income Security Act of 1974 (ERISA), such as a 401(k), profit sharing, health, life, or disability insurance plan. Government plans, such as Social Security, are not employee benefit plans.

Money includes currency, coins, bank notes, travelers checks, register checks, and money orders.

Other property means any tangible property other than money or securities that has value.

Securities are instruments or contracts that represent money or property. Checks, drafts, bonds, certificates of deposit, stock certificates, stamps, and credit card receipts are all considered securities.

Insuring Agreements and Endorsements

The Commercial Crime forms include the following coverages as insuring agreements:

➤ Employee Theft

➤ Forgery or Alteration

➤ Inside the Premises—Theft of Money and Securities

➤ Inside the Premises—Robbery or Safe Burglary of Other Property

➤ Outside the Premises

➤ Computer Fraud

➤ Money Orders and Counterfeit Paper Currency

➤ Funds Transfer Fraud

Although multiple coverages are listed in the form, the insured must select the coverages that will apply to the policy. For each insuring agreement selected, a limit of insurance and deductible must be listed on the declarations. The policy limit and deductible both apply per occurrence. Any insuring agreements the insured does not want must be designated as "Not Covered" on the declarations page.

Employee Theft

Employee Theft coverage pays for loss of or damage to money, securities, and other property resulting from theft committed by an employee, either acting alone or in collusion with others. The employee does not have to be identified for coverage to apply.

There is no coverage for

➤ Any employee who has previously had similar insurance cancelled and not reinstated

➤ Loss resulting from trading, either in the insured's name or in a genuine or fictitious account

➤ Loss resulting from fraudulent or dishonest use of warehouse receipts

Proof of loss may not be based on an inventory shortage or profit and loss computation.

An employee benefit plan may be listed in the declarations as a named insured for Employee Theft coverage. No deductible applies to losses sustained by an employee benefit plan.

Under the Government Crime forms, Employee Theft losses may be written on a *per loss basis*, which means that the limit of insurance applies regardless of how many employees were involved in the loss, or on a *per employee basis*, meaning all loss caused by one employee. Treasurers, tax collectors, and employees required by law to be individually bonded are not covered.

Forgery or Alteration

Forgery or Alteration coverage pays for loss from forgery or alteration of checks, drafts, promissory notes, or similar instruments made or drawn by or on the named insured or the insured's agent. This includes documents that are forged or altered with a mechanically reproduced facsimile signature. Coverage is provided worldwide.

If the insured is sued for refusing to pay a forged or altered instrument and obtains the insurer's written permission to defend the suit, the insurer will pay reasonable defense costs incurred by the insured. These expenses are paid in addition to the limit of liability, with no deductible required.

Inside the Premises—Theft of Money and Securities

Inside the Premises—Theft of Money and Securities coverage pays for theft, disappearance, or destruction of money and securities while inside the insured's premises or a banking premises. If the insured owns or is liable for damage to the premises, this type of insurance also covers damage to the interior or exterior of the premises that results from theft or attempted theft.

Damage to a locked safe, vault, cash register, cash box, or cash drawer that is inside the premises is also covered when the damage results from theft, attempted theft, or unlawful entry.

Inside the Premises—Robbery or Safe Burglary of Other Property

The fourth insuring agreement, *Inside the Premises—Robbery or Safe Burglary of Other Property*, has two primary coverages:

➤ Loss of other property (not money or securities) while inside the premises from actual or attempted robbery of a custodian

➤ Loss of other property from a safe or vault inside the premises from actual or attempted safe burglary

If the insured owns or is liable for damage to the premises, this type of insurance also covers damage to the interior or exterior of the premises that results from actual or attempted robbery or safe burglary. Damage to a locked safe or vault that is inside the premises is also covered when the damage results from actual or attempted robbery or safe burglary.

Outside the Premises

The *Outside the Premises* insuring agreement also provides two types of coverage:

➤ Theft, disappearance, or destruction of money and securities while outside the premises and in the care and custody of a messenger or an armored car company

➤ Loss of other property by actual or attempted robbery while outside the premises and in the care and custody of a messenger or an armored car company

Computer Fraud

Computer Fraud coverage covers loss of or damage to money, securities, and other property because of the use of a computer to fraudulently transfer that property from inside the premises or banking premises to a place or person (other than a messenger) outside the premises. Coverage is provided world-wide. Proof of loss may not be based on an inventory shortage or profit and loss computation.

Money Orders and Counterfeit Paper Currency

The next insuring agreement, *Money Orders and Counterfeit Paper Currency*, covers losses that result when the insured accepts invalid money orders or counterfeit paper currency in good faith.

Suppose that a customer at the insured's clothing store uses cash to purchase $1,000 worth of merchandise. When the insured attempts to deposit the money, she learns that it is counterfeit. The Money Orders and Counterfeit Paper Currency coverage would pay for her loss.

Funds Transfer Fraud

The *Funds Transfer Fraud* insuring agreement covers losses resulting from fraudulent instructions to a financial institution to pay money from an insured's transfer account. Loss resulting from the use of a computer to fraudulently transfer money, securities, or other property is not covered. Fraudulent instructions are defined as instructions by someone who is impersonating an insured or an employee to transfer money without the insured's knowledge or consent. A transfer account is an account maintained at a financial institution that enables money to be transferred electronically, either by phone or in writing.

Extortion—Commercial Entities Endorsement

The *Extortion—Commercial Entities* endorsement pays for loss of money, securities, and other property resulting from extortion. *Extortion* means the surrender of property away from the premises as the result of a threat communicated to the insured to do bodily harm to the insured, an employee, or a relative of either who is being held captive.

Exclusions

The following material summarizes the exclusions that apply to Crime coverages.

For All Coverages

The following exclusions apply to all the coverages in the Crime forms:

➤ Theft or dishonest acts committed by the insured, partners, or members, whether acting alone or in collusion with others.

➤ Theft or dishonest acts committed by any of the insured's employees, managers, directors, trustees, or authorized representatives, except as covered under Employee Theft coverage. The exclusion applies whether the person is acting alone or in collusion with others and while actually working for the insured or otherwise.

➤ Seizure or destruction of property by government authority.

➤ Indirect or consequential losses.

➤ Legal expenses, except as provided under Forgery or Alteration coverage.

➤ Nuclear hazard.

➤ War and similar actions.

For Selected Coverages

In addition to the exclusions that apply to all coverages in the Crime forms, certain exclusions apply only to the Inside the Premises—Theft of Money and Securities, Inside the Premises—Robbery or Safe Burglary of Other Property, and Outside the Premises coverages. These coverages exclude

➤ Loss resulting from accounting or arithmetic errors or omissions.

➤ Loss resulting from giving or surrendering property in an exchange or purchase.

➤ Loss due to fire (does not apply to safes or vaults or destruction of money and securities under Inside the Premises—Theft of Money and Securities coverage).

➤ Loss of property contained in any money-operated device unless it is equipped with a recording instrument.

➤ Loss of motor vehicles, trailers, or semitrailers, including attached equipment and accessories.

➤ Loss of property when it is transferred or surrendered outside the premises or banking premises on the basis of unauthorized instructions or as a result of a threat to cause bodily harm or property damage. This does not apply to loss of money, securities, or other property while outside the premises and in the custody of a messenger if the insured was not aware of a threat at the time the property left the premises.

➤ Loss to the interior or exterior of the premises or to a safe, vault, cash register, cash box, cash drawer, or other property by vandalism or malicious mischief.

➤ Loss resulting from the insured or anyone acting with the insured's authority being induced by any dishonest act to voluntarily part with title to or possession of property.

The following exclusions apply only to the Computer Fraud insuring agreement:

➤ Loss resulting from the giving or surrendering of property in any exchange or purchase

➤ Loss resulting from funds transfer fraud

➤ Loss resulting from the insured, or someone acting on the insured's authority, being induced by a dishonest act to voluntarily part with title to or possession of property

Conditions

Similar to the Exclusions section, the Crime conditions are divided into conditions that apply to all coverages and conditions that apply only to certain coverages. We begin with conditions that apply to all coverages.

Cancellation as to Any Employee

Coverage for any employee is cancelled immediately on discovery of any theft or other dishonest act committed by the employee by the named insured, partners, officers, directors, members, or managers. This is true even when the dishonest act occurred before the employee was hired by the named insured.

The insurance company also reserves the right to cancel coverage for any employee. The insured must be notified in writing at least 30 days before the effective date of cancellation.

Valuation

For loss or damage to *property other than money or securities*, the insurer will pay the lesser of the property's replacement cost, the amount needed to repair or replace the property, or the limit of insurance.

Losses to money are paid at face value, but loss of a foreign currency can be paid at its face value in that other currency or in the American dollar equivalent determined by the exchange rate on the day the loss was discovered. Losses to *securities* are paid at their value at the close of business on the day the loss was discovered, but the insurer also has the option of replacing them in kind.

Other Conditions That Apply to All Coverages

New employees and additional premises obtained through a *consolidation or merger* are automatically covered for 90 days. However, the insured is required to provide written notice to the insurer and pay any additional premium required. This condition does not appear in Crime forms written for government entities.

The *limit of insurance* is not cumulative, regardless of how long the insurance remains in force.

If a loss is covered under more than one coverage in the Crime form, the insurer will pay the actual amount of loss or the sum of the limits of the applicable coverages, whichever is less.

If other insurance applies to a loss, Crime insurance pays on an excess basis, meaning that the other insurance will pay up to its limits first and the Crime policy coverage may apply only to any loss that still remains unpaid.

The insured cannot take legal action against the insurer for 90 days after filing the proof of loss. Legal action must be instigated within 2 years of the date of loss.

The coverage territory includes the United States, its territories and possessions, and Canada.

The insured's duties in the event of loss include the following:

➤ Notifying the insurer as soon as possible

➤ Notifying the police if a law might have been broken (does not apply to Employee Theft or Forgery or Alteration coverage)

➤ Submitting to examination under oath at the insurer's request

➤ Providing a sworn proof of loss within 120 days

➤ Cooperating with the insurer in the investigation and settlement of the claim

Conditions That Apply to Selected Coverages

Other conditions apply only to certain coverages:

➤ **Employee Theft coverage:** Losses that occur outside the coverage territory are covered when the employee is temporarily outside the territory for 90 days or fewer.

➤ **Forgery or Alteration coverage:** In addition to the proof of loss, the insured must submit the instrument involved in the loss or an affidavit describing the amount and cause of loss.

➤ **Inside the Premises—Robbery or Safe Burglary of Other Property and Outside the Premises coverages:** A $5,000 per occurrence limit applies for loss to precious metals, precious or semiprecious stones, furs, pearls, or other articles that contain these materials.

➤ **Outside the Premises coverage:** The insurer will only pay the amount of loss that cannot be recovered under the insured's contract with the armored car company and from any insurance available from the armored car company.

➤ **Computer Fraud coverage:** A $5,000 per occurrence limit applies for loss to manuscripts, drawings, or records, including the costs of reproducing or reconstructing information in them.

Fidelity Bonds

A *bond* is a guarantee that a specific duty will be discharged, a certain performance maintained, or a specific obligation fulfilled. *Fidelity bonds* guarantee an employee's honest discharge of duty and are written to protect an insured from dishonest acts by employees. The Employee Dishonesty coverage we discussed earlier provides coverage comparable to that provided by Fidelity bonds. There is another type of bond, called a *Surety bond*, that we discuss later in the course.

Parties to a Bond

Many similarities exist between insurance policies and bonds (insurance companies often issue both), but there are some important distinctions as well. Insurance contracts include two parties—the insured and the insurance company. Bonds are contracts between three parties:

➤ **Principal:** The party who promises to do (or not do) a specific thing. This is the person or company bonded.

➤ **Surety:** The party (often the insurance company) who agrees to be responsible for loss that might result if the principal does not keep his or her promise.

➤ **Obligee:** Party to whom the principal makes the promise and for whose protection the bond is written.

Suppose that the XYZ Insurance Company issues a Fidelity bond to Baker and Company that covers Baker's treasurer. XYZ Insurance Company is the surety, Baker and Company is the obligee, and Baker's treasurer is the principal.

Types of Fidelity Bonds

Several different types of Fidelity bonds exist:

➤ **Name Schedule bonds** cover each employee named on the policy schedule for the amount listed in the schedule. The limit of liability might vary for different employees on the list.

➤ **Position Schedule bonds** list positions in the company that are covered rather than the individuals who fill these positions. A new employee hired in a scheduled position is automatically covered.

➤ **Commercial Blanket bonds** cover losses arising from the dishonesty of one or more employees acting separately or together (in collusion). Neither the employees nor their positions are specifically named. The bond's limit of liability applies separately to each loss, regardless of the number of employees involved in a single loss.

➤ **Blanket Position bonds** are similar to Commercial Blanket bonds in that employees or positions are not specifically listed. However, the bond's limit applies separately to each employee involved in a loss.

Fidelity bonds are continuous and do not have an expiration date, although they may be terminated by the parties to the bond. Similar to Commercial Crime forms, Fidelity bonds provide a discovery or cutoff period for losses that occurred during the term of the bond, but were not discovered until after its termination.

Exam Prep Questions

1. George Hawthorn is employed by Moison Appliances as a shipping clerk. As he is stacking TVs in the storage room, he is surprised by two men, both carrying guns. They proceed to empty the warehouse of TVs. This is an example of what?

   ○ A. Burglary
   ○ B. Robbery
   ○ C. Mysterious disappearance
   ○ D. A fidelity loss

2. Which of the following must be true in a burglary?

   ❑ A. Property must be taken from a custodian or watchperson.
   ❑ B. There must be no evidence of force or violence.
   ❑ C. The burglary must involve unlawful entry or exit from the premises.
   ❑ D. There must be visible evidence of forcible entry or exit.

3. Theft generally means which of the following?

   ○ A. Any act of stealing
   ○ B. Any act of stealing other than burglary or robbery
   ○ C. Burglary and robbery only
   ○ D. Employee dishonesty only

4. Coverage for defense costs is included in which of the following?

   ○ A. Computer Fraud coverage
   ○ B. Forgery or Alteration coverage
   ○ C. All of the Crime coverages
   ○ D. None of the Crime coverages

5. Who of the following would be considered custodians while having care and custody of company property inside the premises?

   ○ A. A store clerk
   ○ B. A company vice president
   ○ C. A janitor
   ○ D. A night watchperson

6. In a Crime insurance policy, certificates of deposit are considered which of the following?

   ○ A. Other property
   ○ B. Money
   ○ C. Securities
   ○ D. Either money or securities

7. What type of property is protected under Computer Fraud coverage?

○ A. Money

○ B. Securities

○ C. Other property

○ D. All of the above

8. An insured must file a proof of loss within how many days after a loss?

○ A. 90 days

○ B. 30 days

○ C. 120 days

○ D. 60 days

Exam Prep Answers

1. B is correct. In Crime forms, robbery is defined as the unlawful taking of property from the care and custody of another person. The robber must have caused or threatened to cause bodily harm to the person being robbed or must have committed an obviously unlawful act that is witnessed by the person being robbed. Burglary is the taking of property by stealth rather than by force or threat.

2. C and D are correct. Although burglary is not specifically defined in the Crime forms, it still has a specific meaning in the insurance industry. Burglary is the taking of property from inside the premises by a person unlawfully entering or leaving the premises. There must be evidence of forcible entry or exit, such as marks made by tools, explosives, chemicals, or electricity. There is no requirement that the property be taken from a custodian or watchperson.

3. A is correct. Theft means the unlawful taking of money, securities, or other property. This broad term includes burglary, safe burglary, and robbery.

4. B is correct. Under Forgery or Alteration coverage, if the insured is sued for refusing to pay a forged or altered instrument and obtains the insurer's written permission to defend the suit, the insurer will pay reasonable defense costs incurred by the insured.

5. A and B are correct. A custodian is someone who has care or custody of property inside the premises. It includes the insured, the insured's partners or members, or any employee. It does not include a watchperson or janitor.

6. C is correct. Securities are instruments or contracts that represent money or property. Checks, drafts, bonds, certificates of deposit, stock certificates, stamps, and credit card receipts are all considered securities.

7. D is correct. Computer Fraud coverage covers loss of or damage to money, securities, and other property because of the use of a computer to fraudulently transfer that property from inside the premises or banking premises to a place or person (other than a messenger) outside the premises.

8. C is correct. If a loss occurs, the insured must provide a sworn proof of loss within 120 days.

Workers Compensation

Terms you'll need to understand:

✓ Assumption of risk
✓ Contributory negligence
✓ Fellow servant rule
✓ Permanent total disability
✓ Permanent partial disability
✓ Temporary total disability
✓ Temporary partial disability
✓ Private insurer
✓ Monopolistic state fund
✓ Competitive state fund
✓ Self-insurance
✓ Group insurance pools

Concepts you'll need to master:

✓ Common law defenses
✓ Exclusive remedy
✓ Exempt employments
✓ Compulsory compensation laws
✓ Elective compensation laws
✓ Deposit premium
✓ Experience rating

In this chapter, we discuss workers compensation coverage, a type of insurance designed to cover employees who are injured on the job. Workers compensation pays for all medical and rehabilitative care required to recover from the injury and also pays an income to the worker during any period he or she is too hurt to work. Workers compensation also pays benefits to the surviving dependents of a worker killed on the job.

Workers Compensation Laws

Workers compensation laws give employees the right to collect from their employers for injury, disability, or death that occurs in the course of employment.

Prior to the enactment of workers compensation laws, a worker had to sue his or her employer and prove the employer negligent to be reimbursed for a work-related injury. Employers proved successful at avoiding liability through the use of three common law defenses:

➤ *Assumption of risk* allowed the employer to deny liability on the basis that the employee knew what the situation was like before he or she was employed and, therefore, assumed all the risk of injury himself or herself.

➤ *Contributory negligence* was used to deny liability on the basis that no matter how negligent the employer was, the employee had also been negligent; therefore, the employee should be responsible for the consequences.

➤ The *fellow servant rule* was used to deny liability on the basis that the injury was caused by a fellow employee; therefore, the employer could not be held liable.

When workers compensation laws were finally adopted, they were designed to provide a fair means of handling work-related injuries, including occupational diseases. They are based on the idea that the cost of most work-related injuries and occupational diseases should be charged directly to the employer, regardless of who is at fault, and without complex court proceedings. The cost, in turn, would be passed on to the consumer as a cost of production. In return, the benefits stipulated in workers compensation laws are the only means—the *exclusive remedy*—available to employees against employers for injuries covered by those laws.

 Because workers compensation benefits are set by statute, employees cannot sue their employers in court to obtain additional compensation.

Occupations Covered

The early workers compensation laws applied only to hazardous occupations. Over the years, the scope of the laws has expanded to embrace more occupational groups. Every state has exempt classifications, but the majority of the nation's employees are now covered under workers compensation laws. Although the exemptions are not the same in all states, the following classes of employees are typically exempt:

➤ Certain farm and agricultural workers

➤ Charitable organization workers

➤ Domestic employees and casual laborers

➤ Newspaper vendors

In some states, the hours worked or wages earned determine whether an employee is exempt.

 Employers are not required to provide insurance or compensation benefits for exempt employees, but it is often recommended that they do. The fact that a worker is not covered under the law does not preclude legal claims against the employer. Benefits can always be voluntarily provided by purchasing workers compensation insurance to cover exempt employees.

Benefits Provided

Workers compensation laws vary from state to state, but in general they pay benefits in four categories.

➤ **Disability/loss of income benefits** compensate employees who are unable to work as the result of a work-related injury. These benefits are intended to replace a portion of lost income, but not all of it.

➤ **Medical benefits** pay for the cost of various types of medical services required because of an employment-related injury. Almost any type of related medical expense is covered with neither an upper dollar limit nor a limit on the period of time for which expenses are paid.

➤ **Survivor/death benefits** compensate a surviving spouse, children, or other relatives of an employee whose death results from a work-related injury. In general, survivor benefits usually include a weekly benefit and a stipulated amount for funeral and burial expenses.

➤ **Rehabilitation benefits** include medical rehabilitation, such as physical therapy designed to improve physical functioning, and vocational rehabilitation, such as retraining for a different occupation. Workers compensation rehabilitation benefits usually pay any reasonably justifiable expenses for these purposes.

Compensable Injuries

Work-related injuries must arise *out of employment* and arise *in the course of employment* to be compensated under workers compensation laws. Three factors are used to determine if the injury arose in the course of employment: time, place, and circumstances.

Time is important because a compensable injury must occur during the time work is actually performed for the purposes of employment. Place and circumstances are important because the injury must either

➤ Occur at the place of employment

➤ Occur away from the place of employment while employment duties are being performed

Types of Disability

The level of disability suffered by an injured worker is categorized into one of four types:

➤ Permanent total

➤ Permanent partial

➤ Temporary total

➤ Temporary partial

A *permanent* disability is one that will affect the worker for the rest of his or her life, for example, the loss of an arm or a leg. A *temporary* disability is one that will eventually go away, for example, a broken arm or leg that is expected to fully heal.

Determining the difference between a *total* and a *partial* disability depends on what standard the state uses to determine the degree of disability. In different areas, the determination is made by deciding first whether the worker is *industrially disabled* (which refers to an individual's loss of earnings because of an inability to perform the usual duties of his or her job) or *medically disabled* (which refers to a physical condition that might affect functioning and prevent an individual from performing any job). For example, if a factory machine operator who earned $50,000 a year lost the use of her hands, but she could still earn $20,000 a year as a quality inspector for the factory, she would be industrially disabled to the extent of $30,000—the difference between her earnings as a machine operator and her earnings as a quality inspector. If that machine operator lost the use of her eyes so that she could not even be a quality inspector, she would be medically disabled to the extent of her entire pre-injury earnings of $50,000 a year.

Where *industrial disability* is the standard, the difference between partial and total disability depends on whether the individual is able to earn at least some money by working or has completely lost the ability to work for a living. When medical disability is the standard, partial or total disability depends on whether the individual has partial physical functioning after the injury or has sustained a complete loss of physical functioning.

Compulsory Versus Elective

State workers compensation laws are either *compulsory* or *elective*. In most states, the law is compulsory, meaning that the employer must accept and comply with all provisions of the law.

If the state law is *elective*, the employer can choose not to be subject to the law. However, in states where the law is elective, there are still powerful incentives to participate in the system. An employer who elects not to participate loses all common law defenses. As a result, many employers elect to participate because it provides a degree of protection by putting a cap on their potential liability for worker injuries.

Even in elective states, there are certain occupations or groups for which workers compensation is compulsory, such as government employees. And both elective and compulsory states often exclude certain classes of employees, such as farm workers or domestic servants.

Funding

Because workers compensation benefits are often extended to employees over long periods of time, it is important that measures be taken to guarantee that the company has the funds to pay benefits required under the law. There are five basic methods for funding these benefits. Each state requires that employers provide security through at least one of these methods.

The most common way employers meet their workers compensation obligations is through insurance purchased from a *private insurer*. The employer transfers compensation obligations to the insurance company from which the policy was purchased. Then, the insurance company pays the benefits required by law.

Some states have created *monopolistic state funds* that require employers to purchase workers compensation insurance from them. Private insurance companies are not allowed to compete against these funds. To be insured against workers compensation claims, the employer must buy coverage from the state fund.

Other states have created *competitive state funds* that give employers a choice between purchasing workers compensation insurance from a state fund or a private insurance company. Thus, the state fund competes with private insurance.

Some employers assume their own workers compensation liability through the *self-insurance* method. If this method is chosen, the employer sets up a fund to pay workers compensation claims and files evidence of its existence with the state workers compensation authority. The employer must handle benefit costs and claim expenses, as well as medical and legal services.

Many states allow individual employers to form *group insurance pools* to insure the group members' workers compensation exposure in a particular state. Eligibility requirements vary from state to state. For example, in some states, the group members must be involved in the same type of business; in others, the members must have a minimum amount of workers compensation premium.

Workers Compensation and Employers Liability Policy

Almost all states that allow private insurance companies to offer coverage use the standardized Workers Compensation and Employers Liability policy filed by the National Council on Compensation Insurance (NCCI).

Coverages

A complete policy contains an Information Page (similar to the declarations used with other types of policies) and a policy form that contains the following sections:

➤ General Section

➤ Part One—Workers Compensation

➤ Part Two—Employers Liability

➤ Part Three—Other States Insurance

➤ Part Four—Your Duties If Injury Occurs

➤ Part Five—Premium

➤ Part Six—Conditions

The General Section contains definitions and conditions that apply to the policy as a whole.

Part One—Workers Compensation promises to pay all compensation and other benefits required of the insured by the workers compensation law in the state or states where the insured's business operates (which are listed in the Information Page). No dollar limit applies, except for those that are a part of the law. Coverage applies to any work-related accident occurring during the policy period.

Part Two—Employers Liability provides coverage to the insured for sums the insured becomes legally obligated to pay under common law because of a work-related injury or occupational disease. A minimum limit of $100,000 per accident applies. There is also a per employee limit for disease and an overall limit for additional claims.

You might wonder why the insured needs Employers Liability coverage because workers compensation laws were designed to make benefits payable on a no-fault basis. However, there are situations that are not covered by workers compensation laws, such as exempt employments, illegal employments, and non-compensable injuries. An employee who is unable to collect workers compensation under state law may still sue the employer for damages.

Part Three—Other States Insurance is used to provide coverage for states that are not specifically listed in the Information Page for Part One coverage, but in which the insurance company is also licensed to offer workers compensation coverage. The state must be listed in the Information Page for Other States Insurance coverage (or the Information Page might state that coverage is available in all states except those listed), and the insured must provide notice to the insurer as soon as work begins in a new state in order to have coverage.

Anticipated other states should be listed on the Information Page. However, Other States Insurance coverage cannot be used to provide coverage in the five states that have monopolistic state funds (North Dakota, Ohio, Washington, West Virginia, and Wyoming). If coverage is needed in these states, arrangements have to be made with the appropriate state fund.

Part Four—Your Duties If Injury Occurs addresses the insured's obligations when an injury occurs for which there might be coverage. The insured must provide medical services required for the injured party, report the injury to the insurer, and cooperate with the insurer in the investigation and settlement of the claim.

Part Five—Premium explains how the cost of the policy is determined.

Part Six—Conditions sets forth the various conditions that apply to the policy, such as cancellation procedures, subrogation, and the insurer's right to inspect the insured's workplace.

Exclusions

There are very few exclusions that apply to Part One of the workers compensation policy. The following exclusions apply to the Employers Liability section of the policy:

➤ Liability assumed under contract

➤ Punitive damages awarded because a worker was employed in violation of the law

➤ Injury to a worker while employed in violation of the law with the insured's knowledge

➤ Obligations imposed by any workers compensation, occupational disease, unemployment compensation, or disability benefits law

➤ Injury intentionally caused or aggravated by the insured

➤ Injury that occurs outside the United States, its territories or possessions, or Canada (does not apply to residents of these areas who are temporarily outside these areas)

➤ Damages arising out of violations of employment practices laws, such as discrimination or harassment

➤ Injury that is covered under a federal workers compensation law

➤ Injury to the master or member of the crew of any vessel

➤ Fines and penalties imposed for violations of federal or state law

➤ Damages payable under the Migrant and Seasonal Agricultural Worker Protection Act and other federal laws awarding damages for violation of laws or regulations

Endorsements

Coverage for certain types of benefits or certain classes of employees may only be provided by endorsement.

Some workers are required to be covered under the federal Longshore and Harbor Workers Compensation Act, which takes precedence over any state law that might cover the same workers. Under this act, specified benefits must be paid to maritime employees injured while working on navigable waters or shore-site areas of the United States and its territories. Employers whose workers are subject to this act can provide coverage by attaching the *Longshore and Harbor Workers Compensation Act Coverage endorsement* to the policy.

Some types of workers are not covered under a state's workers compensation laws, such as domestic employees and farm workers. An employer can provide coverage for excluded workers by adding the *Voluntary Compensation endorsement* to the policy.

Federal Workers Compensation Laws

Most workers are protected under their state's workers compensation laws. However, some categories of employees are covered under federal workers compensation laws.

In most states, interstate railroad workers are covered under the *Federal Employers Liability Act (FELA)* instead of state workers compensation laws. FELA allows the injured worker or a representative of a deceased worker to sue the employer for negligence and eliminates two of the common law defenses: contributory negligence and assumption of risk. Awards provided under FELA are often more substantial than those provided under state workers compensation laws because FELA does not limit an injured employee's remedies to scheduled benefits.

The *Jones Act* is a federal law that allows members of ships' crews to sue their employer/shipowner at common law for injuries caused by the employer's/shipowner's negligence.

Rating Workers Compensation Coverage

Workers compensation coverage is rated on the basis of the employer's payroll. Published manuals contain listings of numerous rate classifications based on the type of work employees perform and their relative exposures to work-related injuries. For any given employer, one or more of these classifications are selected.

For each classification, the manual provides a rate per $100 of payroll. The rate for each rate class is multiplied by each $100 of payroll applicable to the class. Rates for each class are totaled, and a *premium discount* that varies with the amount of total premium is applied. Because the employer does not know at policy inception what its payroll will be at any given time of the year, payroll is estimated for the purpose of determining a *deposit premium*. Later, the final premium is calculated.

Insureds who have premiums above a certain amount are eligible for *experience rating*. Under experience rating, premiums can be lowered—or raised—depending on the insurance company's claim experience with that insured. The amount of premiums the insured has paid and the amount of losses the insurance company has incurred on behalf of that insured are evaluated over the three years immediately preceding the current policy period. If the insured has a better than average loss history, the insured's premium is reduced by a fraction (called an *experience modification factor*) representing the proportion by which the insured's claim experience is more favorable than the average. If the loss history is worse than average, a surcharge will be applied to increase the premium.

Exam Prep Questions

1. Which one of the following injuries qualifies as a compensable injury under workers compensation laws?

   ○ A. A factory worker fractures her arm while working overtime on the assembly line.

   ○ B. A hotel maid falls down the stairs while cleaning her own home.

   ○ C. A secretary accidentally swallows his gum while in the company lunch-room and chokes when it gets lodged in his windpipe.

   ○ D. An office manager is injured in a traffic accident on his way to work.

2. Which of the following benefits are paid under workers compensation laws?

   ❏ A. Medical

   ❏ B. Rehabilitation

   ❏ C. Disability income

   ❏ D. Pain and suffering

3. In a competitive state, an employer can obtain workers compensation insurance from which of the following?

   ○ A. A private insurance company

   ○ B. The state fund

   ○ C. Either A or B

   ○ D. Neither A nor B

4. In most states, workers compensation laws apply to which of the following?

   ○ A. Only to workers in occupations that are considered extremely hazardous

   ○ B. To most workers except those specifically excluded by law

   ○ C. To full-time workers only

   ○ D. To all workers

5. Under which part of a Workers Compensation and Employers Liability policy would you find a description of the insured's obligations when an injury occurs?

   ○ A. Part One

   ○ B. Part Two

   ○ C. Part Three

   ○ D. Part Four

6. Under which part of a Workers Compensation and Employers Liability policy would you find a description of employers liability coverage provided?

   ○ A. Part One
   ○ B. Part Two
   ○ C. Part Three
   ○ D. Part Four

7. George is a trash collector earning $35,000 a year who hurts his back on the job, so he can no longer go out with the collection trucks. However, he can still be a route coordinator in the office at a salary of $25,000 per year. To what extent is George industrially disabled?

   ○ A. $35,000 per year
   ○ B. $25,000 per year
   ○ C. $10,000 per year
   ○ D. $0 per year

Exam Prep Questions

1. A is correct. Work-related injuries must arise out of employment and arise in the course of employment to be compensable. Time, place, and circumstances are all considered in making this determination.

2. A, B, and C are correct. Workers compensation laws pay benefits in four categories: disability/loss of income benefits, medical benefits, survivor/death benefits, and rehabilitation benefits. They do not pay benefits for pain and suffering.

3. C is correct. Competitive states give employers a choice between purchasing workers compensation insurance from a state fund or a private insurance company. The state fund competes with private insurance.

4. B is correct. Every state has some exempt classifications, but the majority of the nation's employees are covered under workers compensation laws.

5. D is correct. Part Four describes the insured's duties when a worker is injured. Part One describes the general terms of the workers compensation policy. Part Two is Employers Liability Insurance. Part Three is Other States Insurance.

6. B is correct. Part One describes the Workers Compensation coverage, and Part Two describes the Employers Liability coverage. Part Three is Other States Insurance, and Part Four describes the insured's duties upon a loss.

7. C is correct. Industrially disability measures the earnings an injured worker had before and after the injury. George's industrial disability is found by subtracting his route coordinator earnings of $25,000 from his trash collector earnings of $35,000.

19

Miscellaneous Commercial Insurance

Terms you'll need to understand:

✓ Scheduled farm personal property
✓ Unscheduled farm personal property
✓ Breakdown
✓ Expediting expenses
✓ Spoilage damage
✓ Utility interruption

✓ Dollar deductible
✓ Time deductible
✓ Percentage of loss deductible
✓ Self-insured retention
✓ Terrorism Risk Insurance Act
✓ Hull insurance

Concepts you'll need to master:

✓ Farm coverage part
✓ Farm property coverage forms
✓ Farm scheduled personal property
✓ Farm unscheduled personal property
✓ Farm liability coverage
✓ Boiler and machinery coverage part
✓ Equipment breakdown protection coverage form

✓ Suspension provision
✓ Malpractice insurance
✓ Errors and omissions insurance
✓ Employment practices liability insurance
✓ Difference in conditions insurance
✓ Umbrella insurance
✓ Surety bonds
✓ Surplus lines

Some commercial loss exposures are not covered by the policies we've reviewed so far. For example, Commercial General Liability (CGL) insurance excludes losses arising out of professional liability and aviation, and Commercial Property insurance excludes losses resulting from boiler explosions. In this chapter, we review some specialized commercial insurance policies that were developed to cover these exposures.

Farm Insurance

Farmers' businesses and homes are often at the same location, so they need insurance that covers both their personal and business exposures to loss. The *Farm coverage part* can be written as a mono-line policy or it can be included in a Commercial Package Policy. It can include several *Farm Property coverage forms* that cover both the personal and business property exposures of the farmer and a *Farm Liability coverage form* for the personal and business liability exposures of the farmer.

Farm Property Coverage Forms

The *Farm Property coverage forms* cover direct physical loss to a variety of properties. The insured can select any combination of three separate forms.

Covered Property

The *Farm Dwellings, Appurtenant Structures, and Household Personal Property* coverage form is similar to Section I of the Homeowners policy. It contains the following coverages:

➤ Coverage A—Dwellings

➤ Coverage B—Other Private Structures Appurtenant to Dwellings

➤ Coverage C—Household Personal Property

➤ Coverage D—Loss of Use

 As in the Homeowners form, Coverage D includes coverage for additional living expenses and fair rental value.

A special limit of $250 per occurrence applies to loss or damage to outdoor radio and TV antennas and satellite dishes.

In general, growing crops, trees, plants, shrubs, and lawns are excluded. However, a coverage extension for Coverages A, B, and C allows limited coverage for trees, plants, shrubs, or lawns within 250 feet of the covered residence, but only against loss by specified perils.

Causes of Loss and Other Provisions

The *Farm Property—Causes of Loss form* is a separate document listing the perils that the property is insured against. This form offers three separate levels of coverage within the same form: Basic, Broad, and Special. These levels of coverage are very similar to those provided by the Commercial Property Causes of Loss forms reviewed in previous chapters. The declarations indicates what level of coverage the insured has selected for each form. The insured can obtain coverage against earthquake by purchasing the separate *Earthquake Causes of Loss* form.

Perils covered under the *Covered Causes of Loss—Basic* section are the same as those you've studied for other basic property insurance forms.

Property insured under the Farm Property and Farm Structures forms is also covered for collision that results in

➤ Damage to covered farm machinery or other farm personal property

➤ Death of covered livestock

The *Covered Causes of Loss—Broad* section adds additional perils. Some that are unique to the farm risk include

➤ Electrocution of covered livestock

➤ Attacks on covered livestock by dogs or wild animals

➤ Drowning of covered livestock

➤ Accidents involving loading or unloading

➤ Accidental shooting of covered livestock

The *Covered Causes of Loss—Special* section provides open peril coverage, with the excluded losses being those you are already familiar with from your study of other open peril policy forms.

Farm Liability Coverage Form

The Farm Liability coverage form provides the following coverages for liability arising out of farming operations or personal activities:

➤ Coverage H—Bodily Injury and Property Damage Liability

➤ Coverage I—Personal and Advertising Injury Liability

➤ Coverage J—Medical Payments

The exclusions are similar to those found in other liability policies. There is no coverage for losses arising out of the following:

➤ Pollutants

➤ Injury to farm employees

➤ Vehicles, except as specifically described in the policy

➤ The insured's performance of or failure to perform custom farming operations for others

➤ The insured's own products

➤ Aircraft spraying

Other sections of the form—such as definitions, conditions, and additional coverages—are essentially the same as those you studied in connection with other liability insurance policies.

Boiler and Machinery Insurance

Most of the commercial lines policies you studied in previous chapters exclude loss resulting from boiler explosions.

Boilers are used to produce steam. Water in the enclosed vessel is heated to convert it to steam and then heated still further. Steam under pressure can generate the power to drive engines, turbines, and other heavy machinery, and the heat absorbed by the steam can be used in cooling and heating. This steam, however, can cause great destruction. Although boilers are built to withstand great pressure, and safety devices such as safety valves are designed to regulate pressure buildup, there was a time when accidents were all too frequent, resulting in substantial loss in lives and money.

To combat such problems, a group of engineers developed a boiler inspection service that they provided for their customers at a modest charge. As an added attraction, the engineers guaranteed their inspection service by offering insurance against loss that occurred in spite of their careful inspection.

This guaranteed insurance developed into *Boiler and Machinery (B&M) insurance*, and the principles of boiler insurance started being applied not only to boilers, but also to loss exposures arising out of other machines, particularly those that generated power.

 The focal point of Boiler and Machinery insurance continues to be loss prevention. Regular inspection services are provided as an integral part of the insurance coverage. A substantial part of each premium dollar is dedicated to inspection and loss control services. Because of the emphasis on loss prevention and the advance of sophisticated manufacturing processes, boiler explosions now rarely occur.

Boiler and Machinery Coverage Part

Whether boiler and machinery coverage is issued as a mono-line policy or as part of a package, the policy consists of

➤ The Common Policy Declarations

➤ The Common Policy Conditions

➤ A Boiler and Machinery coverage part (and one or more other coverage parts, if it is a package policy)

The *Boiler and Machinery coverage part* consists of

➤ The Equipment Breakdown Protection coverage declarations

➤ The Equipment Breakdown Protection coverage form

➤ Any applicable endorsements

Equipment Breakdown Protection Coverage Form

Although the term "boiler and machinery" is still used in the Common Policy Declarations and in the Commercial Lines Manual for classification purposes, the latest ISO coverage form is called the *Equipment Breakdown Protection* coverage form.

Covered Causes of Loss

Under the Equipment Breakdown Protection coverage form, the only covered cause of loss is "breakdown" to "covered equipment."

Definitions

For insurance purposes, *breakdown* means the following types of direct physical loss that cause damage to covered equipment and necessitates its repair or replacement (unless the loss or damage is otherwise specifically excluded within the coverage form):

➤ Failure of pressure or vacuum equipment

➤ Mechanical failure, including rupture or bursting caused by centrifugal force

➤ Electrical failure, including arcing

However, the term "breakdown" *does not include* any of the following:

➤ Malfunction, including but not limited to adjustment, alignment, calibration, cleaning, or modification

➤ Defects, erasures, errors, limitations, or viruses in computer equipment and programs, including the inability to recognize and process any date or time or provide instructions to covered equipment

➤ Leakage at any valve, fitting, shaft seal, gland packing, joint, or connection

➤ Damage to any vacuum tube, glass tube, or brush

➤ Damage to any structure or foundation supporting the covered equipment or any of its parts

➤ The functioning of any safety or protective device (such as one that turns off equipment to prevent further damage)

➤ The cracking of any part of an internal combustion gas turbine exposed to the products of combustion

One breakdown means that if an initial breakdown causes other breakdowns, all are considered a single breakdown. All breakdowns at any one premises that manifest themselves at the same time and are the direct result of the same cause are considered "one breakdown."

Covered property means property that the insured owns or that is in the insured's care, custody, or control and for which the insured is legally liable.

Covered equipment includes

➤ Equipment built to operate under internal pressure or vacuum other than the weight of contents

➤ Electrical or mechanical equipment used in the generation, transmission, or utilization of energy

➤ Communication equipment and computer equipment

➤ Any equipment owned by a public or private utility and used solely to supply utility services to the insured's premises

Computer equipment means the insured's programmable electronic equipment used to store, retrieve, and process data, as well as associated peripheral equipment that provides communications including input and output functions (such as printing) or auxiliary functions (such as data transmission).

Coverages Provided

This form provides coverage only for the portion of loss or damage that is a direct result of a breakdown to covered equipment. Each of the following coverages is provided only if either a limit or the word "included" is shown for that coverage in the declarations. If neither a limit nor the word "included" is shown, that particular coverage is not provided. An insured can select from among the following coverages:

➤ Property damage

➤ Expediting expenses

➤ Business income and/or extra expense

➤ Spoilage damage

➤ Utility interruption

➤ Newly acquired premises

➤ Ordinance or law

➤ Errors or omissions

➤ Brands and labels

➤ Contingent business income and/or extra expense

Property damage coverage applies to direct damage to covered property located at a premises described in the declarations. The only difference between this coverage and commercial property coverage is the covered cause of loss—the damage must be caused by a breakdown of covered equipment (rather than fire, lightning, windstorm, and so on).

Expediting expenses coverage pays extra costs necessarily incurred by the insured to make temporary repairs and to expedite the permanent repairs or replacement of the damaged property.

Business income and extra expense coverage, or *extra expense coverage only*, are similar to the same coverages under the commercial property coverage part. The only significant difference is the covered cause of loss—the damage must be caused by a breakdown of covered equipment (rather than fire, lightning, windstorm, and so on).

Spoilage damage to raw materials, property in process, or finished products can be covered if these items are in storage or in the course of being manufactured at the time of loss, the insured owns or is legally liable for these items under contract, and the spoilage is because of the lack or excess of power, light, heat, steam, or refrigeration. When this coverage applies, the insurer also pays any necessary expenses incurred by the insured to reduce the amount of the loss, but only to the extent that the expenses do not exceed the amount of loss that otherwise would have been payable.

Coverage for *utility interruption* can be purchased if the insured has business income and/or extra expense coverage, spoilage coverage, or both. This coverage extends the business income, extra expense, and/or spoilage coverage to apply to loss resulting from an interruption of utility services because of a breakdown of equipment that is not the insured's. It applies when there is a breakdown of equipment owned, operated, or controlled by a public or private utility that directly generates, transmits, distributes, or provides utility services received by the insured that are used to supply electric power, communication services, air conditioning, heating, gas, sewer, water, or steam to the insured's premises. When this coverage is written, a waiting period (stated in hours) must be shown in the declarations. After the waiting period is met, coverage commences from the initial time of interruption and is subject to any applicable deductibles.

If coverage for *newly acquired premises* is written, the insurer automatically provides coverage at any newly acquired premises the insured purchases or leases. Coverage begins as soon as the premises is acquired and continues only for the number of days for this coverage shown in the declarations. However, as a condition of the coverage, the insured is required to notify the insurer in writing of the new premises and agree to pay an additional premium.

Ordinance or law coverage is virtually identical to the coverage available under other property coverages. If applicable, the ordinance and law exclusion will not apply and the insurer will pay increased costs resulting from the enforcement of laws or ordinances that regulate the demolition, construction, repair, or use of the building or structure. The only difference is that under this form, the loss must result from breakdown of covered equipment (rather than traditional perils such as fire, lightning, windstorm, and so on).

Errors and omissions coverage pays for loss or damage that would not otherwise be payable under the coverage form, solely because of one or more of the following:

➤ Any error or unintentional omission in the description or location of any property shown in the declarations

➤ Any failure through error to include any premises owned or occupied by the insured at the inception date of the coverage part

➤ Any error or unintentional omission by the insured that results in cancellation of any premises insured under the policy

No coverage is provided as a result of any error or unintentional omission by the insured in the reporting of values for requested coverages. It is a condition of this coverage that errors or unintentional omissions must be reported and corrected when discovered.

Coverage for *brands and labels* is available for businesses that carry branded or labeled merchandise. If such property is "covered property" and is damaged in a breakdown, the insurer can take all or any part of the property at an agreed or appraised value. In such cases, the insured may stamp the word "Salvage" on the merchandise or its containers, or may remove the brands and labels, if doing so will not physically damage the property. The insurer pays the reasonable costs for stamping or removing labels, but the total paid for these costs and the value of the damaged property cannot exceed the applicable limit of insurance for such property.

Contingent business income and/or extra expense coverage is also available. When applicable, it pays the insured's losses resulting from a breakdown of covered property at a premises shown in the declarations that the insured does not own or operate. For example, a loss at another premises that prevents the insured from receiving services or materials—or from shipping them to others—or that results in a loss of sales at the insured's premises might be covered. This is called coverage for "dependent properties" on commercial property coverage forms.

Exclusions

The Equipment Breakdown Protection coverage form lists a number of exclusions that apply to loss or damage regardless of whether any other cause or event contributes concurrently or in any sequence to the loss. A number of these are general exclusions found on many other commercial coverage forms, such as earth movement, water, nuclear hazards, and war or military action.

Additional exclusions also apply, and they address the unique nature of boiler and machinery coverage or the interface between this coverage and commercial property coverages. These exclusions merit some discussion.

Generally, *explosions* are excluded. This means internal or external combustion explosions resulting from the ignition of fuel or dust particles or something else, and not explosions caused by pressure or the centrifugal force of moving parts. The form makes an exception and states that it will cover loss or damage caused by an explosion of any covered steam boiler, electric steam generator, steam piping, steam turbine, steam engine, gas turbine, or moving or rotating machinery when the explosion is caused by centrifugal force or mechanical breakdown.

Any loss because of *fire or combustion explosion* is excluded, including those that result in a breakdown, occur at the same time as a breakdown, or ensue from a breakdown. The reason for this is that fire damage is covered by standard commercial property forms. If a fire causes a breakdown to occur, and the breakdown causes additional damage (perhaps because of a pressure explosion that blew out windows and destroyed furniture and fixtures), the fire is still the *"proximate cause"* of all resulting losses, which is covered by property insurance even if some of the damage was not actually fire damage.

Also excluded are *explosions within a chemical recovery type boiler* or within the passage from the furnace to the atmosphere.

Damage to covered equipment *undergoing a pressure or electrical test* is excluded because during testing, the technicians might push the threshold of tolerance of the equipment to the upper limits of specifications, or beyond; therefore, any resulting damage is not considered accidental and is not what the insurance was designed to cover.

There is no coverage for damage caused by water or other means to *extinguish a fire*, even when the attempt is unsuccessful. Once again, the obligation for this loss should fall back on the property insurance coverage, under the doctrine of "proximate cause."

Generally, there is no coverage for damage caused by *depletion, deterioration, corrosion, erosion,* or *wear and tear*. The insurer will not pay for upgrades to covered equipment. However, if a breakdown occurs, it will pay for any resulting loss or damage.

If coverage is provided by another policy, whether collectible or not, there is no coverage for any loss caused by a limited number of the *broad form perils* found on commercial property causes of loss forms. Specifically, the Equipment Breakdown Protection form excludes losses caused by aircraft, vehicles, freezing, lightning, sinkhole collapse, smoke, riot, civil commotion, vandalism, or the weight of snow, sleet, or ice. But this exclusion applies only if there is other coverage—if it is not otherwise covered, the Equipment Breakdown Protection form provides coverage within the scope of its provisions (damage resulting from a breakdown of equipment, even if because of one of these causes).

There is no coverage for any loss or damage resulting from a breakdown caused by *windstorm or hail*. Although this is similar to the previous exclusion, there is one major difference—it is absolute, and there is no exception even when other insurance does not apply.

There is no coverage for any *delay in or interruption of* any business, manufacturing, or processing activity, except as provided by the business income and/or extra expense and utility interruption coverages.

With respect to *business income and/or extra expense* coverage and *utility interruption* coverage, there is no coverage for

➤ Any business activity that would not or could not have been carried on if the breakdown had not occurred

➤ The insured's failure to use due diligence and all reasonable means to operate the business as nearly normal as practicable

➤ Suspension, lapse, or cancellation of any contract following a breakdown extending beyond the time business could have been resumed if the contract has not lapsed, been suspended, or cancelled

There is no coverage for *lack or excess of power*, light, heat, steam, or refrigeration, except as provided by the business income and/or extra expense, utility interruption, and spoilage damage coverages.

With respect to *utility interruption* coverage, there is no coverage for loss resulting from any of the following, whether or not the insured has coverage under another policy:

➤ Acts of sabotage

➤ Collapse

➤ Deliberate acts of load shedding by a supplying utility

➤ Freezing caused by cold weather

➤ Impact of aircraft, missile, or vehicle

➤ Impact of objects falling from an aircraft or missile

➤ Lightning

➤ Riot, civil commotion, or vandalism

➤ Sinkhole collapse

➤ Smoke

➤ Weight of snow, ice, or sleet

There is no coverage for any *indirect loss* resulting from a breakdown of covered equipment except as might be provided by the business income and/or extra expense, utility interruption, and spoilage damage coverages.

There is no coverage for any loss resulting from *neglect by the insured* to use all reasonable means to save and preserve covered property from further damage at and after the time of loss.

Limits of Insurance

This form can show a variety of limits of insurance in the declarations. The primary limit is an overall *limit per breakdown*—this is the most the insurer will pay for loss or damage resulting from any one breakdown under all applicable coverages.

For each applicable coverage, a limit of insurance or the word "included" must be shown in the declarations. If a *limit of insurance* is shown, that is the most the insurer will pay for that particular coverage. If the word *included* is shown for any coverage, the limit for that coverage is part of, and not in addition to, the limit per breakdown.

For a few coverages, *time limits* must be shown in the declarations. If coverage for an extended period of restoration is elected under the business income and/or extra expense coverages, or if coverage for newly acquired premises is elected, a *number of days* must be shown in the declarations for these coverages. If utility interruption coverage is elected, a *number of hours* that apply as a waiting period must be shown in the declarations.

For the following coverages, the policy automatically provides up to *$25,000 per breakdown* unless a higher limit (or the word "included") is shown in the declarations:

➤ Ammonia contamination

➤ Consequential loss

➤ Data and media

➤ Hazardous substance

➤ Water damage

Deductibles

Deductibles apply separately for each applicable coverage unless the deductibles are shown as "combined" for any two or more coverages. If a *combined deductible* applies, the insurer subtracts the combined deductible amount from the aggregate amount of loss to which the combined deductible applies.

Some coverages are subject to a *dollar deductible*; in which case, the insurer subtracts the deductible amount from any loss it would otherwise pay.

Certain coverages are subject to a *time deductible*, which is usually expressed as a number of days. If a time deductible applies, the insurer is not responsible for any loss that occurs during the deductible period immediately following a breakdown. For example, if business income coverage is elected with a time deductible of seven days, coverage would not begin until after the business has been shut down for more than seven days.

Deductibles can be expressed as a *percentage of loss*; in which case, the insurer would not be liable for the indicated percentage of an aggregate loss. For example, if a coverage is written with a percentage of loss deductible of 15%, the insurer is only obligated to pay 85% of any covered loss.

Business income coverage can also be written with a *multiple of daily value* deductible and with *minimum* or *maximum* deductible amounts that apply to the coverage.

Loss Conditions

The Equipment Breakdown Protection coverage form includes a number of standard loss conditions similar to those found on other commercial coverage forms, including abandonment, appraisal, other insurance, and subrogation.

Additionally, this form includes a provision for paying *defense costs*. If the insurer elects to defend the insured against lawsuits arising from the owners of property damaged by a covered loss, it will do so at its own expense.

The insurer also reserves the right to *adjust losses with the owner* of property. If there is loss or damage to property of others in the care, custody, or control of the insured, the insurer has the right to settle the loss or damage with the owner of that property.

Another condition addresses the issue of *reducing the insured's loss*. As soon as possible after a breakdown, the insured is required to resume business (partially or completely), make up for lost business within a reasonable period of time, and make use of every reasonable means to reduce or avert loss.

A *valuation* condition states that the insurer determines the value of covered property when loss or damage occurs based on the cost to repair, rebuild, or replace the damaged property with property of the same kind, capacity, size, or quality. Some special provisions apply to particular types of property and circumstances.

For business income and/or extra expense coverage, a few additional conditions apply. These address the issues of providing annual reports of values, adjustments of premium, and coinsurance.

General Conditions

The Equipment Breakdown Protection coverage form includes a number of general conditions that are frequently found on other commercial coverage forms, such as concealment, misrepresentation or fraud, no benefit to bailee, and liberalization. It also includes some conditions that are unique to boiler and machinery insurance.

The coverage form includes a *suspension provision*. One of the unique things about boiler and machinery insurance is that the insurer or any representative of the insurer can *immediately suspend* the insurance against loss by breakdown for specific equipment whenever that equipment is found to be in, or exposed to, a dangerous condition. Advance notice is not required, but the insurer must mail or deliver written notice of the suspension to the insured's last known address or the address where the covered equipment is located. The suspension applies only to the particular equipment. After it is in effect, the suspension can be lifted and the insurance reinstated only by an endorsement for that equipment. If insurance is suspended, the insured is entitled to a pro rata refund of premium for the period of suspension.

There is a *joint or disputed loss agreement* condition that is designed to facilitate payment when both a commercial property policy and equipment breakdown protection policy are in effect, damage occurs to property that is covered under both policies, and there is disagreement between the insurers whether there is coverage or as to the amount of the loss to be paid under its own policy. This condition applies only if both policies have a similar provision for resolving disputed losses. Generally, each insurer agrees to pay the full amount of any loss that it agrees is covered under its own policy and a half of the loss that is in dispute. This condition does not apply when both coverages are written by the same insurer.

The last condition addresses *final settlement between insurers*. This condition applies only when two or more insurers are involved in a settlement of a disputed loss or one that is resolved by arbitration. It requires the insurer found responsible for the greater percentage on the ultimate loss to return the excess contribution made by the other insurer(s); plus it must pay interest on the amount from the date the insured invokes this agreement until the date the other insurer(s) are actually reimbursed. Arbitration expenses are apportioned between insurers on the same basis that the loss is apportioned.

Aviation Insurance

Insurance coverages for aircraft are similar to those available for automobile exposures. The most significant differences between aircraft and automobile insurance are the higher dollar exposure to loss and the high degree of care required by the operator of the aircraft. As in automobile policies, the two basic Aviation coverages are Physical Damage and Liability.

Physical Damage Coverage

Aviation Physical Damage coverage, called *Hull insurance*, is much like the Comprehensive and Collision coverages provided by auto insurance. It covers the complete aircraft, including its airframe, engines, controls, and electronic navigation and communications equipment. It does not cover personal effects. Either a *fixed dollar* or a *"percentage of the loss"* deductible usually applies. Coverage can be provided while the aircraft is in one of the following situations:

➤ In the air or on the ground

➤ On the ground only

➤ Not in motion under its own power

The declarations indicate what coverage applies and any special restrictions or deductibles.

Liability Coverage

Aviation Liability insurance for owners of aircraft includes coverage for

➤ Bodily injury liability to persons other than passengers

➤ Bodily injury to passengers

➤ Property damage liability

➤ Medical payments (payable for injuries to passengers, regardless of whether the insured is liable for their injuries)

Professional Liability Insurance

Professional liability—liability arising out of rendering or failing to render services of a professional nature—is excluded under CGL policies. Special *Professional Liability policies* have been developed for many professionals, including physicians, surgeons, dentists, lawyers, insurance agents, architects, accountants, as well as directors and officers of corporations. Each policy is tailored to fit a specific occupational need. Most policies are written on a claims-made basis.

Professionals have two kinds of legal duty to their clients. These are to perform the services for which they were hired and to perform them in accordance with the appropriate standards of conduct. Because of their special skills, professionals are held to a higher standard of conduct.

Professional Liability policies can go by several different names. *Malpractice insurance* is the term commonly applied to Medical Professional Liability policies written for medical professionals or institutions, including physicians, nurses, dentists, surgeons, opticians, optometrists, chiropractors, and veterinarians. *Errors and Omissions (E&O) insurance* is a broad term that refers to Professional Liability policies written for other professionals, such as insurance agents, accountants, architects, stockbrokers, engineers, consultants, and attorneys.

Early in our discussion of the insurance agent's role, we discussed the liability exposure that an insurance agent has and the need for him or her to be properly insured under an E&O policy. E&O insurance is also appropriate for directors and officers of corporations who can be sued as individuals by stockholders. Directors and officers have no coverage under a CGL for personal liability and no coverage under their homeowners contract for liability arising out of business pursuits. This exposure is properly insured under a type of E&O insurance called *Directors and Officers Liability*.

Because Malpractice and E&O insurance cover loss arising from professional acts, or acts that fall within a professional's duties, it is extremely important to distinguish between professional and nonprofessional exposures. Unfortunately, courts have not always been consistent in their interpretations. If the insured wants full coverage against liability exposures arising from business, it might be advisable for the insured to maintain both a CGL policy and the appropriate Professional Liability policy.

Employment Practices Liability Insurance

Both the CGL and Workers Compensation and Employers Liability policies exclude losses arising out of wrongful termination, discrimination, sexual harassment, and other employment-related practices. This coverage is provided by *Employment Practices Liability (EPL) insurance.*

EPL insurance can be issued as an endorsement to a Directors and Officers Liability policy or as a separate policy. Although standard ISO forms are available, many companies issue their own policies. Policy provisions differ greatly among insurers, particularly those regarding the types of wrongful employment acts covered. Most policies cover wrongful acts committed by the employer and its employees. However, typical exclusions include the following:

➤ Wrongful termination practices committed with dishonest, fraudulent, criminal, or malicious intent

➤ Mass layoffs of employees

➤ Deliberate fraud or purposeful violation of laws, rules, or regulations

➤ Bodily injury (BI) or property damage (PD) other than emotional distress, mental anguish, or humiliation

➤ Liabilities of others assumed under contract, except employment contracts

➤ Circumstances reported under prior EPL policies

Difference in Conditions Insurance

In Chapter 13, "Commercial Property Insurance," you learned that although the Commercial Property coverage part provides extensive property coverage, it still contains several exclusions. *Difference in Conditions (DIC) insurance* provides broad coverage to fill those gaps. It is written to exclude the basic fire and extended coverage perils, but include most other insurable perils. Consequently, it is written in conjunction with policies providing the basic coverage excluded by the Difference in Conditions policy. For example, a Commercial Property policy excludes such things as damage caused by insects, birds, rodents, or other animals. If an insured desired such coverage, it could be obtained through a DIC policy.

DIC policies are usually written on large risks with a high deductible. Insurance companies issue their own DIC policies because there is no standardized form for this type of coverage.

 DIC policies provide broad coverage for property insurance exposures only. Although they can fill coverage gaps, they do not provide any liability coverage.

Commercial Umbrella Insurance

Just as Personal Umbrella policies are available to cover the catastrophic liability exposures of personal risks, high-limit *Commercial Umbrella policies* are designed to provide catastrophic Liability coverage for business risks.

Because the umbrella policy is not designed to handle usual or everyday exposures, the insured must have underlying liability coverage, such as Commercial Auto or CGL coverage, before an umbrella policy will be issued. In areas where underlying insurance does not exist, a *self-insured retention* will apply, which is an amount of loss the insured must absorb (in effect, a deductible) before the umbrella coverage kicks in.

A Commercial Umbrella policy provides coverage in three types of situations:

➤ When the policy limits applying to a loss under an underlying policy have been exhausted.

➤ When a loss is excluded under an underlying contract but not excluded under the Umbrella. (The insured must first meet the retention limit.)

➤ When previous losses reimbursed under an underlying policy have reduced its aggregate limit so that a subsequent loss is not fully covered.

 Commercial Umbrella policies provide broad coverage for liability exposures only, which apply as excess above underlying insurance or a self-insured retention. They do not provide any property coverage.

Surety Bonds

As part of our discussion of Crime insurance, we talked about Fidelity bonding, which is a way for employers to protect themselves against an employee's dishonesty. A *Fidelity bond* is essentially a guarantee that certain acts on the part of the employee *will not* be committed.

Surety bonds, on the other hand, emphasize that certain things *will* happen. In broad terms, Surety bonding guarantees one of the following:

➤ *Someone will faithfully perform* whatever he or she agrees to do

➤ *Someone will make a payment* as agreed upon by that person and another party

> One of the key differences between Fidelity and Surety bonding lies in the fact that, in Fidelity bonding, the obligee (the employer) seeks and pays for the bond. The principal (the employee) often does not even know that the bond exists. With Surety bonds, on the other hand, the principal is always the party that both arranges and pays for the bond for the benefit of the obligee.

Before a Surety bond is issued, the principal must submit an application that contains not only the information needed for underwriting, but also an *indemnity agreement* through which the principal agrees to indemnify the surety for any loss sustained. This is necessary because suretyship does not anticipate losses, although they do occur. Instead, it is expected that the principal will perform as agreed and, if not, that the principal will otherwise make it up to the obligee.

If the principal does default, however, the surety company will indemnify the obligee and then attempt to collect from the principal. The premium paid is actually a charge for using the credit of the surety company, without allowance for losses. In addition, in some cases the surety can require that the principal deposit money, called *collateral security*, to protect the surety against possible loss.

Contract Bonds

Many different types of bonds are available for a variety of needs. One of these is *Contract bonds*, which guarantee the fulfillment of contractual obligations. The following are common types of Contract bonds:

➤ *Bid bonds*: Guarantee that if a contractor's bid is accepted, the contractor will enter into a contract and provide the required Performance bond.

➤ *Performance bonds*: Guarantee that jobs will be completed by the contractor according to contract specifications.

➤ *Payment bonds*: Guarantee that bills for labor and materials will be paid by the contractor as they are due. These are sometimes called *Labor and Materials bonds*, and are frequently included as part of a Performance bond.

➤ *Supply bonds*: Guarantee that a supplier will furnish supplies, products, or equipment at an agreed upon price and time.

➤ *Completion bonds*: Guarantee that when contractors borrow money to fund construction projects, the project will be carried out and the work will be delivered free and clear of liens or encumbrances.

Judicial Bonds

Judicial bonds guarantee that the principal will fulfill certain obligations set forth by law. There are two classes of judicial bonds:

➤ *Fiduciary bonds* are commonly used to bond guardians, administrators, trustees, and executors—all of whom are fiduciaries or persons appointed by a court of law to manage the property of others.

➤ *Court bonds* are used to settle legal arguments that do not involve monetary damages. Their primary purpose is to protect obligees against loss in case principals are not able to prove that they are legally entitled to the legal remedy they sought against the obligees.

Other Types of Bonds

Public Official bonds, which are required by law, guarantee that public officials will handle public money correctly and otherwise perform their duties faithfully and honestly.

License and Permit bonds are sometimes required in connection with the issuance of licenses by government agencies. They guarantee that the person who posts the bond will comply with all applicable laws pertaining to his or her activities.

Surplus Lines

Generally, an insurer is not allowed to transact business in a state without having a current Certificate of Authority or license issued by the insurance department specifically authorizing the insurer to transact particular lines of business. These insurers are known as *authorized* or *admitted insurers*, and they transact traditional lines of insurance. In most states, the law prohibits anyone from acting as an agent for an unauthorized company and prohibits an insurer from transacting any line of business for which it is not authorized.

The Unauthorized Market and Surplus Lines

In almost every state, the insurance law makes exemptions that apply to certain transactions that might be legally conducted by *unauthorized* or *non-admitted insurers* without requiring a Certificate of Authority. These transactions usually include certain types of transportation and ocean marine risks, reinsurance, and *surplus lines coverages*. Surplus lines coverages are those that are not available or cannot be procured from authorized insurers within a state. Although surplus lines are considered an unregulated area of insurance, the business must be procured and conducted in accordance with the surplus lines insurance law of the state.

Conditions for Obtaining Coverage

Although there are variations from one state to another, generally three conditions must be met before surplus lines insurance can be obtained from an unauthorized insurer:

➤ The business must be obtained through a licensed surplus lines broker.

➤ It is determined after a diligent search that the full amount of insurance cannot be obtained from authorized insurers who market the insurance in the state.

➤ Coverage cannot be obtained as a surplus lines coverage solely for the purpose of obtaining a better contract or a lower premium than an authorized insurer could provide.

Although surplus lines insurers are "unauthorized," many states issue a list of approved surplus lines carriers and require brokers to place surplus lines business with those insurers.

Federal Terrorism Risk Insurance Act of 2002

We conclude our discussion of miscellaneous commercial insurance policies by covering a federal program that affects most commercial lines of insurance—the *Federal Terrorism Risk Insurance Act of 2002*.

Background

Insurance protection is vital for economic development and stability. Without insurance protection, builders might not build structures, potential buyers might not buy property, and potential business owners might not be willing to operate a business. When faced with catastrophic losses, the insurance industry has often backed away from providing needed coverages, and the federal government has stepped in to provide subsidies, loss sharing, or excess reinsurance in order to make insurance available. The FAIR Plan program was created to make property insurance available in urban areas after the riots during the 1960s. The Federal Crop Insurance Program was implemented when insurers were unwilling to assume the full risk of crop hail damage. The National Flood Insurance Program was created in response to the unavailability of flood insurance in high-risk areas.

After the terrorist attacks on the United States on September 11, 2001, insurers started to attach terrorism exclusion endorsements to commercial property and casualty policies. They did not want to assume the potential catastrophic losses that might result from future attacks. But without insurance for such losses, business owners who were no more capable of assuming such losses would have to bear the risk. This situation created a lot of uncertainty in the U.S. economy, which could have many negative consequences.

As a result, in 2002, Congress enacted and the president signed into law the *Terrorism Risk Insurance Act (TRIA) of 2002*. This federal law provides a federal backstop for defined acts of terrorism and imposes certain obligations on insurers. It is designed to limit the exposure of individual insurers and the insurance industry as a whole, and to make insurance available and affordable, under a system in which the federal government participates and shares the risk of loss. The act voids terrorism exclusions, and state approval of such exclusions, in property and casualty insurance contracts to the extent that they exclude losses that would otherwise be insured losses.

Temporary Program

The program is intended to be a temporary federal program that provides for a system of shared public and private compensation for insured losses resulting from acts of terrorism in order to protect consumers by addressing market disruptions and ensure the continued widespread availability and affordability of property and casualty insurance for terrorism risk. Unless it is extended by Congress, the program will terminate on December 31, 2005.

Definitions

The term *act of terrorism* means any act that is certified by the secretary of the treasury, in concurrence with the secretary of state and the attorney general of the United States, to meet the following criteria:

➤ To be an act of terrorism

➤ To be a violent act or an act that is dangerous to human life, property, or infrastructure

➤ To have resulted in damage within the United States, or outside of the United States in the case of an air carrier, vessel, or the premises of a U.S. mission

➤ To have been committed by an individual or individuals acting on behalf of any foreign person or foreign interest, as part of an effort to coerce the civilian population of the United States or to influence the policy or affect the conduct of the U.S. government by coercion

The term *insured loss* means any loss resulting from an act of terrorism, including an act of war (in the case of workers compensation losses) that is covered by primary or excess property and casualty insurance issued by an insurer if the loss occurs in the following locations:

➤ Within the United States

➤ In an air carrier or to a U.S. flag vessel regardless of where the loss occurs

➤ At the premises of a U.S. mission

General Overview of Program

The program allows for risk sharing when the proper conditions are met. Generally, insurers are subject to *deductibles* (amounts they must pay before federal contributions begin), and when multiple insurers are involved in a loss, the secretary will determine the pro rata share of insured losses to be paid by each insurer. The federal government will pay 90% of insured losses that exceed insurer deductibles. However, there is an annual cap on the maximum obligation of insurers and the federal government under the law.

Insurer Deductibles

Coverage for an individual insurer's losses are subject to a deductible, which is based on a percentage of the insurer's direct earned premiums during the prior calendar year. The percentage ranges from 1% to 15% and varies depending on the program year.

Cap on Annual Liability

If the aggregate insured losses exceed $100 billion during any program year under the shared program, the federal government will not be liable for any portion of insured losses in excess of $100 billion, and no insurer that has met its insurer deductible will be liable for the payment of any portion of insured losses that exceeds $100 billion.

Exam Prep Questions

1. Which of the following may be covered under a Farm coverage part?
   - ❑ A. Farm buildings, equipment, and livestock
   - ❑ B. Liability arising out of farm operations
   - ❑ C. Growing crops
   - ❑ D. Farm dwelling and its personal property

2. A breakdown of equipment covered under the Equipment Breakdown Protection coverage form results in the simultaneous breakdown of three other pieces of covered equipment. According to the form, how many "breakdowns" occurred in this loss?
   - ○ A. One
   - ○ B. Two
   - ○ C. Three
   - ○ D. Four

3. The insured knows that it might take several months for his damaged turbine to be fully repaired, so he authorizes $500 for temporary repairs so that production can resume. This expenditure would be covered under which coverage in the Equipment Breakdown Protection coverage form?
   - ○ A. Spoilage
   - ○ B. Errors or omissions
   - ○ C. Expediting expense
   - ○ D. Contingent business income

4. Under the Equipment Breakdown Protection coverage form, which of the following causes of damage to covered equipment would *not* be a covered "breakdown"?
   - ○ A. Electrical failure, including arcing
   - ○ B. Leakage at any valve, fitting, shaft seal, gland packing, joint, or connection
   - ○ C. Failure of pressure or vacuum equipment
   - ○ D. Mechanical failure, including rupture or bursting caused by centrifugal force

5. Which of the following statements apply to Professional Liability policies?
   - ❑ A. They cover the insured's liability arising out of rendering or failing to render services of a professional nature.
   - ❑ B. They duplicate the coverage provided by the CGL policy.
   - ❑ C. They are tailored to fit specific occupational needs.
   - ❑ D. They cover most general liability and automobile liability losses.

6. A business that wants coverage for its liability for employment-related acts can obtain it by purchasing which of the following?

○ A. CGL insurance

○ B. Workers Compensation and Employers Liability insurance

○ C. Employment Practices Liability insurance

○ D. Any of the above

7. Commercial insureds who need more Liability coverage than provided by a certain policy or want coverage for losses excluded by a certain policy should purchase which of the following?

○ A. Difference in Conditions policy

○ B. Commercial Umbrella policy

○ C. Surety bond

○ D. Fidelity bond

8. Which of these statements regarding Difference in Conditions insurance are correct?

❑ A. It excludes coverage for basic perils such as fire, lightning, and windstorm.

❑ B. It is written in conjunction with policies that cover basic perils.

❑ C. It does not have a deductible requirement.

❑ D. It covers property and liability exposures.

9. Which one of the following answer choices lists all of the parties to a Surety bond?

○ A. Principal and obligee

○ B. Principal, obligee, surety

○ C. Surety and obligee

○ D. Principal and surety

10. All of the following types of losses may be covered by the Equipment Breakdown Protection coverage form *except* which of the following?

○ A. Business income losses and/or extra expenses

○ B. Expediting expenses

○ C. Losses because of spoilage damage

○ D. Damage caused by fire or combustion explosion

11. How do deductibles apply in the Equipment Breakdown Protection coverage form?

○ A. Deductibles apply separately for each applicable coverage unless the deductibles are shown as "combined" for any two or more coverages.

○ B. A single deductible applies to all applicable coverages.

○ C. Deductibles are always stated as a specific dollar amount.

○ D. There are no deductibles under this coverage.

12. Under the terms of the Suspension provision in the Equipment Breakdown Protection coverage form, coverage on dangerous equipment can be suspended when?

  ○ A. On 30 days' advance notice to the insured

  ○ B. At the end of the policy period

  ○ C. Immediately on delivery of written notice to the insured

  ○ D. On 15 days' advance notice when sent by certified mail

Exam Prep Answers

1. A, B, and D are correct. Growing crops are not covered under a Farm coverage part.

2. A is correct. One breakdown means that if an initial breakdown causes other breakdowns, all are considered a single breakdown. All breakdowns at any one premises that manifest themselves at the same time and are the direct result of the same cause are considered "one breakdown."

3. C is correct. This coverage extension covers the reasonable cost of temporary repairs and expedition (speeding up) of permanent repairs.

4. B is correct. Under the Equipment Breakdown Protection coverage form, breakdown means the following types of direct physical loss that cause damage to covered equipment and necessitates its repair or replacement: failure of pressure or vacuum equipment, mechanical failure, including rupture or bursting caused by centrifugal force, and electrical failure, including arcing. Choice B is specifically excluded under this definition.

5. A and C are correct. Liability arising out of rendering or failing to render services of a professional nature is excluded under CGL policies. Special Professional Liability policies have been developed for many professionals, such as physicians, lawyers, and insurance agents. Each policy is tailored to fit a specific occupational need.

6. C is correct. This coverage is provided by Employment Practices Liability insurance. The other policies listed specifically exclude losses arising out of employment-related practices.

7. B is correct. Commercial Umbrella policies provide catastrophic Liability coverage for business risks. Because the Umbrella is not designed to handle usual or everyday exposures, the insured must have underlying Liability coverage before an Umbrella will be issued. The Umbrella can cover certain losses that are excluded by the underlying insurance.

8. A and B are correct. Difference in Conditions insurance is written to exclude the basic fire and extended coverage perils, but to include most other insurable perils that are not covered under Commercial Property coverage. Consequently, it is written in conjunction with policies providing the basic coverage excluded by the DIC policy. DIC policies are usually written on large risks with a high deductible.

9. B is correct. There are three parties to a Surety bond: the principal, the obligee, and the surety.

10. D is correct. Business income and/or extra expense losses, expediting expenses, and spoilage damage are all coverage options in the Equipment Breakdown Protection coverage form. Damage caused by fire or combustion explosion is excluded because it is covered under Commercial Property insurance.

11. A is correct. Deductibles apply separately for each applicable coverage unless the deductibles are shown as "combined" for any two or more coverages. Depending on the coverage, the deductible might be expressed as a dollar amount, a time limit, a percentage of loss, or a multiple of daily value.

12. C is correct. The insurer can immediately suspend coverage whenever covered equipment is found to be in or exposed to a dangerous condition. Suspension applies only to that particular object and takes effect as soon as written notice is delivered to the insured.

Practice Exam 1

This practice exam covers the general insurance concepts covered in this book and is designed to help you evaluate your comprehension of the general insurance concepts for which you will be tested in your insurance license qualification exam. The questions are intended to resemble the types of questions and the range of content on your insurance license qualification exam; however, because insurance license exam questions are kept strictly confidential, you should not expect these questions to be the same as those you will see on your actual exam. Rather, this practice exam is designed to help you evaluate how well you understand the general insurance concepts presented in this book.

What are some effective methods for studying for this practice exam?

➤ Read this exam cram from cover to cover.

➤ Answer the review questions at the end of each chapter and grade yourself.

➤ Take this practice exam and the one that follows it. Grade yourself on these tests as well.

➤ Obtain and use some supplementary study materials such as the *Exam Simulator* and the *Audio Review Program* described in Appendix B, "Need to Know More?"

➤ Before taking your actual insurance qualification license exam, make sure that you obtain and study a BISYS Education Services license training package described in Appendix B.

Practice Exam 1 Questions

1. Which type of insurer consists of an unincorporated group of members who share losses and provide insurance to each other?

   ○ A. Lloyd's Association
   ○ B. Reciprocal exchange
   ○ C. Mutual company
   ○ D. Multi-line insurer

2. Medical payments under a homeowners policy are available for expenses resulting from an injury to which of the following?

   ○ A. The named insured
   ○ B. A residence employee
   ○ C. A person who is on the insured location without permission
   ○ D. Any regular resident of the insured's household who pays rent

3. Some property insurance policies provide for payment of the full policy limit in the event of a total loss by a covered peril, regardless of the actual value of the property. These policies are known as which of the following?

   ○ A. Indemnity policies
   ○ B. ACV policies
   ○ C. Valued or agreed amount policies
   ○ D. Market value policies

4. Which part of an insurance policy sets the rules of conduct, duties, and obligations of the insured and insurer under the terms of the contract?

   ○ A. Declarations
   ○ B. Insuring agreement
   ○ C. Conditions
   ○ D. Exclusions

5. When an uninterrupted chain of events resulting from a negligent act causes a loss, that act is considered to be which of the following?

   ○ A. An assumption of risk
   ○ B. An intervening cause
   ○ C. The proximate cause of loss
   ○ D. A matter of strict liability

6. Policies issued under the National Flood Insurance Program provide removal coverage for property removed to protect it from flood. This coverage applies at another location for up to how many days?

   ○ A. 60 days
   ○ B. 45 days
   ○ C. 30 days
   ○ D. 15 days

7. In legal terms, the actions by one party might have the effect of giving up a known right. When this occurs, the party has created which of the following?

  ○ A. Unilateral contract
  ○ B. Representation
  ○ C. Warranty
  ○ D. Waiver

8. When the special causes of loss form is attached to a commercial property coverage part, coverage for theft of furs and fur garments is limited to how much?

  ○ A. $2,500
  ○ B. $2,000
  ○ C. $1,500
  ○ D. $1,000

9. An insurer's loss ratio is determined by dividing what?

  ○ A. Premiums by combined losses and expenses
  ○ B. Premiums by underwriting losses
  ○ C. Operating expenses by total premiums
  ○ D. Underwriting losses by total premiums

10. Under most property insurance policies, the policy territory includes which of the following?

  ○ A. Only the United States
  ○ B. The United States, its territories and possessions, and Canada
  ○ C. The United States, Canada, and Mexico
  ○ D. All of North America and Europe

11. Apparent authority of an insurance agent is the authority

  ○ A. given by the agent's contract with the insurer.
  ○ B. granted to an agent by state law.
  ○ C. the agent tells an insurance applicant that he or she has.
  ○ D. that members of the public can reasonably assume that the agent has.

12. Claims-made general liability coverage does *not* apply to bodily injury or property damage that occurs when?

  ○ A. On the policy's retroactive date
  ○ B. Before the policy's retroactive date
  ○ C. After the policy's retroactive date
  ○ D. Before the effective date, if there is no retroactive date

13. Under liability insurance policies, what does an "aggregate limit" mean?

   ○ A. It is the most the insurer will pay for any one accident.
   ○ B. It is the most the insurer will pay for all losses during any one policy period.
   ○ C. It is the maximum limit for each claim when multiple claimants are arising out of the same occurrence.
   ○ D. It is the single largest limit that applies when a loss is covered by two or more policies issued by the same insurer.

14. The purpose of FAIR Plans (Fair Access to Insurance Requirements) is to do what?

   ○ A. Give the federal government a major role in providing insurance
   ○ B. Make property insurance available to risks that were otherwise considered uninsurable because of environmental hazards
   ○ C. Require complete disclosure of the reasons for policy cancellations
   ○ D. Force all insurance companies to participate in an insurance pool

15. In the event of a physical damage loss that makes a covered auto unavailable for a period of time, a personal auto policy will provide coverage for transportation expenses at the rate of $20 per day up to how much?

   ○ A. A maximum payment of $300
   ○ B. A maximum payment of $460
   ○ C. A maximum payment of $600
   ○ D. A maximum payment of $740

16. Under the business auto coverage part, each of the following is true about the classifications of covered autos, which are designated by numerical symbols shown in the declarations, *except* for which of the following?

   ○ A. All classes of newly acquired autos are automatically covered.
   ○ B. An insured can select different classifications for various coverages.
   ○ C. "Any auto" is the broadest coverage classification.
   ○ D. "Hired autos" include autos the insured leases, hires, rents, or borrows.

17. Something that might increase the likelihood that a loss will occur, is called what?

   ○ A. Peril
   ○ B. Hazard
   ○ C. Risk
   ○ D. Catastrophe

18. Tom Baxter has an automobile insured by a personal auto policy. He trades in his car and purchases a new private passenger auto as a replacement vehicle. If he does not notify the insurance company, the liability coverage for his replacement vehicle will apply automatically for how long?

    ○ A. 10 days
    ○ B. 30 days
    ○ C. 60 days
    ○ D. Until the end of the policy period

19. A device that is used to minimize small nuisance claims and that helps to keep insurance premiums down is called what?

    ○ A. Arbitration
    ○ B. Deductible
    ○ C. Valued policy
    ○ D. Coinsurance

20. Homeowners coverage for loss of personal property because of "mysterious disappearance" is provided by what?

    ○ A. The special form (HO-3) only
    ○ B. The broad and special forms (HO-2 and HO-3) only
    ○ C. The comprehensive form (HO-5) only
    ○ D. All homeowners forms

21. Which type of insurance professional does not actually sell insurance coverages, but sells advice about insurance coverages?

    ○ A. Excess and surplus lines agent
    ○ B. Solicitor
    ○ C. Consultant
    ○ D. Producer

22. Which of the following is not excluded under commercial general liability coverage for bodily injury and property damage liability?

    ○ A. Injury or damage caused by the operation of mobile equipment
    ○ B. Damage to property rented to the named insured
    ○ C. An injury that is also covered by a workers compensation law
    ○ D. Liability resulting from the accidental escape of pollutants

23. Most liability claims are based on negligence that results in injury or damage. An act of negligence is considered to be a tort. What does the term "tort" mean?

    ○ A. A tort is a criminal act committed with the intent to cause injury.
    ○ B. A tort is a civil wrong that violates the rights of another.
    ○ C. A tort is any act that has the potential to cause financial loss to another person.
    ○ D. A tort is an act that can be prosecuted by the state or federal government even if no injury or damage occurred.

24. Various types of domestic shipments may be covered under a number of inland marine forms. Which of the following is not one of the non-filed marine forms used to insure domestic shipments?

   ○ A. Mail coverage form

   ○ B. Annual transit policy

   ○ C. Trip transit policy

   ○ D. Motor truck cargo shipper's form

25. Claims that are paid by general liability coverage are charged against the aggregate policy limits and reduce the amount of insurance remaining to pay future claims. However, CGL aggregate limits will be reinstated in full

   ○ A. if there are more than five claims during a policy period.

   ○ B. on the next policy anniversary date.

   ○ C. if the insured pays an extra premium for reinstatement.

   ○ D. as soon as the aggregate is actually exhausted.

26. Under the dwelling property forms, personal property moved to a new principal residence will be automatically covered at the new location (subject to policy expiration) for a period of how long?

   ○ A. 60 days

   ○ B. 30 days

   ○ C. 20 days

   ○ D. 10 days

27. Which of the following is not true about insurance binders?

   ○ A. Binders are only valid when issued in writing.

   ○ B. A binder issued by an agent is valid only if the agent has express authority to issue the binder.

   ○ C. Some insurers issue binders directly to let insureds know coverage is in effect until a policy is actually issued.

   ○ D. A binder is a temporary contract of insurance.

28. Under the NCCI workers compensation and employers liability policy form, the basic, or minimum, limit for employers liability coverage is how much per accident?

   ○ A. $50,000 per accident

   ○ B. $100,000 per accident

   ○ C. $250,000 per accident

   ○ D. $500,000 per accident

29. If coverage for towing and labor costs is included in a personal auto policy, labor costs will be covered only if the labor is performed

   ○ A. at a garage by an experienced mechanic.

   ○ B. at the place of disablement.

   ○ C. within 24 hours of the disablement.

   ○ D. within 48 hours of the disablement.

30. Which dwelling policy forms are named peril forms?

   ○ A. All dwelling forms
   ○ B. The basic form only
   ○ C. The basic and broad forms
   ○ D. The special form only

31. The only significant difference between the occurrence and claims-made forms of general liability insurance is found in which of the following?

   ○ A. The coverages provided by the policy
   ○ B. The policy's exclusions
   ○ C. The "trigger," or the way in which coverage is activated under the policy
   ○ D. The policy's conditions

32. Under a homeowners policy, in addition to any payments for damages awarded against an insured, the insurance company will reimburse the insured for reasonable expenses incurred at the company's request, including loss of earnings of up to how many days?

   ○ A. $500 a day
   ○ B. $300 a day
   ○ C. $250 a day
   ○ D. $100 a day

33. If general liability "claims-made" coverage is renewed by "occurrence" coverage and the insured purchases a supplemental extended reporting period (ERP), the period for reporting claims under the policy will be extended for how long?

   ○ A. Indefinitely
   ○ B. 5 years
   ○ C. 3 years
   ○ D. 60 days

34. An insurer has subrogation rights under all personal auto policy coverages except which of the following?

   ○ A. Physical damage coverage
   ○ B. Uninsured motorists coverage
   ○ C. Medical payments
   ○ D. Liability coverage

35. Under liability insurance policies, what does the term "personal injury" usually mean?

   ○ A. Injury for such things as libel, slander, false arrest, or invasion of privacy

   ○ B. Only bodily injuries that are suffered by individuals

   ○ C. Any form of injury that affects a person, including bodily injury, property damage, financial injury, and damage to one's reputation

   ○ D. Injuries suffered by named insureds or family members who are insured under personal lines policies

36. Which of the following coverages may be attached to a homeowners policy only by endorsement?

   ○ A. Coverage for a mobile home

   ○ B. Coverage damage to the property of others

   ○ C. Personal property coverage

   ○ D. Medical payments

37. Under the supplementary payments provided by general liability coverage, when a vehicle to which the bodily injury insurance applies is involved in an accident and bail bonds are required, the insurer will pay up to what amount?

   ○ A. $250 for the cost of the bail bonds

   ○ B. $200 for the cost of the bail bonds

   ○ C. $150 for the cost of the bail bonds

   ○ D. $100 for the cost of the bail bonds

38. Under a personal auto policy, if an insured already has physical damage coverage for at least one vehicle, a new vehicle will be automatically covered from the date it is acquired as long as the insured notifies the insurer and requests the coverage within how many days?

   ○ A. 30 days

   ○ B. 14 days

   ○ C. 10 days

   ○ D. 7 days

39. If Coverage C (personal property coverage) is written on a dwelling form, the Other Coverages section of the policy will extend the insurance to provide worldwide personal property coverage for an amount up to which of the following?

   ○ A. 10% of the Coverage C limit

   ○ B. 25% of the Coverage C limit

   ○ C. 40% of the Coverage C limit

   ○ D. 50% of the Coverage C limit

40. The name of the coverage that provides legal liability insurance for damage to customers' autos that are left with the insured for service, repair, or storage is which of the following?
    - ○ A. Garage physical damage
    - ○ B. Garage errors and omissions
    - ○ C. Garage liability
    - ○ D. Garagekeepers coverage

41. Which of the following is not true about difference in conditions (DIC) insurance?
    - ○ A. DIC policies provide property and liability coverages.
    - ○ B. Traditional perils (such as fire, lightning, and so on) are usually excluded by DIC policies.
    - ○ C. DIC supplements other coverages and fills insurance gaps.
    - ○ D. DIC can provide considerable protection at a reasonable cost.

42. If coverage for personal liability and medical payments is attached to a dwelling policy, what basic limit of coverage applies to medical payments unless a higher amount is purchased?
    - ○ A. $500 per person
    - ○ B. $1,000 per person
    - ○ C. $2,500 per person
    - ○ D. $5,000 per person

43. Which of the following is not true about workers compensation insurance?
    - ○ A. A few states have monopolistic state funds, and employers are required to purchase coverage from the fund.
    - ○ B. Most states allow an employer to self-insure for the required benefits.
    - ○ C. If an employer has coverage in one state, any operations started in other states will be automatically covered.
    - ○ D. Workers compensation benefits are only available for work-related injuries that arise out of and in the course of employment.

44. Under which type of marketing system do agents or agencies operate as independent businesses but agree to represent only one insurance company?
    - ○ A. Direct writer system
    - ○ B. Exclusive of captive agency system
    - ○ C. Direct response system
    - ○ D. Independent agency system

45. Under a personal auto policy, which of the following is not a collision loss?
    - ○ A. Impact between a covered auto and a deer
    - ○ B. Impact between a covered auto and a stationary object
    - ○ C. Impact between a covered auto and another vehicle
    - ○ D. Upset of a covered auto, resulting in damage

46. A commercial property coverage part with the basic causes of loss form attached covers all of the following perils except which one?
    - ○ A. Windstorm
    - ○ B. Explosion
    - ○ C. Volcanic eruption
    - ○ D. Sprinkler leakage

47. Which of the following situations would be covered by liability insurance under a personal auto policy?
    - ○ A. An insured causes injuries while operating a taxi cab.
    - ○ B. An auto mechanic has an accident while road testing a customer's vehicle.
    - ○ C. An insured damages another vehicle while driving a motorcycle.
    - ○ D. Bodily injuries and property damage occur when an insured is involved in an accident while driving co-workers to their job as part of a share-the-expense car pool.

48. Which of the following is not true about homeowners personal property coverage?
    - ○ A. The basic form does not include personal property coverage.
    - ○ B. Personal property of a guest may be covered.
    - ○ C. Special sublimits apply to some types of personal property.
    - ○ D. The full limit applies to personal property anywhere in the world.

49. To avoid problems with underinsurance and overinsurance, a business that has fluctuating inventory values during the year should consider coverage written on
    - ○ A. the value reporting form.
    - ○ B. a replacement cost basis.
    - ○ C. the business income form.
    - ○ D. a blanket basis.

50. The name of a liability insurance policy that provides high limits of coverage above underlying coverage and may fill a number of insurance gaps is
    - ○ A. a general liability policy.
    - ○ B. an umbrella policy.
    - ○ C. an errors and omissions policy.
    - ○ D. a difference in conditions policy.

Answers to Practice Exam 1

Quick Check Answer Key 1

1. B	**18.** D	**35.** A
2. B	**19.** B	**36.** A
3. C	**20.** C	**37.** A
4. C	**21.** C	**38.** B
5. C	**22.** A	**39.** A
6. B	**23.** B	**40.** D
7. D	**24.** A	**41.** A
8. A	**25.** B	**42.** B
9. D	**26.** B	**43.** C
10. B	**27.** A	**44.** B
11. D	**28.** B	**45.** A
12. B	**29.** B	**46.** C
13. B	**30.** C	**47.** D
14. B	**31.** C	**48.** A
15. C	**32.** C	**49.** A
16. A	**33.** A	**50.** B
17. B	**34.** A	

Answers and Explanations

1. Answer B is correct. Reciprocal insurers consist of members who are unincorporated and collectively share losses and provide insurance to themselves. Lloyd's Associations are syndicates of insurance underwriters, and mutual and multi-line insurers are examples of traditional insurance companies.

2. Answer B is correct. Under homeowners coverage for medical payments to others, injuries to the named insured, family members, and any other regular residents are specifically excluded. However, although residents are not usually covered, an exception is made for "resident employees" and they are covered.

3. Answer C is correct. For certain hard-to-value items, the insurance company may issue a valued or agreed amount contract for a specified amount agreed to by both parties. If the item is lost or completely destroyed, the insurer will pay this amount as settlement.

4. Answer C is correct. The conditions state the ground rules for the contract and spell out the responsibilities and obligations of both the insurance company and insured.

5. Answer C is correct. To establish that one person's actions toward another were negligent and caused injury or damage, the negligent act and the damage must be tied together. If there was no intervening cause and the negligent act led directly to the loss in an unbroken sequence of events, the negligent act was the proximate cause of loss.

6. Answer B is correct. Under flood policies, property is also covered at another place, either above ground or outside of the special flood hazard area, for 45 days when removed by the insured to protect it from flood.

7. Answer D is correct. The legal definition of "waiver" is the intentional relinquishment of a known right. Sometimes an insurer or its agent might overlook a provision that might have been grounds for denying coverage or increasing the premium. By doing so, the insurer might have relinquished its right to deny coverage or exercise options at a later date by creating a waiver. A representation is a statement believed, but not guaranteed, to be true, whereas a warranty is a statement guaranteed to be true. A unilateral contract is one in which only one party is obligated to perform its part of the agreement—for example, an insurance contract is unilateral because an insured might choose not to enter the agreement by paying the premium, but if the insured pays the premium, the insurance company is obligated to pay for covered losses.

8. Answer A is correct. The special form is the only causes of loss form for commercial property coverage that provides theft coverage. However, for certain classes of property, various limitations apply, and coverage for theft of furs and fur garments is limited to $2,500.

9. Answer D is correct. The loss ratio is used to compare the company's loss experience from year to year. It is calculated by dividing the amount of incurred underwriting losses by the earned premium. It can be calculated separately for individual lines of insurance or the company's entire operations.

10. Answer B is correct. The policy territory typically includes the United States, its territories and possessions, and Canada. Mexico and Europe are not included.

11. Answer D is correct. Apparent authority is a doctrine that holds an agent may have whatever authority a reasonable person would assume he or she has. An agent acting under apparent authority may bind an insurer as fully as one acting under expressed or implied authority.

12. Answer B is correct. A retroactive date on a claims-made liability policy marks the date on which coverage for reported claims begins. An occurrence on the retroactive date would be covered, but there would be no coverage for bodily injury or property damage that occurred prior to the retroactive date.

13. Answer B is correct. An aggregate limit is a maximum limit that applies to all losses during a policy period. Each individual loss is subtracted from the aggregate limit and reduces the remaining coverage. At each policy anniversary or renewal, the aggregate limit is reinstated in full.

14. Answer B is correct. Essentially, a FAIR plan makes insurance available to risks that were previously considered uninsurable because of environmental hazards.

15. Answer C is correct. In addition to collision and other than collision coverage, if a covered loss makes an insured auto unavailable, a personal auto policy will provide coverage for transportation expenses up to $20 per day, subject to a maximum payment of $600.

16. Answer A is correct. An insured can select which vehicles are to be "covered autos" for each individual coverage. Different symbols can be used for various coverages and autos. With the exception of specifically described autos, autos acquired during the policy period are automatically covered.

17. Answer B is correct. A hazard is something that increases the chance of loss, such as a loose step or flammable materials. A peril is the cause of loss, such as a fire. Risk is any outcome that involves uncertainty. A catastrophe is an unexpected event, such as an earthquake or flood, which is not considered a hazard.

18. Answer D is correct. Under a personal auto policy, if a newly acquired auto replaces another auto, the new vehicle automatically has the broadest coverage for liability, medical payments, and uninsured motorists coverage for any auto shown in the declarations until the end of the policy period.

19. Answer B is correct. Many property insurance policies have a deductible, which is the amount of a claim the insured has to absorb before the insurance applies. Deductibles reduce the cost of insurance by eliminating small claims. The amount of the deductible is stated in the declarations. Arbitration is a means of settling claims disputes when the insured and the company disagree on the value of property. A valued policy is one under which a certain value for property is stated in the policy, regardless of its value at the time of any loss. Coinsurance is a means by which insureds share in partial losses if they have not insured their property for full value.

20. Answer C is correct. The comprehensive form (HO-5) is the only homeowners policy that insures loss of personal property items by what is known as "mysterious disappearance" because it covers loss by "theft, misplacing, or losing." The other policy forms only cover loss because of damage, destruction, or theft of property. The broad form (HO-2) covers only named perils, and mysterious disappearance is not one of them. The special form (H0-3) offers only broad form coverage for personal property.

21. Answer C is correct. Insurance consultants do not actually sell insurance; they sell advice. Agents, brokers, and solicitors are all producers who sell insurance.

22. Answer A is correct. BI and PD coverage for the ownership, operation, or use of mobile equipment is covered by CGL policies. All of the other answer choices are specifically excluded.

23. Answer B is correct. A tort is a civil wrong that violates the rights of another. Unlike the commission of a crime, in which the government may prosecute the wrongdoer, torts are a part of civil law that is concerned with private relationships between people.

24. Answer A is correct. Annual transit policies, trip transit policies, and motor truck cargo policies are all examples of nonfiled inland marine forms used to cover domestic shipments. Although some types of property may be covered in transit by the mail coverage form, it is a filed form that is part of the ISO package policy program.

25. Answer B is correct. Claims paid under general liability coverage are charged against the applicable aggregate policy limits and reduce the amount of insurance remaining to pay future claims during the policy period, but they apply separately to each consecutive policy period and are reinstated on each policy anniversary date.

26. Answer B is correct. Coverage is provided for personal property moved from the described location to a new principal residence. This coverage applies only for 30 days and not beyond the policy expiration date.

27. Answer A is correct. Binders can be issued in writing, but oral binders are valid if the agent is acting within the scope of his or her authority. Binders are temporary contracts of insurance and can be given by agents or insurers.

28. Answer B is correct. Employers liability insurance provides coverage for sums the insured becomes legally obligated to pay under common law because of work-related injuries or occupational diseases. A minimum limit of $100,000 per accident applies.

29. Answer B is correct. Coverage for towing and labor costs will cover labor only if it is performed at the place of disablement. Although the towing charge may be covered if the vehicle is taken to a garage, any work performed after the vehicle is taken to a garage is not covered.

30. Answer C is correct. The basic and broad dwelling forms provide coverage on a named peril basis. The special form provides open peril coverage.

31. Answer C is correct. There are two primary CGL coverage forms: the occurrence form and the claims-made form. Although the two forms contain basically the same coverages, exclusions, and conditions, they only differ in how the coverage under the form is activated, or "triggered" for Coverages A and B.

32. Answer C is correct. As part of the additional liability coverages, a homeowners policy will reimburse an insured for reasonable expenses incurred at the company's request, including loss of earnings of up to $250 a day.

33. Answer A is correct. A supplemental extending reporting period provides an unlimited extension of the time for reporting covered claims. However, in order for a claim to be covered, it must not have occurred before the retroactive date and not after the policy expiration date.

34. Answer A is correct. Under a personal auto policy, an insurer has subrogation rights against third parties who might be responsible for a loss, such as other drivers or uninsured motorists. However, under physical damage coverage, the insured might be the only one responsible for a loss or nobody might be responsible. It would make little sense to pay an insured for a collision loss and then try to recover from the insured. So the policy specifically states that subrogation rights do not apply to physical damage coverage.

35. Answer A is correct. Some policies cover an insured's exposure for "personal injury," which means liability for such things as slander, libel, false arrest, and invasion of privacy. In the insurance business "bodily injury" and "personal injury" have different meanings and are not used interchangeably. The term "bodily injury" is limited to physical injury.

36. Answer A is correct. Mobile homes may be covered only when the Mobile Home endorsement is attached. All of the other answer choices are included in every homeowners policy.

37. Answer A is correct. Under the supplementary payments provided by CGL coverage, when a vehicle to which the bodily injury insurance applies is involved in an accident and bail bonds are required, the insurer will pay up to $250 for the cost of the bail bonds.

38. Answer B is correct. If an insured already has physical damage coverage for at least one vehicle under a personal auto policy, a new vehicle will be automatically covered from the date it is acquired as long as the insured notifies the insurer and requests the coverage within 14 days. It doesn't matter if the new auto is a replacement or additional vehicle.

39. Answer A is correct. In addition to the major coverages written, if personal property coverage is included, a dwelling policy will provide up to 10% of the Coverage C limit for personal property located anywhere in the world. This would include such things as clothing, personal effects, cameras, and luggage taken on vacation.

40. Answer D is correct. The liability section of a garage policy excludes coverage for damage to property of others in the insured's care, custody, or control. For garages, this leaves a significant uninsured exposure, but the specific coverage for this exposure can be purchased under the garagekeepers coverage section of the policy.

41. Answer A is correct. DIC policies do provide broad property coverage intended to supplement other coverages and fill insurance gaps. For this reason, DIC policies typically exclude coverage for traditional perils such as fire, lightning, and the extended coverage perils. DIC policies do not provide any liability coverage.

42. Answer B is correct. Under a dwelling policy, if the endorsement is included, the basic limit of coverage is $1,000 per person for medical payments to others. However, this is a minimum limit, and higher limits can be purchased.

43. Answer C is correct. States where coverage applies must be listed on the information page. Coverage for other states is not automatically provided. In order to have coverage in other states, the states need to be listed on the policy and the insured must notify the insurer as soon as operations begin.

44. Answer B is correct. In the exclusive of captive agency system, the insurance company contracts with agencies, which are independent businesses, to represent and sell insurance only for that insurance company.

45. Answer A is correct. Collision is defined as the impact of a covered auto with another object or vehicle. The policy specifically lists contact with a bird or animal as an "other than collision" loss.

46. Answer C is correct. The commercial property basic causes of loss form specifically lists windstorm, explosion, and sprinkler leakage as covered perils. It provides some coverage for volcanic "action," which might mean cleaning up ash and dust, but there's no coverage for direct damage because of volcanic eruption. The earthquake and volcanic eruption form must be attached in order to have this coverage.

47. Answer D is correct. Although the PAP excludes liability arising out of operation of a public or livery conveyance, such as a taxi business, an exception is made for share-the-expense car pools that are covered. The other answer choices are specifically excluded.

48. Answer A is correct. All homeowner policy forms include personal property coverage. Personal property coverage applies worldwide; at the insured's request, the property of guests can be covered; and special sublimits apply to certain classes of property on all policies.

49. Answer A is correct. The value reporting form is an endorsement specifically designed for businesses with fluctuating inventory values because of seasonal variations in business or shifting inventory between different locations. When this coverage applies, the insured must report values periodically, such as monthly, and the actual amount of insurance in effect will be adjusted accordingly. The final premium will be adjusted at the end of the policy year based on average values.

50. Answer B is correct. Umbrella policies provide high limits of liability coverage above underlying policy limits and might fill a number of insurance gaps. Both Personal and Commercial Umbrella policies are available.

Practice Exam 2

Practice Exam 2 Questions

1. The term "time element coverage" is used when the amount of loss depends on which of the following?
   - ○ A. The time between the date of loss and the policy expiration date
   - ○ B. The time between the policy effective date and date of loss
   - ○ C. The time of year when a seasonal business suffers a loss
   - ○ D. The time it takes to repair, rebuild, or restore damaged property

2. Which of the following is not one of the common law defenses against an employer's liability?
   - ○ A. Assumption of risk
   - ○ B. Fellow servant rule
   - ○ C. Proximate cause
   - ○ D. Contributory negligence

3. Vehicles that might be insured by a personal auto policy are described in the eligibility rules and the policy definitions. Each of the following is true about vehicles eligible for PAP coverage except
   - ○ A. Vehicles with fewer than four wheels are not eligible.
   - ○ B. Vehicles owned by an individual or married couple may be insured.
   - ○ C. Private passenger autos, pickup trucks, and vans used for personal transportation may be insured.
   - ○ D. Vans used in a delivery business are eligible for coverage.

4. Businessowners policies provide an additional coverage for preservation of property when it is removed from the premises to protect it from loss by a covered peril. The coverage will apply at other locations for up to

   ○ A. 60 days
   ○ B. 30 days
   ○ C. 20 days
   ○ D. 15 days

5. Which of the following losses is not excluded under the physical damage coverage of a personal auto policy?

   ○ A. Loss of custom furnishings in a customized van
   ○ B. Loss caused by freezing of the cooling system
   ○ C. Damage to equipment designed for the detection of radar
   ○ D. Damage to a covered auto while being used as part of a car pool

6. Under the business auto coverage part, liability insurance applies to mobile equipment while which of the following occurs?

   ○ A. It is being operated on public roads.
   ○ B. It is being carried or towed by a covered auto.
   ○ C. It is being operated away from the insured's premises and work sites.
   ○ D. It is being used for the purpose for which it was designed.

7. Insurance is a mechanism used to manage which of the following types of risk?

   ○ A. Pure risks
   ○ B. Speculative risks
   ○ C. Both pure and speculative risks
   ○ D. Neither pure nor speculative risks

8. Under the 1989 dwelling policy forms, if coverage for vandalism and malicious mischief is attached to a policy, it will be suspended whenever the building has been vacant for more than how many days?

   ○ A. 45 consecutive days
   ○ B. 30 consecutive days
   ○ C. 20 consecutive days
   ○ D. 10 consecutive days

9. Commercial general liability coverage provides medical expense payments for accidental injuries if the expenses are incurred and reported to the insurer within what date?

   ○ A. Six months after the accident date
   ○ B. One year after the accident date
   ○ C. Two years after the accident date
   ○ D. Three years after the accident date

10. An employer purchases a fidelity bond to protect against potential losses by employee dishonesty. In this situation, each of the employees covered by the bond is considered which of the following?

  ○ A. A fiduciary
  ○ B. A principal
  ○ C. A guarantor
  ○ D. An obligee

11. When insurance is written on a dwelling form, each of the following types of property would be insured under Coverage A (dwelling coverage) except which one?

  ○ A. A storage shed connected to the dwelling by a utility line
  ○ B. A laundry room attached to the dwelling
  ○ C. Building equipment and outdoor equipment
  ○ D. Materials and supplies used for construction or repair of the dwelling

12. On homeowners policies, "insured location" is a broad term describing where liability coverages apply. It includes each of the following except which one?

  ○ A. Family cemetery plots
  ○ B. Any newly acquired premises
  ○ C. Structures on farm land owned by an insured
  ○ D. A nonowned premises used as a temporary residence by an insured

13. The most common definition of actual cash value (ACV) in the property insurance field is which of the following?

  ○ A. Original cost, plus depreciation
  ○ B. Original cost, less depreciation
  ○ C. Replacement cost, plus depreciation
  ○ D. Replacement cost, less depreciation

14. Each of the following is true about the National Flood Insurance Program except which one?

  ○ A. There are maximum limits on the amount of coverage available.
  ○ B. Coverage may be written by private insurance carriers.
  ○ C. Eligibility requirements are set by private insurance carriers.
  ○ D. The federal government reimburses insurance companies for losses that exceed premiums collected.

15. What is meant by the term "adverse selection"?
    - ○ A. Underwriting practices that discriminate against applicants in certain geographical areas
    - ○ B. Selling types of insurance to applicants who do not need that particular kind of coverage
    - ○ C. Agency marketing practices that promote only the policies that pay the highest commissions
    - ○ D. The tendency of people with greater than average exposure to loss to purchase insurance

16. A commercial building valued at $300,000 is insured for $200,000. If the policy is written with an 80% coinsurance percentage and a standard deductible, how much would be paid for a $60,000 loss?
    - ○ A. $60,000
    - ○ B. $49,500
    - ○ C. $40,000
    - ○ D. $39,500

17. Under homeowners coverage for medical payments to others, necessary medical expenses for treating an accidental injury will be covered if it incurred within how many days?
    - ○ A. 90 days of the accident date
    - ○ B. 1 year of the accident date
    - ○ C. 3 years of the accident date
    - ○ D. 5 years of the accident date

18. Under a Personal Umbrella policy, a self-insured retention is an amount that
    - ○ A. is in effect a deductible for insured losses.
    - ○ B. reflects the maximum the insurer will pay for a particular loss.
    - ○ C. applies between underlying coverage and the umbrella coverage.
    - ○ D. reduces the amount of underlying coverage available to cover insured losses.

19. Ocean marine protection and indemnity (P&I) coverage usually insures the ship owner against liability for all of the following except which one?
    - ○ A. Cargo lost or damaged through negligence
    - ○ B. Damage to other vessels when caused by collision
    - ○ C. Damage to or loss of the insured ship
    - ○ D. Job-related injuries to sailors

20. National flood insurance is available for which of the following?
    - ○ A. Private residences only
    - ○ B. Private residences and residential contents only
    - ○ C. Residential and nonresidential buildings only
    - ○ D. Residential and nonresidential buildings and contents

21. Which dwelling forms can provide replacement cost coverage for buildings?

  ○ A. The basic and broad forms only
  ○ B. The broad and special forms only
  ○ C. The special form only
  ○ D. The basic, broad, and special forms

22. Under the commercial property conditions, the coverage territory includes all of the following except which one?

  ○ A. United States
  ○ B. Mexico
  ○ C. Puerto Rico
  ○ D. Canada

23. Which of the following risks might qualify for coverage under a businessowners policy?

  ○ A. A bank or saving and loan association
  ○ B. A bar and grill
  ○ C. An office building of any size
  ○ D. An apartment building of any size

24. Under business auto liability coverage, if an insured takes time off from work at the request of the insurer and suffers loss of earnings, as a supplementary payment, the insurer will pay up to how much?

  ○ A. $150 a day for lost earnings
  ○ B. $200 a day for lost earnings
  ○ C. $250 a day for lost earnings
  ○ D. $300 a day for lost earnings

25. The primary purpose of insurance is to do which of the following?

  ○ A. Avoid risk
  ○ B. Eliminate risk
  ○ C. Transfer risk
  ○ D. Reduce risk

26. Restoring an insured to approximately the same condition that existed before a property loss is an example of what principal?

  ○ A. Insurable interest
  ○ B. Salvage rights
  ○ C. Subrogation
  ○ D. Indemnity

27. Which dwelling forms provide coverage for loss of fair rental value when a dwelling becomes uninhabitable?
    - ○ A. The special form only
    - ○ B. The basic and broad forms only
    - ○ C. The broad and special forms only
    - ○ D. The basic, broad, and special forms

28. On a commercial package policy, interline endorsements are which of the following?
    - ○ A. Attached to the common policy conditions
    - ○ B. Attached to the common policy declarations
    - ○ C. Only apply to commercial property coverages
    - ○ D. Could apply to more than one line of insurance

29. On homeowners policies, personal property used for business purposes is which of following?
    - ○ A. Cannot be covered
    - ○ B. Covered only if an additional premium is paid
    - ○ C. May be covered only while on the residence premises
    - ○ D. Covered up to $2,500 on the premises and up to $500 off the premises

30. When an insured cancels a policy prior to its expiration date, the insurance company will return a portion of the unused premium on a short rate basis. What does the term "short rate" mean?
    - ○ A. The insurer will keep the earned premium plus an additional amount for policy writing expenses.
    - ○ B. There will be a pro rata adjustment of the premium so that the insured is not charged for the full policy term.
    - ○ C. The agent will return the commission paid on the policy to the insurer.
    - ○ D. The insurer will return the unearned premium plus interest on the amount that was not used.

31. The taking of money or other property from inside a premises by someone who has unlawfully and forcefully entered or exited is an example of what kind of crime?
    - ○ A. Robbery
    - ○ B. Burglary
    - ○ C. Embezzlement
    - ○ D. Safe burglary

32. Which method of risk management best describes the use of high deductibles or elements of self-insurance to reduce insurance costs?
    - ○ A. Retention
    - ○ B. Transfer
    - ○ C. Avoidance
    - ○ D. Reduction

33. Office buildings are eligible for coverage under a businessowners policy if they do not contain more than 100,000 square feet of space and do not exceed which of the following?

    ○ A. 4 stories in height

    ○ B. 6 stories in height

    ○ C. 8 stories in height

    ○ D. 10 stories in height

34. An insurance company has made an underwriting profit when which of the following is true?

    ○ A. Its combined ratio is greater than 100%.

    ○ B. Its combined ratio is less than 100%.

    ○ C. Its loss ratio is less than its expense ratio.

    ○ D. Its expense ratio is less than its loss ratio.

35. The commercial Common Policy declarations would include all of the following types of information except which one?

    ○ A. The policy period

    ○ B. The coverage parts purchased and their premiums

    ○ C. The exclusions that apply to the coverages

    ○ D. The identity and mailing address of the named insured

36. Under the loss sustained version of commercial crime coverage forms, the policy will cover losses sustained during the policy period and discovered either during the policy term or no later than which of the following?

    ○ A. Three years after policy expiration

    ○ B. Two years after policy expiration

    ○ C. One year after policy expiration

    ○ D. Six months after policy expiration

37. Under the NCCI workers compensation and employers liability policy form, the employers liability coverage excludes any claim for which of the following?

    ○ A. Care and loss of service

    ○ B. Liability assumed under contract

    ○ C. Damages to a third party

    ○ D. Consequential injury to a spouse or relative of an injured worker

38. Each of the following is true about farm coverages except which one?

    ○ A. Livestock and equipment may be insured.

    ○ B. Property and liability coverages may be included.

    ○ C. The principal residence may be covered by farm or homeowners forms.

    ○ D. Farm coverage may be written as a mono-line policy or part of a package.

39. Because an insurer writes the policy language and the insured has little or no control over the content, any ambiguity in the wording is usually resolved in favor of the insured. Because the design and wording of a policy are in the hands of the insurer, insurance policies are said to be which of the following?

   ○ A. Contracts of indemnity
   ○ B. Unilateral contracts
   ○ C. Contracts of adhesion
   ○ D. Aleatory contracts

40. Which of the commercial property causes of loss forms provide theft coverage?

   ○ A. The basic, broad, and special forms.
   ○ B. The broad and special forms only.
   ○ C. The special form only.
   ○ D. None of the forms provide theft coverage.

41. After a homeowners policy has been in effect for at least 60 days, when the insurer cancels for any reason other than nonpayment of premium, it must give the insured advance written notice of at least how many days?

   ○ A. 60 days
   ○ B. 30 days
   ○ C. 20 days
   ○ D. 10 days

42. Under which policy provision is an insured's right to recover for a loss from a third party transferred to the insurance company?

   ○ A. Abandonment
   ○ B. Pair or set clause
   ○ C. Subrogation
   ○ D. Arbitration

43. A businessowners policy may provide additional coverage for increased cost of construction when required to comply with an existing ordinance or law. However, this coverage is available only for buildings that are insured on a replacement cost basis and it is limited to which of the following amounts?

   ○ A. $10,000
   ○ B. $7,500
   ○ C. $5,000
   ○ D. $2,500

44. Which of the following is not available as one of the farm liability coverages included in an ISO policy?
    - ○ A. Medical payments to others
    - ○ B. Bodily injury and property damage
    - ○ C. Personal injury and advertising injury
    - ○ D. Injury to farm employees

45. Which of the following is not an optional property coverage on homeowners policies?
    - ○ A. Personal property replacement cost
    - ○ B. Permitted incidental occupancies
    - ○ C. Increased limits for jewelry, watches, and furs
    - ○ D. Coverage for loss of use of the premises

46. Which of the following is true about commercial crime coverage written on a discovery policy form?
    - ○ A. In order to be covered, losses must be sustained and discovered during the policy period.
    - ○ B. Losses may be covered if they are discovered at any time up to 18 months after the policy expires.
    - ○ C. No exclusions apply to the types of losses that may be covered by this form.
    - ○ D. A loss discovered during the policy period will be covered even if it was sustained years earlier.

47. Withholding, rather than misstating, a material fact on an insurance application is an act of which of the following?
    - ○ A. Misrepresentation
    - ○ B. Concealment
    - ○ C. Waiver and estoppel
    - ○ D. Fraud

48. When an insurer cancels a commercial package policy for reasons other than nonpayment of premium, it must give written notice to the first named insured at least how long?
    - ○ A. 60 days in advance
    - ○ B. 30 days in advance
    - ○ C. 20 days in advance
    - ○ D. 10 days in advance

49. Which of the following coverages may be included in a personal auto policy without the necessity of issuing an endorsement?
    - ○ A. Miscellaneous type vehicles
    - ○ B. Towing and labor costs
    - ○ C. Transportation expenses
    - ○ D. Named nonowner coverage

50. The commercial building and personal property coverage form provides a number of coverage extensions but only if which of the following is true?

   - ○ A. The coverage for buildings is written on a replacement basis.
   - ○ B. All coverages are written on a blanket basis.
   - ○ C. They are shown in the declarations and an additional premium is paid.
   - ○ D. An 80% or higher coinsurance percentage or a value reporting symbol is shown in the declarations.

Answers to Practice Exam 2

....

Quick Check Answer Key 2

1. D	18. A	35. C
2. C	19. C	36. C
3. D	20. D	37. B
4. B	21. B	38. C
5. D	22. B	39. C
6. B	23. D	40. C
7. A	24. C	41. B
8. B	25. C	42. C
9. B	26. D	43. A
10. B	27. D	44. D
11. A	28. D	45. D
12. C	29. D	46. D
13. D	30. A	47. B
14. C	31. B	48. B
15. D	32. A	49. C
16. B	33. B	50. D
17. C	34. B	

Answers and Explanations

1. Answer D is correct. The term "time element coverage" is used for many indirect losses, such as a business income loss, because the amount of loss might not be directly related to the amount of property damage that occurred, yet it is related to the time it takes to repair, rebuild, or restore the damaged property. Many factors can influence the ultimate loss, including the availability of supplies and replacement parts.

2. Answer C is correct. Assumption of risk, contributory negligence, and the fellow servant rule are the traditional common law defenses against employer liability. Proximate cause is a concept applied to determine which peril or event actually caused a loss.

3. Answer D is correct. Generally, four-wheel private passenger autos, pickups, and vans owned by an individual or married couple are eligible if used for pleasure or general transportation. Pickups and vans used in a business, other than farming or ranching, are not eligible.

4. Answer B is correct. The preservation of property additional coverage under a businessowners policy covers direct physical loss or damage from any cause if the property has been removed to another location in order to protect it from loss by a covered peril. Coverage applies while the property is being moved and while it is temporarily stored at another location, but only for 30 days after the property is first moved.

5. Answer D is correct. Damage to a covered auto while being used as part of a car pool is not excluded. All of the other answer choices are specifically excluded.

6. Answer B is correct. Although mobile equipment exposures are usually covered by CGL insurance, it is covered by business auto insurance while being carried or towed by a covered auto because in such cases it is considered an extension of the covered auto.

7. Answer A is correct. Insurance is only used to manage pure risks that involve only the possibility of loss and no opportunity for gain.

8. Answer B is correct. If a dwelling policy includes the extended coverage (EC) perils, coverage for vandalism and malicious mischief (V&MM) may also be added. However, this coverage will not apply whenever the building has been vacant for more than 30 consecutive days.

9. Answer B is correct. CGL insurance policies provide coverage for medical expense payments for accidental injuries if the expenses are incurred and reported to the insurer within one year after the accident date.

10. Answer B is correct. Fidelity bonds are contracts between three parties. The employees who are required to act honestly are the principals. The surety or guarantor, which is usually an insurance company, agrees to be responsible for a loss if a principal violates the terms of the bond. The obligee, the employer, is the party who is being protected by the bond and who will be paid if a loss occurs.

11. Answer A is correct. A storage shed connected to the dwelling by a utility line would be considered an "other structure" available for insurance under Coverage B. All other answer choices are specifically described in the policy as being part of Coverage A, insurance for the dwelling.

12. Answer C is correct. Family cemetery plots, newly acquired premises, and premises used as a temporary residence by an insured are all included in the policy definition of "insured location." Farm exposures are specifically excluded by the homeowner eligibility rules.

13. Answer D is correct. Many losses are reimbursed on an actual cash value (ACV) basis. Actual cash value is usually calculated by determining an item's replacement cost and subtracting an amount for depreciation.

14. Answer C is correct. The Federal Insurance Administration sets rates, eligibility requirements, and coverage limitations for flood insurance. Maximum limits do apply to the amount of coverage available, coverage may be written by private insurance carriers, and the FIA reimburses insurance companies for losses that exceed premiums collected.

15. Answer D is correct. Adverse selection means the tendency of people with a greater than average exposure to loss to purchase insurance coverage. For example, if insurers only sold earthquake coverage to applicants in earthquake-prone areas, or flood insurance only to those in flood-prone areas, the situation known as adverse selection would exist. Insurers and underwriters guard against adverse selection by trying to sell broad ranges of coverages to a large cross-section of the population in order to increase the premium base and spread the risk of loss.

16. Answer B is correct. The coinsurance requirement is for the insured to carry 80% of the $300,000 building value, or $240,000 of coverage. Because the insured only has $200,000 of coverage, a penalty applies. The formula is that the amount actually carried ($200,000) is divided by the amount required ($240,000) to produce a fraction that will be multiplied by the loss. In this case, the fraction is 5/6 and the loss was $60,000, so the result is a $50,000 covered loss. However, the standard deductible is $500 per occurrence, so the net amount paid will be $49,500.

17. Answer C is correct. Coverage for medical payments to others under a homeowners policy applies to necessary medical expenses incurred within three years of an accident that causes bodily injury.

18. Answer A is correct. A Personal Umbrella may cover losses that are excluded by underlying insurance—in which case, a self-insured retention limit applies. This operates similar to a deductible because it is the out-of-pocket amount the insured must absorb before the umbrella coverage applies.

19. Answer C is correct. Ocean marine protection and indemnity (P&I) coverage provides liability coverage for job-related injuries to sailors, cargo lost or damaged through negligence, damage to other vessels when caused by collision, and a few other things. Damage to the insured ship is not covered under P&I, but the insurance is available under hull coverage.

20. Answer D is correct. Almost any building that is walled and roofed, is principally above ground, and is fixed to a permanent site is eligible to be covered by a flood policy. A policy may cover a building, its contents, or both.

21. Answer B is correct. Although all dwelling forms settle personal property losses at actual cash value, under the broad and special forms (DP-2 and DP-3), replacement cost coverage for buildings is provided if the insured carries insurance equal to at least 80% of the full replacement cost at the time of loss.

22. Answer B is correct. The conditions state that the coverage territory includes the United States, its territories and possessions, and Canada. Mexico is not included in the coverage territory.

23. Answer D is correct. Under the BOP eligibility rules, there is no size limitation on apartment buildings, but a size limit does apply to office buildings. Banks, saving and loan associations, bars, and pubs are specifically described as ineligible risk categories.

24. Answer C is correct. The business auto coverage form includes supplementary payments under the liability section that state the insurer will pay expenses incurred by an insured at the insurer's request, including up to $250 a day for lost earnings because of time off from work.

25. Answer C is correct. The purpose of insurance is not to avoid or eliminate risk, but to transfer risk. Risk reduction efforts play a part in loss control, which helps to keep insurance costs down, but insurance itself is not an example of reducing risk.

26. Answer D is correct. The principal of indemnity states that when a loss occurs, an individual should be restored to approximately the same financial position he or she was in before the loss. Insurable interest is a requirement for the insurance to apply. Salvage and subrogation, which are related to claim settlements, help the insurer recover its losses and to not indemnify the insured.

27. Answer D is correct. All dwelling policies provide coverage for the loss of fair rental value if a building or other structure becomes uninhabitable because of an insured cause of loss. A limited amount of coverage is provided under the Other Coverages section of the policy, but an insured with a greater exposure might purchase a specific amount of coverage.

28. Answer D is correct. Interline endorsements attached to a commercial package policy are endorsements that can apply to more than one line of insurance or coverage part.

29. Answer D is correct. Homeowners policies do cover some property used for business, but the coverage is subject to special limitations. The policy will only provide up to $2,500 of coverage for business property on the residence premises and $500 of coverage for business property away from the premises.

30. Answer A is correct. When an insured cancels a policy prior to expiration, the unearned premium may be returned on a short rate basis. This means that the company not only keeps the earned premium for the insurance provided, but also keeps an additional amount for expenses of issuing the policy.

31. Answer B is correct. Burglary is the taking of money or other property from inside a premises by someone who has unlawfully entered or exited the premises. There must be visible evidence of forced entry or exit. Robbery is taking money or property by force or threat. Embezzlement is taking money by means of bookkeeping fraud. Safe burglary is a special form of burglary that specifically refers only to breaking into a safe to take money or property, as opposed to just breaking in to a premises.

32. Answer A is correct. Risks may be retained in whole or in part by intentionally self-insuring or selecting high deductibles. The other risk management options are not examples of risk reduction. Transfer refers to the purchase of insurance, where the risk of loss is assumed by the insurance company in return for the premium. Avoidance means taking steps to not incur the risk at all, such as never driving a car to avoid the risk of collision. Reduction means taking steps to lower the severity of a loss if it occurs, such as installing a sprinkler system—a fire might still occur, but it won't spread if the sprinkler system puts the fire out.

33. Answer B is correct. Under the eligibility rules, office buildings may qualify for coverage under a businessowners policy if they do not contain more than 100,000 square feet of space and do not exceed 6 stories in height.

34. Answer B is correct. The combined ratio is the sum of the loss ratio and the expense ratio. A combined ratio of less than 100% indicates that the company had an underwriting profit. A combined ratio of more than 100% indicates that the company has had a net loss.

35. Answer C is correct. The Common Policy Declarations contain vital summary information about the contract, such as name and address of the named insured, policy period, coverage parts attached, premiums, and a list of forms attached to the policy. Exclusions are found in the individual coverage parts. Exclusions may be contained in coverage forms, causes of loss forms, or both.

36. Answer C is correct. Crime insurance written under a loss sustained form covers losses sustained during the policy period and discovered either during the policy period or up to one year after the policy expires.

37. Answer B is correct. Liability assumed under contract is specifically excluded under the employers liability section of a workers compensation policy. The other answer choices are not excluded and are commonly covered by the policy.

38. Answer C is correct. Farm property, including the principal residence and other structures, may not be covered by homeowner forms. All of the other answer choices reflect exposures that may be covered by farm forms.

39. Answer C is correct. Insurance policies are contracts of adhesion. The insurer draws up the contract language, and the insured simply adheres to the terms. For this reason, any ambiguity in the wording is usually resolved in favor of the insured by the courts.

40. Answer C is correct. Only the special causes of loss form provides theft coverage for commercial property.

41. Answer B is correct. The insurance company is only required to give notice 10 days in advance when it cancels a policy for any reason during the first 60 days of coverage or for nonpayment of premium at any time during the policy term. However, after a policy has been in effect for 60 days, the insurer must give notice at least 30 days in advance when canceling for any reason other than nonpayment of premium.

42. Answer C is correct. The Transfer of Rights of Recovery clause, also known as subrogation, gives the insurance company the right to recover from a third party who was at fault for a loss, up to the amount that the insurer has paid the insured for the loss. The abandonment provision merely states that the insured cannot decide to surrender damaged property to the insurer in return for full payment. (The acquisition of damaged property is at the option of the insurance company.) The pair or set clause states that the settlement for damage to one item that is part of a pair or set will be made with recognition of the reduction in value of the pair or set. Arbitration is a means of settling claims disputes when the insured and the insurance company disagree on the value of damaged property.

43. Answer A is correct. If a building is insured on a replacement cost basis, a businessowners policy will provide additional coverage for increased cost of construction when required to comply with an existing ordinance or law. This coverage is limited to 10,000.

44. Answer D is correct. Similar to CGL coverage, the farm liability form provides coverage for bodily injury and property damage, personal injury and advertising injury, and medical payments to others. Coverage for injury to farm employees is specifically excluded.

45. Answer D is correct. All homeowner policies provide some coverage for loss of use. The other answer choices reflect available optional coverages, but they must be added by endorsement.

46. Answer D is correct. Commercial crime coverage written on a discovery policy form will cover a loss discovered during the policy period even if it was sustained months or years earlier. It will also cover a loss discovered up to 60 days after the policy expires. Exclusions do apply to this coverage.

47. Answer B is correct. Concealment is similar to misrepresentation, except that it involves withholding a material fact where misrepresentation involves misstating a material fact. Fraud has a more extensive definition, which includes the insurance company relying on and being harmed by the misstatement of a material fact. Waiver and estoppel are terms that involve someone giving up a known right.

48. Answer B is correct. If the insurer cancels a commercial package policy, it must mail a written notice to the last known address of the first named insured. Ten days' notice is required for cancellation for nonpayment of premium; 30 days notice is required for cancellation for any other reason permitted by the policy.

49. Answer C is correct. Coverage for transportation expenses is included in the physical damage section of a personal auto policy. All of the other answer choices are optional coverages that may be added by endorsement.

50. Answer D is correct. The commercial building and personal property coverage form does provide a number of coverage extensions but only if an 80% or higher coinsurance percentage or a value reporting symbol is shown in the declarations.

What's on the CD-ROM

The CD-ROM in this book features a Preview Edition Exam Simulator from BISYS Education Services and includes a 50-question exam that randomly combines questions from all the chapters in this book and the state insurance law topics (state law questions are not provided for California, Florida, Georgia, Oklahoma, or Wisconsin), giving you some practice at answering these questions in a format similar to the one you'll experience on your state insurance licensing qualification exam. In addition to the exam simulator, the CD-ROM includes an electronic version of the book (based on the BISYS Education Services *Property-Casualty Concepts* manual) in Portable Document Format (PDF).

Review Questions and Exam Simulator

The review questions for the various chapters and the state insurance law topics are under separate links so that you can study particular areas in turn. After you answer each review question, you will be told whether your answer was correct, and you will be given feedback on why the answer was right or wrong. In contrast, when you go to the exam simulator, you will not be told after each question whether you answered correctly, or be given feedback on your answer. When you finish all 50 questions on the exam simulator, you will be given a percentage score to show how well you did on the exam as a whole. Each time you take the exam simulator, a different set of questions will be chosen from the chapter and state law review questions, and they will be presented in a different randomized order so that you can use the exam simulator many times to test your comprehension of the material without simply "learning the test."

What we've described are the default settings for each type of quiz or exam, but you have other options. When you access each quiz or exam, you will be given the option (by clicking on the Change Settings button) of changing the setting on each quiz or exam so that you can turn off feedback altogether, see feedback for all questions after you complete the entire quiz or exam, see feedback after the quiz or exam only for those questions you answered incorrectly, or see feedback after each question only for those questions you answered incorrectly. The Change Settings option allows you to tailor the feedback to practice questions and the exam simulator to your preferences.

Installing the CD

To install the CD-ROM, follow these instructions:

1. Close all applications before beginning the installation.

2. Insert the CD into your CD drive.

3. The installation program will start automatically. Click Next.

4. To indicate your consent to the licensing agreement, click Yes.

5. Click Next to copy the installation program to the Bisys CBT folder under the Program Files folder on your computer's hard drive.

6. Click Next to add the BISYS Education Services icon to your Program Folder.

7. The installation program will then copy all the Exam Simulator files to your computer's hard drive (this may take a few minutes). Click Finish to complete the installation process. Note that the installation program will automatically restart your computer when you do so. (If you do not click Finish at this point, you will have to restart your computer later to complete the installation process.)

8. To start your Exam Simulator, click on your Start button, select Programs, BISYS Education Services, and then click on Property-Casualty Exam Cram Review.

9. Press Begin, and then press New User.

10. Fill in the information as required and choose a password. Then click Create Account.

11. Type in the two-letter postal abbreviation of the state for which you will be taking the licensing exam and click Begin.

You are now ready to use the Exam Simulator program. Simply click Exams and you can either take exams with their default settings described here or change the settings as you wish.

Customer Service and Ordering

If you encounter problems with the exam simulator on the CD-ROM, or if you'd like to purchase the full insurance license exam simulator, call BISYS Education Services at 800-241-9095 or visit www.bisys-education.com.

Glossary

Abandonment condition
A condition often contained in property insurance policies stating that the insured cannot abandon damaged property to the insurer and demand to be reimbursed for its full value.

absolute liability
Type of liability imposed by law on those participating in certain activities that are considered especially hazardous. A person involved in such operations may be held liable for the damages of another, even though the individual was not negligent.

accident
An unintentional loss that occurs at a specific time and place.

Accounts Receivable insurance
Filed Commercial Inland Marine form that insures against loss the insured suffers because of an inability to collect from customers when accounts receivable records are damaged or destroyed.

actual cash value (ACV)
The cost to replace an item of property at the time of loss, less an allowance for depreciation. Often used to determine the amount of reimbursement for a loss.

additional coverages
Supplemental insurance coverages that apply only in certain circumstances, have reduced or separate limits of liability, or require the insured to meet certain requirements before they are applicable. Also called *coverage extensions*, *other coverages*, and *extended coverages*.

additional insured
An individual or company, in addition to the insured, who is listed in the declarations. An example is a mortgage company that has an insurable interest in the property insured.

Additional Insured—Lessor Endorsement

Commercial Auto endorsement used to make leased vehicles considered owned vehicles for coverage purposes.

Adhesion contract

A contract where one party has more power than the other party in drafting the contract. An insurance policy is an adhesion contract—the insurer is the one with more power.

admitted insurer

See authorized insurer.

adverse selection

The tendency of insureds with a greater-than-average chance of loss to purchase insurance.

agency

Principles governing the authority of any agent that represents a principal.

agent

An individual or organization that legally represents another; a state-licensed professional who represents the insurance company in the sale and servicing of insurance; the direct link between the insurance company and the policyholder.

aggregate limit

Type of policy limit found in Liability policies that limits coverage to a specified total amount for all losses occurring within the policy period.

Agreed Amount policy

See Valued policy.

Agreed Value condition

Condition found in some Property insurance policies stipulating that a certain value meet the coinsurance requirement. If the policy limit equals or exceeds this amount, the insured will not be assessed a coinsurance penalty. Also called *Stated Amount condition*.

agreement

See offer and acceptance.

aleatory contract

A contract under which one party's performance is contingent on an uncertain event. An insurance policy is an aleatory contract because the insurance company is required to fulfill its promise to pay only if a loss occurs. The monetary value that the insurance company will return to the insured is not known at the time the contract is formed, and it might be more or less than the monetary value the insured provided to the insurance company in the form of the premium.

alien company

An insurance company incorporated in a country other than the United States that is doing business in the United States.

all risk policy

See open peril policy.

A.M. Best company
Organization that rates the financial stability of insurance companies doing business in the United States.

Annual Transit policy
Nonfiled Commercial Inland Marine transportation form that insures a property owner's incoming or outgoing shipments of goods during a year.

apparent authority
Legal doctrine that states that an agent has whatever authority a reasonable person would assume he or she has based on appearances, for example, the use of the principal's logo on the agent's business premises and stationery.

application
Questionnaire filled out by an agent and the prospect who is seeking insurance. The form contains information used to underwrite and rate the policy.

Appraisal condition
Policy condition that outlines a procedure for when the insured and insurer disagree on the amount of a loss. The insured and the insurer each select an appraiser. The two appraisers select an umpire. If the appraisers cannot agree on the amount of loss, the umpire is consulted. The amount agreed to by any two of the three parties is the amount paid for the loss.

appurtenant structures
Buildings of lesser value that are on the same premises as the main building insured under a Property policy. They are usually covered by the policy.

Arbitration condition
Policy condition that is similar to the Appraisal condition; can be used to resolve other areas of disagreement besides those regarding the value of a loss.

assessment mutual company
Mutual insurance company that charges members a pro rata share of losses at the end of each policy period. See mutual company.

Assigned Risk plan
See Automobile Insurance plan.

Assignment condition
Condition in insurance policies specifying that the policy cannot be transferred to another unless the company consents to the transfer in writing.

Assumption of Risk
Defense against liability based on the common law principle that a person who knowingly exposes himself or herself to danger or injury assumes the risk of loss and cannot hold another person responsible for the loss.

audit
See premium audit.

authorized insurer
Company that meets a state insurance department's standards and is authorized to do business in that state. Also called an *admitted insurer.*

Automatic Increase in Insurance endorsement
Dwelling policy endorsement that provides an annual increase in the Coverage A amount of 4%, 6%, or 8%.

Automobile Insurance plan
A state-sponsored plan that provides Automobile insurance to those who are uninsurable under standard Auto insurance policies.

Aviation Hull insurance
Insurance that provides coverage for physical damage to aircraft.

Aviation Liability insurance
Insurance provided for owners of aircraft that covers liability for bodily injury, injury to passengers, and property damage. Also provides Medical Payments coverage.

bailee
A person or organization that has temporary possession of someone else's personal property.

Bailee's Customer policy
Nonfiled Commercial Inland Marine form obtained by a bailee to cover loss or damage to customers' property in the bailee's custody, without regard to liability.

bailment
Delivery of property by the owner to someone else to be held for some special purpose and then returned to the owner.

barratry
Illegal acts committed willfully by a ship's master or crew for the purpose of damaging the ship or cargo. Includes hijacking, abandonment, and embezzlement. This peril is covered in Ocean Marine insurance.

Best's
Organization that rates the financial stability of insurance companies doing business in the United States.

Bid bond
Type of Surety bond that guarantees if a contractor's bid is accepted, the contractor will enter into a contract and provide the required Performance bond.

Bill of Lading
Standardized contract of carriage issued by common carriers to the business for which it is shipping goods.

binder
Oral or written statement that provides immediate insurance protection for a specified period. Designed to provide temporary coverage until a policy is issued or denied.

blanket insurance

Type of insurance policy that covers more than one item of property at a single location or one or more items of property at multiple locations.

Blanket Position bond

Fidelity bond that covers losses arising from the dishonesty of one or more employees acting separately or in collusion. Provides a single limit of liability applicable to each employee involved in a loss.

Boatowners policy

See Watercraft Package policy.

bodily injury (BI)

Defined in most policies to include injury, sickness, disease, and death resulting from any of these at any time.

Boiler and Machinery insurance

Insurance that covers the insured for losses arising out of the use of steam boilers or other machinery or equipment. May be included in the Commercial Package policy.

Broad Theft Coverage endorsement

Dwelling policy endorsement that covers theft, attempted theft, and vandalism and malicious mischief resulting from theft. Property is covered while it is on or off the premises.

broker

Individual who represents the prospect, instead of the insurance company, in the insurance transaction.

Builders Risk Coverage form

One of the Commercial Property coverage forms; covers commercial, residential, or farm buildings that are under construction.

Builders Risk Reporting form

Optional form used with the Commercial Property Builders Risk coverage form; allows insured to purchase a smaller amount of insurance that gradually increases as the value of the building under construction increases.

Building and Personal Property Coverage form

Commercial Property coverage form that covers buildings, the insured's business personal property, and the personal property of others located at the business premises.

burglary

As defined in Crime insurance forms, the taking of property by a person unlawfully entering or leaving the premises as evidenced by visible signs of forced entry or exit.

Business Auto Coverage form

One of the Commercial Auto coverage forms; covers a business's owned, nonowned, and hired autos against liability and physical damage losses.

Business Auto Physical Damage Coverage form

One of the Commercial Auto coverage forms; covers a business's owned or hired business autos for physical damage only.

Business Income coverage forms
Commercial Property coverage forms that pay for loss of income that the insured sustains because of a direct physical loss from a covered peril that forces the insured to suspend operations until the property can be repaired, rebuilt, or replaced with reasonable speed. Available with or without Extra Expense coverage.

Business Income from Dependent Properties—Broad form
Commercial Property coverage form designed for insureds whose business income is dependent on the ongoing operations of other businesses they do not own.

Business liability
Liability that arises out of the conduct of a business.

Business Pursuits endorsement
Homeowners policy endorsement that provides liability coverage for a business conducted away from the residence premises.

Businessowners Policy (BOP)
Package policy designed to provide broad Property and Liability coverage for small businesses. Eligibility requirements are more strict than the CPP (Commercial Package Policy) requirements.

Camera and Musical Instruments Dealers Coverage form
Filed Commercial Inland Marine form written to cover camera and musical instruments dealers; covers the insured's stock in trade as well as customer property in the insured's care, custody, or control.

cancellation
Termination of an insurance policy by the insured or the insurance company during the policy period.

capital
The accumulated, permanent resources a company gets from owners and customers. The value of the portion of assets that a company owns and that are not restricted by obligations to creditors.

captive agent
See exclusive agent.

Cargo insurance
Type of Ocean Marine insurance that covers goods while they are in transit over water.

Casualty insurance
Line of insurance that includes a wide variety of unrelated coverages, including Liability, Auto, Workers Compensation, Aviation, Crime, and Surety bonds.

Causes of Loss form
Separate form used with the Commercial Property coverage part of the Commercial Package policy that lists covered perils and exclusions. Several different versions provide increasingly broader coverage from basic to broad to special. A Causes of Loss form takes the place of the policy's "perils insured against" provisions.

certificate of insurance

Written form that verifies a policy has been written. Provides a summary of the coverage provided under the policy.

claim adjuster

Person employed by or acting on behalf of an insurance company to evaluate and settle insurance claims. The adjuster must determine the cause of loss, whether the loss is covered by the policy, the value of the loss, and the amount of loss payable by the policy.

claims-made form

Commercial General Liability coverage form that pays for BI or PD losses for which a claim was first made against the insured during the policy period.

class rating

See manual rating.

coinsurance

Policy condition that requires an insured to pay part of a loss if the amount of insurance carried on property is less than a specified percentage of the value of the property at the time of loss.

coinsurance penalty

The amount not paid by the insurance company because the insured failed to comply with the coinsurance condition.

Collision coverage

In Auto insurance, a type of physical damage coverage that covers loss that occurs when the insured's auto strikes another object or vehicle. May also include upset or overturn of the insured auto.

combined ratio

The sum of the loss ratio and the expense ratio. A ratio of 100% is the break-even point. A ratio below 100% indicates an underwriting profit; a ratio above 100% indicates a loss. See loss ratio and expense ratio.

combined single limit

See single limit.

Commercial Articles Coverage form

Filed Commercial Inland Marine form that covers photographic equipment or musical instruments used commercially.

Commercial Auto Coverage part

A part of the Commercial Package policy that provides Liability and Physical Damage coverage for a business's autos, including garage, trucking, and motor carrier businesses.

Commercial Blanket bond

Type of Fidelity bond that covers loss arising from the dishonesty of one or more employees acting separately or in collusion. The limit of liability applies separately to each loss, regardless of the number of employees involved.

Commercial Crime Coverage part

A part of the Commercial Package Policy that covers various crime exposures of businesses.

Commercial General Liability (CGL) Coverage part

A part of the Commercial Package Policy that provides liability coverage for businesses.

Commercial Inland Marine insurance

See Inland Marine insurance.

commercial lines

Insurance designed for businesses, institutions, or organizations.

Commercial Package Policy (CPP)

Package policy for businesses developed by ISO. Insureds can select two or more of the following coverages to include in the policy: Commercial General Liability, Commercial Property, Commercial Inland Marine, Commercial Crime, Boiler and Machinery, Farm, and Commercial Auto. Most commercial risks are eligible for the CPP.

Commercial Property Coverage part

A part of the Commercial Package Policy that provides insurance for a business's real and business personal property.

Commercial Property floater risks

Category of the Nationwide Definition that includes a number of Commercial Inland Marine forms, such as Bailee's Customer forms, Equipment forms, Business floaters, and Dealers policies.

Commercial Umbrella policy

See Umbrella policy.

Common Policy conditions

Form that must be included in the Commercial Package Policy; it contains conditions that apply to all coverages issued under the CPP.

Common Policy declarations

Form that must be included in the Commercial Package Policy; contains information about the insured that applies to all coverages issued under the CPP.

Comparative Negligence

Law that allows an injured party to collect from another party for a loss, even when the injured party contributed to his or her own loss. Damages are reduced to the extent of the injured party's negligence.

compensatory damages

Damages that reimburse an injured party for losses that were actually sustained. See general damages and special damages.

competent parties

One of the requirements of a legal contract; states that for a contract to be valid, it must be made between parties who are considered competent under the law.

competitive state fund

Method of providing workers compensation coverage in some states; employers can either purchase insurance from a private insurance company or from a state fund.

Completion bond

Type of Surety bond that guarantees when contractors borrow money to fund construction projects, the project will be carried out and the work will be delivered free and clear of liens or encumbrances.

Comprehensive coverage

In Auto insurance, a broad Physical Damage coverage that covers all property losses except collision and those perils or property that are specifically excluded. Also called *Other Than Collision coverage (OTC)*.

concealment

The withholding of a material fact involved in the contract on which the insurer relies.

concurrent causation

A situation in which two or more perils act concurrently (at the same time or in sequence) to cause a loss. Some courts ruled that losses from concurrent causation are covered even when one of the perils that contributed to the loss is excluded under the policy. These rulings led Property insurers to revise policy language to clarify the intent of the policy.

conditional contract

A contract that contains a number of conditions that both parties must comply with. An insurance policy is a conditional contract.

conditions

Portion of an insurance policy that describes the rights and duties of the insured and the insurance company under the policy.

Condominium Association Coverage form

Commercial Property coverage form that covers the buildings in a condominium complex. Does not cover the condominium owner's personal property.

Condominium Commercial Unit-Owners Coverage form

Commercial Property coverage form that may only be purchased by owners of commercial condominiums; covers the condominium's contents, including business personal property and the personal property of others.

consequential loss

See indirect loss.

consideration

A characteristic of a legal contract; the thing of value exchanged for the performance promised in the contract. With insurance contracts, the consideration that the insured gives is the premium payment. The consideration that the insurer gives is the promise to pay for certain losses suffered by the insured.

consultant

Insurance professional who, for a fee, offers advice on the benefits, advantages, and disadvantages of various insurance policies. Sells advice, not insurance.

contract

A legal agreement between two competent parties that promises a certain performance in exchange for a certain consideration.

Contract bonds

Category of Surety bonds that guarantee the fulfillment of contractual obligations. Includes Bid bonds, Labor and Materials bonds, Performance bonds, Payment bonds, Supply bonds, and Completion bonds.

Contractors Equipment floater

Nonfiled Commercial Inland Marine form that covers the heavy machinery, equipment, and tools a contractor uses in business.

contribution by equal shares

Type of Other Insurance condition found in Liability policies. It calls for all insurers to contribute equally up to the limit of the policy having the smallest limit, whereupon that company stops paying. The other companies share in the remainder of the loss until the loss is paid in full or all policy limits are exhausted.

contribution by limits

See pro rata other insurance.

Contributory Negligence

Common law defense against negligence stating that if an individual contributes to his or her own loss in any way, someone else cannot be held liable for the loss.

countersignature

Signature of a licensed agent that, in most states, must appear on the policy to validate the contract.

Court bond

Type of Surety bond used to settle legal arguments that do not involve monetary damages.

Coverage extensions

See additional coverages.

Coverage form

Document that contains insuring agreements, coverages, exclusions, and conditions. Must be attached to a policy jacket to make a complete policy. Also called a *policy form*.

Coverage part

Combination of forms and endorsements used to provide a particular commercial coverage. The forms and endorsements available under each coverage part can be used to issue a policy covering a single line of insurance or combined to provide a Commercial Package Policy.

coverage trigger

Event that activates (triggers) coverage under a Commercial General Liability coverage form. Under the occurrence form, the coverage trigger is bodily injury or property damage that occurs during the policy period. Under the claims-made form, the trigger is BI or PD that occurs on or after the retroactive date, if any, for which a claim is first made against an insured during the policy period.

custodian

As defined in Crime insurance forms, an insured, partner, or employee who has care and custody of insured property within the premises. Does not apply to watchpersons or janitors.

declarations

Section of an insurance contract that shows who is insured, what property or risk is covered, when and where the coverage is effective, and how much coverage applies.

deductible

The dollar amount an insured must absorb prior to the insurance company paying out for a covered loss up to the limits of the policy.

defense costs

Legal expenses incurred by the insurer to defend suits brought against insureds. Defense costs are paid in addition to payments for BI or PD claims.

definitions

Section of an insurance policy that clarifies the meaning of certain terms used in the policy.

degree of care

Extent of legal duty owed by one person to another, depending on the situation. Also called *standard of care*.

deposit premium

Premium paid at the beginning of the policy period that is based on an estimate of what the final premium will be. This premium is adjusted based on reports submitted by the insured to the insurer. Also called an *estimated premium*.

Difference in Conditions insurance (DIC)

Type of Commercial Property Policy that covers most insurable perils but excludes basic fire and extended coverage perils.

diminution of value

An actual or perceived loss of an auto's resale or market value that results from a direct, accidental loss.

direct loss

Financial loss resulting directly from a loss to property.

direct response system

Insurance company that sells insurance through the mail or over the phone. No agents are involved.

direct writer

Insurance marketing system in which the company's agents are also employees of the company so that there is not only an agent-principal relationship between the two, but also an employee-employer relationship that binds the agent closer to the interests of the company.

Directors and Officers Liability insurance (D&O)

Type of Errors and Omissions policy written for directors and officers of corporations who might be sued as individuals by stockholders.

disability insurance

Line of insurance that protects the insured against loss of income resulting from injury or sickness.

discovery form

Commercial Crime form that covers losses sustained at any time and discovered either during the policy period or up to 60 days after the policy expires. The discovery period for losses related to employee benefit plans extends for up to one year after policy expiration.

Doctrine of Reasonable Expectations

Legal principle that provides that an insurance policy includes coverages that an average person would reasonably expect it to include, regardless of what the policy actually provides.

domestic company

Insurance company doing business in the state in which it is incorporated.

Domestic shipments

Category of the Nationwide Definition that includes coverage for cargo in transit over land.

Drive Other Car—Broadened Coverage for Named Individuals (DOC) endorsement

Commercial Auto endorsement that extends the definition of a covered auto to include autos the named insured does not own, hire, or borrow while being used by the person named in the endorsement.

Duties Following Loss

Condition found in property-casualty policies that explains the insured's responsibilities after a loss occurs.

Dwelling policy

Policy that provides Property coverage to individuals and families. Covers dwellings, other structures, personal property, and fair rental value. Some versions also cover additional living expense. The unendorsed policy does not provide liability coverage.

Dwelling Under Construction endorsement

Dwelling policy endorsement used to provide provisional limits of liability for dwellings under construction. The limits of liability increase as construction of the building progresses.

earned premium

Premium an insurance company has actually earned by providing insurance protection for the designated period of time.

earthquake insurance

Insurance that covers damage to a structure, its contents, or both as the result of an earthquake. Available as a separate policy and as an endorsement to the Dwelling, Homeowners, and Commercial Property policies.

Electronic Data Processing Equipment floater

Nonfiled Commercial Inland Marine policy that provides open peril coverage for computer hardware, computer software, and data that are owned by the insured or in the insured's care, custody, or control. Breakdown coverage, extra expense, and business interruption coverage may also be included.

Employees as Additional Insureds Endorsement

Endorsement used with the Business Auto coverage form that covers employees while they are using an auto not owned, hired, or borrowed by the business in the business or personal affairs of the named insured.

Employers Liability coverage

Coverage included in the Workers Compensation and Employers Liability policy that covers the employer's liability at common law arising out of employees' work-related injuries and occupational diseases.

Employment Practices Liability insurance

Type of policy that covers a business's losses arising out wrongful termination, discrimination, sexual harassment, and other employment-related practices.

Endorsement

Document attached to an insurance policy that changes the policy in some way.

Equipment Breakdown Protection Coverage form

Title of ISO coverage form used to write what is traditionally called Boiler and Machinery insurance. See Boiler and Machinery insurance.

Equipment Dealers Coverage Form

Filed Commercial Inland Marine coverage form that covers mobile equipment and construction equipment dealers; it also covers the insured's stock in trade as well as customer property in the insured's care, custody, or control.

Errors and Omissions insurance (E&O)

Professional Liability coverage that protects the insured against liability for committing an error or omission in the performance of professional duties.

estimated premium

See deposit premium.

estoppel

Principle stating that if one intentionally or unintentionally creates the impression that a certain fact exists, and an innocent party relies on that impression and is injured as a result, the guilty party may be legally prohibited from asserting that the fact does not exist.

excess insurance

When two or more policies or coverages apply to the same loss, the one that applies only after the limits of the primary coverage have been exhausted.

excess lines agent

Agent licensed by the state to handle the placement of business with nonadmitted insurers. Also called *surplus lines agent*.

exclusions

Section of an insurance policy that lists property, perils, persons, or situations that are not covered under the policy.

exclusive agent

An agent who markets insurance for a single company. Also called *captive agent*.

Exclusive Remedy Doctrine

One of the precepts upon which the workers compensation system was founded; stipulates that the only means available to employees to receive compensation from employers for injuries covered by workers compensation laws is through the benefits mandated by those laws.

exemplary damages

See punitive damages.

expense ratio

Ratio that indicates the cost of doing business. It is calculated by dividing the amount of underwriting expenses by the amount of written premium.

Experience Modification factor

In experience rating, the factor applied to reduce the premium when loss experience is better than expected.

experience rating

Type of merit rating that determines premium based on previous loss experience.

exports

Category of the Nationwide Definition that includes risks eligible for Ocean Marine insurance.

exposure

A condition or situation that presents a possibility of loss.

express authority

Legal doctrine stating that an agent has the authority specifically given to the agent, either orally or in writing, by the principal.

extended coverages

See additional coverages.

Extended Nonowned Coverage for Named Individual endorsement

Personal Auto policy endorsement that eliminates most exclusions applicable to autos that are furnished or available for the regular use of the named insured or family members.

extended reporting period (ERP)

Period of time provided by the claims-made Commercial General Liability coverage form during which coverage will be provided for claims made after the expiration date of the policy if certain conditions are met. The Basic ERP runs 60 days and can be extended to 5 years. The Supplemental ERP runs for an unlimited duration, but is available only by endorsement for an additional premium.

Extortion—Commercial Entities Endorsement

Endorsement used with the Commercial Crime policy that covers loss of money, securities, and other property when surrendered away from the premises as a result of a threat to do bodily harm to the insured, an employee, or a relative of either who is being held captive.

Extra Expense Coverage form

Commercial Property coverage form that covers additional expenses incurred by the insured business to continue operations following a direct loss by a peril insured against.

Fair Credit Reporting act

Federal law that allows consumers who are denied insurance because of information contained in a credit report to be notified and allowed to obtain the information used in the report from the reporting agency.

FAIR plan

Program established by law that makes property insurance available to insureds who might otherwise be uninsurable in the standard market. Stands for *fair access to insurance requirements*.

Farm Coverage part

Part of the Commercial Package Policy that provides Property and Liability insurance to farmers for both their personal and business exposures.

Federal Employers Liability Act (FELA)

Federal law that provides benefits to injured railroad workers who are exempt under state workers compensation laws.

Federal Terrorism Risk Insurance Act of 2002

Federal law designed to ensure that insurance coverage for terrorism losses under commercial lines policies will be available and affordable. It requires insurers to pay a specified amount for terrorism losses in a given calendar year; once that limit is reached, the federal government will reimburse insurers 90% of insured losses that exceed the limit.

fellow servant rule

Common law defense against liability that allowed employers to escape liability for injury to an employee if another employee's carelessness had contributed to the loss.

Fidelity bond

Class of bonds that guarantees an employee's honest discharge of duty; written to protect an insured from dishonest acts by employees.

fiduciary

A person or organization who holds, has discretionary authority, and manages the money of another person or organization—for example, a bank officer managing a trust fund for a customer or an insurance agent to whom premiums have been paid for forwarding to the company.

Fiduciary bond

Type of Surety bond that guarantees a fiduciary will fulfill its obligations set forth by law.

Fiduciary Liability policy

Insurance that protects people who manage private pension and employee benefit plans against liability for violation of the federal ERISA law.

field underwriting

Selection of clients by the agent in accordance with company standards.

File and Use

Method of rate and form ratification used by some state insurance departments that allows a company to begin using forms or rates as soon as they are filed by the department. The department eventually reviews the filing and officially accepts or rejects it.

filed form

Standardized Inland Marine form that can be written under the Commercial Inland Marine coverage part of the Commercial Package Policy.

Film Coverage form

Filed Commercial Inland Marine form that covers exposed motion picture film until production is complete and positive prints are made.

Financial Responsibility laws

State laws that require owners or operators of autos to provide evidence that they have the funds to pay for automobile losses for which they might become liable. Insurance is the usual method for providing this evidence to the state.

first named insured

First person listed in the declarations as an insured. The first named insured might have a higher level of duties or rights under the policy.

First Party loss

Property insurance loss.

flat cancellation

Cancellation of a policy by the insured or the insurance company on its effective date.

floater

Insurance policy that covers property wherever it is located. (Inland Marine Coverage—sometimes referred to as a "rider.")

Flood insurance

See National Flood Insurance program.

Floor Plan Coverage form

Filed Commercial Inland Marine form that covers stock that is subject to a *floor plan arrangement*, where a dealer borrows money from a lender with which to pay for merchandise.

foreign company

An insurance company doing business in a state other than the one in which it is incorporated.

fraternal benefit society

An incorporated society or order, without capital stock, that is operated on the lodge system and is conducted solely for the benefit of its members and their beneficiaries, and not for profit. Fraternal benefit societies offer insurance that is available only to members.

fraud

A deliberate misrepresentation that causes harm; an all-out effort by one party to deceive and cheat the other.

freight insurance

Type of Ocean Marine insurance that protects the insured against the loss of shipping costs.

functional replacement cost

Method to determine reimbursement for some losses, particularly those to antique, ornate, or custom construction. The damaged property is repaired or replaced with less expensive, but functionally equivalent, materials.

Garage coverage form

Commercial Auto coverage form designed for garage businesses such as dealers, service stations, garages, and parking lots. It includes coverage for liability arising out of auto and garage operations, physical damage, and garagekeepers' losses arising out of owned, nonowned, and hired autos.

Garagekeepers insurance

Coverage that is part of the Garage coverage form. Covers a garage risk's legal liability for customers' autos in the care, custody, or control of the garage. At the insured's option and for an additional premium, it can also apply without regard to fault.

general average loss

Ocean Marine term used to indicate a partial loss resulting from a sacrifice of cargo to save remaining property (jettison). Each party shares in the loss in proportion to his or her total interest in the property being transported.

General Conditions form

Separate form that lists the conditions that apply to a policy.

general damages

Type of compensatory damages that reimburse the injured party for such things as pain and suffering and disfigurement.

hazard

Something that increases the chance of loss.

health insurance

Line of insurance that protects the insured against financial loss because of medical bills.

Hired and Nonowned Auto Liability endorsement

Businessowners policy endorsement used to cover hired or nonowned autos used by the business.

hold harmless agreement

Contractual arrangement in which one party assumes the liability of a situation and relieves the other party of responsibility.

Home Day Care Coverage endorsement

Homeowners policy endorsement used to provide coverage for home day care businesses.

homeowners policy

Personal multi-line policy for homeowners that includes both Property and Liability coverages. There are different forms that provide varying degrees of property coverage. Liability coverage is the same in all forms.

Hull insurance

Ocean Marine insurance that provides coverage for physical damage to the ship.

implied authority

Authority given by the principal to the agent that is not formally expressed or communicated.

implied warranties

In Ocean Marine insurance, warranties that are not written into the policy, but have become a part of the policy by custom.

imports

Category of the Nationwide Definition that includes risks eligible for Ocean Marine insurance.

imputed liability

See vicarious liability.

incidental contract

See insured contract.

incidental occupancy

A business conducted in a dwelling used primarily as a residence with no other businesses operating on the same premises. Individual insurers have specific guidelines about the types of incidental businesses permitted, but examples include business or professional offices and private schools or instructional studios.

incurred losses

One of the components used to calculate the loss ratio. It includes paid losses and certain expenses associated with claim handling.

indemnity

Principle of insurance that provides that when a loss occurs, the insured should be restored to the approximate financial condition he or she occupied before the loss occurred, no better or no worse.

independent adjuster

Claim handler who works independently instead of for a particular insurer.

independent agent

Agent who represents many insurance companies, rather than a single company. Also called a *nonexclusive agent.*

indirect loss

Loss that is the result or consequence of a direct loss. Also called a *consequential loss.*

Individual Named Insured endorsement

Commercial Auto endorsement that provides coverage similar to that provided under the Personal Auto policy to family members of the named insured while using any auto.

Inland Marine insurance

Form of insurance originally designed as an extension of Ocean Marine coverage to insure transportation of goods over land. Today, it covers a variety of portable property, in addition to goods in transit. Available as personal or commercial insurance. Commercial Inland Marine insurance can be included in the Commercial Package policy.

Installation policy

Nonfiled Commercial Inland Marine policy that covers loss to machinery, equipment, building materials, and supplies in transit to or being used with or during the course of installation, testing, building, renovating, or repair.

Instrumentalities of Transportation and Communication

Category of the Nationwide Definition that includes a variety of forms closely related to transportation or communication, such as bridges, pipelines, and television towers.

insurable interest

Any actual, lawful, and substantial economic interest in the safety or preservation of the subject of the insurance from loss or destruction or financial damage or impairment.

insurance

Contract or device for transferring the risk of loss from a person, business, or organization to an insurance company that agrees, in exchange for a premium, to pay for losses through an accumulation of premiums.

insurance commissioner

Head official of a state insurance department. Can also be called an *insurance director* or *insurance superintendent.*

insurance department

State department charged with controlling insurance matters within the state.

Insurance Guaranty Association

State funds created by law that pay claims to insurers domiciled in that state that become insolvent (bankrupt). Funds are generated by making assessments against other insurers operating in the state.

Insurance Services Office (ISO)

Organization established for the benefit of its member insurance companies and other subscriber companies. ISO gathers statistics, provides loss costs, drafts policy forms and coverage provisions, and conducts inspections for rate-making purposes.

insured contract

Term used in the CGL and Businessowners Liability forms to describe contracts for which contractual liability coverage is available under the policy, such as leases, sidetrack agreements, and elevator maintenance agreements. Also called *incidental contract*.

insuring agreement

Section of an insurance policy that describes what is covered and the perils the policy insures against.

Interline endorsement

An endorsement that modifies two or more lines of insurance.

intervening cause

An independent action that breaks the chain of causation and sets in motion a new chain of events. When this occurs, the intervening cause becomes the *proximate cause*. Can serve as a common law defense against liability.

invitee

A person invited onto a premises for some purpose involving potential benefit to the property owner.

jettison

A voluntary action to rid a ship of cargo to prevent further damage or peril. Jettison is a covered peril in Ocean Marine policies.

Jewelers Block coverage form

Filed Commercial Inland Marine form for jewelers that covers the insured's stock in trade and the property of others while it is on or off the premises.

Joint Ownership Coverage endorsement

Personal Auto policy endorsement that allows the policy to be issued to two or more persons who live in the same household or two or more individuals who are related in another way besides husband and wife.

Jones Act

Federal law that allows members of ships' crews to sue their employer/shipowner at common law for injuries caused by the employer's/shipowner's negligence.

judgment rating

Method of rating that establishes premiums based on a careful evaluation of each individual risk, without the use of manuals or tables.

Judicial bond

Category of Surety bond that guarantees the principal will fulfill certain obligations set forth by law. Includes Fiduciary bonds and Court bonds.

Labor and Materials bond
See Payment bond.

Law of Large Numbers
Principle stating that the more examples used to develop any statistic, the more reliable the statistic will be.

Legal Liability coverage form
Commercial Property coverage form that covers the insured for liability arising out of negligent damage to the property of others while it is in the insured's care, custody, or control.

legal purpose
One of the characteristics of a legal contract; means that contracts are enforceable only if they are not obviously illegal, immoral, or against the public good.

liability insurance
Type of insurance that protects an insured from financial loss arising out of liability claims by transferring the burden of financial loss from the insured to the insurance company.

Liberalization condition
Condition found in Property insurance contracts providing that if the insurer broadens coverage under a policy form or endorsement without requiring an additional premium, all existing similar policies or endorsements will be construed to contain the broadened coverage.

License and Permit bond
Type of Surety bond that is sometimes required in connection with the issuance of licenses by government agencies. They guarantee that the person who posts the bond will comply with all applicable laws pertaining to their activities.

licensee
Person on the premises with the property owner's consent, but for the sole benefit of the visitor.

life insurance
Insurance that pays a stipulated sum to a designated beneficiary upon the death of the insured. Protects the insured's beneficiary against the financial consequences of the insured's premature death.

limit of coverage
See policy limit.

limit of insurance
See policy limit.

limit of liability
See policy limit.

limitations
Policy language that eliminates or reduces coverage under certain circumstances or when specified conditions apply.

Liquor Liability coverage form
CGL coverage form that provides coverage for liquor liability excluded by standard CGL policies for those who are in the business of manufacturing, distributing, selling, serving, or furnishing alcoholic beverages.

Livestock coverage form

Farm coverage form used to provide separate coverage for livestock.

Lloyd's Association

A voluntary association of individuals or groups of individuals who agree to share in insurance contracts. Each individual or "syndicate" is individually responsible for the amounts of insurance they write.

Longshore and Harbor Workers Compensation Act Coverage endorsement

Endorsement used with the Workers Compensation and Employers Liability policy that covers the additional benefits required by federal law for maritime workers injured while working on navigable waters or shore-site areas.

loss cost

Factor used in figuring insurance rates that represents how much an insurance company needs to collect to cover expected losses.

Loss Payable condition

See Mortgage condition.

loss provisions

General term used to describe policy conditions that specify what the insured and insurer must do after a loss.

loss ratio

Method used to determine an insurance company's success in covering current losses out of current premium income; determined by dividing incurred losses by earned premium.

Loss Sustained During Prior Insurance condition

Condition found in loss sustained version of the Commercial Crime forms that allows losses that occurred during a prior policy period to be covered under the current policy if certain conditions are met.

Loss Sustained form

Commercial Crime form that covers losses sustained during the policy period and discovered either during the policy period or up to one year after the policy expires.

Mail coverage form

Filed Commercial Inland Marine form that covers property in transport by registered, first class, certified, or express mail.

Malpractice insurance

Term used to describe Professional Liability insurance issued to medical professionals or institutions.

manual rating

Method of premium determination that uses rates based on collected statistics. The rates, which apply per unit of insurance, are published in manuals. Also called *class rating*.

market value

The amount property could be sold for at the time of loss. Can be used to determine the amount of reimbursement for a loss.

material fact
A fact that would cause an insurer to decline a risk, charge a different premium, or change the provisions of the policy that was issued.

MCS-90 endorsement
Endorsement attached to the Truckers coverage form to provide public liability coverage.

merit rating
Method of determining premiums where a manual rate is modified to reflect the risk's unique characteristics. See experience rating, retrospective rating, and schedule rating.

messenger
As defined in Crime insurance forms, an insured, partner, or employee who has care and custody of insured property outside the premises.

Miscellaneous Type Vehicle endorsement
Personal Auto policy endorsement that provides coverage for vehicles that are usually excluded by the policy, such as motorcycles, motor homes, golf carts, mopeds, and other recreational vehicles.

misrepresentation
Written or verbal misstatement of a material fact involved in the contract on which the insurer relies.

Mobile Agricultural Machinery and Equipment coverage form
Farm coverage form that provides separate coverage for a farmer's mobile agricultural machinery and equipment.

Mobile Equipment endorsement
Commercial Auto endorsement in which mobile equipment is considered a covered auto for coverage purposes.

Mobile Home insurance
Coverage that protects both a mobile home structure and its contents. Some companies have Mobile Home package policies that provide Property and Liability insurance for owners of mobile homes. In addition, there is a Mobile Homeowners endorsement that can be attached to an HO-2 or HO-3 to modify coverage for mobile homeowners.

mono-line company
Insurance company that writes a single line of insurance.

mono-line policy
Insurance policy that provides one type of insurance coverage.

monopolistic state fund
Method of providing workers compensation coverage used in some states; employers must purchase workers compensation insurance from a state fund; private insurance companies are not allowed to compete.

moral hazard
Hazard created by an individual who would be willing to create a loss situation on purpose just to collect from the insurance company.

morale hazard

Hazard created by an individual's tendency to contribute to a loss through his or her own irresponsible actions or carelessness.

Mortgage condition

Condition found in property insurance policies that specifies the rights and duties of the mortgagee under the policy. Also called the *Loss Payable condition or mortgagee clause.*

mortgagee rights

Rights granted to a mortgagee under a property contract issued to a mortgagor by virtue of the mortgagee's financial interest in the property.

Motor Carrier Act of 1980

Federal regulation that requires truckers and other commercial carriers to certify that they are able to meet financial obligations if they become liable for injury or damage arising from their trucking operations.

Motor Carrier coverage form

Commercial Auto coverage form that is an alternative to the Truckers Coverage form. It can be used to cover anyone who transports property by auto in a commercial enterprise.

Motor Truck Cargo policy

Nonfiled Commercial Inland Marine policy that protects a carrier against its liability for damage to domestic shipments in its custody.

multi-line company

Insurance company that writes more than one line of insurance.

multi-line policy

See package policy.

mutual company

Insurance company owned by its policyholders. The policyholders share in profits made by the company through dividends or reductions in future premiums.

mysterious disappearance

Vanishing of property with no explanation.

Name Schedule bond

Type of Fidelity bond that covers loss only from named employees.

named insured

Person, business, or other entity named in the declarations to whom the policy is issued.

Named Nonowner Coverage endorsement

Personal Auto policy endorsement that provides coverage for the use of nonowned autos to individuals who do not own a car.

named peril policy

Insurance policy that insures only against perils specifically listed in the policy. Also called *specified peril policy.*

National Association of Insurance Commissioners (NAIC)

Organization made up of individual state insurance commissioners whose purpose is to promote uniformity in regulation by drafting model laws and regulations.

National Flood Insurance Program

Program run by the federal government that makes flood insurance available to eligible communities at subsidized rates. Includes coverage for both buildings and personal property.

Nationwide Definition

Document that categorizes and classifies risks that are eligible for Ocean or Inland Marine insurance.

negligence

The lack of reasonable care that is required to protect others from the unreasonable chance of harm.

No Benefit to Bailee condition

Condition found in some Property insurance contracts stating that a bailee is not covered under an insured's policy while the bailee has possession of the insured's property.

No-Fault insurance

Form of Automobile insurance in which each insurance company pays the damages of its own insureds, regardless of who was at fault for the accident. No-fault insurance has been enacted in several states.

nonadmitted insurer

Company that is not authorized to do business in a particular state. Also called an *unauthorized insurer.*

nonconcurrency

Situation that exists when the same property is covered by more than one policy, but the policies are not identical as to the extent of coverage provided.

nonexclusive agent

See independent agent.

nonfiled form

Type of Commercial Inland Marine form that is not standardized and cannot be included in the Commercial Inland Marine coverage part of the Commercial Package Policy.

nonrenewal

Decision made by an insured or insurance company to not continue coverage for another policy period after the current policy period expires.

nonreporting policy

Type of insurance policy for which a flat premium is charged every time the policy is renewed.

obligee

In bonds, the party to whom the principal makes the promise, and for whose protection the bond is written.

occurrence

A loss that occurs at a specific time and place or over a period of time.

Occurrence form

Commercial General Liability coverage form that covers bodily injury or property damage that occurs during the policy period, regardless of when the claim is made.

Ocean Marine insurance

Insurance designed to provide broad coverage for cargo and ships in transit over sea. Includes Cargo insurance, Hull insurance, Freight insurance, and Protection and Indemnity insurance.

offer and acceptance

One of the elements of a legal contract; means that a contract must involve two parties: one who makes an offer and another who accepts the offer. Also called *agreement.*

Open Competition

Method of rate and form regulation used by some state insurance departments that allows insurance companies to compete openly with the forms and rates they select, subject only to requirements of adequacy and nondiscrimination.

open peril policy

Insurance policy that protects the insured from losses caused by any peril that is not specifically excluded by the policy. Also called *all risk* and *special coverage.*

Optional Limits Transportation Expenses Coverage endorsement

Personal Auto policy endorsement that allows the insured to select the daily and maximum limits of coverage provided for transportation and loss of use expenses.

Ordinance or Law Coverage endorsement

Endorsement used with the Commercial Property coverage part to provide coverage for demolition costs and increased construction costs required or regulated by law or ordinance.

other coverages

See additional coverages.

Other Insurance condition

Policy condition that sets out how any other insurance that applies to the same loss will affect reimbursement under the policy. See contribution by equal shares, excess insurance, primary insurance, and pro rata other insurance.

Other Than Collision coverage (OTC)

See Comprehensive coverage.

Outboard Motor and Boat insurance

Insurance against physical damage to boats. Usually provided by Inland Marine forms.

Owners and Contractors Protective Liability coverage form

Commercial General Liability coverage form that covers claims caused by the negligence of a contractor or subcontractor hired by the insured.

package policy
Policy that includes more than one type of insurance coverage. Also called a *multi-line policy*.

Pair or Set condition
Loss settlement condition found in property insurance contracts stating that when part of a set is damaged or destroyed, the insured will not be reimbursed for the value of the entire set. Various methods are used to determine the amount of reimbursement.

Parcel Post policy
Nonfiled Commercial Inland Marine policy that covers mail sent by parcel post.

particular average loss
In Ocean Marine insurance, any partial loss that does not arise from a general sacrifice of property (jettison).

Payment bond
Type of Surety bond that guarantees bills for labor and materials will be paid to the contractor as they are due. Also called *Labor and Materials bond*.

Peak Season endorsement
Endorsement attached to the Commercial Property coverage part to provide increased coverage during particular seasons of the year when the insured's inventory is at higher levels than usual.

Performance bond
Type of Surety bond that guarantees jobs will be completed by the contractor according to the contract specifications.

peril
The cause of loss.

perils of the sea
Perils to which property in transit by water is exposed. Includes unusual action of wind or waves, stranding, lightning, collision, and sinking.

Permitted Incidental Occupancies endorsement
Homeowners policy endorsement that covers the insured's business activities conducted on the residence premises.

Personal Articles form
Personal Inland Marine form that provides scheduled coverage for nine optional classes of personal property: jewelry, furs, cameras, musical instruments, silverware, golf equipment, fine arts, stamp collections, and coin collections.

Personal Auto policy
Auto policy that provides Property and Liability coverage for both owned and nonowned autos used, maintained, or operated by the insured and his or her family members.

Personal contract
One of the characteristics of an insurance contract; means that an insurance contract insures a person, not property.

Personal Effects form
Personal Inland Marine form that covers an insured's personal belongings, such as baggage, while traveling.

personal injury
Injury other than bodily injury arising out of such things as libel, slander, false arrest, wrongful entry, violation of privacy, and malicious prosecution.

Personal Injury endorsement
Homeowners policy endorsement that modifies the definition of bodily injury to include personal injury.

Personal Inland Marine insurance
See Inland Marine insurance.

Personal Liability and Medical Payments to Others endorsement
Endorsement to the Dwelling policy that provides liability coverage similar to that provided by Section II of the Homeowners policy. Can also be purchased as a separate policy.

personal lines
Insurance coverages that protect individuals and their families.

Personal Property form
Personal Inland Marine form that provides open peril coverage for personal property.

Personal Property floater risks
Category of the Nationwide Definition that includes risks eligible for Personal Inland Marine insurance.

Personal Property Replacement Cost endorsement
Homeowners policy endorsement that adds replacement cost coverage for personal property.

Personal Umbrella policy
See Umbrella policy.

Personal Yacht insurance
Type of personal watercraft policy written for large pleasure boats.

physical hazard
Hazard that arises from the condition, occupancy, or use of the property itself.

Physicians and Surgeons Equipment form
Filed Commercial Inland Marine form that covers medical instruments on and off the premises and furniture and fixtures at the doctor's office against direct physical loss.

policy
An insurance contract.

policy form
See Coverage form.

Policy Jacket
Document used to assemble an insurance policy. Contains general conditions or the declarations page, but provides no coverage in and of itself. A policy form must be attached to make it a complete policy. Also called a *skeleton policy*.

policy limit

Maximum amount the insurance company will pay for a particular loss, or for losses sustained during a period of time. Also called *limit of coverage, limit of insurance,* and *limit of liability.*

policy period

The date and time specified in the declarations for when coverage begins and ends.

policy territory

Place where coverage under a policy applies.

Pollution Liability Coverage Extension endorsement

Commercial General Liability endorsement that provides coverage for BI and PD claims arising out of pollution losses. Excludes coverage for pollution cleanup costs.

Pollution Liability coverage form

CGL coverage form that provides certain pollution coverages that are excluded under the standard CGL. Includes coverage for pollution cleanup costs.

Pollution Liability—Limited coverage form

CGL coverage form that provides certain pollution coverages that are excluded under the standard CGL. Does not include coverage for pollution cleanup costs.

Position Schedule bond

Fidelity bond that covers specifically named positions in the company, rather than the individuals who hold these positions.

postjudgment interest

Interest accruing on a judgment after an award has been made, but before payment is made by the insurance company. Usually covered as a supplementary payment in liability policies.

prejudgment interest

Interest awarded to compensate a third party for interest he or she might have earned if compensation had been received at the time of injury or damage, rather than at the time of judgment.

Premises and Operations

Business liability exposure arising out of the business location or the activities of the business. Covered under the CGL.

premium audit

Survey of the insured's financial records to gather information used to calculate the premium, such as exposures and limits.

primary insurance

When two or more coverages or policies apply to the same loss, the one that pays first, up to its limit of liability or the amount of the loss, whichever is less.

principal

In bonds, the party who promises to do or not do a specific thing. In agency law, the person or company being represented.

prior approval

Method of rate and form ratification used by some state insurance departments that requires a company to obtain official approval before using new forms or rates.

pro rata other insurance

Method of handling insurance when more than one coverage applies to a loss. Each coverage pays a portion of the loss in proportion to the relationship its limit of liability bears to the total limit of liability under all applicable insurance. Also called *contribution by limits*.

producer

General term used to describe someone who sells insurance, such as an agent, broker, or solicitor.

Products and Completed Operations

Business liability exposure arising out of defects in the company's products or completed operations. Covered by the CGL.

Professional liability

Liability arising out of rendering or failing to render services of a professional nature.

Professional Liability policy

Insurance coverage issued to a professional that covers the rendering or failing to render services of a professional nature. Policies are tailored to fit specific occupational needs.

Proof of Loss

Form completed by an insured after a loss that provides an official inventory of damages.

property damage (PD)

Damage to or destruction of property, including loss of use of the property.

property insurance

Line of insurance that includes many types of coverages designed to handle the risk that a person will suffer financial loss because something he or she owns is damaged or destroyed.

Protection and Indemnity

Form of Ocean Marine Liability insurance that covers a variety of types of liability, such as damage to cargo through negligence and damage to other property or another boat resulting from collision.

Protective Safeguards endorsement

Businessowners policy endorsement that requires the insured to maintain fire or security service on specified property as a condition of the policy.

proximate cause

An action that, in a natural and continuous sequence, produces a loss.

Public Official bond

Type of Surety bond furnished by principals who are elected or appointed to fill positions of trust that guarantee their faithful and honest performance in office.

punitive damages

Type of damages intended to punish the defendant and make an example out of him or her to discourage others from behaving the same way. Also called *exemplary damages*.

pure risk

A risk in which there is no chance of gain, only loss.

quotation

A summary of coverages and premiums proposed by an agent to a prospective client.

rate

The basic charge an insurance company sets for various types of insurance.

reasonable person rule

Principle of law stating that each person must behave like a prudent person, following those ordinary considerations that guide human affairs.

rebating

Giving or offering some benefit other than those specified in the policy to induce a customer to buy insurance. Rebating is illegal in most states.

reciprocal company

An unincorporated group of members who share insurance responsibilities with other members. It is managed by an attorney-in-fact, an individual whose management authority is spelled out in a legal document like a power of attorney.

reinsurance

Acceptance by an insurer, called a reinsurer, of all or part of the risk of loss of another insurer.

repair cost

The cost to repair a damaged or destroyed item of property. May be the basis of reimbursement for a loss.

replacement cost

The cost to replace a damaged or destroyed item of property, without deduction for depreciation. May be the basis of reimbursement for some losses.

Reporting policy

Type of policy that does not charge a flat premium. The insured pays a deposit premium, and then submits periodic reports to the insurer showing the status of the factors on which the premium is based. From these status reports, premiums are calculated and charged against the deposit.

representation
Statements on an insurance application that the applicant believes are true. A representation is not considered a matter to which the parties contract, so a policy cannot be voided on the basis of a representation.

Residual Market insurance
Insurance that is not ordinarily available from private insurers and may be provided by the government. Examples include Flood insurance, which is provided by the federal government, and workers compensation benefits, which might be provided by state funds.

retention limit
In an Umbrella policy, the amount the insured must pay for a loss that is not covered by an underlying policy before the Umbrella will begin to cover the loss. Also called the *self-insured retention*.

retroactive date
Under the claims-made CGL form, a date stipulated in the declarations as the first date on which an event may occur and be covered by the policy if a claim is filed.

retrospective rating
Type of merit rating that bases the insured's premium on losses incurred during the policy period.

risk
The chance or uncertainty of loss.

risk retention group
Insurance company formed by several organizations to cover those organizations' liability loss exposures. Risk retention groups are exempt from most state laws that govern insurance companies.

robbery
In Crime insurance, the taking or attempted taking of property by one who has caused or threatened to cause bodily harm, or committed a witnessed, obviously unlawful act.

Running Down clause
Provision found in Ocean Marine Hull policies that provides protection if the ship owner is held liable for the negligent operation of the vessel in damaging another ship.

salvage
Damaged property that can be retrieved, reconditioned, and sold to reduce an insured loss.

schedule rating
Type of merit rating that applies a system of debits or credits to reflect characteristics of a particular insured.

scheduled coverage
Property that is specifically listed in the declarations and covered for a specific amount. Also called *specific insurance*.

Scheduled Personal Property endorsement

Homeowners policy endorsement that provides open peril, scheduled coverage for nine optional classes of property.

self insurance

Alternative to purchasing insurance in which a company or individual assumes the risk of paying for its losses and sets aside the necessary funds to pay for such losses.

self-insured retention

See retention limit.

service bureau

Organization that gathers, pools, and analyzes statistics from its member insurance companies to establish loss costs used to determine insurance rates.

Signs Coverage form

Filed Commercial Inland Marine form that insures businesses against loss to neon, fluorescent, automatic, or mechanical electric signs and lights.

single limit

One policy limit that applies to both BI and PD losses. May also be called a *combined single limit*.

skeleton policy

See Policy Jacket.

solicitor

Insurance professional who sells insurance and collects premiums, but cannot issue or countersign policies.

special coverage

See open peril policy.

special damages

Type of compensatory damages that reimburse the injured party for direct and specific expenses involved in the loss, such as medical expenses and lost wages.

specific insurance

See scheduled coverage.

Specified Causes of Loss

One of the physical damage coverage options in the Commercial Auto coverage forms; provides more limited coverage than Comprehensive coverage, insuring only against specified perils such as fire, flood, or explosion.

specified peril policy

See named peril policy.

speculative risk

A risk that might result in a loss or gain.

Split Limits

Policy limit that provides separate limits for BI and PD.

Spoilage endorsement

Endorsement used with the Building and Personal Property and Condominium Commercial Unit-Owners Commercial Property coverage forms. It adds coverage for the insured's perishable stock—personal property that must be maintained under controlled conditions to protect it from loss or damage.

Spread of risk

Principle of insurance stating that insurers should spread their insured risks over a large geographical area, rather than insuring a large number of people in a small area.

Standard & Poor

Organization that rates the financial stability of insurance companies doing business in the United States.

standard of care

See degree of care.

stated amount condition

See Agreed Value condition.

statute of limitations

Law providing that certain types of suits must be brought within a specified time of the occurrence to be valid under the law.

stock company

An insurance company owned by its stockholders. Profits are shared by the stockholders. Policyholders are not entitled to share in company profits.

subrogation

The transfer to the insurance company of the insured's right to collect damages from another party.

supplemental extended reporting period

See extended reporting period.

supplementary payments

A payment that provides extra coverage over and above the insured's limit of liability. Commonly included are defense costs, first aid expenses, bond premiums, and postjudgment interest.

Supply bond

Type of Surety bond that guarantees a supplier will furnish supplies, products, or equipment at an agreed upon time and price.

surety

In bonds, the party (often the insurance company) that agrees to be responsible for loss that can result if the principal does not keep his or her promise.

Surety bond

Bond that guarantees someone will perform faithfully whatever he or she agrees to do, or that someone will make an agreed upon payment to another party.

surplus

The difference between what a company owns (assets) and what it owes (liabilities).

surplus lines agent

See excess lines agent.

Theatrical Property coverage form

Filed Commercial Inland Marine form that covers scenery, props, and costumes used by a theater group in a specific production.

theft

In Crime insurance, a broad term encompassing any unlawful taking of property, including burglary and robbery.

third party loss

A liability loss.

Time Element coverage

Coverage for the loss of business income over a period of time that results from direct physical loss.

tort

A civil wrong for which monetary damages may be provided. Does not include losses arising out of contracts.

Towing and Labor Costs endorsement

Personal Auto policy endorsement that covers towing and the costs of labor performed at the site the car was disabled.

Trailer Interchange insurance

A coverage provided under the Truckers and Motor Carrier coverage forms. Covers damage to a specific trailer under the policy of the trucker who has possession of the trailer at the time of loss, provided that the trucker is liable for the damage under a written interchange agreement and the damage is caused by a covered peril.

trespasser

A person who is on the premises without the property owner's express or implied permission.

Trip Transit policy

Nonfiled Commercial Inland Marine policy that covers a single shipment of goods.

Truckers coverage form

Commercial Auto coverage form written specifically for the trucking industry.

twisting

Illegal activity in which an agent convinces a prospect to cancel existing insurance and buy another policy from the agent, to the detriment of the prospect.

Umbrella policy

Type of policy that provides broad coverage for an insured's liability over and above liability covered by an underlying contract. May also cover losses that are excluded by the underlying policy. Available as personal or commercial insurance.

unauthorized insurer

See nonadmitted insurer.

Underinsured Motorists coverage

Auto coverage that pays the difference between the insured's actual damages for bodily injury and the amount of liability insurance carried by the at-fault driver. May be added to the Personal or Commercial Auto policy by endorsement.

underwriting

Insurance company function that involves researching and evaluating insurance applicants to decide which ones are acceptable to the company as insureds.

underwriting expenses

One of the components used to calculate the expense ratio. Includes all costs required to acquire and maintain a book of business, such as expenses for commissions, salaries, and other administrative and regulatory costs.

unfair discrimination

Applying different standards to insureds that have the same risks of loss.

unilateral contract

A type of contract that is "one-sided." An insurance policy is one-sided because only the insurance company is legally bound to perform its part of the agreement.

Uninsured Motorists coverage

Automobile coverage designed to provide protection for the insured if he or she is involved in an accident in which an uninsured motorist is at fault. Uninsured motorists include those who do not carry insurance, motorists whose insurance does not meet the state's minimum financial responsibility laws, drivers whose insurance companies are insolvent, and hit-and-run drivers who cannot be identified.

unoccupancy

The absence of people from a premises. Property coverage is often restricted if there are long periods of unoccupancy.

use and file

Method of rate and form ratification used by some state insurance departments that requires insurance companies to file rates and forms within a certain period of time after they are first used.

Utility Services—Direct Damage Coverage endorsement

Businessowners policy endorsement that covers loss or damage to property caused by an interruption in water, communication, or power service. For coverage to apply, the property must be listed on the endorsement and the utility equipment must be damaged by a covered cause of loss.

Utility Services—Time Element Coverage endorsement

Businessowners policy endorsement that covers loss of business income and extra expense that occurs because of an interruption in water, communication, or power service. For coverage to apply, the property must be listed on the endorsement and the utility equipment must be damaged by a covered cause of loss.

utmost good faith

A characteristic of insurance contracts meaning that the insurance company must be able to rely on the honesty and cooperation of the insured, and the insured must rely on the company to fulfill its obligations.

vacancy

The absence of both people and property from a premises. Property coverage is often restricted when there are long periods of vacancy.

Valuable Papers and Records insurance

Filed Commercial Inland Marine form that provides coverage for valuable papers such as manuscripts, blueprints, records, and other printed documents.

valuation

Method used by the insurance company to determine the appropriate payment for a loss.

Value Reporting endorsement

Endorsement used with the Commercial Property coverage part to provide coverage based on the actual values of property at certain locations at specific times.

Valued policy

Policy written for a specified amount that lists the value of the insured property as agreed to by both the insured and the insurer. This amount is used to value losses. Also called an *Agreed Amount policy.*

vandalism and malicious mischief (V&MM)

Coverage provided in many Property insurance policies that protects property against damage caused by vandals.

vicarious liability

Liability that a person or business incurs because of the actions of others, such as family members or employees. Also called *imputed liability.*

Voluntary Compensation endorsement

Endorsement used with the Workers Compensation and Employers Liability policy that adds coverage for employees who are excluded from the state's workers compensation law.

waiver

The intentional relinquishment of a known right.

Warehouse to Warehouse clause

Provision found in Ocean Marine Cargo policies that extends coverage for the cargo from its point of origination to its point of destination.

warranty

A specific agreement between the insured and the insurer that becomes a part of the insurance policy. A breach of warranty can void the policy.

watchperson

As defined in Crime insurance forms, someone retained specifically by the insured whose sole duty is to have care and custody of property inside the premises.

Watercraft endorsement

Homeowners policy endorsement that provides coverage for BI or PD arising out of the use of watercraft.

Watercraft Package policy

Package policy that provides Property, Liability, and Medical Payments coverage for losses arising out of the ownership, maintenance, or use of watercraft.

Workers Compensation and Employers Liability policy

Insurance that covers an employer's obligations under workers compensation laws, which make the employer responsible for stated damages in the event of a work-related injury or illness. Also covers the insured's liability for work-related injuries under common law.

written premium

One of the components used to calculate the expense ratio. It is the gross amount of premium income on the company's books, which includes both earned and unearned premiums.

Index

E

F

How can we make this index more useful? Email us at indexes@quepublishing.com

Q – R

reporting forms, 70
representations, 50
residual market insurance, 23
retaining risks, 3
retroactive dates (claims-made forms),
   309-310
retrospective ratings, 48
riot insurance (FAIR Plans), 197
risks, 2
   field underwriting, 24
   ineligible, 212
   managing, 2-3
   pure/speculative, 4
   reducing, 2
   retaining, 3
   retention groups, 22
   transferring, 3
robberies, 356
RRGs (risk retention groups), 22

S

safe burglaries, 356
salvage condition, 66-67
Scheduled Personal Property endorsement
   (homeowners), 144-145
securities (commercial crimes), 357
self-insure, 22
service bureaus rates, 36
service needs (agents), 25
sets, replacing, 65
short rate basis, 51
Show Windows coverage (Jewelers Block),
   292
Signs coverage forms (Inland Marine policies), 291
solicitors, 28
special forms (homeowners), 125, 135-136
specific damages, 83
specific insurance, 57
speculative risks, 4
spoilage damage coverage (Equipment
   Breakdown Protection coverage forms),
   390
spoilage endorsements (commercial properties), 270
standards of care, 79
state regulations, 33
statistical departments, 30
statutes of limitations (negligence), 81
stock companies, 20
strict liability, 82
subrogation condition (properties), 67

Supplemental Extended Reprinting Period
   endorsement, 311
supplementary payments
   BOPs, 229
   Business Auto coverage liabilities, 337
   CGL, 318
   insuring agreements, 85
   PAPs, 163
supply bonds, 402
support departments, 32
Surety Association of America, 37
Surety bonds, 400-401
   Contract bonds, 401
   judicial bonds, 402
   License and Permit bonds, 402
   Public Official bonds, 402
surplus lines, 28, 402-403
survivor/death benefits, 371
suspension provision condition (Equipment
   Breakdown Protection coverage), 396

T

temporary substitute autos, 172
termination condition (physical damage
   PAP coverage), 176
terms (policies), 50
territory (policies) (properties), 70
Theatrical Property coverage forms (Inland
   Marine policies), 286-287
thefts, 356
third party losses, 83
time deductibles, 395
torts, 78
Towing and Labor Costs endorsement, 177
trailer interchange insurance (Truckers coverage forms), 343
Transfer of Rights of Recovery Against
   Others to Us condition (commercial properties), 246
Transfer of Your Rights and Duties Under
   This Policy condition, 205
transferring risks, 3
Transit Coverage in the Event of
   Cancellation condition, 294
transportation expenses (physical damage
   PAP coverage), 173
trees, shrubs, and other plants coverages
   Dwelling policies, 106
   homeowners, 130
Trip Transit policies, 297
Truckers coverage forms, 343
twisting, 35

How can we make this index more useful? Email us at indexes@quepublishing.com